THE FEATURE FILM DISTRIBUTION DEAL

A Critical Analysis of the Single Most Important Film Industry Agreement

John W. Cones

Southern Illinois University Press

Carbondale and Edwardsville

Library of Congress Cataloging-in-Publication Data

Cones, John W.
    The feature film distribution deal : a critical analysis of the
single most important film industry agreement / John W. Cones.
        p. cm.
    Includes bibliographical references and index.
    1. Motion picture—United States—Distribution. 2. Motion
pictures—Distribution. 3. Motion pictures—United States—
Marketing. 4. Motion pictures—Marketing. 5. Motion picture
industry—United States—Finance. 6. Motion picture industry—
Finance. I. Title.
    PN1993.5.U6C634   1997
    384'.83'0973—dc20   96-33733
    ISBN 0-8093-2081-9 (alk. paper). —   CIP
    ISBN 0-8093-2082-7 (pbk. : alk. paper)

This book is dedicated to independent feature film producers, along with all net and gross profit participants (including the Hollywood outsider investors) who rely on the producers' ability to negotiate with film distributors and to monitor distributor implementation of the film distribution deal.

Contents

Appendixes

Introduction

THIS IS A book about one of the most critical factors in determining whether any profit participants (particularly net profit participants, who make significant contributions to the financing or production of a feature film, including producers, directors, actors, investors and others) will actually share in a portion of the revenue generated in any or all markets by the exploitation of their own motion picture. That single factor is referred to herein as "distributor business practices." In certain situations, however, these practices may actually be occurring at the studio level, but since it is often difficult to separate the activities of the studio from its affiliated distributor and the distribution arm of the vertically integrated major studio/distributors dominate the conglomerate anyway, the phrase "distributor business practices" will suffice for these purposes. Unfortunately, feature film distributor business practices run the gamut from industry level problems to rather obscure distribution agreement drafting issues. This book focuses only on issues relating to the distribution agreement. Many of these other distributor or studio business practices are discussed in this book's companion volume *How the Movie Wars Were Won* (self-published, 1995).

This book does not represent an attempt to accuse any specific major studio/distributor, or other distributor, of questionable or unethical conduct, creative accounting, sharp negotiating tactics or anticompetitive practices in any specific instance. Nor should it be interpreted as an indictment of the entire distributor segment of the industry. It also does not attempt to achieve any specific level of "proof" with regard to any reported business practice. There is also no attempt made here to quantify the likelihood that any given discussed practice may or may not occur within the context of an actual and specific industry relationship. Rather, this book is merely an attempt to compile and discuss in one place a written presentation of distributor practices that have been reported from time to time in various trade publications, books on the film industry and in discussions with large numbers of feature film producers, other profit participants and attorneys, accountants, auditors and broker/dealers (whose clients work in or relate in some way to the film finance and distribution arenas), mixed with my own opinions regarding such practices, for the primary purpose of alerting concerned individuals in and out of the film industry to the possibility that such business practices may actually be occurring and to help them understand how such practices may adversely affect them.

Thus, the information relating to such reported film distributor practices and provided here is offered for the purpose of making those profit participants just mentioned and others interested in the financial aspects of the film business more aware of the potential breadth of the problem and to aid in the long-term correction of the abuses herein described, if in fact they are occurring. The book is specifically designed to help future independent producers and other net and gross profit participants to be more alert to the possible occurrence of such practices, to aid such producers and others whose interests are aligned with them in negotiating film distribution and other entertainment industry agreements that are fairer to all parties and to aid such profit participants in more effectively monitoring the implementation of such agreements.

Since the consistent and persistent occurrence of such practices over a lengthy period of time tends or would tend to facilitate the concentration of decision-making authority and creative power in the hands of a few distributors and/or studio/distributor executives in the film industry, it is also hoped that this book will at least slightly inhibit the ability of such persons to continue such practices. Thus, to the extent that this book may help preserve a vigorous independent film community, it is also hoped that it may contribute in a modest way toward the preservation of a more healthy marketplace for ideas as expressed through the important communications medium—feature films.

Who should read this book? This publication is written for and may prove useful to independent producers; executive producers; associate producers; producers' representatives; directors; actors/actresses; screenwriters; the talent guilds; distributors; entertainment, antitrust and securities attorneys; securities issuers and broker/dealers; investment bankers; money finders; financiers; both passive and active investors; corporate distributor shareholders; profit participation auditors; completion guarantors; subdistributors; end users; territorial distributors; foreign sales agents; production payroll accountants; interactive media and virtual reality entrepreneurs; film finance consultants; cable company executives; pay-per-view proponents; video companies and merchandisers, all of which may have a significant financial stake, from time to time, in a feature film distribution deal. In addition, this book may be of interest to Congress, its research staffs, government regulators at the Internal Revenue Service, the Securities and Exchange Commission, the Federal Trade Commission and law enforcement officials such as the Los Angeles district attorney and the U.S. Justice Department.

Since the book has been primarily written for people already associated with the industry in some way, little if any time has been spent on explaining the very basics of the film industry. However, for any interested reader looking for an overview of the film industry, see Appendix A "Motion Picture Industry Overview." Also, my earlier work *Film Finance and Distribution—A Dictionary of Terms* (Silman-James Press, 1992) provides definitions of most of the technical terms used in this book.

Books and lectures. This book and others in my series on the Hollywood-based U.S. film industry (see list of other books by the same author in the Selected Bibliography in the back of this book) have grown out of a series of lectures presented by the author during the period from 1987 through 1995 on topics relating to business and legal aspects of film finance and distribution. The lectures were sponsored by the American Film Institute, the UCLA (graduate level) Independent Producer's Program, the USC Cinema-TV School, UCLA's Anderson Graduate School of Management, the USC Cinema-TV Alumni Association, UCLA Extension, Loyola Marymount, the Idaho Film and Video Association, the Samuel French Bookshop, the Cinergy Group of Sacramento, Cinewomen, Cinetex, The Midnight Special Book Store, Teknifilm Labs of Portland, IFP/West and other film industry organizations.

This work is specifically an outgrowth of another study of the author (i.e., the above-mentioned dictionary of film finance and distribution terms) and represents a more narrowly focused book (relating more specifically to distributor business practices as opposed to the more general terminology of film finance and distribution). On the other hand, most all of the concepts discussed in this book are defined in the former publication. This book, however, expands the discussion of such topics.

The underlying research, which has supported the author's lecture series and the material in this book, was developed from 1987 through 1995 and includes the books and articles listed in the Selected Bibliography that appears at the end of the book as well as discussions with thousands of independent feature film producers, distributors, exhibitors, entertainment attorneys, profit participation auditors, film finance consultants, entertainment lenders, film teachers and film students.

The missing authors. This book could have been written (and some will argue that it should have been written) by one of the film industry profit participation auditors (see the list of profit participation audit firms in Appendix B). Unfortunately, even though I have suggested on several occasions that such a book be written by certain members of those film industry audit firms, none were willing to step forward and author such a book. Their privately expressed reason: "If we put this all down in writing and really explain in detail what the distributors are doing, there will be less need for feature film profit participants to hire us!" In other words, the distributor practices described and in many instances criticized in this book have resulted in the creation of a cottage industry in Hollywood, the profit participation auditing industry. And, to the extent that more people are aware of and really understand the specific distributor practices involved, or even worse (from the distributor and profit participation auditors' points of view), to the extent that anyone is actually able to demand or negotiate more favorable treatment or is able to bring about some modest reforms in such distributor practices, that would tend to diminish the need for profit participation auditors and thus would ultimately diminish the income of the profit participation audit firms. Welcome to Hollywood!

Notice

All statements made in this book,
other than those attributed to
another cited source, are the
opinions of the author.

THE FEATURE FILM DISTRIBUTION DEAL

1 | Feature Film Net Profits

I<small>T IS THE</small> primary contention of this book (and its companion volume *How the Movie Wars Were Won*) that the pervasive market power of the major studio/distributors in the United States (the MPAA companies, generally)[1] has been gained and is maintained by engaging in numerous questionable, unethical, unfair, unconscionable, anticompetitive, predatory and/or illegal business practices.[2] Many but not all of these business practices revolve around language found in (or in some cases language purposefully omitted from) the feature film distribution agreements utilized by these major studio/distributors. Such practices are often referred to as "creative accounting" or "creative contract interpretation."

In the not too distant past, the CBS television network's *Sixty Minutes* program "did a story on 'creative accounting' in the movie business. The *Los Angeles Times* published several lengthy articles on the same subject. Cliff Robertson appeared for an hour on Phil Donahue's television program, asserting, 'We're trying to stop a corruption that has become malignant in our industry and grown every year.' Along the way, the media cumulatively pointed out that nearly every major star in Hollywood, in addition to a lot of directors and writers, had disputed studio accounting practices at one time or another and in some instances had begun lawsuits. Most cases were settled out of court."[3]

More recently (1988), Art Buchwald and producer Alain Bernheim filed their now-famous lawsuit against Paramount (with Pierce O'Donnell as their attorney). In the meantime, profit participation auditors Steven Sills and Ivan Axelrod wrote an article about some of these same studio business practices (published in 1989).[4] The *Buchwald* case then came to trial in December of 1989 and law student Hillary Bibicoff followed in 1991 with an extensive examination of the net profits situation, which was published in a law journal.[5] Also in 1991, Adam Marcus wrote his *Cardozo Arts & Entertainment Law Journal* article about the *Buchwald* case and the future of net profits.[6] Hundreds of other articles have been written about the *Buchwald* lawsuit, the trial phase of which did not end until March of 1992.

Los Angeles entertainment attorney Peter Dekom published his brief but important article about the net profit system in the summer of 1992.[7] Attorney

Pierce O'Donnell and *Los Angeles Times* reporter Dennis McDougal published their book about the *Buchwald* case and its implications for the net profit system, also in the summer of 1992.[8] My earlier book, *Film Finance and Distribution—A Dictionary of Terms*, was published about the same time in the summer of 1992. It contains a discussion of all of the 337 reported distributor practices covered a year or so earlier in the self-published monograph *337 Reported Distributor Practices* and is written with a distinct editorial slant that provides a critical look at the studio net profit system. *Hollywood Reporter* writer David Robb published a series of articles on the net profit system in August and September 1992. Following all of these reports, studies, articles, books and lawsuits, the question may be fairly raised, "What has been the result of all of this criticism of and attacks on the Hollywood net profit system?" The answer is a resounding, "Not very much!"

Many of the problems with the Hollywood net profit system referred to in the books, articles and lawsuits cited above stem from the distribution deal itself and the way the feature film distribution deal defines and handles the concept of net profits. This book seeks to delve into the specifics of the film distribution deal even more critically than those predecessor inquiries and to lay additional groundwork for the ultimate reform of the Hollywood net profit system.

In film industry parlance, the net profit is a form of percentage participation in a motion picture's revenue stream that has been characterized by some as "the customary form of participation" although it has not always been so, nor is it likely to continue to be, since more and more prospective net profit participants within the industry understand how unlikely it is for a film to generate net profits. As a result of the high profile *Buchwald v. Paramount* case, some in the industry have started referring to net profits as net proceeds, so as to avoid any suggestion that anything resembling profits are involved and to remind us that the term is a contractually defined term. That appears to be the typical film industry answer to problems (i.e., to make a cosmetic change). The film industry leaders have used a similar approach with the MPAA ratings system on more than one occasion.

Generally speaking, net profits are "what remain after the studio has recouped from gross receipts (a) distribution fees (based on gross receipts without any deductions), (b) distribution expenses, (c) interest on negative cost, (d) negative cost (plus overhead) and (e) deferments and gross participations."[9] Of course, this definition of net profits only applies to studio financed films. Net profits for independently financed films would call only for the deduction of distributor fees and expenses from distributor gross receipts (see Chapter 2 discussion, "The Five Major Film Finance/Distribution Scenarios").

Net profit participations are percentage interests based on net profits as defined in the distribution agreement.) They are payments to talent or others computed as a percentage of the profits generated by a film or fixed sums to be paid if a movie's profits reach a certain level. Movie revenue participations are supposed to be negotiable and thus may be based on gross receipts, net profits or other stages in a movie's revenue stream. If reasonable controls and/or limitations are not imposed on the distributor's claim to distribution expenses, its distribution fees are not reasonable and other parties are allowed to participate in the distributor's gross film rentals, net profit participations are not likely to occur. Such practices could impact adversely on the financial interests of investors, producers, executive producers, directors, screenwriters, actors/actresses or others who have negotiated a profit participation interest in a given motion picture.

The phrase "contractually defined profits" is a reference to the fact that the terms "profit," "gross profit" and "net profit" and many other terms used in distribution agreements are actually subjective terms and that their meanings may vary somewhat in each film deal depending on how the term is specifically defined in the contract, a contract that is typically negotiated between a very powerful party (the major studio/distributor) and a weaker party (the producer). In other words, although the terms used may be very similar, there really is no industry standard definition for such terms since no one individual or organization has the authority to impose such definition on two individuals or entities negotiating a contract containing those terms and the negotiations are generally between parties of grossly unequal bargaining strength.

The producer's share is a term defined in some distribution agreements as the accountable gross remaining after the deduction, on a continuing basis, of the aggregate of the distributor's distribution fees, distribution expenses and gross participations, if any. Some distribution agreements provide that third party participations, if any, be deducted from the producer's share. The reasoning used to support this position is that the producer, to a greater or lesser extent, is responsible for the production of the motion picture, including all of the associated costs (i.e., the producer is responsible for negotiating and allowing such third party participations, which include talent participations since talent is not a party to the distribution agreement between the producer and distributor). Thus, logically (from the distributor's point of view) the producer should pay the costs of these contingent commitments to talent out of the producer's portion of the film's revenue stream (i.e., out of the producer's share of net profits).

The producer may readily agree with this analysis since the producer and all other net profit participants are likely to fare better if they are paid on a pari passu (pro rata and concurrent) basis with the talent as opposed to allowing talent to receive gross participations. After all, in the studio/distributor financed films, gross participations are generally defined as a production cost and thus the studio/distributor collects interest and overhead charges on these "expenses" that were never actually paid out by the studio/distributor.

Creative accounting is, of course, a derogatory term. It is commonly used by people in the film industry to refer to the accounting practices of studio/distributors and may include everything from actual dishonest practices in reporting and dividing up the revenues generated by a given film at the exhibitor and distributor levels to sharp negotiating tactics used in conjunction with the drafting of a distribution deal by an overly powerful party. Such deals often result in agreements weighted heavily in favor of the distributor as opposed to the producer (who actually represents all other net profit participants). The studios like to take the position that although mistakes and misapplication of contractual terms do occur in the industry, often what is sometimes called creative accounting is no more than the film distributor's following the terms of the negotiated distribution deal. On the other hand, because of the huge disparity in the bargaining power of the parties to the contract the terms of that deal were clearly disadvantageous to the producer in the first place. The studio continues by saying that in some instances what producers call creative accounting is merely the result of their own lack of preparation for the distribution negotiation process. Some in the industry then conclude that independent producers must therefore work harder to improve their (or their representatives') negotiating skill and leverage and insist on broad audit rights that are implemented. This book says that is not enough and it is misleading to suggest otherwise.

Instances of "creative accounting" might involve account numbers, adhesion contracts, allocations, anticipated expenses, apportioned expenses, bad debts, combination ads, the commingling of funds, cross-collateralization, the use of deal memos, direct distribution expenses, discretion, facilities allocations, front-end loads, improperly claimed expenses, kickbacks, overhead, rolling break-evens, settlement transactions, so-called standard contracts, studio accounting practices, subjective terms, the "sue-us" tactic, underreported rentals and/or usury.[10] Outside investors may look at this situation and determine that they might be in a better position to benefit from such distributor practices if they were shareholders in the distribution companies engaging in such practices and so long as the distribution companies did not get caught. On the other hand, why would any distributor who utilized the practices described herein be inclined to be any more fair and honest with its own shareholders?

As entertainment attorney Mark Litwak points out in his book *Dealmaking in the Film & Television Industry*, "Creative accounting problems are widespread in the industry."[11] The phrase "studio accounting" is also sometimes used in a way that is synonymous with "creative accounting" to describe various methods of accounting for motion picture revenues that have long been alleged to be unfair. Such methods include the practice of charging unauthorized and excessive expenses to a given film being produced at the studio, the rolling breakeven that keeps rolling just beyond net profits and unfair overhead charges imposed by the studio on net profit participants. In other words, the studio has the books and records, it interprets the production/distribution agreement, it computes the profit and it decides how much should be paid. Industry insiders have long maintained that there is a certain amount of inadvertent and some intentional abusive or unconscionable accounting practices regularly occurring at the studios.

The very slippery concept of "breakeven" is an important concept to understand in analyzing the net profit situation. Breakeven in most industries is the point at which sales equal costs. In the film business, it is the specific point at which an exhibited motion picture neither makes nor loses money (i.e., receipts cover all costs attributed to the picture by the individual or entity calculating breakeven). Above this point, a film begins to show a profit, below it, a loss. In other words, breakeven is the point in a movie's revenue stream at which the income to the exhibitor, distributor or producing entity is said to equal such entity's cost of producing and/or distributing the movie. Breakeven, thus, may be different for many of the different individuals or entities involved with a film, although the most commonly referred to "breakeven" is the distributor's breakeven. Generally, this is the point at which deferred or contingent compensation is paid. In many cases, the costs of distribution continue to escalate ahead of the pace at which receipts are generated. Reportedly fewer than 5 percent of motion pictures released in recent years and using the major studio/distributor net profits definition have earned a profit (i.e., achieved breakeven).

Unfortunately, distributors use a number of variations of breakeven in their distribution deals:

1. *Actual breakeven.* The point at which revenue generated by exploitation of a motion picture equals the costs incurred in the production and/or distribution of such motion picture for the applicable entity (e.g., the film's distributor). Breakeven in a film context is a contractually defined term, and a significant number of variations have been used to signify specific points in a film's revenue stream (e.g., artificial breakeven, breakeven, cash breakeven, first breakeven, rolling breakeven, etc.).

2. *Contractual breakeven.* The point in a motion picture's revenue stream that is defined by agreement to constitute breakeven. Since there are many ways to define breakeven in film distribution agreements and certain breakeven points may never be achieved due to the effect of the so-called rolling breakeven, it may be advantageous for all profit participants at whatever level actually to negotiate a contractually defined breakeven for purposes of triggering the payment of bonuses, escalations or various levels of participation.

3. Rolling breakeven. The point at which a film's revenues are equal to expenses on a continuing basis, (i.e., after all appropriate deductions are taken from film rentals in each accounting period, those persons who have been able to negotiate a percentage or fixed participation at such accounting stages may be paid if the film is in a profit position). Too much discretion, latitude, flexibility in the standards of conduct, lack of definition and too little auditing leeway in the distribution deal create opportunities for the distributor to keep pushing breakeven back, no matter how it is defined.

4. Second breakeven. A contractually defined point in a motion picture's revenue stream when revenues equal costs again (i.e., following the first such occurrence).

5. Cash breakeven. A concept that may be defined in several ways, but which in its most favorable form for a gross participant is defined as that point in a film's revenue stream at which gross receipts equal the film's negative cost, plus interest and distribution expenses excluding production and advertising overhead. A more favorable definition from the studio/distributor's point of view also takes into consideration some distribution fee, although lower than normal (e.g., 17.5 percent, to reimburse the studio for its internal costs of distribution, plus some level of production overhead). The concept of cash breakeven is sometimes used by the studio/distributors to make sure they have recouped their real costs (as opposed to their real costs plus some profit factor) before the payment of gross participation obligations is triggered. For example, if gross participations are to escalate at different levels of breakeven, cash breakeven is usually considered the first breakeven.

6. Artificial breakeven. Another contractually defined multiple of a film's negative cost (e.g., when gross receipts equal three times the negative cost of the motion picture) that may be treated as actual breakeven in a given deal.

7. Initial actual breakeven. Another contractually defined breakeven point in the revenue stream of a motion picture, which commonly means that point at which net proceeds or net profits are reached.

The Make-a-Great-Movie Myth

The Net Profit Problem. The following two quotes illustrate some aspects of the feature film net profit problem: "In mid-1982, it was estimated that 80 percent of the films released in the United States during 1981 lost money."[12] "The standard studio deal produces a profit to the participant in less than 5 percent of the pictures released today."[13]

The major studio/distributors routinely generate information purporting to show that most films do not make money and the profit participation auditors estimate that only a small percentage of such films actually generate net profits.

The myth. Many independent producers and other prospective net profit participants apparently believe that all they have to do is make great motion pictures and that will solve the problem (i.e., they will be able to participate in the upside profit potential of their own movies).

The reality. A short list of good to excellent motion pictures which have failed to generate net profits should demonstrate that making a good movie is not all that is necessary to solve the net profit problem.

1. *The Blues Brothers*—"*The Blues Brothers*, released in 1980, was still showing a net deficit of more than $7 million as of Sept. 29, 1990, and will probably never hit break-even."[14]

2. *Ruthless People*—The Touchstone Pictures 1986 feature *Ruthless People* reportedly was still showing an $11 million dollar deficit as of July, 1987, although it had grossed $90 million dollars worldwide.[15]

3. *The Untouchables*—Paramount's *The Untouchables* (1987) showing gross receipts of $106,240,936 as of November 24, 1990 but a deficit of $19,3454,497.[16]

4. *Fatal Attraction*—"A studio profit statement for the runaway hit movie (*Fatal Attraction*) released in September 1987, showed that a little over two years later it had grossed $166 million for the studio. But . . . [the net] profit statement . . . still show[ed] a net deficit of $100,000."[17]

5. *Frantic*—"Over at Warner Bros., Roman Polanski's *Frantic*, starring Harrison Ford, remained $28.4 million in the red six months after its February 1988 release, despite the fact that it had already taken in more than $26 million in gross receipts."[18]

6. *Rain Man*—A participation statement for United Artists' big 1988 hit, *Rain Man*, starring Dustin Hoffman and Tom Cruise, "showed gross receipts totaling $189 million as of November 1989, but for net profit participants the movie remained $24.3 million in the hole."[19] The film reportedly generated a box office gross of more than $300 million as of May 1989 but was still showing a loss in excess of $25 million.[20] As of July 1991, the same film reported a $400 million box office gross but according to the MGM/Pathe accounting statements for the period from November 1990 to February 1991, it was $27 million away from breaking even.[21] "Worse, because of a complex deal with actors Dustin Hoffman and Tom Cruise and director Barry Levinson as well as escalating interest charges, the film is actually generating more costs than revenues. The statement indicates that *Rain Man* earned about $830,000 compared with expenses of more than $2 million during the four months' interest fees were roughly $591,000."[22]

7. *Who Framed Roger Rabbit?*—Another Touchstone Pictures release *Who Framed Roger Rabbit?* (released in June of 1988) reportedly grossed $150 million by January, 1989 but was still showing a loss.[23] This film "had returned more than $205 million to Disney in the form of gross receipts as of

Dec. 31, 1990, but was still showing a net deficit of $19.6 million" for purposes of net profit calculations.[24]

8. *Coming to America*—At one point in early 1990, Paramount's 1988 release *Coming to America* was reported to have "gross receipts in excess of $160 million . . . while still showing a loss of $18 million."[25] In March of that same year, worldwide box-office receipts were reported to be approximately $250 million, but the film was still showing a $17 million dollar loss.[26] *Premiere* magazine reported in June of 1992 that *Coming to America* "was still in the red, despite grosses in excess of $350 million."[27]

9. *Batman*—The Warner Bros. 1989 release *Batman* was the fifth-highest grossing motion picture in history as of September of 1990 (at $253.4 million) and the No. 1 box-office hit of all time for Warners but was still $35.8 million in the red and not likely to ever show a profit, according to financial statements obtained by the *Los Angeles Times*.[28]

It would appear from this limited survey that making a good movie does not solve the problem of major studio/distributor business practices that tend to result in significantly reduced gross and net profit participations for others besides such distributors. A complete analysis of the net profit status of all of the feature films released by the major studio/distributors in the last ten years would be even more revealing, but that cannot be done, because the major studio/distributors will not make that information available. If the major studio/distributors wish to refute this apparent problem, let them step forward with a more complete factual picture (i.e., how many motion pictures released by each of the major studio/distributors in the past ten years resulted in gross or net profits for others besides the distributors, which movies and what were the percentages of such movies as compared to the total number of films released by each such distributor?).

During the Buchwald v. Paramount case the studio provided figures to counter the argument that net profits are seldom paid. The studio maintained that during the period from 1975 through 1988 "twenty-nine Paramount movies in all had generated $153,394,000 in net profits for ninety-four participants."[29] That's an average of $10,956,714 in net profits per year or $1,631,851 per participant (of those who actually received net profits). This may sound favorable to net profit participants, but it might not look quite so generous if the studio would permit a comparison of what the net profit participants received as a group to what the studio/distributor received. Furthermore, these figures would not seem so favorable if the studio would release accurate statistics on how many net profit participants during that same period received nothing for their interests. After all, in five of those years, only one film out of all of the films released by Paramount in each of those years generated net profits. In another five of those years only two of the Paramount releases generated net profits. At no time during the period covered by the figures released by Paramount did a significant percentage of the films released generate net profits. During the three-year period 1985 through 1987, Paramount actually released 32 films. Only five of those generated net profits (a 16 percent ratio) which is more favorable than the estimates of industry commentators for all of the major studio/distributors, but still low. Note that Paramount did not release a list of all of its films during those years, thus anyone seeking to develop a more accurate picture of the company's net profit situation would have to do additional research. For that reason, David Robb's series in *The Hollywood Reporter* does not tell the whole story.

Critics of the Film Industry Net Profit System

People inside and outside the U.S. film industry have been critical of the net profit system for many years. So as not to underestimate the level of criticism a considerable number of quotes relating to the net profit problem are included here:

1. *Comedian's heirs.* "Groucho Marx's estate [had to hire a profit participation auditor] . . . in trying to extract more profits out of the 1930s comedy *A Night at the Opera.*"[30]

2. *Anthropologist.* "Back in the forties, the anthropologist, Hortense Powdermaker, observed, 'In all field work there is usually one piece of esoteric data which is hidden by the natives. Among the Melanesians in the Southwest Pacific it is black magic. Among the Hollywood executives it is net profits.' "[31]

3. *Granddaughter of industry mogul.* "Even the granddaughter of Cecil B. De Mille . . . [had] to go back to Paramount nearly forty years after the studio released 'The Ten Commandments' (1956) and demand her late grandfather's full and up-to-date profit participation in the movie."[32]

4. *Film director.* Director Jules Dassin after leaving Hollywood for Europe following his blacklisting by the studios in the 50s, did go on to produce the hit film *Never On Sunday* (1960) as a low budget movie with his own money (a total production cost of $105,000) and the film's worldwide box office approached $10 million. But when Dassin's agent inquired of the chief executive of the film's distributor (Arthur Krim at United Artists) about Dassin's share of the net profits, he was told: "You're entitled to it, but you must bear in mind . . . that we lost money with some other movies. Therefore, we have to compensate for the losers with the winners."[33] In other words, the major studios are going to arbitrarily take some of the money that would have been paid to others to be sure the studios do not lose, although those others will.

5. *Writer.* "Academy Award-winning writer William Peter Blatty complained that Warner Bros. unfairly siphoned off his profits from the 1973 hit,

The Exorcist." Actors Sean Connery and Michael Caine similarly objected to their sparse net profits for *The Man Who Would be King*, a 1975 Allied Artists picture."[34]

6. *Independent producer.* There may be a difference in how the major studio/distributors handle net profits and the experience of people contracting with independent distributors, such as Roger Corman's New World Pictures. Roger Corman reports in his 1990 book that David Carradine who appeared in the 1975 New World film *Death Race* and "negotiated a percentage of the profits, has come back . . . and done a half-dozen pictures over the years because he knows we pay off on our back-end commitments on percentages."[35]

7. *Another quote from Roger Corman (producer/director).* Independent producer/director Roger Corman (talking about his tenure at independent New World Pictures) reports that by "the late 1970s . . . we had some major low-budget hits with huge profits, (and) . . . we also had earned a reputation for paying off and for being honest. We have never been sued—or even threatened with a suit—over profit participation; our books have been audited numerous times and the books always pass inspection. We have paid off more consistently, I believe, than any other company, and I believe too that our company has often had the highest profit ratio in the industry—profit in relation to money invested. Actors . . . came back and worked again for us because of this."[36]

8. *Actor.* Paul Newman challenged the accounting on his 1981 film *Fort Apache: The Bronx.*[37]

9. *Screenwriter/author.* Screenwriter/author William Goldman pointed out that "*Rocky* cost barely over one million and took in, worldwide, probably close to a hundred million. When money comes in over the transom like that, no bookkeeper in Hollywood can hide it all."[38]

10. *Author/studio executive.* "Profit participation was one of the backbones of independent production, but the feeling was widespread (not entirely without reason) that 'profits are meaningless,' because back room chicanery, 'creative bookkeeping,' and studio overheads pushed profits ever farther from the pockets of the creative 'partners,' while plushly lining those of the studios."[39]

11. *Entertainment attorney.* In his 1986 book, Los Angeles entertainment attorney Mark Litwak reported that profit participation auditors say studio errors "are of two types . . . clerical errors . . . and contract interpretation errors . . . [clerical errors] arise because studio accountants don't read the contracts made with filmmakers . . . [the contract interpretation errors occur because] the studios operate under the philosophy 'When in doubt resolve it in our favor and we will fight it out later if it is contested.' "[40] Since the studios are primarily responsible for the language used in their distribution agreements

and they have had staffs of attorneys working on those agreements for years, it is odd that the studios would have trouble interpreting their own contracts.

12. "Forbes" magazine reporter. In 1990, *Forbes* magazine writer Dana Weschler reported that according to "industry insiders, the studios have, over the years, devised a definition of net profits that guarantees that profit participants will rarely receive anything substantial no matter how successful the film."[41] Unfortunately, very few industry insiders will speak on the record about the net profit scam.

13. Corman back for more. In his 1991 book, Roger Corman says: "After a series of disagreements . . . I finally left Columbia and moved to Twentieth Century-Fox for one more try at working within the studio system. . . . I made *The St. Valentine's Day Massacre* on a budget of slightly over $1 million. . . . For one of the key roles I wanted Jack Nicholson, but I had to hire an actor under contract to the studio [and] . . . Fox's own accounting department was in charge of the costs. They sent me the first report on costs for construction. It took me five minutes to see what was going on. It wasn't that they were out to get me, but they had a multimillion-dollar overhead, which they had to spread around to whatever was shooting. 'Throw that report out,' I told [an associate] . . . and never look at another one they send us. This picture is going to cost whatever Fox says it's going to cost and there's nothing we can do about it.' "[42]

14. Another quote from Roger. In further commenting on studio bookkeeping, Roger Corman said "without question there is . . . deviousness in the accounting." He goes on to report on an incident relating to his production of *Capone* for Twentieth Century-Fox in which a subsequent accounting statement indicated "that the total advertising costs were to be deducted twice from the gross." Corman says he vigorously complained and threatened "to put everybody in jail for fraud." The double deduction was subsequently withdrawn by the studio.[43]

15. Author. Also in 1991, Nicolas Kent pointed out that "overhead costs and expenses are open to interpretation—and it's the studio's accountants who are doing the interpreting. Studios are notoriously tetchy about their accounting practices. The true figures are hard to come by."[44]

16. Trade press reporter. Today, "Almost everyone agrees that it is becoming increasingly difficult for actors, writers, producers and directors to ever see a dime in net profits from their movies."[45]

17. Profit participation auditor. Profit participation auditor Philip Hacker says: "in the vast majority of cases, the audits [we conduct] result in resolutions that are beneficial to our clients."[46]

18. Another profit participation auditor. "The studios accumulate the costs of poorly performing films, development, etc. and write them off against their successful movies."[47] Unfortunately, in many instances, these "costs" are very arbitrary and highly exaggerated.

19. *Writer/producer/director/actor.* Mel Brooks says: "Studio accounting should be a Busby Berkeley musical. When do they stop taking money? They take overhead on interest and interest on overhead. If a picture costs a million dollars to make, it's a third more just because of studio accounting procedures. If it's $15-million to honestly and actually produce, it will cost $26-million for the same picture to be done at a major studio."[48] On the other hand, Brooks also says: "I . . . have a good business manager-accountant, Robert Goldberg, who protects me from studio accounting." It would be more honest to say that Mel Brooks, like other members of the Hollywood insiders group do not need to be protected from studio accounting as much as the Hollywood outsiders.

20. *More from the profit participation auditors.* "Philip Hacker (an experienced motion picture profit participation auditor) . . . said . . . ' . . . it's getting harder and harder for net deals to pay out . . . ' for two basic reasons. 'First . . . it's getting harder because of the large sums that certain gross participants are paid. The other reason is that the cost of producing and distributing films has become much higher in recent years.' "[49]

21. *Nationally syndicated columnist.* Columnist Art Buchwald in his introduction to the book about his suit against Paramount described the litigation as "a minor breach of contract case which turned into an historic legal battle over the way the motion picture studios keep their books and diddle their talent."[50]

22. *Litigation attorney and playwright.* Pierce O'Donnell quotes from the David Mamet play *Speed-the-Plow*: "Two things I've learned, twenty-five years in the entertainment industry . . . two things which are always true . . . one . . . there is no net. . . . And I forget the second one."[51]

23. *Former studio executive and playwright.* Commenting on the same line in the Mamet play, former studio executive Dawn Steel said: "There's a great line David Mamet used in his play, *Speed-the-Plow*. 'There is no net.' It was a joke about the movie business. But it's no joke."[52]

24. *Attorney/author.* "The net profit formula is looked upon with contempt by many in the Hollywood community."[53]

25. *Profit participation auditor.* "Creative accounting is generally merely creative interpretation of the contract in favor of the distributor."[54] In order for the contract to be creatively interpreted, there needs to be a certain amount of ambiguity in the contract language used. Again, since the major studio/distributors have been using similar agreements for many years and are primarily responsible for the language used, it is fair for the courts to construe any ambiguities against them. The problem is getting them to court.

26. *Litigation attorneys.* In their 114-page "Preliminary Statement of

Contentions Concerning Damages and Accounting Issues" in the *Buchwald v. Paramount* case, Buchwald's attorneys stated that each studio "exploits . . . ambiguities [in its own standard profit participation contract] to the great financial detriment of profit participants. . . . And each studio abuses its awesome power and unconscionable contract terms to manage the venture by making hidden profits, charging exorbitant interest and utterly destroying any hope of 'net profits' by self-interested acts."[55]

27. *Attorney/author.* "Paramount's argument that the need to recoup its investment on financially unsuccessful films requires the current accounting procedures is questionable."[56]

28. *Attorney/author.* "The choice before the studios (following the *Buchwald* case) is whether they would rather return to the net profit formula as it was originally conceived—as a risk reducer which decreased immediate production costs by lower 'up-front' compensation—or continue to make deductions that discourage faith in a formula that currently offers little incentive to talent to accept less compensation 'up-front.' "[57]

29. *Profit participation auditor.* "According to [Philip] Hacker, who estimates that he has conducted more than 500 net profit audits, there are three basic problems that can arise during the course of a net profit audit of a studio's books . . . the studios 'occasionally make clerical mistakes' in their net profits calculations. . . . A second, more common problem . . . involves the interpretation of the profit participant's contract. . . . There is also the problem of allocations—particularly the allocation of money from 'packages' of films."[58] We have to understand that all of the profit participation auditors owe their prosperous livelihoods to the unscrupulous accounting and creative contract interpretation policies of the studios, thus the auditors do not want to be too critical of such studio policies, nor do they seriously propose radical changes for the system for fear such changes will result in less need for their services. Unfortunately, the profit participation auditors, like the entertainment attorneys have a certain amount of self-interest at stake and thus cannot be relied on to be overly enthusiastic about describing the wrongdoings of the major studio/distributors. After all, if the studios actually cleaned up their act, the profit participation auditors would be out of business.

30. *Entertainment attorney.* Entertainment attorney Peter Dekom "who has negotiated hundreds of participation deals on behalf of talent, says that 'the meaningfulness of net profits has deteriorated over the years . . . it is becoming harder and harder for films to break even—the point where production and distribution costs and fees equal income—and pay out net profits. Pictures use[d] to break [even] at three times negative costs, on average . . . but now they're breaking at five to six times negative costs, on average."[59]

31. *Attorney/author.* "Were the studios to make the net profit deal more

attractive to talent by decreasing, or even eliminating, interest and overhead charges, the studios could achieve a reduction in 'up-front' compensation and thus diminish immediate production costs."[60]

32. Entertainment attorney. "The studios have created a system in which virtually nobody who has anything to say about costs has any meaningful reward if the costs are brought under control."[61]

33. Trade press reporter. "Tom Girardi, the attorney representing the executive producers in their suit against Warner Bros. over net profits from *Batman* . . . maintains that net profit deals are 'fraudulent.' "[62]

34. Litigation attorney and newspaper investigative reporter. "An invisible hand took hundreds of millions of dollars out of the pockets of the film industry's creative talent every year. Over the fifty years that net profits had been part of the industry's compensation package, billions had been diverted into the studios' coffers. It was the financial 'crime' of the century."[63] Although, some of O'Donnell's statements in his book are obvious exaggerations, this seemingly outrageous statement appears to be right on the mark. My book attempts to go beyond the O'Donnell book in discussing and explaining the very many facets of what is essentially the white-collar "crime of the century," including studio business practices not considered in the *Paramount v. Buchwald* case.

35. Litigation attorney and newspaper investigative reporter. While Paramount representatives were telling the court in the *Buchwald v. Paramount* case that "most Paramount movies didn't earn a dime, the company's money men were seeking—and getting—millions in bank loans on the strength of their movie profits!"[64]

36. Litigation attorney and newspaper investigative reporter. Pierce O'Donnell and Dennis McDougal actually maintain that "Paramount maintained two accounting systems: one for itself and another for its net profit participants. They were as different as profits and losses. The first set of books, based on what accountants call generally accepted accounting principles (GAAP), was how Paramount was legally obligated to account to its stockholders, the IRS and the Securities and Exchange Commission. The other set of books was maintained according to the net profit definition included in Paramount's 53-page, single-spaced standard form contract. Instead of GAAP accounting, Hollywood's wags called this second brand of bookkeeping GAP accounting: revenues rarely bridged the gap between costs and profits."[65]

37. Movie star's production company. "Even Eddie Murphy was not exempt from Hollywood accounting. Personally, he earned a fortune because his contract called for a percentage of the gross. But his production company had the standard Paramount net profit deal and, unlike Murphy himself, the company earned nothing from *Coming to America*."[66]

38. Profit participation auditor. Profit participation auditor Bennett Newman was quoted in the February 20, 1978, issue of *Newsweek*: "The studio has the books and records, it interprets the contract, computes the profit and decides how much should be paid out. There's a certain amount of screwing going on all the time, but it's a mixed bag of inadvertent and intentional screwing."[67]

39. *Author/studio executive.* "The great majority of films today never achieve profit—that is, a level of financial return at which the filmmaker will share in revenues. But the distributor's 30 percent is inviolate and in what is called first position. The distributor is simply closer to the well, and once the machinery for film distribution was in place, the great controlling fact of the movie business as business became and remains: the machine must be fed."[68]

40. *A newswire service.* "Though hundreds of motion picture profit participation deals are made annually by stars with the major studios, fewer than 10 percent result in a check to participants."[69]

41. *Litigation attorney and newspaper investigative reporter.* "The studio system systematically drained its biggest hits of all money before any of its profit participants got anything."[70]

42. *Independent producer/director.* Roger Corman in talking about his independent film company New World Pictures said: "We functioned outside the mainstream but boasted a strong profit margin on many projects, enabling us to become known as a 'studio' that paid off on profit participation when it was offered. The tradition of never seeing profits in Hollywood simply did not apply to New World."[71]

43. *Independent producer/director.* In his book *How I Made a Hundred Movies in Hollywood and Never Lost a Dime*, low-budget filmmaker Roger Corman tells about the time he produced the film *Secret Invasion* on a budget of $592,000 for release by United Artists. "*Secret Invasion* looked like a big movie and we did it for exactly $592,000. It grossed somewhere around $3 million. The reason I remember the exact negative cost was that we got a distribution report from UA that said we were still a couple hundred thousand dollars from breaking even. I called the head of UA and said, 'Look, either straighten this report out or I'm sending in the auditors. There is no way $3 million in collected gross still leaves us $200,000 short of breaking even on $592,000.' 'Tell you what,' he said 'Don't audit. Well buy out your participation for $400,000. You can have a check tomorrow. But,' he added, 'you sign away all your rights, your piece is paid off, and you attest that our books are true and accurate. . . . We don't want anybody claiming our books aren't true and accurate.' I signed the paper attesting to UA's true and accurate bookkeeping methods and collected the $400,000."[72]

44. *Entertainment attorney.* "It is apparent that net profit participants have been taken for a major ride that does not have economic justification."[73]

45. *Independent filmmaker.* Independent filmmaker Henry Jaglom says:

"Another part of the formula to keep costs low is that I pay all my actors union scale. If they happen to be stars whose names help sell the picture . . . I give them a percentage of the profits, which in my case is actual profits, as opposed to the fancy bookkeeping 'profit participation' of studio pictures."[74]

46. *Author/screenwriter.* "Pressures are mounting from net-profit participants, who also want a piece of the pie in spite of extremely lopsided contractual definitions. One such participant, Art Buchwald, has even managed to convince a trial court that such net-profit definitions are unconscionable and represent contracts of 'adhesion.' Clauses that charged expenses on an accrual basis but included income on a cash basis, included gross participations as negative-cost items that accrued both overhead and interest, and provisions relating to the charging of interest and overhead against each other were rejected by the court."[75]

47. *Entertainment attorney.* "With rare exceptions for that tiny handful of producers with extraordinary bargaining power, it is . . . clear that a producer works on the movie pretty much for the fee paid up front. On most profitable pictures, net profits are clearly meaningless because of the high costs of production, marketing and the rather huge participations in dollar one gross given to major actors and, occasionally, to directors. So if the producer knows that he or she is never going to see any upside from the movie in question, the name of the game is to put as much money into the picture to make it look as good as possible so that it has the best possible chance of raising that producer's price on the next deal, even if putting that money into the motion picture is not necessarily economically sound."[76]

48. *Profit participation auditors.* "The standard studio deal produces a profit to the participant in less than 5 percent of the pictures released today."[77]

49. New York Times *reporter.* "There are almost never any net profits on films with gross-profit participants, and actors, writers, directors and others often resent watching a handful of people walk away with huge sums while they get nothing beyond their salaries."[78]

50. *Entertainment attorney.* "It is difficult for the studio to argue that they are attempting to share the benefits of a film with a writer or producer (typically those stuck with a net definition) when virtually no net profit definition today has any value."[79]

51. *Writer/producer/director/actor.* As much fun as most of Mel Brooks' movies have been, even he is critical of the studio net profit system saying: "It's impossible for a profit participant to make any money on a movie unless it's a gigantic hit because overhead and interest are always being charged to the film."[80] On the other hand, the above Brooks quote is wrong in at least three ways: (1) it is not impossible for profit participants to make any money on a movie, it is just extremely difficult; (2) the question of whether the movie is a "gigantic hit" is not as relevant to the profit participant as the difference be-

tween what the movie makes and what it costs (e.g., some recent studies have shown that many of the medium-budget pictures are more profitable than the big-budget films even though they are not "gigantic hits"); and (3) overhead and interest are charged only against the studio produced pictures. No studio production overhead is charged against films produced on a negative pickup basis, and interest will not be charged against a picture produced by an independent producer using investor money (as opposed to loaned funds or studio-provided funds).

52. Litigation attorney and newspaper investigative reporter. O'Donnell and McDougal say the studios have a "bizarre canon of ethics that allow[s] . . . studios to shaft their most profitable assets—their stars, their storytellers and their directors—while rewarding their most irresponsible and often useless executives."[81]

53. Independent producer/director. Again, illustrating the point that net profits can be generated by well intentioned companies that desire to allow others to share in the profit potential of their own motion pictures, Roger Corman says, "While there's a tradition in Hollywood that no one sees profits on a movie no matter what the box office, I've seen profits on probably 280 of . . . 300-odd pictures."[82]

54. Profit participation auditor. Profit participation auditor Phil Hacker estimates that "99 percent" of the cases he undertook in "two decades of challenging the studios . . . resulted in recovering the cost of the audit and extra money for his clients."[83] Phil Hacker is perfectly willing to offer such a self-serving statement but more hesitant to admit that the same is true for most all of the profit participation auditors, thus revealing that the favorable results for the net profit participant clients of profit participation auditors are not so much the result of the abilities of any individual profit participation auditor or firm but a consequence of the pervasive cheating of the major studios.

55. Attorney/author. If we assume that the studios are seriously interested in lowering production costs, the net profit scam does not make sense. "It is in the studios' interest to maintain the distribution fee which represents the major component of profit for the studios, yet reduce or eliminate interest and overhead charges. Profit participants would then have more confidence in net profit and would thus be more willing to accept lower 'up-front' compensation. To the studios, this should be a welcome occurrence, especially in a financial climate of increasing demands for higher fees."[84] In at least one sense, it may be argued that the studios are shooting themselves in the foot by continuing to support such an unreliable net profit system of contingent compensation. Obviously, anyone with any bargaining strength at all is going to insist on a gross profit participation as opposed to a net profit participation, since net profits are so unlikely to appear. This in turn significantly adds to the negative cost of the film, an issue which the studios are constantly complaining about. On the other hand, it would appear that since the net profit situation has continued for so long (at least fifty years), the studios must like it that way. This book explores the reasons why the studios pretend to want lower production costs but behave in a way that is inconsistent with that charade.

56. Screenwriter. William Goldman says: "Personally, I don't blame the stars for grabbing every cent they can. They all know the studios are going to rob them of as much of a film's profits as they can."[85]

57. Former studio executive. As an example of how high salaries for talent relates to the net profit problem, Peter Bart, in his book *Fade Out*, referred to the time when Frank Yablans was president of MGM the studio approached Sylvester Stallone about doing *Rocky IV*. The actor, however, wanted "a hefty boost in pay. And he wanted it up front—Stallone did not want to be at the mercy of some anonymous studio accountant to compute the film's gross and report his cut." Stallone wanted and got $15 million in cash.[86] Some might argue that this is a case where an actor with a considerable amount of bargaining power was able to demand and obtain substantial upfront compensation, thus confirming the fact that with enough leverage important issues in the film distribution deal are negotiable. On the other hand, this is really more of an indication as to just how much money is actually being made by the major studio/distributors. They would not give away that kind of money on the front end of a film project if they thought they would not be able to get their money back and more on the current film or unless the star's previous films in the series had been so profitable for the studios that they felt he was due to be cut in on a small part of the booty.

Masters of Understatement and Euphemistic Language

Thus far we have seen former studio executives, litigating attorneys, profit participation auditors, authors, screenwriters, entertainment attorneys, producers, directors, movie stars, newspaper reporters, a syndicated columnist, trade press reporters and a newswire service make critical and in some cases blistering statements about the major studio/distributor net profit scam. Can all of these people be wrong?

There is another entire group of people who either do not want to come right out and be critical of the major studio/distributors since their very livelihoods are determined to some extent by maintaining good relationships with those same studios or simply because they have a different perspective on net profits. Nevertheless, this group has provided us with some entertaining examples of understatement and euphemistic language in their descriptions of the major studio/distributor net profit scam.

1. Movie star. For example, actress Jane Fonda says: "Certain personalities in our community [are] . . . somewhat cavalier in terms of accounting. There doesn't seem to be any logic when you look at how much movies cost, and how often they go way over budget. It's totally incomprehensible to outsiders."[87] One of the purposes of this book is to make it comprehensible to outsiders.

2. *Wall Street financial analyst.* Merrill Lynch financial analyst and author Harold Vogel provides the opinion that "standard . . . accounting and forecasting methods as taught in the business schools don't seem to work very well when applied to this industry. In fact, nowhere does the notion of financial artistry become more evident . . . than in accounting for film-company profits—a subject on which cynicism abounds."[88]

3. *Writer/producer/director/actor.* Producer, director, writer, actor Mel Brooks softens his tone a bit by saying: "In the movie business it's important to understand the nature of money and how to sail through those terrible white waters with reefs and sharks, where art and money meet."[89]

4. *Entertainment Attorney.* Entertainment attorney Mark Litwak says that his "experience with distributors has taught [him] . . . that filmmakers need to be very careful when entering distribution agreements."[90] Of course, this may be viewed as another of those self-serving statements by an industry professional who stands to gain by persuading film producers that negotiating distribution agreements without the advice of counsel is reckless indeed.

Early History of Profit Participations

Now there also seems to be some confusion about the history of the net profit deal. Most writers report that the 1950 Universal deal with James Stewart was the first net profit participation. For example, Nicholas Kent reports that "in 1950 James Stewart's agent, Lew Wassermann, made a deal with Universal whereby Stewart waived his customary fee of $250,000 in return for a half-share in the net profits of the movie, *Winchester 73*. . . . Today [Kent says], some stars share the profits without sharing the risk."[91]

Screenwriter/author William Goldman cites the approximate same time period, although a different movie, saying that "*Bend of the River* changed everything. In many ways, this little-remembered 1952 Jimmy Stewart Western is as important as any film ever in its effect on the industry. Stewart's agent . . . Lew Wassermann [who went on to become the head of MCA-Universal] . . . arrange[d] for Stewart to take less than his usual salary in exchange for a percentage of the film's potential profits. It was a gamble that worked: *Bend of the River* was the number-two box-office film of its year, and Stewart cleaned up. Nothing has been the same since. Today, all stars command a percentage of the profits and, if they are superstars, a percentage of the [distributor's] gross [receipts], [net] profits being like the horizon, receding as fast as you approach."[92]

Profit participation auditor Steven Sills also claims Jimmy Stewart was the first net profit participant. He says: "The very first net profit participant was Jimmy Stewart. He accepted the offer of Samuel Goldwyn to take a net profit participation in lieu of his regular salary because Goldwyn did not have the money to pay his regular salary. The movie was a financial success and Stewart profited from his net profit participation. Subsequently others wanted net profits too."[93]

Also, somewhat consistent with these reports on the beginnings of the net profit deal (although he allows for the possibility that other net profit deals may have existed) investigative reporter and author Dan Moldea reports that "Associated Press Hollywood correspondent James Bacon credited MCA's Lew Wassermann with saving Universal Pictures by getting his client Jimmy Stewart to play the lead in the 1950 Western drama *Winchester 73*." According to Moldea, Bacon said, "Bill Goetz was head of the studio and it was in financial trouble. . . . There were no star names on the roster (and) . . . Goetz . . . needed a star name to sell the picture. Wassermann . . . demanded—and got— a fabulous deal for Stewart that netted him fifty percent of the profits. The movie was a blockbuster at the box office. Jimmy got rich. Goetz got blasted by all the other studio heads for ruining the industry. Percentage deals for stars were practically unheard of in those days."[94] Of course, as this book reveals the percentage deals have hardly ruined the industry for the major studio/distributors and their top executives as claimed.

Finally, Mel Stattler, a 43-year veteran of the motion picture industry and (at the time of his testimony in the *Buchwald v. Paramount* case) senior executive consultant for MCA/Universal Studios (another of the major studio/distributors) agreed with Dan Moldea and James Bacon on the Stewart deal. Stattler testified in the *Buchwald* case that "the first net profit deal was struck in 1950 in actor Jimmy Stewart's contract for the motion picture *Winchester 73*. Unable to provide Stewart with the $200,000 to $250,000 he usually commanded per film, Universal, in lieu of fixed 'up-front' compensation, gave him a fifty percent share of the film's 'net profits,' defined in the contract as the point at which the film earned in gross receipts twice its negative cost. This was the contractually defined breakeven point."[95]

In truth, neither of these now-famous Jimmy Stewart deals appear to be the first example of a net profits arrangement. According to Patrick Robertson, author of *The Guinness Book of Movie Facts & Feats*, "The first American artist . . . to receive a percentage deal was James O'Neill (father of Eugene) who played the wronged Edmond Dantes in Famous Players' maiden production *The Count of Monte Cristo* (1913)." O'Neill was offered "20 per cent of the net profits . . . [the film] eventually grossed $45,539.32, of which O'Neill received $3,813.32."[96]

In addition, Hollywood historian Neal Gabler reports that "Paramount . . . [was] formed in 1914 by five exchangemen to distribute films on a reliable and national basis. Producers got $35,000 per film, in advance, and 65 percent of the profits of each film."[97] Gabler does not distinguish, however, between net and gross profits in reporting this Paramount deal, and the deal was with producers not actors, although still a profit participation.

Harry Warner's granddaughter Cass Warner Sperling provides another early report (1917) of a profit participation (although for an author not an actor). In her book *Hollywood Be Thy Name—The Warner Brothers Story*, she reports that when Harry Warner was seeking to buy the motion picture rights to Ambassador James W. Gerard's newly published book *My Four Years in Germany*, Warner told Gerard: "We can't offer a lot of money. . . . But we can assign you a good percentage of the profits." Ultimately, they struck a deal for a $50,000 up-front payment, "plus twenty percent of the profits."[98] Again, in this report, no distinction was made between net and gross profits, although it might be safe to assume that the early distributors were smart enough not to give away gross participations.

On the other hand, academic Gorham Kindem reports that "major movie stars in the 1920s had often received a percentage of the net movie profits."[99] And, in a second reference to profit participation deals, Neal Gabler reported that after the Frank Capra film *It Happened One Night* won an unprecedented five Oscars, for the 1934 release, Columbia's Harry Cohn "tore up Capra's contract and tendered him a new one, giving him $100,000 per picture and 25 percent of the profits."[100]

Patrick Robertson also reports that as "an inducement . . . RKO producer Pandro S. Berman has attested that Fred Astaire received a percentage of the profits on several of his RKO musicals of the 1930s, though this was kept a closely guarded secret at the time."[101] Even first-time feature film producer Orson Welles (at age 24) received a 20 percent net profit participation in "the two-film contract" he signed with RKO on July 22, 1939.[102]

Patrick Robertson did subsequently write about the famous James Stewart deal saying, "A breakthrough came with the deal negotiated with Universal by James Stewart's agent Lew Wassermann for *Winchester 73* (1950). Stewart was able to command up to $250,000 as a fixed fee for a picture, but this was beyond the resources of Universal after a series of flops. It was agreed that Stewart should receive a 50 percent share of the picture's net profits. These were to be defined as anything over twice the negative cost of the film . . . his share of the profits was $600,000. . . . For subsequent films Stewart received his standard $250,000 up front plus 10 percent of the gross."[103]

Net Profits as Risk Reducer

The history of net profits in the film industry "reveals that the original formulation, in its unadulterated form, operated as a risk reducer; it decreased immediate production costs by lowering 'up-front compensation.' "[104] On this point, Mel Stattler further testified in the *Buchwald* case that the "studio gave [Jimmy] Stewart . . . his [early net profit] participation to minimize its risk by immediately reducing the film's production cost. Thus, at its inception, the net profit deal was intended to be a risk reducer for the studio because it spread part of the risk of filmmaking to the performer. Sattler asserted that '[net profit] . . . deals soon ceased being a way to share the risk of failure and instead, became a way for performers to share only the rewards of success.' Agents began demanding such compensation on behalf of their clients in addition to, rather than in lieu of, their salary. In essence, these demands undermined net profit's risk reducing function. The studios responded in the mid-1950s, modifying the amount of revenue needed to breakeven by increasing distribution fees and charging interest on money borrowed and advanced for production costs."[105]

Actually, no one including Mel Sattler is in a position to make a blanket characterization of all net profit deals today as "bonus" deals as opposed to "in lieu of" deals. Only the agent, talent and studio/distributor involved in the specific negotiations can make such a claim and they might disagree as to the characterization in many cases. If the studio wants to characterize net profit participations as "bonuses" (as opposed to "in lieu of compensation") then they should state that in the contract, so that it becomes an issue that is negotiated, even if the parties are of unequal bargaining strength.

The Industry Apologists

In all fairness, there are a number of trade press reporters, industry commentators, financial analysts, university professors, entertainment attorneys, studio executives, accountants and producers who sometimes actually argue in support of the studios' position regarding net profits. For example, the *Hollywood Reporter*'s David Robb was basically repeating the industry line regarding net profits when he stated that "public perception has come to confuse net profits, which is a term of art, with real profits" and that such perceptions are "fueled by erroneous news accounts of the *Coming to America* and *Batman* lawsuits."[106] This film industry propaganda suggests that the term "net profits" is a somewhat meaningless technical term that should not raise any expectations of real profits, and, of course, that all of the business practices routinely utilized by the major studio/distributors to make certain that there are no real profits to be shared with others are perfectly legitimate.

Others, like attorney Paul Lazarus, would suggest that its all just a misunderstanding. He says, in "the film business, actors, directors and producers—third-party profit participants—often cry foul when it comes to what they claim is their fair share of profits of what appears to be a hugely successful motion picture. Phrases like 'creative accounting' are used to characterize the actions of distribution companies that allegedly have siphoned off these profit participants' 'just rewards.' Indeed, the popular perception—even among industry insiders—is that only when a film is a megahit will there be enough net profits to prevent a studio from 'hiding' all the money."[107]

Financial analyst Harold Vogel rationalizes studio accounting by saying that "intelligent and honest people can have significant differences in opinion as to how best to account for their incomes and costs."[108] On the other hand, if there were no concerted effort to cheat net profit participants the studios would have been able to eliminate any "differences in opinion" about how the language used in their contracts ought to be interpreted by "intelligent and honest people" by now. But that is exactly the point. Since most people negotiating with the studios do not have the leverage to insist on more fair provisions, the studios must be the entities responsible for the language and the results. In addition, the studios must intend those results.

University professor David Prindle states that one "financial strategy used systematically by the major studios is referred to informally as creative accounting. This is not, as the phrase implies, the practice of out-and-out embezzlement. Rather, it is wielding the power of distribution to forcibly extract payments from the revenue stream that would otherwise be used to calculate the return to various profit participants."[109] Embezzlement, on the other hand, is the fraudulent appropriation to one's own use of someone else's property. So, what's the difference? Maybe a more accurate description of the studio net profit scam would be grand theft.

Attorneys David Nochimson and Leon Brachman suggest that the problem really is false or unreasonable expectations. They say that "net profits conjures up in the minds of profit participants an accounting concept, and when . . . expectations are not realized, the . . . studio—is accused of chicanery and sometimes worse. What must be kept in mind—the discrepancies revealed by audits notwithstanding—is that net profit participations (and other forms of contingent compensation) are negotiated contractual definitions which have evolved within the motion picture industry and have little to do with the real profit of a picture as measured by generally accepted accounting principles."[110] These attorneys are completely ignoring the problems relating to contracts of adhesion and unconscionability (see discussion of those concepts below).

Paramount attorney Chuck Diamond stated in a radio interview during the *Buchwald v. Paramount* trial that "The contractual terms of net profits really have little to do after all is said and done [with] whether the studio has lost money or made money." He said, "We're not talking about profits the way accountants talk about profits."[111]

"Despite all the recent hype and hoopla to the contrary, the major motion picture studios each year pay out millions of dollars in net profits to writers, producers, directors and actors who don't otherwise have the clout to get better back-end deals or more money up front. . . . Most standard net profit deals never pay out a dime, and they are often one-sided, with the studios dictating the terms. Still, the fact remains, net profits are not a hoax."[112] No, but net profits can be granted or taken away at the complete discretion of the distributor because the film distribution agreements contain excessive amounts of ambiguous language or provisions providing enormous amounts of discretion to the distributor. It is impossible to imagine that anyone in their right mind, who understood the terms of these agreements, would sign them except under the duress of "take it or leave it" and without it such persons do not have a career in the film industry.

Tom Pollock, chairman of the MCA Motion Picture Group admits that there are "fewer net proceeds (same as 'net profits') today" but he says, "It's a myth that major studios are cooking the books, that the books are getting juggled." Pollock says, "The profit margins are shrinking in the industry overall . . . because there's some large gross players pushing break-even back."[113] This Tom Pollock quote provides an example of a studio executive trying to shift the blame for high production costs to major talent, another very common practice.

Producer/author Art Linson points out that "even waitresses know that very few people ever see money once the movie is in release."[114] Thus, Linson is making the argument that since nearly everyone knows net profits are not likely to appear, then no one should count on getting them and no one should be disappointed. Of course, what Art Linson is conveniently overlooking is the fact that very few people in the industry on the talent side have the clout to demand all of their compensation up front, therefore such persons must rely to some extent on net profits, in order to participate equitably in the upside potential of their own movies.

Studio executives have even come very close to bragging about keeping most of the money generated by a film. In her book *They Can Kill You But They Can't Eat You* Dawn Steel reports that "*Flatliners* was to become one of the most profitable films in Columbia's history. The profit-to-cost ratio was huge, particularly because the back-end participation was virtually nonexistent; none of the cast was . . . a big movie star [and] . . . Except for Michael Douglas's gross participation as a producer, all the other players were net participants. . . . We were able to put virtually all the profits in Columbia's pockets."[115]

Police Academy producer Paul Malansky received net profits on the Police Academy series of films. He says: "It's possible to get net profits even in the context of some of these net profit definitions . . . that's what keeps independent producers going—the hope of catching the golden ring. . . . The secret to net profitability . . . is to keep the costs of producing and exploiting a picture within reason. . . . If negative costs are reasonable . . . and the costs of exploiting the picture are not exaggerated, and there are no gross participants and the picture does reasonably well . . . there is no reason why net profit participants shouldn't see a little money."[116] What Paul Malansky is not admitting here is that he may be getting favored treatment since he is one of the members of the so-called Hollywood insider's club. In addition, this book is filled with reasons why profit participants are not likely to see any money regardless of the other factors Malansky cites. Thus, it would appear more likely that Malansky is, at the very least, participating in a shared objective by the Hollywood insider community to mislead the rest of the film community and the public about the fairness of its net profit system.

Former studio accountant David Leedy also likes to suggest that there are consistent winners in the film industry because they understand the deal. He says that "while it is possible to play the game without knowing the rules and many movies are made without careful profit projections, the most consistent winners are individuals and companies who take the time to understand the potential financial effects of their decisions and actions."[117] This appears to be another position inspired by the studios and it reaches the wrong conclusion for the wrong reason. Of all the authors cited in this work, Leedy appears to be as consistently supportive of the studio system as anyone.

Another proponent of the "it's the fault of ignorant people" argument, Leedy, suggests that "the reason participants 'cry foul' is primarily because neither they nor their advisors reviewed all of these facets before signing their agreements. For example, [Leedy says] it is obvious that Fess Parker's problem in not seeing any profits from the Daniel Boone series is due to unanticipated interest accruing on unrecouped costs. Mr. Buchwald's problem was not foreseeing the effect on the net profits computation of two very substantial participations in gross (Landis and Murphy). Seldom, if ever, is the problem due to 'cheating' by the Distributor."[118] Again, what is obvious is that David Leedy is on the side of the major studio/distributors. It could just as accurately be argued that the way the studios handle interest is unconscionable.

Another oversimplified approach is put forward by the president of an independent distributor who says: "The common misconception is that the accounting abuses create the lack of a net. In fact the real problem is that there is so much general mistrust in the Hollywood system that stars and star directors demand larger and larger gross participations. A film with these kinds of participations has what is called a floating breakeven point, which is responsible for the fact that there will never be a net profit on paper, even if the film is earning a lot of money. Again indies have the advantage . . . they are dealing with films that usually don't have personnel of the caliber that can command these gross participations. Also, the films are more modestly budgeted and efficiently marketed. Therefore if a film hits, there is a much greater chance that net points will be quite meaningful."[119]

The Lawyerly Perspective

Entertainment attorneys sometimes bring a unique perspective to the net profit debate. For example, attorneys Nochimson and Brachman concluded their 1986 article by saying:

> Contingent compensation is a sophisticated, complex and often misunderstood area of the motion picture business and requires careful analysis of many issues, the effect of which can best be understood during actual negotiations. It must be kept in mind, however, that like any contract negotiation, the negotiation of net profits involves a real participant and a real studio where the relative bargaining position of the parties may depend on a number of circumstances which will affect the result. Each side has a valid interest to protect. The participant wants to share in the fruits of his labor if the picture in which he has played a part has been successful. The studio wants to recover its costs and obtain a fair return for taking the risk before sharing the profits with others. It is the measurement of this success that underlies the negotiation of net profits and determines how the negotiating lines between participants and studios are drawn.[120]

Hillary Bibicoff, meanwhile, suggests an even more simplistic approach, saying that "whether or not [the net profit participant] . . . receives any return from his profit participation deal depends on the wording of his contract"[121] and that "negotiating some small changes in the studio contracts would result in large differences in the amount of revenue that profit participants could realize."[122]

In the tradition of other practicing entertainment attorneys, Gunther Schiff also suggests that the "battle is often lost in advance because the Participant or his/her representatives do not examine and negotiate the 'standard definition,' which is usually only referred, but sometimes attached, to an initial deal memo. A careful reading of the boilerplate contained in contracts defining the elements of accounting for the Participation . . . which are quite similar in the contracts of most of the production and distribution companies . . . will prove that the Studios provide delineations, in excruciating detail, of their procedures for calculating the Participations . . . the Participant . . . has a plethora of possible changes which may be negotiated. . . . A Participant who has enough clout and determination should obtain substantial relief from some of the more onerous provisions of the 'standard terms.' . . . In order for a Participant to gain a maximum share in the bonanza from a successful project, the effort must be made at the time the deal is negotiated, in order to obtain as many modifications in the Studio's standard definition as possible."[123]

In fact, the stated purpose of the Hillary Bibicoff article in the *Loyola Entertainment Law Journal* was "to create a guide which can be used by profit participants to clarify what an investment in a movie will net them. This allows profit participants to either negotiate for changes in the contract terms, or at least enter into the contract knowing what they are getting."[124] This view represents the hopelessly naive perspective of a law student who has not had the opportunity to work for any significant time in the film industry. This particular law student's article was also encouraged by a law professor who professionally benefits from his support for the positions of the major studio/distributors.

The bottom line according to Gunther Schiff is that so-called standard provisions "are customarily drawn to favor the entity preparing the contract. . . . If the other party fails to examine the document and be fully informed of, and satisfied with, its contents before signing on the dotted line, the agreement will probably result in disappointed expectations. Participants must bite the bullet and try to negotiate improvements in the Definition, and follow up by audit if they are not to be disappointed when a payoff seems certain."[125] This argument is short-sighted in the sense that the vast majority of participants simply do not have the leverage to negotiate a significantly improved definition of net profits and the profit participation audit is limited in its utility, simply because the studios routinely respond to the audit demand for payment with a perfunctory "sue us" (see discussion of this litigation strategy of the major studio/distributors in *How the Movie Wars Were Won*).

Rudolph Petersdorf, a former vp business affairs at both Universal Pictures and Warner Bros in his July 4, 1990, deposition as an expert witness for Art Buchwald, said that "under the system in use for computing net profits, when you combined a system of escalating production costs, escalating distribution costs, which the studio felt was necessary in order to support the heavy investment in the production, and then when you add on top of that the participation of a gross participant, that the amount of money necessary for a film to reach net profits was being pushed back to a point almost impossible to reach."[126] On the other hand, if we combine a system of artificially inflated production costs, with artificially inflated distribution costs and gross profit participations demanded by greedy agents, this really results in a systemized method of cheating net profit participants.

Entertainment attorney Norman Garey (now deceased) said: "It is imperative that the distributors who are responsible for the payment of these participations be policed, because they do make mistakes, both from an accounting and from a contract-interpretation standpoint."[127]

All of these lawyers seem to be suggesting that most of the film profit participants' problems can be solved through negotiation. Of course, this less than forthright self-serving position is actually designed to bring in more clients for the attorneys. This is an example of how the entertainment attorneys who are "players" participate in the film industry's net profit scam. If they can convince gross and net profit participants through lectures, articles, books and word of mouth that the lawyers can solve the prospective profit participants' problems with the film industry's net profit system through study and negotiation, then the profit participants will continue to engage the services of such attorneys and pay considerable amounts of money, only to discover after the fact, that the problem had really not been solved, only modified slightly. Generally speaking, these attorneys know in advance they cannot solve the problem through negotiation; they can only make it a little less onerous for their clients.

Of course, one of the things, that helps the lawyers make their argument that smarter and better negotiating is the answer to the net profit problem is the occasional spectacular success of a filmmaker. "When he was negotiating to make *Star Wars* for Twentieth Century-Fox (for example), Lucas persuaded the studio to give him control of the movie's merchandising rights as well as control of any future sequels in return for paying a smaller fee upfront."[128] The results made George Lucas a very rich man. But such successes are so rare that they should be considered anomalies.

The creative accounting/contract interpretation problem may not only exist at the distributor level. As Triad Artists' Lee Rosenberg says: "The agency commission is 10% of all gross monies received by the writer (or other client), whether from profit participation or from payment made for rights and/or services. All monies go directly to the agency. We usually deduct the commission and issue the client's check within three to five days."[129] This means that talent not only has to wait for the exhibitor and distributor to take their deductions before talent is paid, but the talent agency also gets to take its respective cut out of the film's revenue stream before talent. Thus, at least three different entities have an opportunity to make "mistakes" before monies are paid to talent. Also, when talent agencies are involved in packaging a deal, they may demand an executive producer fee of more than 10 percent in lieu of or in addition to their normal cut. This book merely focuses on the specific problems relating to the distributor transaction and those specific problems relating to the film distribution deal. A look at agency and exhibitor accounting, however, might also prove revealing.

2 | The Five Major Film Finance/Distribution Scenarios

Now that we have framed some of the issues by setting forth a sampling of the rather inflammatory statements from both sides of the net profit debate, it would be helpful to develop a better understanding of the environment in which the feature film distribution agreement is made and what specific distributor business practices have prompted all of the controversy. The following analysis and discussion of the five major film finance/distribution scenarios is provided to help meet that objective. As mentioned earlier, most feature film distribution agreements have some of the same provisions, although the specific language and the terms may differ. In any case, film finance and distribution arrangements typically fall within one of the following described general categories:

(1) *In-house production/distribution.* With the in-house production/distribution arrangement, the studio/distributor develops the film project at the studio, gives a "greenlight" to studio production funding and distributes the completed film through its studio affiliated distributor who distributes using the distributor's funds. An independent producer may have originally submitted the idea, concept, underlying property, outline, synopsis, treatment or screenplay to the studio, but rights to produce as a motion picture were then acquired by the studio and if the producer remained attached, he or she did so as an employee of the studio.

(2) *Production-financing/distribution agreement.* In the production-financing/distribution (P-F/D) arrangement, the studio/distributor's money is used to produce and distribute the film that is brought to the studio by an independent producer with a fairly complete package, that is, acquisition, development and packaging costs have already been incurred by the independent producer. The distribution agreement is entered into (theoretically) prior to the start of production, or at least before the end of production. The studio/distributors provide production and distribution funds.

(3) *Negative pickup.* In the negative pickup deal, the distributor makes a contractual commitment to distribute the film and to pay the production costs and associated fees if the film meets specified delivery requirements (as set out in the distribution agreement), and the producer uses this contractual commit-

ment to secure production financing from a third party lender or financier. The distributor <u>only provides distribution funds</u>. Thus, using a negative pickup arrangement to finance the production costs of a motion picture will eliminate some of the "unconscionable" practices of distributors, at least with respect to studio interest (see discussion of interest below). The negative pickup agreement is typically entered <u>into prior to the production of</u> the film. Note that many in the film industry confuse the negative pickup deal with what is more accurately described as a pure acquisition deal, as described below.

Acquisition deal. In the acquisition deal, nondistributor funds are used to acquire the rights to a property, develop the screenplay, package and produce the film, but <u>distributor funds are used to distribute the motion picture.</u> In addition, the distribution agreement is entered into after the film is produced (i.e., the film is already "in the can"). Theoretically, the terms of the distribution deal will be more favorable to the producer and all parties the producer represents with the acquisition deal as opposed to the three previously discussed film finance/distribution scenarios.

Rent-a-distributor. In a rent-a-distributor situation, nondistributor funds are used to acquire the rights to a property, develop the screenplay, package and produce the film as well as to provide most if not all of the distribution funds. Just as with the acquisition deal, the distribution agreement in the rent-a-distributor scenario is generally entered into after the film is produced. Distributor fees are generally at their lowest with this transaction(e.g., 15 percent).

The following chart illustrates the essential differences between these five film financing/distribution scenarios:

	In-house production/ distribution	Production-financing/ distribution	Negative pickup arrangement	Acquisition deal	Rent-a-distributor
Source of production funds	Studio/ distributor	Studio/ distributor	Lender	Third party	Third party
Source of P&A funds	Distributor	Distributor	Distributor	Distributor	Non-distributor
Time of agreement	Prior to production	Prior to production	Before film completed	After film completed	After film completed

3 | Types of Distribution Deals

DURING THE NEARLY one-hundred-year history of the film industry, the deal between producers and distributors, (i.e., the way in which film revenues are split as between the distributor and the production group) has evolved considerably. Although, the following does not attempt to provide an accurate chronological presentation of that distribution deal evolution, it does represent, as a practical matter, most of the important distinguishable forms through which the feature film distribution deal has passed during the history of the industry.

First dollar gross deal. First-dollar gross deal (an extremely rare arrangement that is all but extinct) provides that the producer or other profit participant gets a stated percentage (e.g., 30 percent of the distributor's gross until a multiple of print and ad expenditures is reached, at which point the producer's share escalates to a larger percentage). Obviously, the profit participant would have to have an extremely powerful package to command a first-dollar deal, even to get one with distributor deductions for checking, collection, conversion, transfer, taxes, residuals, licenses and import and other distribution expenses off the top. In a first-dollar gross deal the distributor has a lot of upside potential and little downside protection, hence it is not a common deal. The producer in this first-dollar gross deal must have faith in the picture because no advance comes with the gross. Hence, the producer is also sacrificing downside protection for upside potential.

The 50/50 first dollar split. A rare but desirable variation from the producer's standpoint is a 50/50 split from the first dollar with no advance. The theory here is that since the producer financed the film (if that's the case), and the distributor is financing the distribution, they are taking an approximately equal risk and should therefore share equally from first dollar.

Modified gross deal. In a modified gross deal the producer gets an advance and the distribution company recoups a multiple of the advance plus its distribution expenses off the top, before splitting the remainder with the producer. This provides protection for both producer and distributor depending on the amount of the advance. However, as a gross deal it is extremely modified, so much so that in any other industry it would be considered a "net" deal.

The 70/30 major deal. In a slightly more common deal, the 70/30 major deal, the distributor deducts all distribution expenses off the top before dividing the receipts 70/30 with the producer.

The sliding scale. A variation from the 70/30 major deal is a sliding scale whereby the distributor pays for all promotional costs and receives 70 percent from the first million, 60 percent from the second million, and 50 percent thereafter. The argument in favor of the sliding scale is that the majority of the distributor's expenses for prints and advertising are incurred during the initial opening of the film.

The 50/50 net deal. In the 50/50 net deal, all distribution costs are deducted off the top and then the net is split on a 50/50 basis between the distributor and the producer group.

The net deal. The net deal is the distributor's favorite and with good reason. The distributor deducts its distribution fee then recoups all costs before giving the producer a cent. The producer's share may be some percentage of the net at that point or 100 percent. This is a high-risk situation for the producer and other net profit participants, especially if any production or completion money has been borrowed from a lending source that is not collateralized by a distributor's guarantee or if the repayment of such a loan is the producer's personal responsibility. With a strong heart and an even stronger picture, the producer has the potential for almost unlimited profits but also the potential for almost nothing. In the current marketplace, the net deal is probably the most common.

Comparing deals. Most distributors today will offer the net deal (i.e., the distributor will deduct its distribution fee and expenses out of the distributor's gross receipts revenue stream then give 100 percent of the balance, if any, to the producer). In a few instances, distributors may offer a deal in which the distributor's expenses are deducted from the distributor's gross receipts before the distributor's fee is deducted. If the producer is comparing that arrangement with a deal which provides for the distributor to deduct its fee from gross receipts before expenses, this makes it difficult to compare deals. In other words, if a distributor's distribution fee is 50 percent of what's left over after distribution expenses are first deducted, the distributor's fee ultimately may not be as much as a 35 percent distribution fee applied against all of the distributor's gross receipts, even if the distribution expenses are the same. Of course, it is generally to the distributor's advantage to deduct distribution expenses after its distribution fees because the fees are a percentage based on the earlier and larger portion of the revenue stream, whereas most of the distributor's expenses are flat, stated costs. Distributors' percentage fees based on some form of gross receipts may range from 15 percent to 40 percent depending on the medium and market.

Theoretical approaches. Distributors are fond of arguing that they are the ones risking their money so they have a right to recoup their money first. That is not always true and that is why it is important to recognize the distinctions between the five different film finance/distribution scenarios discussed above. In many instances, for example, independent producers have expended significant amounts of acquisition and development funds for a film before its production costs are financed by a major studio/distributor on a production-financing/distribution basis. The same is true for negative pickups and in that case the distributor does not put up any acquisition, development or production monies, only distribution expenses. Further, when an independent producer makes a deal with a distributor on acquisition basis (i.e., the distributor acquires the right to distribute the film after the film has been completed), the producer and/or the producer's investors' money has already been at risk for a period of time before the distributor ever becomes involved. Only in the in-house production arrangement is the distributor the sole funding source for development, production and distributor costs, thus, in all fairness, only in that situation, should the distributor be allowed to recoup its expenses before the producer and or third party investors recoup their expenses.

On the other hand, setting the "distributor takes all the risk" myth aside, the above described reasoning is not consistent with the typical reality of the respective bargaining power of the parties as between the film distributor and the producer. Thus, the distributor will generally take advantage of the producer at the negotiation stage and impose an onerous deal on the producer and all other net profit participants represented by the producer. In a market where the parties were of equal bargaining strength, the percentages paid out of the distributor's gross receipts would very likely approximate the value of the time, effort, skill and money each party had contributed to the project and had placed at risk, including the respective investments of all of such items during the development, production and distribution stages of the film.

4 | Negotiating the Distribution Deal

W HEN AN independent feature film producer or the entertainment attorney representing such a producer is negotiating the finer points of the film distribution deal with the distributor, there can be hundreds of issues and subissues theoretically on the table. The discussion below reviews some 135 or so of the most important questions that can be raised in the context of feature film distribution deal negotiations. The discussion does not attempt to place any actual dollar comparative value on the deal points presented or evaluate whether any particular producer or film has any realistic chance of favorably negotiating any specific issue in the current marketplace. The producer may be further assured that the distributor will object to many of these suggestions and will in some cases be able to conjure up persuasive sounding rhetoric to support the distributor's position, (e.g., "take it or leave it"). Preliminary concepts to keep in mind follow.

A. Deal memo versus long form agreements. A deal memo is a shortened version of a contract (e.g., a distribution agreement utilizing a letter agreement format), which theoretically covers the main points (deal points) agreed to by the parties, such as salary, time schedule, screen credit and percentage participation in the film's profits, if any. A deal memo is often used by the major studio business and affairs departments to get the film production process underway on a given film, with the intent that the studio's legal department will ultimately negotiate and draft a full agreement. For smaller independent producers and distributors, the deal memo may not be necessary or even desirable, since these smaller entities do not have the bureaucracy of a major studio that often slows the negotiating and drafting process, and in fact a deal memo may be dangerous since the more detailed provisions of the full contract may be much more burdensome or onerous for the producer and may even conflict with the original provisions of the deal memo.

Long form agreements are contracts that are fully negotiated (theoretically) and contain all of the terms and provisions intended by the parties thereto. Long form film distribution agreements, for example, relating to the licensing of feature films, are negotiated by and between the film's producer and a distributor (or their legal representatives) and usually include long lists of delivery items, detailed lists of what will be considered distribution expenses, extensive producer warranties, the laboratory access letter and an instrument of transfer. Sometimes, negotiators will opt for a letter agreement, deal memo or short form agreement in order to save time, although such a tactic involves certain risks if a dispute on a question not covered by the shorter form of agreement arises before the long form agreement is signed.

B. *Negotiated contractual terms*. The phrase "negotiated contractual definitions" refers to terms used in certain motion picture industry agreements, such as film distribution contracts, whose meanings have been specifically bargained for or settled on after some discussion between the parties to the contract. As seen earlier, some spokespersons for the major studio/distributors are fond of explaining that most if not all of the alleged "creative accounting" practices are really the result of disappointed net profit participants who did not understand the effect of the contractually defined terms in their agreements. It is probably more accurate to observe that most of these terms, whose defined meanings in film industry contracts sometimes vary considerably from the meanings of the same terms as used in the agreements of other industries, are not negotiated at all, and if they are negotiated, the negotiations are between parties with such a disparity in bargaining power that there is an absence of any meaningful choice on the part of the weaker party.

C. *Standard terms and conditions*. The standard terms and conditions section of the film distribution agreement is actually another variation on the distributor discretion problem. This section of the agreement purports to set out the terms and provisions relating to the distribution of a feature film that the studio considers to be its standard deal. It is important to recognize that what is considered standard for that studio may or may not be standard for another major studio/distributor or for an independent distributor, regardless of the fact that such provisions are often similar. After all, in theory (that is, if anyone was watching), it would be a violation of the antitrust laws for competitors like the major studio/distributors, even through the facilities of their trade association (the MPAA) to get together and agree on standard terms and conditions. Thus, the phrase "standard terms and conditions" does not necessarily mean that such terms and conditions are standard in the industry, nor should independent producers allow themselves to be led to believe that is the case. In other words, to the extent that the language in a feature film distribution deal is negotiable, the distributor's standard terms and conditions should also be negotiable.

Generally, the studio/distributor distribution agreement will also contain a provision which says, "To the extent any terms or conditions of the Standard Terms and Conditions are inconsistent with the Deal Terms, the Deal Terms shall govern." Thus, the studio is setting out in the "Standard Terms and Conditions" section what it would prefer with respect to certain issues and if producers want something different, they need to speak up during the negotiations and ask that the language in the "Standard Terms and Conditions" section be crossed out, modified or otherwise altered or that different language be included in the "Deal Terms" section of the agreement that overrules the "Standard Terms and Conditions" section. Of course, the resulting agreement becomes so cumbersome, disorganized and complex that even the most experienced producers have little chance of fully understanding its implications, even if they tried.

D. Fiduciary duty. Probably all of the feature film distributors will absolutely refuse to permit language in the distribution agreement that would create a fiduciary relationship between the distributor and the film's producer or other net profit participants. Court cases seeking to impose such a relationship without supporting contractual language between the parties have generally failed. On the other hand, the feature film distributor in its dealings with subdistributors, exhibitors and other film licensees (those to whom licenses are granted) is clearly supposed to be acting at least partly for the benefit of the net and gross profit participants (in addition to its own benefit) in such transactions. Unfortunately, the history of the U.S. film industry appears to indicate that at least the major studio/distributors have consistently acted for their own benefit to the detriment of such other parties.

E. Adhesion contracts and unconscionability. It bears repeating that the major studio/film distributors are fond of pointing out that many of the business practices that are complained about by others are actually practices authorized by the language of the film distribution agreement. However, such contracts have been found to be so heavily restrictive of one party (the distributor) while so nonrestrictive of another (the producer) that doubts arise as to its representation as a voluntary and uncoerced agreement. Such contracts are referred to as contracts of adhesion or unconscionable contracts. Courts have recognized there is often no true equality of bargaining power in such contracts and have accommodated that reality in interpreting such contracts. The concept implies a grave inequality of bargaining power between the parties. It often arises in the context of so-called "standard-form" printed contracts prepared by one party and submitted to the other on a "take it or leave it" basis.[1]

Although the concept of adhesion contracts has more typically been applied to consumer transactions, some courts have used this legal theory to reinterpret commercial agreements.[2] It is more common, however, for the legal concept of unconscionability to be applied to such transactions. Unconscionable contract provisions are so unreasonably detrimental to the interests of one of the contracting parties as to render the contract unenforceable. As pointed out above, the major studio/distributors have the market share and market power to overwhelmingly dominate the production, distribution and exhibition of U.S. made motion pictures, and thus it may be fair to characterize all feature film distribution agreements between independent producers and MPAA companies as unconscionable and therefore unenforceable. On the other hand, once the distributor takes control of the movie, there is no mechanism for enforcing compliance, except the audit and a lawsuit after the fact (often many years down the road).

In a further explanation of the relationship between the concepts of adhesive contracts and unconscionability, Adam Marcus explains that "once adhesiveness is found [in a contract], a court must then determine whether the whole contract or any individual provisions were contrary to the 'reasonable expectations' of the weaker or 'adhering' party . . . [or whether they are] unduly oppressive or 'unconscionable.' "[3] On the other hand, Marcus states that "in an analysis of the enforceability of contract provisions claimed to be unconscionable, the first step is to make a determination of whether the contract itself is adhesive."[4]

The *Buchwald* court, "relying on *Graham*, noted that part of the contract was negotiated . . . but stated that this did not require a conclusion that the contract was not adhesive."[5] The *Graham* court also stated there are circumstances where "the presence of other assertedly negotiable terms [will not act] to remove the taint of adhesion."[6]

"Utilizing the California Supreme Court's decision in *Graham*, the *Buchwald* court concluded that [the producer plaintiff's] . . . deal memo [with Paramount] contained 'boilerplate' language that was not negotiated, and that other clauses of the contract were presented to [the producer plaintiff] . . . on a 'take it or leave it' basis."[7] The judge in the *Paramount v. Buchwald* case ruled that the "standard form contract was a contract of adhesion, all the other studios' contracts were virtually identical, and seven provisions were unconscionable."[8] Barron's Law Dictionary defines "unconscionable" as a provision that is so "unreasonably detrimental to the interest of a contracting party as to render the contract unenforceable." Barron's further provides that the "basic test is whether, in the light of the general commercial background and the commercial needs of the particular trade or case, the clauses involved are so one-sided as to be unconscionable under the circumstances existing at the time of the making of the contract." Thus, an unconscionable contract or provision is a bargain so one-sided as to amount to an "absence of meaningful choice on the part of one of the parties together with contract terms which are unreasonably favorable to the other party." Barron's continues by saying that "ordinarily, one who signs an agreement without full knowledge of its terms might be held to assume the risk that he has entered into a one-sided bargain. But when a party of little bargaining power and hence little real choice, signs a commercially unreasonable contract with little or no knowledge of its terms, it is hardly likely that his consent . . . was ever given to all the terms. In such a case, the usual rule that the terms of an agreement are not to be questioned should be abandoned and the court should consider whether the terms of the contract are so unfair that enforcement should be withheld."[9]

In her unpublished paper, UCLA law student Teresa Garcia states that "unconscionability is a defense based on the gross unfairness and one-sidedness of a contract." Garcia says that generally, unconscionability means "no reasonable person would not be shocked by the terms of a contract that a party is asking the court to enforce against another party."[10] Unfair surprise and oppression are "the principal targets of the unconscionability doctrine."[11]

In its lawsuit against Buchwald, "Paramount argued that because the net profit provisions contained in [the] . . . contract have existed in Hollywood for years and were well known to [the plaintiff producer] . . . , he was in no way surprised and, therefore, the provisions cannot be found unconscionable."[12] On the other hand, the "*Buchwald* court cited the *Graham* case[13] as an example of a case where a contract provision was found to be unconscionable despite the absence of surprise on the part of the plaintiff."[14] The Graham case, on the other hand, "did not refer to 'surprise,' as such. Rather, it indicated that the provision 'was in [no] way contrary to the reasonable expectations of [the] plaintiff.' "[15]

The legislative history of the unconscionability defense in California "indicates that [it] . . . serves a dual purpose: the prevention of unfair surprise and oppression. 'Surprise' is defined as 'the extent to which the supposedly agreed-upon terms of the bargain are hidden in a prolix printed form drafted by the party seeking to enforce the disputed terms.' 'Oppression' occurs when there is 'an inequality of bargaining power which results in no real negotiation and 'an absence of meaningful choice.' "[16] A plaintiff, however, "need not prove both 'surprise' and 'oppression' to successfully assert the [unconscionability] defense. According to [the] *Buchwald* [case], 'the absence of surprise . . . does not render the doctrine of unconscionability inapplicable.' "[17]

Paramount further argued that California law bars "the offensive use of the unconscionability doctrine . . . [that the unconscionability doctrine is only available] . . . when used by a defendant as a 'shield,' not when used by a plaintiff as a 'sword.' The court's acceptance of such a limitation would have precluded the [*Buchwald*] plaintiffs from asserting a claim of unconscionability. . . . However . . . the *Buchwald* court agreed with the plaintiffs and concluded that the defense is not barred when it is raised in response to a defendant's reliance on a contract." That principle may be stated as follows: "where a defendant relies on a contract as written—when confronting a breach of contract or declaratory judgment action—the plaintiff can assert unconscionability."[18]

The Second Restatement of Contracts at Section 208 provides that a court may decline to enforce all or part of a contract if the court as a matter of law finds that the contract or a clause of the contract is unconscionable at the time of formation of the contract. On this issue, the Restatement is almost identical to the Uniform Commercial Code (at Section 2-302). The U.C.C. is a model code designed to bring about uniformity in commercial transactions. All of the U.S. states, except Louisiana, have adopted the Code. However, the Code does not define "unconscionability." Instead in Comment 1 to Section 2-302 it provides a test for unconscionability: "Whether, in light of the general commercial background and the commercial needs of the particular trade or case, the clauses involved are so one-sided as to be unconscionable under the circumstances existing at the time of the making of the contract." The commentary goes on to provide that the main purpose of the unconscionability doctrine is "the prevention of oppression and unfair surprise."[19]

In response to the studios' suggestion that the unconscionability defense undermines the sanctity of traditional notions of freedom of contract, legal commentator T. Quinn points out that limits often need to be imposed to achieve "balance and basic fairness . . . [To] stress freedom of contract and to overlook its limiting principles paradoxically leads to an erosion of freedom itself in that the exercise of true freedom gets limited to the powerful."[20] This statement provides an excellent analysis of exactly what has happened over the years in the U.S. film industry (i.e., the major studio/distributors have become so powerful as compared to all other parties in the industry that they are the only ones who have the freedom to function in what they claim is a free marketplace).

With few exceptions, independent feature film producers in the current industry environment have little or no real negotiating power when it comes to determining the terms of the distribution deal. In the first place the basic economic law of supply and demand is working against the independent producers (i.e., there are too many films being produced each year). More films are being produced than there are available distributors who are willing to distribute, and even though many of the films being produced arguably do not deserve to be released, there are still too few distributors that are both capable and willing to distribute the worthy films. Thus, even though the available distributors may be willing to negotiate on certain aspects of the distribution deal, as to any given issue, distributors pretty much have the power to say "take it or leave it." And the excessive power of the major studio/distributors has grown until now it is consistently abused. Of course (as pointed out earlier), many independent producers foolishly believe that by producing a "great" film all of their problems associated with their inherent "inferior bargaining position" will go away. Unfortunately, by concentrating most if not all of their time, energy and skill on the creative side of the film business equation as opposed to the business side of the business, many independent producers end up winning the "film" but losing the "deal."

5 | Terms of the Deal Itself

Now that the respective positions on both sides of the net profits debate have been set forth and preliminary concepts relating to the feature film distribution deal have been discussed, here is a review of specific issues that come up within the context of the feature film distribution deal and which are theoretically negotiable. The readers of this book will have to determine for themselves whether the negotiations of such issues are likely to result in unconscionable language in the specific agreements. It may be fair to say that of the 135 or so issues discussed in this book, all but a very limited number are in reality nonnegotiable for all but a handful of Hollywood insider producers.

Gross Receipts Exclusions

The earliest and most important opportunities for film distributors to minimize the amount of film revenues that may eventually be available for distribution to profit participants (both net and gross) is to define more narrowly what revenues will be included in distributor gross receipts (or in the alternative to exclude more items of revenue from gross receipts).

Distributor gross receipts. Gross receipts in the context of a feature film distribution agreement is another one of those contractually defined terms, generally referring, in this case, to all monies actually received by the distributor (or its subsidiaries or affiliates) from the exploitation of any rights granted pursuant to the distribution agreement, from all sources, stated in U.S. dollars, and not subject to forfeiture or return, including nonreturnable advances and guarantees. The major areas from which gross receipts are derived include home video, theatrical revenue or "film rental," nontheatrical, pay television, network television, television syndication and ancillary rights (both foreign and domestic).

Thus, gross receipts exclusions is another term defined in some distribution agreements as the amounts of all adjustments, credits, allowances (other than advertising allowances), rebates and refunds, given or made to subdistributors, exhibitors and licensees, which are excluded from the distributor's gross receipts, adjusted gross or accountable gross (whichever term is used). Also monies in the nature of security deposits, or advance or periodic payments are not included in the distributor's gross receipts (accountable gross or adjusted gross) until they have actually been earned (such as by the exhibition of the film) or forfeited. In other words, some distribution deals will allow the distributor to not count, and therefore not be obligated to include in its net profit calculations, certain items that otherwise might be included in gross receipts (and the subsequent net profits calculation) if the negotiating producer had enough leverage.

Distributor rentals. It is also important to know and recognize the difference between the distributor's gross receipts and gross rentals. The term "rentals" refers to the aggregate amount of the film distributor's share of monies paid at theatre box offices computed on the basis of negotiated agreements between the distributor and the exhibitor. Note that gross receipts refers to amounts actually received and from all markets and media, whereas gross rentals refers to amounts earned from theatrical exhibition only, regardless of whether received by the distributor. Thus, gross receipts is the much broader term and includes distributor rentals.

The issue of film rentals (i.e., what percentage of a film's box office gross comes back to the distributor) is of key importance. In 1956, the chairman of the Allied States Association of Motion Picture Exhibitors was quoted as saying: "Film rentals dominate every other issue in the business."[1] Issues relating to film rentals continue to be important today, although the home video revenue stream has been generating a larger share of the distributor's gross receipts on many films for several years now, thus surpassing film rentals in importance as a revenue source.

One of the ongoing misconceptions about film rentals is that the distributors generally get an amount equal to 50 percent of the box office gross. "While major studios are able to extract distribution terms for a major motion picture which call for the payment of 70 percent and more of the box office receipts (in its initial weeks of release), the industry average for all pictures continues to fall and distributors during 1985 received an average of 35 percent to 40 percent of box office receipts, which varied with the type of the motion picture and its distributor."[2] More current numbers suggest that the distributor rentals for the major studio/distributor released films average in the neighborhood of 43 percent of box office gross. Again, however, such an average is based on widely divergent distributor rental ratios on individual films. The percentage of distributor rentals as compared to box office gross on any given film ranges widely (e.g., from 25 percent to 65 percent) depending on the distributor, the exhibitor, the film and other factors.

Film rentals are one of the earliest forms of film revenue that becomes part of a distributor's gross receipts, thus any transaction which tends to reduce the amount of film rentals actually paid on any given film will correspondingly lower the distributor's gross receipts at an early stage.

The settlement transaction. While film rentals are generally included among distributor gross receipts, the little known and less discussed settlement transaction may effectively eliminate a large portion of any given movie's distributor rentals, thus significantly reducing the distributor's gross receipts. Thus, the single most important exclusion from gross receipts, which is not even mentioned in the distribution agreement, may come about indirectly as a result of the settlement transaction as between the distributor and exhibitor.

Simon Whitney reports that the settlement transaction has been occurring for at least forty-five years. He states that an exhibitor tactic complained of by distributors "was to sign a contract, run the picture, and then refuse to settle at the terms agreed upon if attendance was poor. This practice was said to result in a lawsuit only 'occasionally,' and in fact the practice predated the Paramount case."[3]

The settlement transaction is a conclusive fixing or resolution, usually a compromise, between the distributor and exhibitor or distributor and subdistributors relating to the amount of monies due to be paid to the distributor for a film's exploitation. Generally, settlements are calculated or negotiated on a weekly basis, at least initially between the individual theatre and the branch office of the distributor. According to profit participation auditors, the amount actually settled upon may be 10 percent to 30 percent below what the contractual amount to be paid to the distributor would have been. There is almost never any written communication between the distributor and exhibitor relating to such settlement negotiations (i.e., it's all oral). Thus, the net profit participation auditor can only compare what was paid with what should have been paid pursuant to the contract between the distributor and exhibitor, if the auditor can gain access to that third party contract. These settlements between the distributor and exhibitor can significantly reduce the chances that a given film will ever reach net profits and can have a greater negative impact on the likelihood of net profits occurring than the gross participations that studio executives are so fond of blaming as the culprit. These oral negotiations not only have an impact on the financial interests of a film's producer and its net profit participants, but they also have an adverse impact on the film's gross profit participants, since their effect is to reduce the amount of gross receipts received by the distributor.

On the other hand, why would any distributor be willing to accept less than the contractual amount due from the exhibitor? A distributor may be willing to settle for less than the money actually owed by an exhibitor on a given film in order to help the distributor obtain (read: extort) more favorable exhibition terms on its next film or to get a future somewhat mediocre film into that theatre, to the exclusion of more deserving and competing films.

Some entertainment attorneys have suggested that these settlement transactions would not hold up in court if challenged because the distributor, in its distribution agreement, generally has contracted to maximize its distribution revenue on the film on behalf of all gross and net profit participants. Few if any producers or other profit participants, however, have chosen to litigate this issue and even when confronted by profit participation auditors, this appears to be one of those issues the distributors routinely respond to by saying "sue us."

These settlement transactions as between distributors and exhibitors also often cover the receipts, deductions, fees and so forth for several movies exhibited by such exhibitors and distributed by such distributors (or subdistributors). The actual numbers in such transactions are typically rounded off, averaged or compromised, thus making it difficult for a producer of a movie involved in such a transaction to determine what amount paid to the distributor should be properly allocated to such producer's motion picture.

Most of the MPAA companies routinely settle with exhibitors for a lump sum payment after the run of a motion picture, as stated earlier, for an amount that is somewhere between 10 percent to 30 percent less than what is owed to the distributor by the exhibitor. Universal reportedly does not engage in the practice of settling with exhibitors. Consequently, industry insider's say that Universal is not able to book its films into the best theatres, a situation which suggests that exhibitors also engage in questionable business practices that force the distributors to settle. Such an arrangement might otherwise be referred to as collusion. If the film in question was produced by a major studio/distributor that practice may be of little concern to third parties. But in instances where the film in question was produced by an independent producer and where other third party net profit participants are involved, the above described settlement transaction might be considered a violation of the distributor's fiduciary duty to protect the interests of parties with whom it has contracted (assuming that a fiduciary relationship has been established).

The exhibitor/distributor settlement transaction is also sometimes referred to as selling subject to review. Selling subject to review is the same film industry practice as the settlement transaction. It occurs as between exhibitors and distributors who orally renegotiate the film rental due the distributor after the film's theatrical engagement has been completed. From the distributor's point of view, such a practice may be considered necessary because the film performance at the box office was poorer than expected and the distributor wants to book its next film at the same theatre under the best available terms. Unfortunately, for the other gross and/or net profit participants on the first movie, who are not likely to be affiliated in any way with the distributor's next movie in release, this practice is blatantly unfair, because if the distributor accepts a smaller amount of film rentals from the exhibitor on the first film just so it can get better terms on a second film, the financial interests of the participants in the first film have been sacrificed for the benefit of the distributor. In the context of a so-called "relationship-driven business," it would appear that the relationship that means the most to the distributor is the distributor's relationships with the exhibitors as opposed to its relationships with other gross or net profit participants. This is also a business practice that even if addressed at the negotiating stage of the distribution agreement is most likely to be presented on a take it or leave it basis, and if the distributor is confronted by an auditor who questions the practice, the auditor is likely to get the "sue us" response. Thus, instead of "our films did not do well at the box office," this pervasive practice and others discussed herein are the real reasons the major distributors and exhibitors have done so well in the film business for so long while the smaller and less powerful independent production companies and distributors routinely fall by the wayside.

The settlement transaction as between the distributor and exhibitor clearly involves a conflict of interest for the distributor of an independently produced motion picture. In other words, the distributor is giving away money that belongs to others. A second answer to the question of why a distributor would settle for less money on a given picture is that, by settling for less on the independently produced film, the exhibitor is more likely to pay the distributor more on the films produced by the distributor and subsequently exhibited by the same theatre.

When entertainment attorney Mark Litwak says "collections are a special problem for smaller distributors, " he is touching on one aspect of the settlement transaction. As attorney Litwak says, "The majors can threaten to withhold the next blockbuster until past accounts are settled [but] . . . smaller distributors lack such a club."[4] In other words, the smaller distributors do not have the financial wherewithal to allow the exhibitor to keep a larger percentage of distributor rentals and they also do not have the supposed big blockbuster to offer the exhibitor in the future, thus, most of the small independents are not in a very strong position when it comes to negotiating with exhibitors at settlement time. Producer Martin Ransohoff agrees with the Litwak statement, saying that the "independent film is told to wait four months or take twenty-five percent. . . . The ability to collect is all based on clout."[5] Julian Schlossberg of distributor Castle Hill also confirms that "the deals made by distributors and exhibitors really don't mean much because after the run, according to business done, they renegotiate."[6]

Independent producer Frank Gilroy's notes (published in book form) further confirm the ability of the major studio/distributors to collect more effectively from exhibitors. In another conversation with Castle Hill's Julian Schlossberg who, when "asked what the majors or minimajors could do that he couldn't, Julian said for one thing, because they had a regular flow of product, they could collect more readily since their clout was the next picture."[7] In other words, what Julian Schlossberg and others in the industry are saying is that if you are an independent distributor without a continuing supply of quality film product, you will not have as much leverage with the exhibitors when it comes time to be paid, thus you will not be paid as much as you would have been paid if you had other desirable motion pictures in the pipeline. This means in turn that the payments by the exhibitor to the distributor are not determined by the contract between those same two parties but by the power and discretion of the parties at settlement time. This also means that independent distributors generally do not have the prospect of offering a potential blockbuster, thus, the exhibitor may well opt for a mediocre film released by a major studio/distributor to preserve the exhibitor's ability to get that major's next potential blockbuster. In addition, to the very scary financial implications of the settlement transaction, this all means that independent distributors simply cannot effectively compete for most of the desirable theatres against the major studio/distributors, regardless of the quality of their motion pictures.

Fine Line Features president Ira Deutchman adds a little confusion to the debate by making a carelessly worded statement designed to preserve the prestige and power of the independent distributor (at least that of Fine Line Features). He says: "One myth that can be shattered is the commonly held notion that the studios are better able to collect their share of box-office receipts from exhibitors than the independents. Exhibitors are notorious for paying slowly, and for holding off payment in order to force a renegotiation of terms on less successful pictures. The fact is that the larger, more stable independents have the same tool at their disposal to collect money as the major—future product. In fact struggling studios, with dubious upcoming product lineups, will no doubt have more difficulty with collections than a secure independent. Further, because cash flow is so important to smaller companies, they tend to be more aggressive in collections and settlements with exhibitors than the studios. Indeed, smaller theatre chains are likely to pay smaller distributors more swiftly, simply because their mutual interests are at stake."[8]

Unfortunately, an independent distributor's ability to collect and the willingness of that independent distributor to settle are two different things, often motivated by different considerations. Further, it would be more accurate to point out that Fine Line Features and its affiliated New Line Cinema make up the strongest independent production/distributor combination in the contemporary U.S. marketplace. Only Miramax and Samuel Goldwyn come anywhere close to the combined market share of New Line/Fine Line, but all three of these top independents (Miramax is now owned by Disney) together with all the other independent distributors in the country do not regularly exceed 8 percent of the domestic theatrical gross. In other words, the films released by the seven MPAA companies routinely generate about 92 percent of the domestic theatrical box office gross revenues. Thus, Deutchman's statement may be accurate for his own company and its sister company New Line (or it may be so much film industry hype), but it certainly is not an accurate statement for all or even most independent distributors.

Former distribution and marketing executive Fred Goldberg also tries to suggest that the settlement transaction is not that common: "Not all distributors allow these adjustments. Many settle all of their contracts on the agreed terms. The companies with the clout and the strong line-up of product usually do not have to make settlements to ensure relationships. They feel that exhibitors want and need their product and therefore must honor the terms of the license agreement if they want to play the product."[9] This statement by Fred Goldberg directly contradicts the information provided by many profit participation auditors, distributors and exhibitors. They report that most distributors, including the major studio/distributors, the distributors with the most "clout," settle with exhibitors.

Goldberg's analysis is also limited to consideration of ensuring relationships as the sole motivating factor in determining whether a distributor settles. He refers to the settlement transaction as a "look see." He says, "Adjustments called look-sees will be arranged after the engagement is completed. If the movie does poorly at the box office, the distributor may agree to a reduction of the percentage terms agreed upon."[10] Thus, Goldberg seems to suggest that distributors will routinely agree to accept less money than the contract calls because they feel sorry for the exhibitor and without exacting something valuable in return.

The settlement transaction is also sometimes referred to as an "adjustment." These reductions of film rentals owed by an exhibitor to a distributor pursuant to a film license agreement, which occurs following a poorer than expected performance at the box office (or for other reasons), may be allowed by a distributor in contravention of its obligations to maximize the exploitation of a given film on behalf of net profit participants.

Loews Theatres chairman Alan Friedberg (an exhibitor) makes another point that, oddly enough, argues in favor of even higher settlements for distributors. Friedberg says that "exhibitors are collecting cash at the box office in a cash business, and distributors are arguably entitled to start using the theatres' money, especially since settlement doesn't occur until perhaps months after a picture's run is over."[11]

Friedberg also confirms the occurrence of the settlement transaction saying: "Today the majority of licenses are the result of negotiations, not bids. . . . In a nonbid situation there is generally an opportunity to renegotiate the terms after the fact in the form of a settlement if a picture performs poorly."[12] Friedberg continues: "The real dance goes on once box-office figures are a matter of record. In the case of settlement renegotiation after a run (assuming the picture was not bid), reasons generally relating to expenses are offered on both sides—sometimes leading to acrimonious debate—as to why one party should ultimately receive a greater share than the original deal would allow. In the end, agreement is reached and payment is made."[13]

Merrill Lynch's Harold Vogel erroneously suggests that the settlement transaction only occurs when the film is a real "flop." He says, should "a picture not perform up to expectations, the distributor . . . usually has the right to a certain minimum or 'floor' payment. These minimums are direct percentages (often more than half) of box-office receipts prior to subtraction of house expenses, but any previously advanced (or guaranteed) exhibitor monies can be used to cover floor payments owed. For a film that is a total flop, though, the distributor may reduce the exhibitor's burden through a quietly arranged settlement."[14] Harold Vogel is merely restating the major studio/distributor position (i.e., that settlements are adjustments made in response to the poorer than expected performance of a movie).

Former studio accountant David Leedy did go one step beyond Vogel in his discussion of the settlement transaction, referring to it as "selling subject to review," and saying, "Regardless of the contractual terms (sliding scale, minimum percentage, etc.), most distributors (Universal being an exception) are willing to renegotiate the film rental after the engagement has been completed. This practice . . . may be necessitated due to the poor performance of a particular movie and the distributor's desire to book the next picture at optimum terms."[15] Thus, Leedy offers an additional explanation as to why the distributor might settle for less than the contractual amount due (i.e., such a settlement may help the distributor get its next movie into that theatre). Of course, what Leedy is not saying is that the "next picture" is more likely to be a film produced by the studio/distributor, whereas the film whose rentals were sacrificed (by means of settlement) was more likely to be an independently produced film merely being distributed by the studio/distributor. As profit participation auditor Steven Sills accurately points out, "In the settlement transaction the distributor is actually trading the net profit participant's economic benefit for its own."[16]

Other specialized film industry terms in addition to "the settlement transaction," "selling subject to review," "adjustments" and "look sees" have developed around this clandestine transaction. The phrase "settlement ratio," for example, refers to the percentage below which the final accounting as between distributors and exhibitors is compared to what the accounting should have been if paid in accordance with the original contractual arrangement. Another term, the "film rental ratio," is the percentage of film rentals paid to the distributor compared to box office gross. Again, this ratio may range anywhere from the neighborhood of 25 percent to 65 percent depending on the picture, distributor, exhibitor and when they settle. As stated earlier, the film rental ratio for movies produced by the MPAA companies averages about 43 percent. The ratio for independent productions released by these same MPAA distributor companies has been consistently lower.

In order to provide some historical perspective on these distributor rental ratios, consider the study of Sindlinger & Company, "a firm that has specialized in motion picture statistics." Sindlinger "used exhibitor sources to estimate that film rentals increased steadily from 27.1 percent of box office receipts in 1947 to 33.6 percent in 1955—or from 32.6 to 35.9 percent of receipts excluding admission taxes. Price Waterhouse & Company, using data supplied by the ten largest distributors, found an upward trend from 1947 to 1953, but a sharp drop in 1954 and 1955, and a slightly lower ratio than Sindlinger throughout the period—26.0 percent in 1947, 35.0 in 1953 and 27.8 in 1955. . . . Whatever the precise figures, the ratio of rentals to box office receipts has clearly increased."[17] We can now see that the distributors have continued to exercise their clout with exhibitors because as the figures in the paragraph above indicate, the contemporary distributor rental ratio figures are substantially higher still. These historical figures also illustrate the difficulty of obtaining reliable statistical information in the film industry, another problem which continues through today.

It is fair once again to ask the question why would a distributor settle for less than the actual amount owed based on the terms of the contract as between the exhibitor and distributor? Aside from the motivations already suggested above, that is, the film has performed below expectations or that the distributor wants to assure that its next film (which may be a mediocre film) gets into the theatres, the real answer may lie in the fact that distributors routinely distribute films produced by their own affiliated production companies as well as films produced by independent producers. Thus, if the distributor accepts less money at exhibitor settlement time on the independently produced motion pictures but insists on being paid the contractual amount or slightly more (or slightly less) on movies its affiliated production company produces, both the distributors and exhibitors benefit financially at the expense of the independent producers and all of the profit participants (gross and net) of the independently produced films.

If for example, 75 films are produced by independent producers and distributed by major studio/distributors during the course of a given year, and these films average $10 million in domestic film rentals and an average 20 percent of the film rentals that would have been included in the gross receipts revenue stream of each of such pictures is cut off or diverted by virtue of the settlement transaction, then the $10 million film rental figure per picture equals 80 percent of what should have been included in gross receipts (per the exhibitor/distributor contract terms). Thus, approximately $2.5 million is being deducted from the gross receipts revenue stream for each of these independently produced motion pictures, and of course, $2.5 million × 75 films equals $187.5 million that hypothetically could be (and very likely is) siphoned off each year by virtue of this settlement transaction alone.

A three-year study by film students in the UCLA graduate and extension programs confirmed that for the years 1989–91 distributor rentals received by the major studio/distributors on films produced by those same major studio/distributors were consistently higher than the rentals received by those same entities for the films released through the same distributors but which were produced by independent producers. The students developed these statistical studies by: (1) listing all of the feature films released by the major studio/distributors for a given year in a vertical column on the left-most side of a line legal-size sheet of paper; (2) dividing those films into two groups [a] those produced by the major studio/distributors and [b] those produced by independent production entities (source: Academy of Motion Picture Arts and Sciences Annual Index to Motion Picture Credits); (3) the reported box office gross for each of the films was then set forth in the next vertical column to the right of the first column;[18] (4) another vertical column of the reported distributor rentals for each of the films was set forth to the right of the box office gross column;[19] (5) another column showing the calculated rental ratio on each film was then added [i.e., the percentage of box office gross represented by the distributor rental figure]; (6) all of the rental ratio percentages for the major studio/distributor productions were totaled and averaged and the rental ratio percentages for the independently produced films were totaled and averaged; (7) when compared, the two resulting rental ratio averages provided clear evidence as to which group of films received the highest level of distributor rentals as compared to box office gross; (8) when compared with the same calculations for other years these rental ratios provide some indication as to whether a consistent pattern existed [i.e., whether the distributor rentals received on independently produced features released by the major studio/distributors, were consistently lower than the distributor rentals received by the major studio/distributors for films produced by those same major studio/distributors].

As noted above, in the three years compared to date, the rental ratios for all three years favored the major studio/distributors.[20] In addition, future studies covering an extended time period, say ten years, would further help to determine whether the above-reported three-year pattern extends over a longer period of time, and in the process reveal just how massive this problem really is. In effect, the settlement transaction is another form of cross-collateralization (see discussion of cross-collateralization below).

The exhibitor/distributor deal. Another factor that makes the settlement transaction even more complicated and difficult to monitor is the original contractual arrangement between the exhibitor and distributor. The contractual revenue split as between the distributor and exhibitor is typically handled (and referred to) as a 90/10 deal. In other words, for the first (and sometimes the second) week, 90 percent of the balance of box office gross remaining after the exhibitor's house allowance (sometimes referred to as the house nut) is deducted from the gross box office is paid to the distributor, unless that amount is less than 70 percent of the box office gross for that week, in which case the 70 percent of box office gross is paid to the distributor. This 70 percent figure is referred to as a floor. In other words, the distributor's take will not fall below 70 percent of box office gross for that week. Thus, the 90 percent is based on the exhibitor's net, whereas the 70 percent is based on box office gross. In the 90/10 deal the distributor gets the greater of the two (i.e., 70 percent of the box office gross is the minimum due to be paid, but 90 percent of the balance after deducting the house allowance from box office gross will be the amount due if it is greater than the 70 percent of box office gross).[21] Each subsequent week (or in two-week increments) these percentages then may change during the course of the film's run, so that, for example, in week two, the distributor may get 80 percent of the exhibitor's net with a 60 percent floor, and in the third week, the distributor may get 70 percent with a 50 percent floor and so on, although the major studio/distributors seldom receive less than a 35 percent floor of box office gross.

Outstandings. Additional aspects of the settlement transaction that add further complications to the settlement transaction and thus make it even more difficult to monitor, for all other profit participants except the distributor and the exhibitor, fall within the discussion of a film industry concept referred to as "outstandings." The term "outstandings" is often used among film distributors and exhibitors to refer to the money for advertising expenses or film rentals that the distributor owes the exhibitor or the exhibitor owes the distributor. If the distributor and exhibitor disagree as to the correct amount due on a given film or several films from the same distributor (and disagreement is the general rule rather than the exception), such amounts may remain unsettled for a period of time and may have to be settled on the basis of a compromise figure relating to more than one film. In addition to settling on more than one movie, the distributor and exhibitor may settle their respective accounts relating to cooperative advertising expenses right along with the film revenues. This all contributes to the creation of an impossible auditing task for the profit participation auditors and their clients, the net and gross profit participants, who are relying on the honesty of the distributor and exhibitor to treat them fairly in their secret and oral settlement negotiations. What are the chances that the distributor and exhibitor would actually look out for the best interests of the net and gross profit participants in such a situation? Zero is the probable answer.

Again, this entire settlement transaction scenario can have an extremely adverse impact on a movie's profit participants, particularly if the exhibitor owes the distributor (which is usually the case) and the distributor agrees to settle for an amount that is substantially less than the amount owed (also quite common). In addition, the profit participants can be further hurt if the distributor unfairly allocates the revenues paid by the exhibitor under such circumstances among several films involved (see discussion of revenue allocations below).

Producer advances. Another typical distributor exclusion from distributor gross receipts is the producer advance. The major studio/distributors will generally take the position that producer advances should not be included in gross receipts until earned, in other words, the distributor will want to deduct from the film's revenue stream (i.e., from monies received by the distributor) an amount equal to any advance that has been paid to the producer and will not want to consider such amounts as part of gross receipts for any calculations based on gross receipts. In other words, the distributor will not start counting its gross receipts for purposes of calculating gross and net profit participations until after it has recouped any advance paid to the producer at the time of the delivery of the film. This accounting practice has a tendency to postpone further the likelihood and/or timing of net and gross profit payments. The fact that the producer advance has already been paid has nothing to do with whether it ought to be included in gross receipts for purposes of calculating net profits.

The allocation of revenue problem. The feature film distribution deal will often provide a considerable amount of discretion to the film distributor to allocate film revenues among more than one film. Thus, the allocation of film revenues often involves self-serving decisions by the distributor as to what will be included in gross receipts. For example, to the extent that the distributor's decision does not allocate monies to a particular film that could have been so allocated, this decision has in effect arbitrarily excluded monies from the gross receipts of such film. Just as with the settlement transaction, this gross receipts exclusion, in turn, affects all gross and net profit calculations down the line.

In addition, "Allocation issues abound in the accounting of gross receipts in areas other than theatrical exhibition. Noteworthy are the allocation issues in the licensing of films in a package for television, whether for network or syndication. . . . In the foreign area, the allocation of a portion of film rentals to shorts and trailers . . . percentages may have no reasonable relation to the value of the short or trailer compared to the value of the particular picture."[22] Not surprisingly, the discretionary judgment of the distributor more often than not results in accounting decisions in favor of the distributor.

Distributors sometimes will also seek to make outright sales of a picture in certain territories as part of package of several films for a lump sum price. Such outright sales for a package of films also raise allocation problems.

Although not as common today, the double feature (double bill) also raises such allocation issues. A double feature involves the exhibition of two motion pictures in the same theatre (one after another) for which patrons are only charged the price of a single ticket. During the Great Depression motion picture theatre ticket sales fell significantly and the "double-feature" was created by independent exhibitors in an effort to reattract audiences. The distributor of such a pairing must allocate (based on a predetermined formula, at the distributor's discretion or otherwise) the film rentals generated by the joint exhibition of the films between the two films for purposes of calculating payments due to profit participants, if any.

As mentioned above, the revenue allocation issue also arises within the context of syndicated films, that is, motion pictures that are licensed for use by individual television stations or cable systems for exhibition in their own local markets. Films are usually packaged as a group for television syndication. There are some 200+ television syndication markets in the U.S. The syndication of films may create an allocation issue with respect to how the fee paid for syndication rights is allocated among the various films in the syndication package. Generally, a rather arbitrary syndication formula is imposed on the producers of the various films in the package by the distributor and the application of this formula does not vary from market to market. Generally, the allocation formula will favor the distributor's film in the package over the independently produced films.

These allocation formulas for the packaged films are generally arbitrary and unfair in many instances, but not all. Some major artists can insist that their film be sold individually in the foreign market but the distributors don't want to negotiate fifty separate deals on fifty films in a package, so they want to package for foreign territories. If the artist insists, the distributor will tell the foreign buyer to write up a contract for the other forty-nine films and do the paperwork separately on the one film but the price is still based on all fifty. Foreign buyers may be limited in how much they can pay for a given movie, so the distributor will package a good movie that the foreign buyer wants with a number of other movies and charge a higher price. The foreign buyer will pay the higher price and sometimes leave all the other movies at the port of entry, so as to avoid paying any more required fees.[23] This distributor practice is precisely what the prohibited practice of block booking was all about.

According to profit participation auditor Steven Sills, the studio allocation formulas for packaged films are not designed to hurt the net profit participants but to hurt the corporation's shareholders. Sills says that Financial Accounting Standards Board guidelines (FASB 53) require that production costs be capitalized, that is, carried on the books as an asset, not an expense. The asset is then depreciated and the cost can never be greater than expected revenue, otherwise write-downs are required and that affects the price per share. If a movie is packaged with other movies, the distributor allocations allow this calculation to be handled in a manner that favors the corporation but not the shareholders. The calculation also is not in the economic interest of net profit participants.[24] All of these allocation of revenue issues involve a distributor conflict of interest situation, and film distributors do not have a history of handling such situations in an evenhanded manner.

Charitable contributions. Another instance of film revenues being excluded for purposes of calculating net and gross profit participations based on distributor gross receipts occurs in the form of a charitable contributions exclusion often found in the distribution agreement. Some distributors will include language in the distribution agreement that permits the distributor to exercise its discretion in excluding from the gross receipts pool any contributions the distributor chooses to make to a favorite charitable organization. This may not involve a significant amount of money and in fact may be most typically associated with revenues generated by a charitable premiere of the film. On the other hand, there is no reason that a producer or other net profit participant should agree to allow such gross receipts exclusions, particularly since such net profit participants may never see any profit participation at all. Another aspect of this particular gross receipts exclusion that is even more offensive is that the distributor will most likely be able to take a U.S. income tax deduction for such charitable contributions.

Foreign receipts or overseas rentals. Most of the film distributor definitions of gross receipts state that monies are not included in gross receipts until such funds are collected in dollars in the United States. Foreign receipts are monies earned by the exploitation of a film outside the U.S. and received by the distributor. The term is broader than blocked currencies, thus, in some circumstances may include monies under the control of the distributor, but still in a foreign territory and not blocked by virtue of any restricted currency provisions. The most important issue involving foreign receipts is whether the producer and other participants receive the benefit of monies collected that could but have not been remitted to the United States.

Blocked or restricted currencies. A more specialized form of foreign receipts is the blocked or restricted currencies. These are monies that are or become subject to moratorium, embargo, banking or exchange restrictions, or impediments against remittances to the United States. In other words, they are monies earned by banks or corporations in a foreign country that cannot be removed from that country except under limited circumstances and thus generally have to be spent within its borders. In the film industry, blocked currencies may be foreign film rentals or other film revenues generated by the exploitation of the film in all media in that market. Distributors will typically want to exclude blocked currencies from gross receipts.

Prompt payment. Another issue relating to gross receipt exclusions focus on when certain monies are included. For example, a distributor may seek to avoid any language in the distribution agreement that will obligate it to include promptly funds received for television and cable sales, but instead will allow the distributor to hold such funds until the actual play dates of the movie on such media. Sometimes this lag time, which allows the distributor to benefit from the use of such monies can be as much as one to two years. Thus, the reporting of the receipt of such funds by the distributor may be delayed through four to eight accounting periods.

Videocassette revenue reporting. Video revenues have been setting new records each year for the past several years and have outpaced theatrical revenues both in the foreign and domestic market for several years. Thus, video revenues have become a more important revenue source for motion pictures than even theatrical revenues, although there is still a critical relationship between how a film does in its theatrical release and how it performs on video, preserving great significance for the theatrical release. As Nelson Entertainment President and Chief Operating Officer (COO) Richard "Reg" Childs says, "Domestic gross sales of all home videos are about twice that of box-office gross, but home video needs that theatrical launching of its titles in order to perform at that level."[25]

In an effort to take advantage of this growth in the videocassette market, the major studio/distributors have all created wholly owned subsidiaries or joint ventures to act as videocassette manufacturer/wholesalers for their films. Today "every studio has a home-video division."[26] These manufacturer/wholesaler entities typically only pay 20 percent of wholesale receipts as a royalty fee to the parent company (the film distributor). In other words, unlike other areas of motion picture revenue reporting, home video is handled on a royalty basis (more like the record industry) rather than remitting the distributor's share of the wholesale revenues on a distribution fee basis. The system then arbitrarily switches back, however, to the distribution fee basis at the distributor level, since the parent distributor, in turn, charges a distribution fee (usually about 30 percent) leaving only an extremely small percentage of the videocassette revenue stream remaining for inclusion in the distributor's gross receipts pool. This again significantly and adversely impacts all net and gross profit calculations down the line. In addition to allowing a studio/distributor to take a fee on a related company transaction whose fees were not negotiated in an arm's length transaction, this structure also allows the distributor effectively to deduct monies from the videocassette revenue stream at two different levels, thus permitting the distributor to keep a disproportionate share of videocassette revenues, an even more disproportionate share than it keeps for theatrical revenues.

To provide some idea as to how much money can be generated from the foreign territories alone through the sales of video rights, the following chart depicts the approximate license fees that would have been paid in recent years on a royalty advance for a seven year term for videocassette rights in the territories shown. An "A" level film is one in which the film enjoyed a theatrical release on 800 or more U.S. screens and had at least a $5 million dollar publicity and advertising budget (or the equivalent). A so-called "A–" movie had a theatrical release on at least 400 screens and a P&A budget between $3 and $5 million dollars or its equivalent. A "B" movie had a regional theatrical release on 50–250 screens and a $1 to $3 million dollar P&A or equivalent. A "B–" film had no theatrical release in the domestic market (U.S. and Canada) but was made for video.[27]

Territory	A movie	A– movie	B movie	B– movie
U.S./Canada	$4–$6 million	$3–$4 million	$1–2.5 million	$.5 mil. or less
U.K	$1–$1.5 million	$500,000–$750,000	$250,000–$300,000	$50,000 or less
Japan	$1–1.5 million	$500,000–$750,000	$125,000–$150,000	$50,000 or less
Germany	$500,000–$800,000	$300,000–$375,000	$100,000–$200,000	$50,000 or less
Australia	$400,000–$600,000	$200,000–$300,000	$100,000–$150,000	$50,000 or less
Spain	$350,000–$450,000	$150,000–$250,000	$50,000–$75,000	$50,000 or less
France	$150,000–$250,000	$75,000–$100,000	$30,000–$40,000	$25,000 or less
Italy	$100,000–$150,000	$60,000–$100,000	$25,000–$50,000	$25,000 or less

Note again, that these figures only show the range of advances for territorial video rights expected to be paid not the total anticipated video revenues in each market.

The above-mentioned 20 percent royalty paid to the major studio/distributors by their video manufacturer/wholesaler subsidiaries occurs pursuant to what is often referred to as the 20 percent rule. It is an informal guideline used by most of the home video companies that are wholly owned or controlled by the major film studio/distributors for determining what portion of wholesale video revenue is to be remitted to the studio/distributor as part of the studio/distributor's gross receipts. Pursuant to such rule, an arbitrary share of 20 percent of the total of such monies is remitted to the studio/distributor. If, for example, wholesale revenues to the video company owned by a film distributor are $100.00, the video company will keep $80.00 leaving only 20 percent as a royalty for the film's distributor, that is, $20.00 The distributor will then take a 30 percent distribution fee (30 percent of the $20 or $6.67), leaving only 13.33 percent of the $100.0 in wholesale revenues to add to distributor gross receipts ($13.33), which is still subject to many of the other revenue reducing techniques described in this book. Meanwhile, the distributor is also enjoying a portion of the video company's share since the distributor owns or has a financial interest in the video company.

This so-called 20 percent rule is based on an early estimate of what video profits would be and has no relationship to the actual current numbers. By uniformly applying this 20 percent rule, the studios may in fact be conspiring (or acting in combination) to deny profit participants in movies and television shows their fair share from the sale of videocassettes. Since the major film distributors are also affiliated with production entities in their vertically integrated major studio/distributor organizations, it is quite conceivable that the major studio/distributors might be engaging in a conspiracy or combination in restraint of trade with respect to the small production company competitors of the major studio/distributor production company affiliates.

The video royalty issues is also a gross receipts exclusion problem because "the film distribution agreement will generally define the distributor's wholly owned home video subsidiary as a separate entity from the distributor, thus video revenue coming back to this separate subsidiary will not be part of the distributor's gross receipts."[28] Thus, "Only 20% of the revenues the studio [affiliated video wholesaler] receive[s] from home video sales and rentals are deemed [distributor] 'gross receipts.' The other 80% is set aside as income retained by the studio's home video operation."[29]

From a historical point of view, "Home video started in late '70's; the 20% royalty made sense then because of the costs of manufacturing the cassettes and creating the market, thus the 20% royalty became the industry standard and the majors do not want to set an unfavorable precedent (i.e., an unfavorable precedent for the majors) by changing that."[30]

"Guild residuals are also not paid on secondary market revenue and home video is considered a secondary market. Thus, not only are the distributors reducing net profit participants' participation in video revenues but the guild members' participations as well. Reportedly the guilds agreed to this arrangement because at the time of negotiations on this point, one of the guilds had a serious deficiency with its pension fund and the major studio/distributors contributed to the fund to make it whole."[31]

Paul Newman's long-time attorney Irving Axelrod asks the question, "Isn't it a simply amazing coincidence that they all got together and gave only 20% of video revenue as profits."[32] In his lawsuit against the distributor of *The Sting*, Newman alleged "there was indeed a conspiracy. The reason for the conspiracy is to put money in their pockets that belongs to somebody else."[33] Axelrod says, "The U.S. Supreme Court refused to hear the Newman-Hill case not on the merits of its allegation, but on a technicality: that the so-called conspiracy did not exist until after Newman and Hill signed their contracts for the movie in question, *The Sting*."[34] This appears to be a spurious argument being made by the Court, but maybe a class action lawsuit filed against all of the major studio/distributors by the thousands of net and gross profit participants who have been cheated over the years could overcome such a technicality.

Attorneys Nochimson and Brachman explain that "unlike the other areas of the motion picture business, home video has been treated on a royalty basis (akin to the record industry) rather than on a distribution fee basis. . . . One source of controversy centers around the fact that the studios all have their own video cassette affiliates and the participants complain that the studio is in effect taking a fee on a related company transaction. The studio rebuttal is that the deal with its affiliate company is on an arm's length basis, since the royalty received is the customary 20 percent."[35] It is easy to see the fallacy of the studio argument. The studios are saying that the 20 percent royalty fee on video revenues is the norm in the industry. On the other hand, it is only the norm in the industry because all of the major studio/distributors are doing the same thing. The fact that it is the norm has absolutely nothing to do with whether it is fair or appropriate. In addition to creating another elaborate mechanism for shifting monies from the revenue stream of all third party gross and net profit participants to the pockets of the major studio/distributors, these distributors are also guilty of circular reasoning.

On this issue, entertainment attorney Mark Litwak lines up as a studio apologist. He says: "When the [home video] industry began, most of these transactions were at arm's length. . . . Now most are with home video subsidiaries. Then it becomes a question of how much a subsidiary should keep as its share of the revenues." Litwak defends the major studio video royalty scam contending that Hollywood will never be culpable on the 20 percent rule as long as some people get one amount and others get a different amount. "Everything is open to negotiation [according to Litwak] . . . the fact that, more or less, they all charge the same percentage is not automatically a conspiracy."[36] That is a rather safe statement and it is true. But the same percentage adopted by all major studio/distributors is certainly an indication that there may be a conspiracy and one that should be investigated by the U.S. Justice Department and appropriate Congressional committees with oversight responsibilities for the enforcement of the U.S. antitrust laws. Further, profit participation auditor Steven Sills seems to disagree with Litwak in certain respects, saying bluntly, "Net profit participants and guild members do not get their fair share of video revenues."[37]

Even the generally pro-major studio entertainment attorney Peter Dekom denounces the practice in very strong terms, saying: "There is absolutely no justification on earth for the 20% video royalty. It was created specifically to mirror the record industry, but at a point in time where video [revenue] clearly outstrips theatrical, this anachronism must be eliminated."[38] Finally, Judge Schneider in the *Buchwald* case ruled that the home video royalty provision was as least unconscionable,[39] without ever reaching the antitrust issues.

In summary, there are at least four problems with the way the major studio/distributors handle home video revenues: (1) they are handled on a royalty basis instead of on a subdistribution fee basis; (2) the royalty paid to the distributor is only 20 percent of the wholesale price; (3) the distributors that have ownership interests in the video manufacturer/wholesalers get to participate twice in the video revenue stream, since these distributors also take a distribution fee out of the 20 percent received from the manufacturer/wholesalers; and (4) in addition, the expenses for marketing the video are deducted by the distributor. Thus, it seems quite fair to say that all net profit participants and guild members do not get their fair share of video revenues.

Reserve for returns. In addition to the above shenanigans relating to the home video revenue stream for motion pictures, the film distributor will also typically seek to include language in the distribution agreement permitting it to set aside a reserve for video returns (i.e., a deduction by the distributor from video gross receipts to account for the estimated dollar value of videocassettes sent back to the distributor from the video wholesaler because they were defective or for other reasons). The distributor may want to hold back as much as 25 percent of the video gross receipts as reserves for video returns. Again, the effect of setting aside video reserves for returns is to exclude such revenues from the distributor's gross receipts, at least temporarily, and since all other distributor calculations, such as the net profit calculation, are based on distributor gross receipts, this video revenue exclusion again substantially reduces the prospects for generating net or gross profits.

Ancillary rights. Ancillary rights are the additional powers or privileges to which a film's producer or distributor or other person or entity is justly entitled to exercise with respect to the original literary property and the feature film that the producer may have owned prior to selling or assigning the producer's rights to the distributor. Thus, ancillary rights are additional to theatrical exhibition. Such rights may include the right to produce a remake, sequel, television series, stage play and/or soundtrack recording. Some distributors will seek to exclude ancillary revenue sources from being included in the film's gross receipts or if revenue from ancillary sources is included in gross receipts the studio/distributor may seek to use an approach similar to that used for home video wherein the distributor only gets a small royalty payment out of the revenues generated at the wholesale level (a royalty payment instead of a distribution fee), and quite often the distributor is an owner of the wholesale entity handling the ancillary exploitation. The "threshold issue is whether these sources of revenue are included in gross receipts at all."[40]

Discounts, rebates and kickbacks. MPAA distributors sometimes negotiate reductions in the prices they pay for goods or services such as advertising, film labs, print transport, and so forth based on the volume of pictures provided by the distributor. They may also obtain rebates on such goods or services. The distributors generally do not allow the value of any discounts or rebates that they receive to be passed along to net profit participants.[41] Thus, distributors will in fact exclude the value of such discounts in profit participation calculations, arguing that the distributor's activities are solely responsible for earning such credits.

In addition, from an auditing point of view, it is sometimes difficult to determine the difference between a discount, a rebate and a kickback. Discounts involve a reduction in price, whereas a rebate is a return of a portion of a payment. On the other hand, the term "kickback" refers to the practice of a seller of goods or services paying the purchasing agent of those goods or services a portion of the purchase price in order to induce the agent to enter into the transaction. In most commercial transactions, kickbacks are illegal and prohibited by criminal commercial bribery statutes. The principal of the purchasing agent may also have a cause of action against the agent to recover the amount of the bribery. Also for tax purposes, amounts paid as kickbacks or bribes generally are not deductible.

Trailer revenues. Although not as common today, legal requirements in some countries have provided that a short or trailer be included with any film sent into such country, thus raising allocation issues with respect to what portion of a film's rentals should be allocated to the costs associated with producing the short or trailer. Distributors often seek to exclude its revenues from trailers and accessories from its gross receipts. Although the revenues are thus not counted in calculating net and gross profit participations, a portion of the costs of producing the trailers and film shorts may still be charged off against the producer's film.

Distributor commercials and product placements. Distributors often seek to exclude revenues generated through so-called distributor commercials from gross receipts. In a feature film context and in its broadest sense, a distributor commercial may be defined to include a trailer or product placement (i.e., any paid appearance of a product, commodity or service in the film), appearing before, after or during a feature film.

To provide some indication as to the value of product placements, "when the movie *E. T.* was released in 1982, it contained a scene in which the friendly alien was fed some candy by a child. That candy was Reese's Pieces, and as a result of showing that candy in the film, sales shot up 65%. . . . This incident was widely reported in the trade press, encouraging manufacturers to place their products in films. They realized that product placement in a film could be more rewarding than television advertising, which cost a great deal and often produces meager results."[42] "Nabisco paid $100,000 to have its Baby Ruth candy bar displayed in *The Goonies* (1985). The company also agreed to provide $15 million of network advertising and to give away free movie posters with the purchase of its candy from displays in 37,000 stores."[43]

Sometimes product placements are considered annoying to moviegoers and critics. For example, the way *Regarding Henry* (1991) made a connection "between Ritz Crackers and the Ritz-Carlton hotel [was considered] . . . especially annoying [for film critic Roger Ebert] . . . combining cheap sentiment with a cheap laugh and cheap product placement."[44] One rather ironic example of a product placement was Walt Disney's *Oliver & Co.* (1988) which contained "an extraordinary number of subliminal plugs for Coca-Cola."[45] Disney is the same company that subsequently forbade exhibitors from showing commercials prior to a Disney feature, although Disney features contained product placement and in some instances were nothing more than feature-length commercials for Disney products, characters and theme parks. This Disney episode is an example of the arrogance of power running amok.

Product tie-ins. The distributor may also consider revenue generated by product tie-ins to be inappropriate to include as part of the distributor's gross receipts. As Mark Litwak points out, "Product tie-ins are a no-lose proposition for a studio. The right to market products is licensed to outside companies, which incur all manufacturing and distribution expenses. The studio receives an advance, sometimes as much as $100,000 per product, and royalty payments, typically 7 percent of the revenues that the licensing company receives from retailers. Even if the products are not profitable, the studio benefits from free publicity for its movie."[46] Regardless of how profitable the product tie-in may or may not be, there is an issue as to whether the advance and royalty should be included in the distributor's gross receipts, which in turn will benefit all gross and net profit participants downstream.

Stock footage. Some of the major studio/distributors also exclude from the distributor's gross receipts "all monies received from the 'exploitation or use of stock footage, film and sound materials retained for library purposes, featurettes and still photographs which relate to or are derived from the . . . [net profit participant's motion picture].' . . . [Again] [u]nder most studio contracts . . . the studios do not have to share these proceeds with the net profit participants."[47] In this instance, monies used to produce the film (the film's negative cost) are recouped by the studio/distributor out of its gross receipts and a portion of the film is then used to generate revenue as stock footage. Thus, in effect, all of the gross and net profit participants are paying for the cost of creating a revenue producing asset for the studio/distributor.

Sales of physical properties. Some major studio/distributors exclude from the distributor's gross receipts any revenues received from the sale, rental or other disposition of any physical properties, materials and/or supplies acquired in conjunction with the production of a motion picture. This includes the sale of "movie paraphernalia." Such revenues are sometimes deemed to belong to the studio "although the costs of these materials and supplies were included in the negative cost of the motion picture. Thus, the costs of the materials are included in the movie's budget, but the profits from the disposal of these materials are not included in the profits of the movie."[48] This exclusion of revenues from gross receipts, again, deprives the gross and net profit participants of potential income.

Salvage exclusion. Some major studio/distributors exclude from the distributor's gross receipts all revenues generated from the sale of physical properties that are sold for salvage (i.e., the cost of the items are included in negative cost, while the earnings from disposal of the items are not included in gross receipts).[49]

Uncollectible indebtedness or bad debts. Distributors often seek to exclude uncollectible indebtedness (i.e., bad debts) from distributor gross receipts. Uncollectible indebtedness is debt owed that is determined to be impossible or impractical to collect (e.g., debts owed by a subdistributor, exhibitors or licensees to a film's distributor, that the distributor has determined to be uncollectible). Uncollectible indebtedness may also include amounts earned by a specific film and which are owed to the distributor of the film but which the distributor will not be able to collect because the debtor is insolvent. Unscrupulous distributors may fraudulently claim that such debts cannot be collected when in fact they have been or will be in the future. Or, even worse, a distributor may barter for something of value in exchange for forgoing a debt. In that situation, the distributor gets something of value equal to the value of the debt without having to claim that value as having been received for purposes of calculating gross or net profits.

Ownership/film library. Under some circumstances, the film distributor will require that actual ownership of the film be transferred by the producer to the distributor, thus whatever revenues the film generates as part of the distributor's library of films, following the exploitation of the film in all other markets and media, will be retained by the distributor. In other situations (e.g., when the distributor is acquiring the rights to distribute the film throughout the universe and in perpetuity) the distributor retains the rights to benefit from all revenues generated by the film forever, even without owning the film.

Net recoveries. The distribution agreement will often authorize the distributor to deduct any expenses incurred in litigating or defending against (a) any claims for unauthorized exhibition, distribution or other use of the film and/or (b) for any infringement, plagiarism or other interference by any party with the copyright of the film or (c) for breach of contract in connection with the distribution and/or exhibition of the film. On the other hand, many of these same distributors will seek to exclude from distributor gross receipts all revenues on any related settlement, court judgment or decree. In other words, the film's profit participants are burdened with the costs but are not allowed to benefit from any revenues generated through such activities.

Scrapping of prints. Eventually film distributors will sell their stockpile of used and unneeded feature film prints (used in the theatrical exhibition of the film) for their salvage value. Typically, any revenues generated from this activity will be excluded from the distributor's gross receipts.

All of the above described distributor gross receipts exclusions can in the aggregate substantially reduce the chances of anyone ever receiving net or gross profits from the exploitation of a motion picture. All such reductions in the size of this initial distributor's gross receipts fund negatively impact all other calculations downstream.

Distributor Fees

Once the distributor has determined what its gross receipts are during any given accounting period (and theoretically in accordance with the distribution agreement that has supposedly been negotiated between the producer and distributor) it will start deducting its distribution fees for each market and media. According to former studio accountant David Leedy the distributor's distribution fee "is intended to compensate the distributor for its selling efforts and the maintenance of its home office, branch offices, world-wide sales organization, the use of monies for releasing costs, and other costs."[50] Another of the problems in the film industry is illustrated by this Leedy quote. Although it may be about the best definition of what the distributor's fee covers, it still is not as precise as it could be. The only way anyone can determine whether any of the monies received by the distributor is in the form of a distribution fee is to know exactly what the distribution fee is supposed to cover. For example, a more precise definition of what is covered by the distribution fee might undermine the distributor's argument for a distribution overhead charge. In addition, if the distribution fee covers "the use of monies for releasing costs" as Leedy suggests, a similar duplicate charge under the category of distribution expenses might be eliminated.

Entertainment attorney Mark Litwak also suggests that distribution fees are significantly inflated: "Although the net-profit participant may not see any money from his points, or percentage of profits, the studio may make a 'profit' because it receives 30% to 40% of the gross as a distribution fee. This fee is usually far more than the actual costs the studio incurs to distribute a film.

Thus the release of a picture may be very profitable to the studio although technically there are no 'profits' for the participants."[51]

As marketing and distribution executive Fred Goldberg explains, the "distribution fee is always based on the gross receipts before . . . [any] deductions [distribution expenses, costs of production, etc.] are made. In other words, the distributor's fee comes off the top."[52] Thus, according to Goldberg, it "is to their advantage to generate a high gross."[53] That sounds persuasive but it is not always true. It depends on the movie. If the major studio/distributor has one or more large gross participants on a movie it may be to its advantage to allow the exhibitor to retain larger settlements on this film with the implied agreement that on a later film which has no gross participants, the distributor will be allowed to secure the higher settlement figures. After all, the informal settlement transaction takes place among friends, people who regularly barbeque in each other's back yards. Who's to know the difference?

Distributor fee examples. The chart below shows sample distribution fees for a major studio/distributor, a so-called mini-major (when they still existed), two independent distributors and a small distributor whose name would not even be recognizable to most people involved in the film industry. These figures are not averages. They are the actual percentages offered in recent years in specific distribution deals by distribution companies in the various categories listed.

In the deal memo describing the basic terms of the deal involving the first independent distributor, the production company (shown in the chart below) receives 100 percent of net profits, the domestic home video is not treated as a royalty, a minimum prints and ads commitment of $6 million has been offered, the producer has a right of approval over the distributor's marketing plan, but the distributor is going to deduct 110 percent of its distribution expenses (an effective 10 percent distribution overhead charge).

In the deal involving the second independent distributor (shown in the chart below), the producer has to provide the entire production budget and the distributor gets worldwide distribution rights, pays all distribution expenses and agrees to market the film at a level commensurate with comparable movies typically marketed by that distributor. In addition, the distributor has approval rights over the production budget, principal cast, individual producer, the director and shooting script. The deal further provides that the producer will own the copyright to the film and the distributor guarantees that the producer will recoup 60 percent of the producer's investment no later than 12 months after the film's initial release. The distributor commits to release the film no later than 90 days after delivery. The distributor's deal memo provides that reasonable and actual out-of-pocket distribution expenses are to be deducted by the distributor, then any remaining gross receipts received by the distributor are to be divided one-third to the distributor and two-thirds to the producer.

The producer is to be responsible for any profit participation interests of the creative personnel ("creative participations").

	Major	Mini-major	Name	independents	No name indie
U.S. theatrical	30%	27.5%	20%	20%	21%–25%
Canadian theatrical	35%	27.5%	20%	20%	35%
Domestic pay TV	30%	25%	25%	17.5%	15%
Domestic free TV					
Network	30%	37.5%	30%	17.5%	15%
All other	30%	37.5%	30%	17.5%	35%
Foreign (all media)	35%	37.5%	15%	17.5%	20%
Domestic home video	30%	35%	22.5%	17.5%	15%
Domestic non-theatrical	30%	40%	25%	17.5%	40%
Music recording (all territories)	30%	40%	30%	17.5%	15%
Music publishing (all territories)	30%	40%	30%	17.5%	15%
Merchandising, literary publishing & other	30%	40%	30%	17.5%	25%
Ancillary distribution (all territories)	—	—	—	—	—

As you can see, the terms of the distribution deal will vary considerably among the independent distributors who do not have as much leverage as the major studio/distributors, but who still may be in a stronger bargaining position than the vast majority of the independent producers. Also, note that no fees are provided for ancillary distribution, presumably because such revenues are excluded from the distributor's gross receipts anyway. In other words, there is no need for the distributor to charge a fee on revenues earned in ancillary distribution of the film because the distributor keeps all of that money.

Retroactive distribution fee increases. Some film distribution agreements provide for distribution fees that escalate retroactively, that is, the distribution fee percentage increases in size after a specified event occurs. When such a retroactive increase is authorized, it may also permit the distributor to go back to the first revenue dollars relating to the transaction and recoup at the higher rate from the beginning of the film's revenue flow.

Subdistribution fees. In situations in which a film's distributor utilizes the services of a subdistributor in certain markets or territories, the film's producer and other profit participants may be subjected to distribution fees from both entities, portions of which are redundant. In other words, depending on the size and extent of the distributor's organization, it may contract directly with exhibitors or it may utilize subdistributors (i.e., distributors who handle a specific, limited geographic territory for a film or territorial distributors who have contracted to represent an independent distribution company). Subdistributors subcontract with the main distributor who coordinates the distribution plans and marketing for all the subdistributors of a film. Subdistributors specialize in cities, states or territories. For foreign distribution, the distributor may contract with subdistributors who cover entire countries. Since subdistributors handle a limited territory or "exchange," they generally have an excellent working knowledge of their markets. However, they are paid a commission for booking a film and this system of subdistribution often makes it difficult to audit the independent distributors.

Distributor failure to license. Regardless of the reasons, sometimes distributors fail to license a film in a given territory, in which case, no revenues from that territory for the exploitation of the film in all media will be generated for the benefit of the distributor or any profit participants.

Distribution Expenses

Another set of problems is presented by the list of cost items that the feature film distribution agreement defines as distribution expenses and which in turn are deductible from a specified level of gross receipts. The following discussion covers issues that arise in this area of distribution expenses.

Production or distribution expense. One of the first questions raised with respect to film distribution expenses relates to whether a particular expense item is properly characterized as an expense of distribution or as a production cost.[54] When a film is produced pursuant to a production/financing-distribution deal, the distributor will most likely seek to classify as many expenses as possible as production costs so such expenses will bear interest, but the distributor will generally seek to characterize more of the expenses as distribution costs on negative pickups and pure acquisition deals so as to maximize distributor overhead, if any.

Direct distribution expense. Generally, the film distribution agreement will provide a definition of the expenses that may be deducted by the distributor out of its gross receipts revenue stream. For such purposes distributor expenses may be defined as all costs and expenses incurred, paid, payable or accrued, in connection with the distribution, advertising, exploitation and turning to account of the film (i.e., the activities directly related to the distribution of a film). A key question relates to whether the word "directly" is included in the definition as a modifier of "related." If not, the distributor may be authorized to charge other costs that are only indirectly related to a particular film. Such indirect charges are the same as distribution overhead charges.

Typically, the largest two items relating to the release of any picture are prints and advertising/publicity costs. Other direct expenses may include, but are not limited to, such things as checking costs, freight, guild payments and some taxes. A distributor may try to accomplish the same thing (i.e., deduction of indirect costs) by stating that it will be allowed to recoup more than 100 percent of its out of pocket expenses (e.g., 110 percent), or in the alternative, the distributor may simply provide a distribution overhead charge of 10 to 15 percent to cover its indirect costs.

Off-the-top expenses. Off-the-top expenses are contractually defined feature film distribution costs that represent the first group of expenses deducted by the distributor from the distributor's gross receipts. Off-the-top expenses typically include licenses and taxes, checking and collection costs, any expenses associated with converting foreign currency into U.S. dollars, residual payments to guilds, trade association dues and assessments and local advertising. The major studio/distributors rather uniformly deduct their distribution fees first (i.e., they base the percentage calculation on the largest pool of money received by the distributor, 100 percent of the distributor's gross receipts), then they deduct off-the-top expenses, if any, before paying any contractual gross participations out of this remaining fund which may be labeled "accountable gross" or "adjusted gross." Some independent distributors may deduct certain distribution expenses off-the-top before computing their distribution fee. Note that a lower distribution fee percentage is most likely to result in higher distribution fees if the fee calculation is applied to the larger pool of money (i.e., before the off-the-top expenses are deducted). As can be seen from the distribution fee chart above, the major studio/distributors typically charge the highest distribution fee and may well deduct their fee at the earliest point in the revenue stream. Other distributors may deduct all distribution expenses off-the-top and then divide up the balance between participants pursuant to pre-agreed percentages (i.e., without even charging a distribution fee).

Gross participations. The customary form of gross participation in the contemporary marketplace is based on a gross receipts figure that is somewhat less than pure gross. Before paying gross participations, the distributor is likely to deduct "what are commonly called the small 'off-the-top,' expenses, which include: (1) checking costs, (2) collection costs, (3) taxes, (4) guild payments (residuals), (5) trade association dues and assessments, and (6) conversion/transmission costs."[55]

In other instances, these off-the-top expense deductions from gross receipts may include prints and advertising costs and advances paid to the producer, among other specified items deductible from first position gross. If deductions for enough different items are demanded by the distributor and accepted by the prospective adjusted or accountable gross participant, the resulting gross participation may have only slightly more value than a net profit participation. For example, the cost of prints and advertising alone may diminish the value of an adjusted or accountable gross participation to the point that no money will ever be paid to persons or entities with rights to receive such funds.

Checking costs. Attendance checking involves the activities undertaken on behalf of a distributor (or producer in self-distribution situations) designed to verify the actual number of paid moviegoers in attendance at a showing or showings of a film. Such activities may include the hiring of checkers to go to the theatre and count those in attendance or to purchase the first and last ticket of the day at a given theatre to then compare the ticket numbers with the exhibitor's attendance reports.

There are organizations that provide such checking services for producers and distributors. Independent checking companies are businesses that can be hired by a producer or distributor to verify the number of paid ticket-purchasing moviegoers in attendance at showings of a given movie and which is not the checking service normally used by the major studio/distributors. A checker is a person hired by producers or distributors or by checking services on behalf of producers or distributors to verify the number of paid ticket-purchasing moviegoers in attendance at showings of a given movie. Checking costs are distributor expenses incurred in monitoring the activities of exhibitors to ensure that reported film attendance and receipts are accurate and in investigating the unauthorized usage of motion pictures. These are important activities that can benefit the producer too.

The checking services are sometimes asked to conduct open checks, in which the person doing the checking (i.e., the checker) identifies himself or herself to the theatre manager and asks permission to monitor the conduct of the theatre's box office personnel. Such observation enables the checking entity, usually the film's distributor, to compare box office receipts on the day checked with a day in which ticket sales were not observed (a blind check). A blind check involves the covert monitoring of the activities of a theatre's box office personnel by a checker who is posing as a regular patron and observing such activity.

Collection costs. Collection costs are distributor expense items incurred in connection with the collection of gross receipts, including attorney and auditor fees and costs associated with any liability incurred by the distributor in connection with such collection activities. Collection costs are typically deducted as off-the-top expenses.

Foreign taxes. Foreign taxes are often mishandled by the MPAA distributors to the detriment of other interested parties. Foreign taxes generally represent the largest part of the distribution expense item "taxes." Many foreign countries will levy some form of gross receipts, remittance or other tax on the exploitation of the film in their country. The distributors will seek to provide in the distribution agreement that the payment of such taxes constitute authorized deductions as distribution expenses. However, the distributor will also claim a U.S. tax credit for the payment of such taxes, which in reality were charged against the producer and other net profit participants (i.e., since such payments were deducted from distributor gross receipts as a distribution expense). Foreign tax credits are dollar for dollar deductions from an individual or entity's U.S. income tax for the payment of foreign taxes levied by countries as a remittance or gross receipts tax. This distributor practice wrongfully takes money away from a film's producer and other net profit participants and unjustly enriches the distributor.

Residuals and royalties. Residuals (or residual payments) are percentage participations for television reruns of a film (i.e., payments to actors, writers or others for each rerun after the initial showing and pursuant to a union agreement). Residuals are generally based on the number of times the film is exhibited on television, or as a percentage of revenues from television exhibition. Royalties, on the other hand, are payments to the holder for the right to use property such as copyrighted material (i.e., a negotiated percentage of income paid to an author or composer for each copy of the work sold). A royalty is a share of the product or of the proceeds therefrom reserved by an owner for permitting another to exploit and use his or her property (i.e., the rental that is paid to the original owner of property based on a percentage of profit or production). Royalty is compensation for the use of property, but it is based as to amount entirely upon the use actually made of the property. The residual and royalty provision in a film distribution agreement is language or a paragraph which provides for the payment of residuals and royalties associated with the picture (e.g., that the distribution company agrees to make all residual and supplemental payments required to be made in the distribution of the picture).

Dues and assessments. The dues and assessments distributor expense item refers to the charges levied by the Motion Picture Association of America (MPAA), the Association of Motion Picture and Theatrical Producers (AMPTP) and other industry groups for their work in representing the interests of their respective segments of the motion picture industry. These dues payments are allocated to each film based on a percentage of the gross receipts generated by the film. Thus, such payments are considered a distribution expense and are paid prior to any payments to net profit participants. The MPAA distribution companies reportedly extract these dues allocations from theatrical revenues generated by MPAA distributed films whereas the percentage used is based on the anticipated revenues from television, video and theatrical distribution.

Fifty percent plus of association dues and assessments are related to fighting piracy (i.e., protecting the video revenue stream which mostly goes to the distributor or its subsidiary). On the other hand (as stated above) the dues and assessment distributor expense deduction comes out of the domestic theatrical revenue stream, usually one of the "off-the-top" expense deductions. Thus, in effect, the theatrical revenue stream is paying for expenses primarily associated with the home video revenue stream, most of which goes to the distributor, as opposed to net profit participants.

As an example, the John Landis' contract for off-the-top expenses contained this explanation of "trade dues" to be deducted: "Allocable portion of dues, assessments, including legal fees and costs and contributions to MPAA, AMPTP or similarly constituted or substitute organizations throughout the world (including legal fees to counsel respecting anti-trust matters) . . . up to a maximum of $75,000."[56]

Thus, this category of distributor expense may include legal fees to such association's outside counsel (not its in-house counsel) relating to antitrust matters, which means the major distributors are deducting from gross receipts (i.e., reducing the amount of funds that other participants may share in, to pay for activities which help to continue or improve their position of market dominance). Since most independent producers have to wait until a film's revenue stream reaches net profits, they are contributing to the payment of the distributor association's costs incurred in conjunction with fighting antitrust claims or taking positions on legislative issues most of which would be opposed by the independent producer whose funds are being used.

Conversion and transmission costs. Conversion costs refer to a specific kind of distribution expense (i.e., costs, discounts and expenses incurred in obtaining remittances of receipts to the U.S., including costs of contesting imposition of restricted funds). Conversion costs are generally treated as off-the-top distribution expenses. Transmission costs are expenses incurred by film distributors in bringing funds earned in foreign territories to the U.S. They are also typically treated as off-the-top distribution expenses.

Adjusted or accountable gross. After the off-the-top expenses are deducted from the distributor's gross receipts, the remaining funds are often referred to as adjusted gross or accountable gross, depending on the distributor. Again, these are defined terms (supposedly negotiated) in a movie distribution deal, which typically refer to gross receipts minus certain specified deductions (the off-the-top expenses). The gross participations granted either by the production company or the distributor to creative talent are then generally paid as a percentage of this adjusted or accountable gross figure. Thus, such gross participations are not actually based on the distributor's true gross receipts. This interim category of distributor revenues appears to have been created as a way to avoid paying gross profit participants based on pure gross (i.e., to protect certain expense items from incursions by the gross profit participants).

Off-the-bottom expenses. Another contractually defined term sometimes used in feature film distribution agreements to describe another category of distributor expense deductions that are taken by the distributor after payment of gross participations, if any, but before net profits. For example, in a distribution arrangement where production costs are provided by a limited partnership or a third party financier (other than a bank/lender) the distributor may want to deduct first from gross receipts its distribution fee, then any off-the-top expenses, then gross participations, if any, then off-the-bottom expenses and remit all of the balance to the producer's group. This producer's group is then responsible for providing the partnership or financier with recoupment of the negative costs plus whatever return they contracted for and the producer's group is responsible for dividing up the balance of the net profits as between deferrals, net profit participations and the producer's share. On the other hand, if a bank or lender were involved in a negative pickup situation, the negative costs plus interest and fees would be paid by the distributor to the bank or lender first (prior to the actual release of the film), then as gross receipts are generated, the distributor might take its distribution fees, off-the-top expenses, pay gross participations, if any, then take off-the-bottom costs and remit the balance to the producer's group as net profits. In the studio financed production-financing/distribution arrangement, the distributor typically takes its distribution fees first, then off-the-top expenses, pays gross participants, if any, takes off-the-bottom costs, deducts interest payments, then recoups the negative costs and finally, if anything is left, remits the balance to the producer group as net profits.

Improperly claimed expenses. Auditors who regularly audit MPAA distributors on behalf of producers and other net profit participants often find that the distributors have wrongfully or unfairly allocated certain of their incidental expenses or costs to a film, or have completely fabricated distribution expenses that are allocated to a film. A single example of the many instances of these occurrences, involved studio executive David Begelman who, "while in Florida overseeing location-filming on *The Greatest,* starring Muhammad Ali, had used limousines for personal purposes having nothing to do with business, and had charged their $6,000 cost to the budget of the film."[57]

Account numbers. Studios routinely assign an accounting number to be used for expenses incurred by each film being produced at the studio, and the account number is often all that is required of someone to charge expenses for goods or services to the account of such a film. In other words, if a studio's financial accounting procedures are somewhat lax, and most people in the industry agree that they are, it is entirely possible for someone to gain access to a film's account number and to charge something to the budget of that film, even though that particular cost item had nothing to do with the production of the film (e.g., sexual services of so-called Hollywood "party girls"). Such improperly claimed expenses effectively provide unauthorized perks for individuals working on or close to studio-financed film projects and may reduce the available monies that the corporation could use to pay dividends to its shareholders while also reducing the prospects for payment of net profits to profit participants. Many in the film industry believe that distributors or the distribution division of the studio routinely claim improper expenses. In such cases, the distributor wrongfully or unfairly allocates certain of its incidental expenses or costs to a film, or completely fabricates distribution expenses that are allocated to a film.

Anticipated expenses. Major studio/distributor film distribution agreements often contain language that permits the distributor to deduct from gross receipts an amount adequate to cover future estimated distribution expenses. Such provisions often provide that the distributor may in good faith retain sums necessary to pay for costs reasonably anticipated to arise in connection with the picture being distributed. Unfortunately, such provisions are typically worded in a very vague manner and permit the distributor to exercise its un-fettered discretion in determining how much to set aside to cover such future expenses. Thus, the producer and other net profit participants are at the mercy of the distributor, since if at the end of any given accounting period, the distributor chooses not to permit a small amount of net profits to flow through to the net profit participants, this provision allows the distributor to claim higher reserves, that is, reserves far in excess of the amounts needed to cover reasonably expected expenses.

Allocated or apportioned expenses. Allocated or apportioned expenses are costs that are divided according to the parties' interests; proportionately. Many distribution agreements allow the distributor the discretion to apportion numerous distribution expenses relating to advertising, facilities, employees, and so forth among films that are marketed in a package. As entertainment attorney Mark Litwak points out, "The cost of limos, lunches, executive travel and other expenses that were incurred on flops may find their way on the books of hits."[58] Of course, if those hits were produced by independent producers, this simply is another instance of the studios illegally shifting the costs of their "losers" to the independent "winners" (produced by independents but released by the major studio/distributors).

Studios have also been known to "charge all the expenses related to the promotion of a picture at such events as the Cannes Film Festivals to each picture the studio presents, rather than assigning each film a pro-rata share of the total."[59] Attorneys Nochimson and Brachman also raise questions relating to "whether distribution expenses cover more than one picture."[60] The distributor will often try to permit itself the discretion to allocate expenses as it sees fit, in which case, it will typically allocate certain of the larger expenses to the independently produced films and the smaller expenses to its own films. In some instances, the distributor may even allocate duplicate expenses to several films when the expenses were incurred only on behalf of one of the motion pictures. A profit participant cannot make an informed judgment as to whether such apportionments are fair without having access to the information upon which such apportionments are based.

Advertising costs. As stated above, the MPAA company distribution deals are often drafted so as to allow the distributor a great deal of discretion in making allocations. This becomes particularly troublesome when the distributor is allocating the costs of advertising several films among such films. Since advertising is generally the single largest expense item of the distributor and the distributor is usually able to deduct such expenses from the revenue stream before any net profits are declared, there is a built-in incentive for the distributor to overstate and wrongfully allocate such expenses. As attorney Litwak points out, "A studio may try to deduct the cost of an ad used to promote a different movie."[61]

Again, if the distributor is handling the distribution for two films, one produced by the distributor's affiliated production company and the other produced by an independent producer, and the distributor utilizes the services of its own in-house advertising department or an outside advertising agency to execute media buys on behalf of both films, all over the country, in several different media, including radio, television, newspapers and magazines, it would be extremely difficult for any auditor of the independently produced film's net profit participants to determine accurately which advertising costs are truly associated with which film. This creates an opportunity for distributors and their advertising agencies or in-house advertising departments to make more "mistakes" in favor of the distributor, "mistakes" which cost the net profit participants of the independently produced film, substantial amounts of money.

Cooperative advertising. Film advertising and promotion in which the cost is shared between the distributor and exhibitor or other entity is referred to as cooperative advertising. Such costs are generally calculated on a weekly basis. The exhibitor's contribution toward the total cost of the ads is either a predetermined fixed amount set out in the contract between the distributor and exhibitor (but decreasing from week to week) or a negotiated formula based on mutually agreed ad expenditures. The distributor's contribution may be a fixed amount or a percentage arrangement similar to that used for film rentals. Expenditures for cooperative advertising are more advantageous from a tax standpoint since such costs can usually be deducted in the year in which they are incurred, whereas national advertising may have to be capitalized and amortized over the period in which the major portion of gross revenue from the picture is recorded. As discussed earlier, distributors and exhibitors commonly negotiate and settle their accounts relating to several motion pictures, including their respective obligations with respect to cooperative advertising, with the result that it is often difficult to determine exactly what portion of cooperative advertising costs incurred by a distributor should be allocated to a given producer's film.

Combination and cooperative ads. The allocation of expense problem crops up with combination ads (i.e., where one print advertisement is used to advertise two different films). If such combination ads are used and they are cooperative ads (i.e., the distributor and exhibitor share the costs), not only will the distributor and exhibitor allocate the costs between the two films, but they also will allocate the costs between the two entities. Otherwise, the exhibitor and distributor are free to engage in difficult to prove collusive activities (among friends) which allocate most of the cost of such ads to the independent producer's film as opposed to the studio produced film.

Inflated advertising costs. Many film distributors utilize the services of outside advertising agencies to help design a film's marketing plan and to make the many media buys associated with advertising a given film. There is very little, if anything, to prevent an outside advertising agency from charging more than is warranted for its services, since it knows that such expenses are going to be reimbursed to the studio/distributor by deductions from the movie's revenue stream. In an insular community like Hollywood, such situations may also involve outside advertising agencies run by friends and family of the studio executive who is all too willing to overlook the advertising agency's overcharges since the only people getting hurt by such a scam are the particular film's net profit participants and the major studio/distributor's stockholders. In addition, these are the kinds of situations that are ripe for the questions raised in the section of this book relating to discounts, rebates and kickbacks. Since there is so much money involved in the advertising of a motion picture, it may be quite easy and tempting to make arrangements for the outside advertising agency to overcharge advertising expenses to a film and then provide some direct or indirect benefit to the studio executive who has the discretion to place such advertising accounts with the advertising agency.

Excessive advertising ("buying a gross"). Some distributors will engage in an activity referred to in the industry as buying a gross, which means the distributor has spent an excessive amount of advertising and promotional dollars in an effort to achieve a higher level of distributor rentals during a film's theatrical release while also creating a loss for the film during its theatrical release. Such distributor tactics may make it impossible for the films involved ever to generate net profits. The distributor expenses will, of course, be deducted from the distributor's gross receipts (thus recouped), but may also help to generate significantly higher revenues from the video, cable and foreign markets wherein the distributor has a better deal and its expenses are not as great. Such excessive advertising during a film's theatrical release may also then contribute to higher revenues during the film's video release, and since the distributor generally is able to extract an even higher percentage of monies out of the film's video revenue stream, it may be to the advantage of the distributor to buy a gross.

Advertising fees. Some major studio/distributors routinely charge a 10 percent advertising fee simply for administering a movie's advertising program, even when the program is actually conceived, planned, created and implemented by an outside advertising agency. Such percentage-based fees may go far beyond what is actually necessary to cover the activities of the studio's employees, particularly on the films that expend large amounts of money on advertising.

Advertising overhead. Other studios may characterize a cost item similar to the advertising fee as advertising overhead. "Most major studios charge 10% of the total advertising and publicity expenditure as a contractual overhead amount. . . . In the December 21, 1990 decision on the *Buchwald vs. Paramount* case, Judge Schneider found Paramount's charge of 10% advertising overhead unconscionable."[62] Such charges are imposed by many of the major studio/distributors and some independent distributors to cover the costs of operating their internal advertising and publicity departments. Generally, the charge equals 10 percent of all distribution expenses, a percentage that has no relation to actual costs since certain pictures bear a disproportionate share of such expenses. In many instances this overhead charge will exceed the actual costs of the services actually provided for a given motion picture.

Distributor employee time allocations (shared employee salaries). Some distribution companies allocate the time that their "publicity people spend on a specific movie and charge their time and expenses against the P&A (prints and advertising) budget . . . the salary and the expenses of the project manager are proportionally charged against the movies he or she supervises."[63] Such allocations may also occur for studio/distributor employees performing functions other than advertising or publicity. They are employees of the studio/distributor whose salaries are shared among several films that the employees are supposedly working on. If such allocations are made and thus the time such employees spend working on a given film project is charged against the distribution expenses of the film, this may constitute a double charge, in the sense that the distributor may also be charging overhead that is designed to cover just such expenses. In addition, it is very difficult to determine whether the time being reported by such employees is accurately stated. Actual instances of studio executives being given time cards to fill out arbitrarily so that the studio can allocate their time as a cost of a given film (even though the employee did not work on that film at all) have been reported.

Contractual distributor overhead. Motion picture distributors may also seek to deduct a stated percentage of all distribution expenses (as opposed to a specific advertising overhead charge) that cannot be directly allocated to a specific motion picture distributed. This more general distributor overhead is deducted from gross receipts as a distribution expense for a specific film by authority of a provision in the distribution agreement that permits such deductions. Nearly all if not all major studio/distributors impose such contractually defined overhead charges on the producers of films they distribute, thus it may be fair to assume that few, if any, feature film producers have the bargaining power to eliminate such charges.

Distributor cost allocations. Cost allocation issues also arise in the licensing of films in a package for television, whether for network or syndication; and in foreign distribution, such issues arise with respect to the allocation of a portion of film rentals to shorts and trailers. Distributors often demand language in their distributor agreements that provide them with the discretion to make such allocations without reference to any objective criteria.

Facilities allocations. The major studio/distributors will also seek to allocate the cost of utilizing their facilities among the various films produced and/or distributed (i.e., they will apportion studio or distributor operating expenses among the studio's various components for the purpose of charging such expenses against a given film's costs). If facilities allocations are made by an independent distributor, such expense allocations are no different than studio overhead, since independent distributors do not have studio facilities.

Below-the-line fringes. Compensation paid to or for the benefit of a film's crew in addition to their salaries is referred to as below-the-line fringes. When such individuals are members of a guild or union, these benefits may include vacation pay and health, welfare and pension contributions. Also, such payments may be made directly to the guild or union. Studios often overstate the cost of such benefits in determining the negative cost of a movie (i.e., they deduct an overstated amount as a distribution expense, but pay a smaller amount to the guilds, keeping the balance and depriving the net profit participants of any participation in such funds).

Exhibitor allowances. Often film distributors will grant certain allowances (sums granted as reimbursement for expenses) to exhibitors for advertising and exploitation of a film. Such allowances are granted in lieu of revenues that would have otherwise been paid by the exhibitor to the distributor. Thus, these allowances are the equivalent of a distributor deduction from its gross receipts, a deduction that reduces the monies available to contribute toward net profits.

Over-reported travel expenses. Another of the alleged wrongful studio accounting practices sometimes complained about by producers is the overreporting of travel expenses. In other words, the studio inflates the travel expenses associated with the production of a film being produced in conjunction with the studio. As with advertising expenses, this may occur as part of a scheme implemented through an outside agency, through travel agencies that may be owned and operated by friends or relatives of the studio executive with the authority to select the travel agency for travel associated with the production of a movie. Of course, on films that have been produced or distributed using the studio/distributor's funds, these inflated expenses will be deducted from revenues generated by the exploitation of the film.

Print costs. The expenses incurred in making a film's release prints for theatrical exhibition are referred to as print costs. The cost of a single print may be in the $2,000 range, thus if a distributor were to effect a two-thousand print release, its print costs would equal $4,000,000. Clearly then, print costs are one of the major distribution expenses (advertising being the other) and present a significant opportunity for overstating the amount or for possible kickback arrangements from favored or distributor-owned film labs. The cost of the print containers and for shipping the prints may also be included in this distributor expense item, making the print costs category of distributor expenses even more difficult to judge.

Unauthorized distribution. Individual distributors may claim to incur costs in preventing unauthorized distribution of their films (i.e., the sale, rental or other exploitation of a film without a grant of distribution rights). The distributor, of course, would seek to define such costs as deductible distribution expenses, thus, to the extent they are overstated or improperly claimed, the distributor has again succeeded in fraudulently depriving all net profit participants of their opportunity to benefit from net profits or a greater amount of net profits. Further, distributor association dues, fees, assessments or other levies are typically made to cover the costs of such activities conducted on behalf of the association's distributor members. In situations where an individual distributor is also claiming such costs, the activity may have been paid for twice.

Ongoing distribution expenses. Certain of the film distributor's expenses continue to accrue (e.g., any of the distributor expenses that are based on some percentage of a defined portion of the film's revenue stream would be considered ongoing costs, so long as there was no ceiling on such expenses). Thus, residuals, taxes, trade association dues, gross profit participations and even interest up to a point all might be considered ongoing costs. This ongoing cost phenomenon (also referred to as the rolling breakeven) helps to explain why a motion picture may never achieve net profits or achieves net profits for one accounting period but not on the next accounting statement (i.e., the ongoing costs may have increased substantially during the next accounting period).

Interest

The major studio/distributors engage in a number of unconscionable practices relating to the charging of interest on motion pictures whose production financing has been provided by such companies. For definitional purposes, interest is consideration or compensation paid for the use of money loaned. It represents the cost of using someone else's money (in this case the studio's money) expressed as a rate per period of time, usually one year, in which case it is called an annual rate of interest. In studio financing, interest is typically deducted from the net profit calculation after distributor expenses and before the cost of production. Most of the interest problems discussed here only arise within the context of the production/financing-distribution deal, but the interest issue creates problems for independent producers at several levels.

Interest plus profit participation. Distribution agreements involving studio financing of the negative cost of a film often allow the studio to charge interest on its unrecouped negative cost in addition to permitting the affiliated distributor to retain a substantial if not overwhelming interest in any profit participation. Neither banks providing production money loans nor their affiliates are generally permitted to participate in a film's revenue stream.

Excessive interest rates. The interest rate charged by the studio is often not in proportion to the actual cost of funds. Studios have been known to charge interest rates of 20 percent to 30 percent.

Delayed interest payments on negative cost balances. In calculating this interest on the studio's unrecouped negative costs, all distribution fees and direct distribution costs are typically first deducted from gross receipts, thus significantly decreasing the amount of gross receipts, if any, that may apply toward recoupment of the studio's contribution toward production costs. Thus, at many early stages of earnings statements, no recoupment of negative costs is achieved and the interest charges simply continue to accrue. Thus, the overall amount of interest charges paid are increased due to the expanded time period during which interest is accruing. This self-dealing arrangement allows the studio to make more money on the interest payments. In contrast, with a bank-financed motion picture production, the bank will recoup its loaned amount (including the negative cost, plus interest and fees) long before the distributor deducts its distribution fee and expenses.

Interest on advances. The studio/distributors typically will take the position that advances should not be included in gross receipts until earned, in other words, the distributor will want to deduct an amount equal to any advance that has been paid to the producer from monies received by the distributor and will not want to consider such amounts as part of gross receipts for any profit participation calculations that start with a gross receipts figure. On the other hand, these same studio/distributors often seek to charge interest on such advances. In other words, they want to be paid interest on funds that are not advanced as part of the film's negative cost but funds advanced as the first part of the producer group's share of the film's revenue stream. At the same time, such advances are not allowed by the distributor to be counted as part of the distributor's gross receipts in the distributor's net profit calculations, thus the producer group has to pay interest on the money advanced but is deprived of the benefit of such money for purposes of calculating net profits.

Interest on monies not spent. Interest is commonly charged by the major studio/distributors on monies not yet spent. The studio will calculate interest on negative costs from the point at which such expenses are incurred (as an accounting entry), as opposed to when such expenses are actually paid to the provider of a product or service. Thus, the studio is actually getting interest on monies that were not actually out-of-pocket.

Premature deductions from gross receipts. In preparing an earnings statement for a film, the studio's affiliated distributor may show as a deduction the print and advertising costs that have been incurred but have not yet been paid, and this accounting procedure may prevent the interim participation statement from showing a net profit. This premature accrual of expenses also eliminates some of the film's gross receipts that would have been used to reduce the film's negative cost, thereby also effectively creating higher interest charges than would otherwise be the case.

When interest charges stop. Studios also commonly seek to continue charging interest on the negative costs of a film until the end of the accounting period in which payments reducing the negative cost total and/or interest are received by the studio. In other words, if the studio/distributor receives gross receipts that apply toward recoupment of the film's negative cost, interest will still accrue on that portion of the negative cost until the end of that accounting period (i.e., for another couple of months). Such a policy would be more reasonable if the studio's accounting policy was consistent and interest charges did not start until the end of the accounting period.

Interest on overhead. In most cases, studio/distributors providing production monies pursuant to a P-F/D deal will charge a 10 to 15 percent production overhead charge on the production cost of the picture and characterize such a charge as a cost of production for purposes of calculating interest. Thus, interest is again being charged on monies not actually loaned or expended by the studio. Further, some studio-affiliated distributors will include some or all of their indirect distribution costs (i.e., the normal costs of doing business as a distributor that are not specifically tied to a particular film being distributed — the same as distribution overhead), and this distributor's overhead charge is recouped by the distributor from its gross receipts as a distribution expense. Thus again, such amounts are not available for recoupment of the negative cost, with the result that the producer and other net profit participants end up paying more interest than necessary on the negative cost of the picture. As stated earlier, the distributor may also seek to characterize incorrectly certain of its distribution overhead charges as production costs, thus getting even more interest on these indirect distribution expenses.

Simple vs. exact interest. Studio/distributors also typically insist on using a form of simple interest, based on a 360-day year, instead of exact interest (based on a 365-day year), and that practice, particularly when dealing with substantial amounts of money in the form of negative costs, will sometimes result in the payment of a significantly greater amount of interest to the studio/distributor for that final partial interest-bearing accounting period.

Interest on gross participations. Studio/distributors often engage in this variation on the practice of charging interest on monies not actually spent. In this situation, a studio/distributor that has financed the production costs of a motion picture categorizes gross participations (i.e., monies paid to talent, and sometimes others, out of some level of the distributor's gross receipts) as production costs (as opposed to distribution expenses or some other noninterest-bearing accounting entry) and thus charges interest and overhead on such participations.[64] Thus, the studio/distributor is being paid interest on monies that were never actually expended. The gross participations were merely deducted from the distributor's gross receipts revenue stream long after the film had been produced.

Production Cost Issues

Production costs are generally going to be under the control of the independent producer and director in all but the studio in-house production deals. On the other hand, if a producer is attached to a project being financed as a production-financing/distribution deal and the director is actually named by the studio, the producer may not have the real authority to prevent the director from spending too much money. In addition, as pointed out by Peter Dekom in his *American Premiere* article on the motion picture net profit scam, none of the people who are in a position to lower the production costs of films are given any incentive to do so.[65]

Production or distribution expense. As pointed out above in the discussion on distributor expense deductions, when a studio/distributor finances the production costs of a film, there may be a tendency for this self-dealing combined entity to characterize some of what are actually distribution costs as production costs, with the result that interest being incurred by the production cost side is inflated. The term "negative cost" for a studio/distributor not only may include the out-of-pocket production expenses but also a nonallocated overhead percentage charge which may range from 10 percent to 15 percent. Interest charges will also normally be charged against such overhead charges. Thus, the characterization of distribution costs as production expenses becomes very important with respect to keeping production costs down.

Talent participations. The high up front salaries paid to talent is without question one of the factors contributing to the high cost of production for major studio/distributor films. Talent participations in the backside revenue earnings (revenue stream) of the film, specifically, gross participations which are arbitrarily characterized by the distributor as a production expenses, inflate production costs even further. Talent participations generally are financial interests of writers, directors and/or actors who negotiate percentage participations based on a film's earnings at some specific level of the film's revenue stream. Such participations are often expressed as points (i.e., a percentage of the revenue at a given level). For example, "gross points" can be defined on a number of different levels of distributors' gross receipts. Net points may also be defined at different levels of a film's revenue stream, such as the film's net profits, the producer's share of net proceeds or partnership net receipts for films financed by means of a limited partnership. Net points are also commonly referred to as net profits or net proceeds. As has been stated, however, the presence of gross participations with respect to any given feature film all but destroys any possibility of net profit participations. Thus, anyone who negotiates a net profit participation (whether outside investor or a member of the film's creative team) who also does not have the leverage to limit the ability of the producer or the major studio/distributor from permitting gross profit participations on the same film (and few, if any, possess such leverage) has just wasted his or her effort and has negotiated a worthless provision. This in turn suggests that most all of such net profit arrangements are unconscionable.

Gross participants. Gross participants are those persons or entities who have negotiated or are awarded a percentage participation in a movie's gross receipts (i.e., prior to net receipts or net profits). Gross participations and gross participants have been around for some time. "For directing *North by Northwest* (1959)," director Alfred Hitchcock "received a fee of $250,000 plus 10 percent of the movie's gross receipts above $8 million . . . by 1962, Hitchcock was the third-largest stockholder in MCA, the owners of Universal."[66]

The gross participation amounts involved are even more significant today. "Warner Brothers . . . agreed to pay Jack Nicholson a hefty upfront fee—$7 million—to play the over-the-top villain, the Joker, in *Batman*. In addition to that, Nicholson took home a 15 per cent share of the gross . . . Arnold Schwarzenegger commanded the same 15 per cent gross share in *Total Recall*, as well as the $10 million fee Carolco paid him upfront."[67] On the movie *Twins*, the "two stars, Arnold Schwarzenegger and Danny DeVito, together with the director, Ivan Reitman, took a nominal salary upfront in return for a share of the studio's gross profits."[68] This is exactly what Peter Dekom suggests in his article ought to happen, but since the major studio/distributors have such a terrible reputation when it comes to allowing films to achieve net profits, few in the ranks of talent are willing to give up their upfront salaries for a share of net profits and fewer still have the leverage to obtain gross participations.

These huge gross participations paid to a few actors, directors or producers not only spell the death knell for net profit participations but also confirm just how much money is actually being made by the studios with these films. In other words, if the value of Jack Nicholson's gross participation rises to $50 million and that only represents 20 percent of the film's gross receipts, then obviously the distributor would be dividing up the other 80 percent of gross receipts between its distribution fee (33 percent or $82,500,000) and an inflated distribution expense recoupment along with an inflated negative cost plus interest on films handled as in-house productions or on a production-financing/distribution basis.

As discussed above, first position gross is a share of the gross receipts or total revenues from a given source or stage in a movie's revenue stream, such as film rentals or home video, which is accounted for before distribution fees, distribution expenses, negative costs or other gross participations are deducted. First position is generally considered to be the most sought-after participation in a movie deal but it is seldom awarded by movie studio/distributors, except to a handful of the most-recognized talent in the industry, if any. Again, to the extent that anyone other than the distributor is participating in distributor gross receipts in a first position, the chances that such a film will generate net profits for anyone else are probably zero.

Reporter David Robb confirms the point made earlier that "there is no such thing as a 'true' gross deal because every gross deal—even the first-dollar gross deal—is computed after certain 'off-the-top' expenses are deducted. There are usually seven or eight of these 'off-the-top' items; principally taxes, residuals and trade dues, that are deducted from a film's gross receipts before gross participation payments are paid."[69]

Even agents sometimes overstate the value of gross participations. For example, agent Ed Limato says: "The best deal that you can make for any actor is what we call a first dollar gross deal . . . that is when an actor gets a percentage, usually starting at ten per cent, of every dollar that goes into the studio's coffers. That simply means that there is no way the studio can lie to you (about the movie's receipts) or tack on this expense or that expense. When you make that kind of deal for an artist, you know that he's home."[70]

This view is somewhat naive, considering the fact that a gross participation does not eliminate any of the problems described previously relating to distributor gross receipt exclusions, since if monies are effectively excluded from the distributor's gross receipts, they will certainly not benefit any gross profit participant (even the first dollar gross participant). And as discussed earlier, there are a number of techniques used by the major studio/distributors to exclude revenues from the distributor's gross receipts pool including the exhibitor/distributor settlement transaction and the home video royalty scam.

Also, in today's Hollywood, gross participations are typically based on some modified level of the distributor's gross receipts, such as adjusted gross or accountable gross. In other words, some deductions are made by the distributor prior to the payment of any so-called talent gross participations, thus the talent is not participating in pure gross or 100 percent of the distributor's gross receipts. Thus, it is not accurate to suggest that an actor has a realistic possibility of being paid a percentage of "every dollar that goes into the studio's coffers."

On the other hand gross points "are so sought after because the alternative, net points, are virtually worthless."[71] Although partly true, this Nicolas Kent statement is also an exaggeration. Net points are not worthless, they just seldom materialize. That is not the same as saying they never appear. They do sometimes occur, only not very often. Peter Dekom directs equally strong language toward the gross and net profit participation relationship, saying "the deduction of gross participants against net profits, particularly after the deduction of a distribution fee, absolutely renders net profits meaningless, even if the . . . video calculation were fairly computed."[72]

As a consequence, there has to be a certain amount of tension between gross profit participants and net profit participants. It would be difficult to believe that most of the net profit participants on the all-time box office champ for Warner Bros. *Batman* would not resent the fact that Jack Nicholson, in addition to a reported up front fee advance of $6 million, was successful in negotiating one of the richest deals in Hollywood history: 15 percent of the gross with an escalator clause that boosted his take to as high as 20 percent the more money the film took in. Thus Nicholson's earnings alone accounted for more than $50 million of *Batman's* production costs according to industry sources, and along with the distributor's fees and expense reimbursement, plus interest and other distributor tactics described in this book, eliminated all possibilities that net profit participants on that film would ever see another dime.

As lawyers David Nochimson and Leon Brachman point out, it "is customary for studios to treat prebreak participations as elements of negative cost, the effect of which is to delay the point at which net profits are reached because of the application of overhead and interest on such participations."[73] And apparently, this studio characterization of gross participations will hold up in court. In the *Alperson v. Mirisch* case,[74] the California Court of Appeals affirmed the trial court's holding that percentage of gross receipts agreements (gross profit participation agreements) are properly deductible as costs of production (negative cost) in computing a film's net profit."[75] On the other hand, that does not mean that a producer has to accept the distributor's characterization of gross participations as costs of production. In my view, gross participations should not be characterized as either a cost of production or distribution. It should have its own separate accounting category.

Negative costs. A film's negative cost (or production cost) is the total of all of the various costs, charges, and expenses incurred in the acquisition and production of a motion picture, in all its aspects prior to release (i.e., to produce the final negative). Such costs are generally incurred in four stages: story rights acquisition, preproduction, principal photography and postproduction and the complete production process can take a year to eighteen months. Production expenses may include the cost of the story, salaries of cast, directors, producers, and so forth, set construction and operations, wardrobe, sound synchronization, editing and any other costs necessary to create a finished film negative. Other components of movie production costs might include (depending on the form of film finance used) residuals, participations, allocated studio overhead, abandonment costs and capitalized interest. Production costs may also include contractual overheads and contractual facility and equipment charges in excess of actual costs, rebates and receipts from sales of props and sets, provision for self-insurance, a completion bond charge, participations before breakeven and overhead thereon and deferments, along with actual or imputed interest. Negative costs are also distinguished from distribution, subdistribution and exhibition costs.

Inflated costs. The production cost for studio financed films does not mean the studio's cost in providing a certain service or product but what it arbitrarily decides to charge the film for such service or product and the studio markup for such items is often extremely high (ranking right up there with the 800 percent markups a hospital emergency room might charge for a Band-Aid or other items furnished). The average negative cost for films is an industry statistic that is generally only available for MPAA films, since no other film industry organization has undertaken the job of calculating such statistics. Of course, the MPAA figures only cover the films produced by MPAA member companies, thus the figures can be very misleading when considering the industry as a whole. The MPAA average negative cost figure represents a statistical median for a given year. The average negative cost for an MPAA movie in 1991 was reportedly in the neighborhood of $26 million and in 1992, $28 million.

Studio executives and their representatives are fond of pointing to escalating advertising expenses, high labor costs and the demands of gross profit participants as the primary culprits in the escalation of negative costs. Spokespersons for "A" level talent counter that if the studios would quit playing games with their books (thus making net profits virtually obsolete) there would be little need to demand gross participations. Studio producer Art Linson also oversimplifies the issue, saying "because of overhead and union contracts, the costs for the major studios far exceed those for small independent companies."[76] The costs for the major studios far exceed those for the small independent production companies for many more reasons that are cited here by Art Linson and not only include high labor costs, demands of gross profit participants and their agents, agency packages, inflated costs of all property and services provided by studios, entertainment attorneys who work off a percentage of a film's budget and excessive interest rates, but also the high salaries of studio executives.

Many in the film industry have complained for the last several years about the rising production costs that have been occurring during a period that has witnessed declining theatrical admissions, a slowing of home video cassette sales worldwide, a leveling off of U.S. made programming sales to Europe and reduced margins of profit. The warning has gone out that this lack of profitability in the film business will make it more and more difficult to attract capital. But it appears that the only thing the business leaders in various segments of the film industry can suggest to lower production costs is for the other guy to quit being so greedy. For example, the studio/distributors complain that the agents and their actor clients need to reduce their up front and gross participation demands. In response the high priced talent attorneys counter that they will consider such a proposal if the studio/distributors will handle net profit participations more fairly, particularly in the area of home video. This intra-industry economic warfare is unfortunate, in light of what has happened in recent years to other great American industries that could not downshift across the board as the rest of the world became increasingly more competitive and globally integrated.

Production overhead. Production overhead charges, in a general sense, are the costs of operating a business that are not directly associated with the production or sale of goods or services. "Production overhead" may also be referred to as indirect costs. In the film industry, the term production overhead refers to those costs and expenses incurred by a studio/distributor in the business of producing motion pictures generally that cannot be directly charged to specific pictures, regardless of whether or not such facilities or staff are actually used on a given picture. In other words, "Negative cost for studio(s) does not only include the out-of-pocket production costs but includes a nonallocated overhead percentage charge (typically 15%) for the major studio/distributors."[77]

For example, the "actual production cost for *Coming to America*—the so-called negative cost—was about $36 million, according to [Ned] Tanen. But the profit partcipation statement . . . showed a negative cost of $50,127,544 . . . much of the $14 million difference was probably overhead."[78]

There does seem to be some disagreement among the industry commentators about what percentage the studios charge for production overhead. Nochimson and Brachman say 15 percent (above), but Buck Houghton says, "If you are in a studio, there is an overhead charge of thirty to forty percent of direct costs."[79] Other industry observers say studio production overhead, generally ranges between 10 percent to 25 percent of the movie's production costs or budget. In any case, these indirect costs may include such things as rental of sound stages or other studio facilities such as dressing facilities, vehicles, telephones, office space and equipment, secretaries' salaries, messenger services, photocopying, computer services, studio executives' salaries and their expenses, development and story-abandonment costs and general administrative costs relating to the production area or other costs of doing business which are all absorbed on a supposedly pro rata basis by each film produced and possibly even distributed by the studio in a given year.

One of the problems with the studio production overhead charges is (as profit participation auditor Steven Sills points out) that "some of the things covered by production overhead are already covered in the production costs."[80] Former studio executive and author Steven Bach agrees, saying studio overhead is "viewed as pure gravy by producers because every studio facility or property used by the production, from sound stages to arc lights to typewriters to thumbtacks, is charged to the picture anyway, so that the overhead charge is, from the producer's point of view, at best an override and at worst legalized larceny."[81]

It is particularly troublesome for some to have a studio/distributor finance the production costs of a film, then add such overhead to the negative cost of the film and charge interest on that overhead while delaying recoupment of the negative cost until after distribution fees are collected and distribution expenses are recovered, if ever. The concept of studio production overhead does not apply to films financed and distributed on a negative pickup, pure acquisition and rent-a-distributor basis, so long as no studio facilities were utilized.

The actual accounting entry for such costs is referred to as the overhead surcharge. Since it is expressed as a flat percentage, it has no relation to actual costs. Interest is usually charged on the overhead surcharge and the overhead surcharge amount is generally deducted prior to the calculation of net profit participations, thus adding significantly to the amount that must be recouped by the studio before a motion picture can realize net profits. Studios have also been known to charge an overhead fee on other expenses that are in themselves overhead.

Overbudget penalties. In production-financing/distribution agreements and negative pickup deals the studios will commonly insert overbudget penalties in the distribution agreement. The overbudget penalty is a form of financial punishment or forfeiture imposed by a studio when a producer of a studio-financed film goes over budget. While the terms "forfeiture" and "penalty" are often used interchangeably, the generic term "penalty" includes forfeiture and the term "forfeiture" in a more narrow sense relates to a loss of real or personal property, while a penalty most often relates to the loss of money. In either case, the major studio/distributors will try to avoid the use of these particular words in describing their overbudget policy relating to the production of a motion picture, since contract law may not allow unreasonable penalties to be enforced in commercial transactions. The overbudget penalty is one of the few techniques the studios use to keep costs down, but as usual, they seem to go overboard.

The double add-back provision, for example, permits the studio to recoup from the film's producer or director twice the amount of the overage prior to breakeven on the film. In another form of overbudget penalty sometimes imposed by a studio that is financing the production of a film, the studio will withhold a significant amount of the producer's fee until delivery of the film's answer print. If the picture is delivered within budget the producer receives his or her complete fee, but if the film has gone over budget, the producer has to wait until first net profits to receive the balance on a deferred basis.

Creative Control Issues

Creative control relates to the power and authority to make creative decisions with respect to a film being produced and with respect to significant creative aspects of the film (i.e., the appearance and content of the final feature film product). Creative control issues often become a major point of negotiation between a producer and distributor (or between the producer/director team and the distributor). The issue comes up in the context of a distribution agreement in several respects.

Approved elements. Approved elements are significant aspects of a film that have been reviewed and approved by the distributor who has committed to distribute the film once it is produced (e.g., script, budget, director and lead actors). If the film as produced does not contain the elements approved in advance of production by the distributor, that distributor may be able to avoid its obligation to distribute the film. As an example, "a typical UA contract reserved to itself standard approvals of script, director, cast, production manager, cameraman, budget, playing time, rating, composer, technical personnel, locations, raw stock, aspect ratio, processing laboratory, number of release prints, advertising campaign and budget."[82]

Script changes. If the film being produced (as an in-house production, under a production-financing/distribution agreement or as a negative pickup) significantly departs from the approved script, the distributor may avoid its obligation to distribute the film (assuming the final product is not to its liking anyway). The question of what constitutes a significant change may provide an opportunity to disagree. Such changes will inevitably occur during production of a picture and may create problems with a distributor and/or the completion guarantor (always required with a negative pickup). In the event that a distribution agreement was negotiated and signed prior to principal photography, the distributor typically includes a provision providing for distributor script approval.

Editing rights. The editing rights provision (sometimes referred to as the "final cut" clause) sets forth who has the right to make editing changes (i.e., who has final editing rights or the authority to produce the final cut of a movie). Such rights, to some extent, depend on the parties' relative bargaining strength and the stature, as well as the rights of the producer and/or director as between them, the nature of the film and other factors. Under some circumstances the producer may have made commitments to the director that prevent the producer from allowing the distributor to make changes in the director's final cut. Also, the director's guild rules may provide some protection for the director with respect to his or her final cut. On the other hand, some editing changes may be required as per government regulation or in order to get a certain motion picture rating. If granted, such rights should be subject to a producer's right of approval, rather than just unlimited editing rights.

Television cover shots. Standards and practices are the guidelines and procedures imposed by the Standards and Practices Departments of the major free television networks on material presented for broadcast. For example, "R" rated feature films are generally not considered in compliance with these more restrictive free television requirements. Film distribution agreements typically require that additional television cover shots be provided on such movies. If such cover shots are not provided and/or the movie does not meet the networks' standards the film distributor may avoid its obligation to make payments to the producer or distribute the film in that market.

Censorable material. Censorable material is a part of an audio or visual presentation in a film that may be considered objectionable in a given jurisdiction (typically, foreign countries). This definition actually appears in some film distribution agreements as a producer warranty (i.e., the producer promises not to include any "censorable material" in the film). This language may produce a chilling effect on the First Amendment freedoms of producers. In other words, the typical language used may be so vague as to prevent the producer from including certain desired scenes in the film.

Cast member approvals. In all but the pure acquisition and rent-a-distributor deals, the distributor will insist on cast approval rights. In the pure acquisition and rent-a-distributor situations, the distributor is not approached until the film is completed, and thus the distributor still effectively has cast approval rights (i.e., if the distributor does not approve of the cast already in the film it will probably not distribute). Thus, in those situations, the producers are still trying to anticipate the likes and dislikes of the distributor regarding casting decisions. In the other three film finance/distribution scenarios (i.e., in-house production, production-financing/distribution arrangement and the negative pickup deal) the distributor is at a minimum committing in advance to expend monies in the distribution of the anticipated film and thus has a reasonable right to know who is going to be in the film.

Producer consultation rights. Many film distribution agreements provide that the distributor is obligated to consult with the film's producer regarding various matters relating to marketing the film, distributor editing and so forth.

However, there is rarely any effective way for the producer to enforce such consultation right, other than the leverage of the future relationship.

Minimum rating. The feature film distribution agreement will invariably impose a producer commitment regarding the film's MPAA rating (a commitment made by a feature film producer to a distributor that the film being produced will receive an MPAA rating not worse than a specific rating (e.g., an "R" rating). If the producer fails to deliver the agreed upon rating, the distributor may be relieved of its obligation to pay monies or release the picture. Such situations which involve an MPAA member distributor and an independent producer may raise the question relating to the inherent conflict of interest involved in rating films through the facilities of an MPAA sponsored organization. With that in mind, it should be obvious that any review and rating function for movies should be performed by private sector entities with no ties to the film community.

Running time. Many distribution agreements specify a range in which the film's running time must fall and may make compliance a condition of delivery. A film's running time refers to the total length of time needed to project a film at its normal speed. Feature films usually require a running time of 90 to 120 minutes. If the producer comes close but fails to come within the prescribed running time, the distributor may be able to use this technical default to avoid its obligations to distribute a film or make payments to the producer pursuant to presale or negative pickup agreements. Again, this scenario assumes that the distributor has determined that the film has little commercial value anyway.

Waiver of droit moral. In many civil law countries in the world, an author or artist (such as a film producer or director) has the right to object to any deformation, mutilation or other alteration of his or her work. Such rights are known as droit moral (French for moral right). Unfortunately, for U.S. producers and directors, the concept of droit moral is not mentioned in the U.S. Copyright Act. Nevertheless, a right analogous to a moral right has been recognized in this country in several situations (but not yet in film) in which the integrity and reputation of an artistic creator was protected by the courts. The express grounds on which common law protection has been given include libel, unfair competition, copyright and the right of privacy. The right of droit moral gives the author of a work certain power to prevent changes, notwithstanding the provisions of his or her contract (e.g., a director may be able to prevent cutting and editing of his or her picture, except for editing for television and censorship). Consequently, film distributors in the U.S. routinely include in their distribution agreements a waiver of droit moral, a contractual provision through which the producer and/or director intentionally and voluntarily give up, relinquish or surrender the rights known as droit moral.

Considered on the basis of their cumulative effect, the above-discussed and described issues provide a considerable amount of creative control to the feature film distributors. In other words, the major studio/distributors who are very quick to complain about any possible censorship from outside third parties (real or threatened) have no hesitation to censor the efforts of filmmakers in a number of ways, based on provisions in the distribution deal itself, provisions that are effectively imposed on the producer and director (i.e., not actually negotiated). Thus, the distributors (specifically the U.S. major studio/distributors) determine to a great extent which movies are made by the U.S. film industry and also to a large degree the content of those movies. At the same time, the distribution deal provisions discussed in this book, some of which can be accurately characterized as unfair, unethical, anticompetitive, predatory and/or illegal, have helped to keep the major studio/distributors in their position of power over other segments of the film industry, segments that might like to see other kinds of movies produced with substantially different content.

General Contractual Provisions

The distributor discretion problem. A number of linguistic devices are used by film distributors in the film distribution agreement to provide them with incredibly excessive discretion. The exercise of discretion by film distributors has long been a significant problem in the film industry for everybody else but the distributor.

Discretion refers to the reasonable exercise of a power or right to choose between alternative courses of action or inaction. Many film distribution agreements are currently drafted so as to include numerous situations in which the distributor is allowed to exercise its discretion. Such discretion is exercised, for example, in the manner and extent of the film's release and the markets selected, as well as the theatres in each such market, with respect to sales methods, policies and terms, by refraining from commencing distribution or discontinuing distribution in any country or place at any time, in allocating license payments among films marketed as a package and more.

One such distributor discretion provision seeks to establish a false standard for distributor conduct such as "customary in the industry." The distributors would like to lead others in the film industry to believe that what is customary in the industry is customarily and routinely agreed upon in the business. Unfortunately, about the only thing customary in the industry is that the major studio/distributors along with the closely associated talent agencies have a habit of exploiting most everyone else. Other examples of the distributor discretion problem appear in the form of vague and subjective standards governing distributor conduct in distributing films, including such language as "customary practices," "usual and customary manner," "long-standing and well-established practices in the industry" or "customary terms and conditions for agreements of this nature in the motion picture industry." The truth is that no such objective standards exist, thus such language pretty well gives distributors a free hand to distribute films as they please.

Another aspect of the distributor discretion problem occurs in many motion picture industry agreements which provide that certain terms not otherwise defined within the agreement are to be defined as "commonly understood" in the industry. Such provisions merely provide a mechanism for determining the meaning of a term that comes into question, thus in the context of arbitration or litigation the fact finder will have to entertain testimony from persons with expertise in the industry to determine whether there actually is a commonly understood meaning for such a term. Unfortunately, many terms are not commonly understood in the industry and it is likely that experts with equal authority may be produced to define such terms to favor both sides of a dispute, leaving the fact finder to have to decide between differing interpretations of the same term. If the negotiating parties have a fairly equal bargaining position, the better practice would be to negotiate a definition of the term for the purposes of the agreement and include the definition in that original agreement, otherwise the party implementing the agreement has a certain amount of discretion in its conduct until challenged by the other party. Again unfortunately, the bargaining power of contracting parties in the motion picture industry is often vastly unequal, and thus the party with the most power tends to get the definitions it wants.

A third example of the distributor discretion problem comes up in the context of the books and records provision. The distributor will often provide that the books and records it keeps are to be maintained in its own unique way (i.e., in its usual and customary manner or "as customarily kept by the distributor"). Thus anyone accepting that language has just agreed that if the distributor has been routinely lying, cheating and stealing from its net and gross profit participants, it is permissible to continue to do the same thing under this new agreement.

Another vague term used by film distributors to gain discretion is "ordinary course of business." Such a term can actually be defined (i.e., according to the common practices and customs of commercial transactions; the usual and necessary activity that is normal and incidental to a business). Occasional isolated or casual transactions are not frequent or continuous enough to constitute the ordinary course of business. This phrase is commonly seen in feature film distribution agreements when the parties have failed to negotiate more specific language. Again, the phrase "ordinary course of business" is a very vague standard of conduct for business practices. It is not a precise standard that can be applied in advance. It is merely a standard that can be applied after the fact, in arbitration or litigation, by bringing in various persons with expertise in the industry to explain what is usual and customary with respect to such practices. Thus the distributor using this language in its distribution agreement has a lot of leeway pursuant to such language to do whatever it desires, on a given issue, knowing that it may take a complaint from the other party and either an arbitration proceeding or a trial and court judgment to firm up the standard of conduct. The distributor knows that the producer is not likely to sue anyway, and even if the producer does sue, the distributor will most likely settle out of court for a smaller amount of damages, thus also rendering the contested definition moot.

An additional distributor term that provides unreasonable discretion is "reasonable and customary." Again, this term provides only a very general standard of conduct for commercial affairs that may only be ascertained on a case by case basis after the fact by testimony in the context of litigation. Although this standard of conduct is somewhat more fair than just "customary" by itself, it still does the nondistributor-contracting party little good unless such a party is willing to challenge the distributor's interpretation of such language after the fact.

Film distribution agreements also often provide that certain things may be deemed to be so by the distributor. The word "deem" is a verb meaning to come to think of as true (whether actually true or not). Such a provision is another example of distributor discretion.

Such vague standards may often appear in so-called short form feature film production documentation or deal memos along with a statement of the intention of the parties to negotiate, draft and sign a more complete written agreement to include such terms at a later date. However, even though there may be a certain level of unanimity regarding the type of provisions that ought to be included in the same or similar feature film related agreements, the specific wording, the application of such terms or their interpretation by the distributors or the courts in any given circumstance is by no means standardized. In addition, some view the use of such vague standards by the major studios as a means of continuing their dominance and control over the rest of the industry.

Distributor commitments. Some distributors are willing to include agreements or pledges in their distribution agreements to perform certain services or at specified levels. Distributor commitments are the pledges, promises or guarantees of a film distributor relating to the distribution of a given film (e.g., agreements by a distributor to spend a certain amount of money on prints and advertising and/or to release a film in the major population centers in the United States). A distributor may also commit to provide a domestic or foreign theatrical release for a film. Such commitments are usually required by home video companies before such companies will provide a home video advance or guarantee. Other such distributor commitments include a trailer commitment, a release window commitment and a commitment to avoid distributing a conflicting film during the same time period (i.e., a film that competes for the same or a similar audience).

Best efforts versus reasonable efforts. The best efforts clause is a provision in film distribution contracts that obligates the distributor to put forth its best efforts in distributing the film. In the event that a dispute arises between the producer and the distributor relating to the distributor's efforts in distributing the film, this clause would serve as a standard by which an arbitrator or court would determine if the distributor had met its obligations under the agreement. Although still vague, best efforts is a higher standard than reasonable efforts. A reasonable efforts clause is a provision in film distribution contracts that merely obligates the distributor to put forth reasonable efforts in distributing the film. Less effort is required of the distributor pursuant to a reasonable efforts clause than a best efforts clause.

Deferments or deferrals. Film industry deferments are salaries or compensation for cast, crew or others providing property or services for the production of a movie paid (by agreement) on a delayed basis after the property and/or services have been provided and after the sale or release of the film. The concept of deferments is not typically utilized in a major studio/distributor production whether financed as an in-house production, as a production-financing/distribution deal or on a negative pickup basis. Whenever such deferments are to be paid, however, they are typically paid at the time a project is sold to a distributor (out of the advance, if any) or out of monies generated by the exhibition of the film. In either case, such payments are also by definition contingent upon the film's earning enough money to pay such deferments.

Grant of rights. In the context of a motion picture distribution agreement, the grant of rights provisions confers the power or privilege for exploiting the movie in specified markets and media. Such rights have presumably been previously granted to producers in the acquisition of literary properties, then are granted to distributors by the producers through the distribution agreement and to subdistributors and others (by the distributor) through various licensing agreements. The phrase "grant of rights" also refers to the provision in such an agreement that sets out what rights are being granted. Generally, in a film distribution deal, such rights will cover markets, changes to the title, the use of music on a soundtrack, dubbed versions and trailers, reediting, advertising and publicizing the picture, use of excerpts, use of the names and likenesses of cast members, commercials, publishing a novelization, adding the name and trademark of the distributor, merchandising, music, publishing and radio rights, remakes and sequels, assignment of producer's rights and warranties from the producer not to encumber the rights granted nor grant the same rights to others.

Ownership. In situations where the distributor is providing development, production and distribution funds (in-house production) or providing production and distribution monies (production-financing/distribution deal), the distribution agreement will typically provide that the producer has transferred ownership rights to the property to the distributor. In situations where the distributor was not originally at risk for the production costs (negative pickup) or where the distributor is only providing distribution monies (acquisition deal), it is possible, in some instances, for the producer to negotiate a mere licensing arrangement with the distributor (i.e., the distributor does not acquire full ownership rights to the film property). If the producer transfers ownership of the picture (worldwide and in perpetuity) to the distributor for an advance and is not likely to see additional monies beyond the advance, the effect of the transaction is to transfer title to the film property to the distributor for the price of the advance only, and thus the producer's participation (and the participation of all net profits participants) in the upside potential of his or her film project has been taken away by the distributor. In other words, if the film makes a considerable amount of money in all markets and all media, the distributor will make most of that money, and the producer (in addition to other net profit participants, including outside investors) are not likely to receive any additional monies.

Term of agreement. The feature film distributor will often seek to distribute the film in perpetuity in all markets and media or in specified markets and media. In that case, even a licensing arrangement, as opposed to transfer of ownership, results as a practical matter in a transfer of all financial benefits generated by the exploitation of the film in the specified markets and media to the distributor forever. Perpetuity means until the end of time (i.e., forever). Feature film distributors, particularly in situations where a studio/distributor provides funding for both the production costs of a motion picture and the distribution expenses will want to obtain a grant of distribution rights in perpetuity, effectively adding that film to its library of films even though copyright ownership stays with an independent production company.

Turnaround provision. The turnaround provision is a clause in the studio development deal (which may ultimately lead to a distribution deal) that provides the right to the original owner of the project before it was accepted by the studio for development (i.e., typically a producer, screenwriter or director) to submit a film project to another production company or studio if the original developing production company (studio) at which the project was being developed elects not to proceed with the production of the film (e.g., "the film project will be turned back to the producer for twelve months if the studio does not begin production within six months after the 120-day development period"). Such right is often contingent upon the original developing production company's development expenses to date being repaid, and sometimes the original development company may retain an interest in the film's earnings.

Takeover provisions. A production-financing/distribution agreement will typically set out the studio's takeover rights (the assumption of control over the production of the motion picture). Such rights may be triggered by fairly subjective events. For example, the distribution agreement provides that if, based on the information available (including, but not limited to, the weekly reporting papers furnished by the production company), the distributor reasonably believes that the estimated cost of production of the picture will exceed the contingency, the studio may enter into negotiations with the production company in an effort to come up with a plan designed to reduce the projected negative costs, but if not successful the studio may take over primary responsibility for the continued production of the picture. With respect to a completion guarantor takeover, the completion bond company may assert its contractual rights to assume responsibility for completing the film since the producer defaulted in some way (e.g., went overbudget or did not complete the film on time). Generally, the event which triggers the takeover rights of the completion guarantor is the subjective judgment of its on-site representative that the film is probably going overbudget.

Substitution clauses. In some situations, involving a preproduction distribution deal with a smaller independent distributor, the distributor may allow a substitution clause to be inserted into the distribution agreement. Such a provision in a film distribution agreement would permit the producer to choose an alternate distributor under specified circumstances. Such provisions are included to protect the producer who may produce a movie that is desired by a much stronger distributor who can provide a wider release and more distributor support. Usually, like a turnaround provision in a studio deal, the substitution clause will require that the original distributor's expenses be reimbursed, that a substitution fee be paid and sometimes a percentage participation be retained by the original distributor. To some extent, the substitution clause serves a purpose similar to the turnaround provision in a studio deal.

Most favored nations clause. The most favored nations clause is a contractual provision by which each signatory grants to the other the broadest rights and privileges that it accords to any other entity with which it deals. In entertainment agreements the clause may be used to denote a level of profit participation, the size and placement of billing, the calibre of dressing rooms or motor homes on location and other such matters. Producers and other profit participants may also need such a provision to help protect their interests in the feature film distribution deal. For example, in film contracts with multiple percentage participants, this provision insures that one participant's terms will be no less favorable than those of any other participant of like standing.

The cross-collateralization scam. Feature film distributors have developed an almost unlimited number of ways to offset their losses in one market against profits in another on a single film, several films produced by the same producer or on films produced by different producers. Cross-collateralization is actually an accounting practice used by and which benefits distributors whereby distributors offset their profits in one market against losses in another or on one film against another. In a worldwide distribution deal the studios typically seek to cross-collateralize profits and losses among territories. With cross-collateralization the producer can only share in the profits of one territory to the extent that the profits of that territory exceed the combined losses of all other territories worldwide. In situations where multiple films of a single producer or production company are being distributed by a single distributor, the distributor may seek authorization in the distribution agreement to cross-collateralize the financial performance of each of such films with the others. The following terms have been developed to describe some of the various forms of cross-collateralization created by film distributors:

1. *Discretionary cross-collateralization*—Discretionary cross-collateralization is the offsetting of motion picture profits by a distributor between markets or films in situations where the distribution agreement does not address the practice (i.e., such cross-collateralization is left to the discretion of the distributor).

2. *Unauthorized cross-collateralization*—The term "unauthorized cross-collateralization" refers to the feature film distributor's unauthorized offsetting of the profits of a movie (a) against the same movie's profits in another market, (b) against the profits of one movie, (c) against the profits of another movie produced by the same production company or (d) against the profits of another movie produced by a different production company. A cross-collateralization provision in a feature film distribution agreement may authorize one form of cross-collateralization but omit one or more of the others. Or, it may fail to say anything about cross-collateralization, thus ostensibly authorizing all forms.

3. *Cross-collateralization of unrecouped expenses*—Cross-collateralization of unrecouped expenses occurs when the expenses incurred in the production or distribution of a film that have not been recouped in distributing the film are recouped by the same distributor as expenses for another film released by the same distributor. In all too many instances, the film that is victimized by this ruse is a film produced by an independent producer.

4. *De facto cross-collateralization*—De facto cross-collateralization is the unauthorized arbitrary allocation of gross receipts to a motion picture marketed as part of a package either to networks, cable, syndication markets or foreign territories. Such allocations effectively cross-collateralize the profits of one movie with the profits of other movies in the package.

5. *Slate cross-collateralization*—Slate cross-collateralization is the feature film distributor practice in which the distributor offsets the financial performance of one motion picture against the financial performance of other films

produced by the same production company. Such cross-collateralization may or may not be authorized by the producer.

6. *Film package cross-collateralization*—Licensees of film packages (a number of films offered to territorial distributors as a package) may also cross-collateralize the results of the exhibition of such films in foreign territories.

7. *Settlement cross-collateralization*—This term describes the shifting of film revenues from the revenue stream of one film to another pursuant to the settlement transaction between the distributor and exhibitor (as described earlier).

8. *Outright sales cross-collateralization*—This is the shifting of film revenues from the revenue stream of one film to another pursuant to outright sales of film rights in foreign territories.

Cross-collateralization, in its multiple forms, is one of the ways the studios implement their winners versus losers approach to distribution. In other words, they take the position that their winners must subsidize their losers in any given year and that this is a legitimate approach to accounting for the profits and losses of the films they release whether authorized or not. Unfortunately, many of the films released or produced by independent producers and the profits or losses of those films should not be cross-collateralized with the films produced by the studio. The settlement transaction, offset rights and special allocations relating to both expenses and revenues are forms of cross-collateralization. In the truest sense, unauthorized cross-collateralization is nothing more than grand theft or some other form of sophisticated white-collar crime.

Offset rights. An offset rights provision in the feature film distribution agreement provides the distributor with the authority to adjust accounting records to compensate for a credit or loss incurred by a second party (e.g., a subdistributor or an exhibitor). In the producer/distributor agreement the distributor may seek offset rights to adjust the accounts between the two parties. Also, if a distributor/exhibitor agreement provides for offset rights, the exhibitor is able to deduct co-op advertising or other expenses owed to the exhibitor by the distributor from distributor rentals that would have otherwise been paid to the distributor. Lending banks will typically require that the distributor's offset rights as to the producer be waived so as to insure more rapid payment to the bank. Offset rights with regard to exhibitors and others with whom the distributor deals may effectively reduce the level of distributor gross receipts, thus negatively impacting the financial interests of all net and gross profit participants.

Outright sales. An outright sale is a transaction defined in some distribution agreements as a license to any person, by the distributor or any franchised subdistributor, to distribute the film for theatrical exhibition, in a particular geographic area and for a particular period of time (other than any such license for a period of less than one year for theatrical exhibition in a part of any country), without any obligation of such person to account for or report to the distributor or such franchised subdistributor on the amount of any proceeds or expenses of such distribution or sublicensing. In the motion picture industry, an "outright sale" does not refer to a true sale but instead to the license of a right for a flat fee instead of a percentage. Flat fee arrangements are commonly employed with certain territories and particular media (e.g., some foreign territories and video or cable). The outright sale provides a lump-sum payment or payments and minimizes the distributor's expenses since it will not have to monitor subdistribution and provide periodic accounting statements for those territories. Outright sales in the major foreign territories may provide the distributor with another opportunity to cross-collateralize the profits of an independent producer's film with the losses of the studio's own film through collusion with the foreign distributor. Films can generate as much as ten times the rentals in certain foreign markets as compared to a flat sale price if the distributor operates its own branch office in the foreign territory and handles the distribution directly.

Foreign markets. Distributors recognize that some movies do better overseas than in the U.S. (e.g., *Ghost* did $120 million foreign and only $80 million in the U.S.). Some films are also released theatrically in the foreign marketplace before the U.S. (e.g., *Come See the Paradise* opened in Europe seven months before the U.S.). Also, Catholic countries apparently loved *The Exorcist*, for example. Thus distributors will often seek to gain distribution rights in all markets and all media throughout the universe, so that in effect the profits and losses of the film in all such markets and media can effectively be cross-collateralized.

Holdback periods. If the distributor is given a broad grant of rights in the distribution agreement (i.e., covering most if not all markets and media), the distributor will want to make its own internal decisions regarding appropriate sequential distribution in various media in the territory. Those distributor decisions may or may not maximize the financial benefits of the film's exploitation for the producer and other net profit participants.

Errors and omissions insurance. Errors and omissions (E&O) insurance coverage is intended to protect against claims based on certain types of occurrences in the course of a film's production and distribution, such as the failure to obtain requisite releases. The producer usually pays for such coverage, at least initially. In some instances, the coverage is expanded to include possible distributor error.

Outside service agreements. Feature film distributors often do business with affiliated or friendly subdistributors, theatres, video companies, outside advertising agencies and other individuals or entities providing support services to the distributor through something less than on an arms-length basis. In other words, the distributor is getting a special deal or favored treatment from such persons or entities. In some cases, these special deals or this favored treatment will not benefit the producer or other net profit participants.

Distributor credit. Distributors often provide extensions of the payment terms to subdistributors and/or exhibitors on indebtedness owed to the distributor by such entities. The abuse of such extensions may delay payments to the producer and other net profit participants.

Distributor contingencies. In the negative pickup distribution agreement, the distributor will seek to include a number of contingencies that must be met before it becomes obligated to distribute the picture. Some of these contingencies may be unreasonable or very subjective.

Distributor assignment rights. The distributor in a film distribution deal typically insists on the right to assign parts of the agreement to subdistributors and other companies for purposes of meeting its distribution obligations. Such assignments may have been contemplated by both parties and may be necessary in order for the distributor to fulfill its obligations. On the other hand, if the language is not properly drafted, such an assignment may also relieve the distributor of its liability for performance.

Assignment of profit participation interest. Quite often the distributor will also insist on a right of first refusal to acquire the net profit participant's interest.

Covenant of good faith and fair dealing. A covenant of good faith and fair dealing is a specific contractual provision imposing an agreement or promise to conduct one's business dealings with another in good faith and fairly (i.e., to conduct such business dealings honestly, in fact, to observe reasonable commercial standards of fair dealing in the trade and not to deny the existence of the contract). Some states provide that the covenant of good faith and fair dealing is implied in every contract executed in these states.

Good faith. Good faith means being faithful to one's duty or obligations (i.e., a total absence of any intention to seek an unfair advantage or to defraud another party; an honest and sincere intention to fulfill one's obligations). Film distribution agreements often utilize this rather vague standard for distributor conduct. Unfortunately it can only be applied after the fact like most other standards of conduct.

Warranties. A warranty is an assurance by one party to a contract of the existence of a fact upon which the other party may rely, intended precisely to relieve the promisee of any duty to ascertain the fact, and amounting to a promise to indemnify the promisee for any loss if the fact warranted proves untrue. Such warranties are either made overtly (i.e., express warranties), or by implication (i.e., implied warranties). In a film distribution agreement producer warranties and representations are likely to be made regarding the quality of the picture (i.e, it will be fully edited, titled, synchronized with sound and of a quality, both artistic and technical, for general theatrical release), as well as for numerous other matters relating to content, ownership, the discharge of the producer's obligations, no infringements, no advertising matter, no impairment of rights granted, valid copyright and MPAA rating. On the other hand, film distributors seldom provide many warranties relating to their side of the bargain, if any.

Warranty of quiet enjoyment. In the context of a feature film distribution deal, the warranty of quiet enjoyment is a warranty given by the producer assuring that the distributor has the right to the unimpaired use and enjoyment of the film property and that the producer does not know of any actual, or potential, adverse claims which might be made against the distribution of the picture that would interfere with the distributor's rights.

Delivery. Production-financing/distribution and negative pickup agreements generally impose specific delivery requirements on the film's producer. The delivery requirements section is a provision in a film distribution agreement that sets out the actions to be taken and the items to be delivered to a film's distributor pursuant to the distribution agreement. Delivery in legal terminology, amounts to a voluntary transfer of title or possession from one party to another. The delivery provision usually appears in a film distribution agreement as a schedule that lists the physical items which are to be provided by the producer to the distributor (through the lab or otherwise) and sets the deadlines for such items to be delivered. Delivery is usually defined as a series of objective events and does not rely on distributor approval.

The audit rights provision. "The natural progression of a participant's deal with a studio from beginning to end is to negotiate the contract, make the film and have it released, receive participation statements, and then 'audit' those statements. The final step is to have the claims made by the auditor negotiated and settled, thereby producing additional payments to the participant. Since the distributor makes all the sales, collects the revenues, pays the expenses and interprets the contract to determine how much the participant is going to receive, the artist has but one safeguard: the contractual right to audit."[83] This is a statement of the natural and self-serving conclusion of a motion picture profit participation auditor. A litigating attorney would add those steps involved in suing and possibly going to trial for those cases in which the profit participant refuses to settle for the small amount offered by the studio in response to the auditor's demand.

Attorney Mark Litwak, once again offers the pro major studio view that most films "are not profitable by any standard, so the profit participants don't bother with an audit." He goes on to say, however, that for "those films that do generate significant revenue, audits invariably pay for themselves."[84] Unfortunately, no one, including attorney Litwak is in a position to make the statement that most films are not profitable by any standard. After all, this book and all of the other cited works by Steven Sills, Ivan Axelrod, Peter Dekom, Hillary Bibicoff, Adam Marcus, Pierce O'Donnell and Dennis McDougal ought to raise the question in any reasonable person's mind, that the rest of the film industry and the world actually has no idea how much money is being made by the major studio/distributors, and therefore whether most films should or should not actually show a profit. There are so many ways that the studios play loosely with their bookkeeping, accounting, contract drafting and/or contract interpretation, that it is absolutely nonsense to naively accept and repeat the oft-stated studio claim that "most films are not profitable."

The second part of attorney Litwak's statement is more reasonable, and knowledgeable persons in the industry agree with him. Retired tax attorney and CPA Bennett Newman, who has audited the books of hundreds of movies and television series, including *The Exorcist*, *Star Wars*, *All in the Family*, *M*A*S*H* and *On Golden Pond*, in referring to the major studio/distributors, says he "wouldn't put a halo on any of them." Newman goes on to say that some "audits don't pay for themselves, but that's rare . . . when [his] . . . firm did go in to scrutinize the studio's books, it invariably found evidence of underreporting."[85]

An audit (generally) is an inspection of the accounting records and procedures of a business, government unit, or other reporting entity by a trained accountant for the purpose of verifying the accuracy and completeness of the records. It may be conducted by a member of the organization (internal audit) or by an outsider (independent audit). An IRS audit consists of the verification of the information on the income tax return. A film distribution audit should be conducted by an accounting firm with this specialized expertise, hired by the producer and other net profit participants. So far as the producer and other net profit participants are concerned the auditor should be allowed to conduct the audit with as few restrictions imposed on the audit as possible.

Again, attorney Litwak makes a somewhat oversimplified and suspect statement when he says: "There are two types of errors revealed by an audit. The first are clerical errors. . . . The other type of error arises out of contract interpretation."[86] This is exactly what the profit participation auditors would lead us to believe. Unfortunately, as can be seen from the above discussion, some of the problems relating to film net profits do not fall neatly within these two categories and some are not errors at all. Still others go far beyond the scope of the net profit audit, effectively making the audit only a partial solution. On the other hand, attorney Litwak is absolutely correct in stating that the "philosophy of most studios is 'When in doubt, resolve it in our favor and we will fight it out later if it is contested.' "[87] Most of those studio decisions made in their favor are not contested, and of those that are contested, most are settled for a round-dollar amount far less than the amount actually owed by the studio. Thus the studio has little if anything to lose in following such a philosophy.

Distributors typically want to limit audit rights by restricting when the audit may be started and conducted, limiting the purpose of the audit, restricting who may conduct the audit, requiring that copies of all reports made by the producer's accountant be delivered to the distributor at the same time as to the producer, placing limits on the amount of time an audit may take, allowing only one audit each year, only permitting individual records to be audited once, limiting the period during which objections may be made, providing that all statements by the distributor are binding unless objected to in writing within a certain period of time, forever barring the producer or other profit participants from instituting any lawsuit unless timely objection is made and only permitting review of the books of the subject picture even when the picture is marketed with other pictures as a package. Distributors will also insert language that permits them to keep records in their own unique way, whatever that is.

The major studio/distributors also will typically limit the authority of anyone to conduct an examination of its books and records separate from an authorized entity. For example, in a film distribution agreement, the distributor will undertake the responsibility for paying directly to third party participants any portion of the production company's share of gross or net proceeds as assigned by the production company, provided that no such third party has an independent audit right (i.e., other than that granted to the production company).

The Buchwald profit participation auditor in describing the circumstances under which he and an associate conducted the Paramount audit said we "were not allowed to photocopy documents, had to work in a cramped, windowless room . . . on the lot, were forbidden to ask Paramount employees routine questions . . . were not allowed to inspect records in chronological sequence. Instead [we] . . . were given a mishmash of boxes of receipts, canceled checks, financial statements, expense reports, computer printouts and microfiche . . . [and] couldn't even buy . . . lunch at the Paramount commissary."[88] This report provides a glimpse of just how obnoxious the studios can be when challenged.

Unfortunately "most of the larger accounting firms find themselves facing conflicts of interest between their prospective profit-participant clients and the companies whose books would be audited."[89] Thus most of the larger accounting firms in Los Angeles do not provide profit participation audit services for clients seeking to audit the books of a major studio/distributor.

Liability limitation. If a distributor assumes the burden of protecting a film's copyright against infringement (through language in the distribution agreement), it may also incur some potential liability if it fails to act conscientiously in the protection of such copyright. Thus the distributor may seek a provision in the distribution agreement that limits its liability for its own conduct in attempting to protect the film's copyright. Such a provision may not provide enough incentive for the distributor to act conscientiously to protect the copyright.

Litigation disclaimer. The distributor will generally require that the distribution agreement include a litigation disclaimer by the producer. This clause, among the producer warranties in the distribution agreement, is a general disclaimer by the producer stating that there is no litigation pending that could impair distribution of the picture.

Final judgment. Many of the MPAA company distribution agreements require the producer to reimburse the distributor for legal fees if the producer files a lawsuit against the distributor but fails to obtain a final judgment against the distributor. Most lawsuits are settled prior to "final judgment" and before substantial legal fees may have been incurred. Thus this provision is simply another way of discouraging producers from suing distributors.

Arbitration. An arbitration clause provides for the submission of a controversy, by agreement of the parties to persons chosen by the parties for resolution. Arbitration is an informal, nonjudicial method for resolving disputes that is usually quicker and less expensive than litigation. Major studio/distributors generally refuse to include arbitration provisions in their distribution agreements, for the purported reason that too much money is involved to allow an arbitrator to decide a dispute. On the other hand, distributors prefer to place the heavy burden associated with pursuing litigation on the producer and other net profit participants, so as to discourage taking the distributor to court. A court case is more likely to take more time and cost the plaintiff producer group more money than an arbitrated matter. The time factor can also be critical in production-financing/distribution deals because the studio will be charging interest on negative cost and production overhead.

Entire agreement clause. The entire agreement clause is a provision included in most contracts, including film distribution agreements, which provides that the written agreement constitutes the entire agreement and supersedes and cancels all prior negotiations, undertakings and agreements, both written and oral, between the parties with respect to the subject matter of the agreement. The clause may provide further that no officer, employee or representative of either party has any authority to make any representations or promises not contained in the agreement and that neither party has signed the agreement in reliance on any such representations or promises. In film distribution situations, statements regarding the manner in which the distributor intends to distribute a given film are often made orally in various conversations between a film producer and representatives of the distributor. This may lead to problems if such statements are not included in the written memorialization of the parties' negotiations (i.e., the written distribution agreement).

6 | Feature Film Distribution Deal Negotiating Checklist

N*egotiating the distribution deal.* More effectively negotiating the numerous provisions in the film distribution agreements that impact on their future potential profit participation may result in improved financial results for the producer and all other net profit participants. Former studio accountant David Leedy suggests that all issues are on the table. He says: "Starting with the highest leverage position, for the producer, assume he approaches the studio with a completed motion picture including well known talent, funds for releasing costs (a rent-a-distributor deal) and worldwide rights. The studio is going to be concerned with the motion picture and whether it has commercial potential, but they will probably be willing to deal. The producer has a blank paper upon which he can structure all kinds of deals."[1] The list that follows provides suggested language for producers to put on Leedy's mythical "blank paper."

Deal memo versus long form agreement. Avoid the use of the deal memo if possible and go straight to the negotiation of the long form agreement. If that is not possible, make sure that the provisions in the deal memo are consistent with the other provisions, or in the alternative that the provisions in the deal memo (assuming they have been negotiated and are mutually satisfactory) override conflicting provisions found elsewhere in the distribution agreement. Watch for important inconsistencies between any preliminary letters from the distributor or deal memos and the actual distribution agreement offered. It is really not reasonable for a distributor to expect a producer to go forward with the production of a film based merely on a so-called "deal memo" when the more detailed provisions of the long form agreement may be much more burdensome or onerous for the producer and may even conflict with the original provisions of the deal memo. Unfortunately, few producers or in a position to demand the long form agreement before production starts.

Negotiated contractual terms. Recognizing that many important terms included in the feature film distribution deal are, at least theoretically, contractually negotiated terms, the producer should carefully review the definitions of such terms, seek to modify them to better suit the needs of the producer and net profit participants and reduce the overly expansive language, so often used. Also, try to keep such concepts simple, so there is less question about how the studio accountants, an auditor or a court should apply the terms. In short, make sure that the definitions used in the film distribution agreement really are negotiated (but see discussion of unconscionable contracts herein).

Fiduciary duty. Add language to the distribution agreement that clearly establishes a fiduciary obligation on the part of the distributor with respect to its conduct on behalf of the producer and other net profit participants. The producer should argue that the distributor should have a legal duty, created by its undertaking, to act (if not primarily for the benefit of the gross and net profit participants) at least equally for their benefit and the self-interest of the distributor; that in any aspect of the transactions between the distributor and all of its licensees, in which there is a conflict of interest as between the interests of the distributor and its net and gross profit participants, the distributor will use its best efforts and act in good faith to maximize the benefits for all concerned. The producer should seek to insert language that states that the distributor agrees it is acting as a fiduciary on behalf of the film's net and gross profit participants.

A gross floor provision. The producer should try to negotiate a minimum level of backend participation (gross floor) for the producer group in the picture's revenue stream regardless of the number or amount of distributor or other deductions from gross receipts. This device permits a producer or other person relying on a percentage participation in net profits to receive at least this minimum (i.e., a gross floor regardless of all of the distributor's gross receipts exclusions, regardless of how many gross points are awarded to others and regardless of the distributor deductions otherwise made from gross receipts). It may be necessary to include such a gross floor to preserve some profit participation for the producer and others participating in the producer's share. In light of the reported figure that only about 5 percent of movies using the major studio/distributor net profits formula ever reach breakeven (i.e., generate net profits), it would seem to be quite essential for every producer to insist on at least some small percentage of a gross floor until distribution deals begin resulting in more films that generate net profits. The distributors do the same with most all of their agreements with exhibitors and other sublicensees, thus why is it not appropriate for producers to do the same with distributors? It is appropriate, but it is not done because producers and net profit participants generally do not have the bargaining strength to see that such language is included in the distribution agreement, which suggests on its face that such agreements are contracts of adhesion.

In lieu of. Because of the specious argument made by the studios that the net profit participation has come to be looked upon as a "bonus" and not as compensation in lieu of salary not paid, the producer should seek to include language in the distribution deal that specifically characterizes the net profit participation as compensation in lieu of salary paid during the production of the movie, as opposed to a bonus.

No distributor participation in net profits. If the distributor insists on deducting its distribution fees and distribution expenses (however defined) prior to any revenue sharing with the producer and/or others, provide that the producer group receive 100 percent of net receipts (also sometimes called net profits or net proceeds) after the distributor has deducted its distribution fees and expenses.

Artificial breakeven. If possible, establish a mutually satisfactory definition of breakeven at some specified level of gross receipts in lieu of traditional concepts of first breakeven, rolling breakeven and so forth.

Incremental bonuses. Negotiate a specified bonus for the producer group for every increment of film rentals or gross receipts that exceed agreed-upon levels of revenue.

Turnaround provision. Even though the turnaround provision appears in the development deal as opposed to the distribution deal, the producer needs to be certain that reasonable time limits and other conditions are imposed on the studio in relation to releasing the project to the producer for acquisition by others. Some distributors have been known to inflate their development costs of projects put into turnaround. The producer may want to seek an agreement that only half of the studio's development costs will be repaid when the project is assigned to another production company or studio and the balance is to be repaid out of the new distributor's gross receipts.

Gross receipts exclusions. Generally speaking, the producer or the producer's counsel should carefully review the proposed distribution agreement to determine what revenues generated by the exploitation of the subject motion picture are being included or excluded from the contractually defined term "gross receipts." Do not allow the distributor to exclude arbitrarily any revenues from gross receipts without a sound reason for doing so.

In negotiating the feature film distribution agreement, watch for and seek to prevent the distributor from excluding the following items from distributor's gross receipts: (a) charitable contributions, (b) advances from exhibitors and other licensees, (c) ancillary rights revenues, (d) the exploitation or use of stock footage, film and sound materials retained for library purposes, featurettes and still photographs, (e) the sale of physical properties the cost of which was included in the negative cost of the picture and (f) salvage revenues. Since gross receipts to the distributor is the earliest and largest defined pool of monies in a motion picture's revenue stream, any unreasonable effort by the distributor to exclude any revenues generated by the exploitation of the motion picture in all markets and media should be resisted.

The settlement transaction. As noted earlier, the settlement transaction is actually a form of cross-collateralization that producers should object to. To prevent this problem, the producer should attempt to require that the distributor insert "floors" in its agreements with subdistributors and exhibitors. A "floor" is a minimum percentage of the box office gross receipts, with the floors or percentages varying from territory to territory on a sliding scale over time. In addition, the producer should see that a "good faith" standard is inserted as part of the distributor's obligations relating to such settlements. Although distributors will generally not allow such language, it would be in the producer's interest (theoretically) if the producer could get the distributor to agree not to settle its accounts with exhibitors and its other licensees on less advantageous terms than those specified in the original contract between such parties. Thus, the producer should seek a warranty from the distributor stating that the distributor will not settle with any third party for less than the amounts due. This one issue alone may account for a 10 percent to 30 percent reduction in the gross receipts revenue stream at this earliest and most critical stage. This reduction in what would have been gross receipts will significantly affect all gross and net profit participants.

Also, the producer should seek to limit the distributor's discretion to allocate revenues to each of the films involved when the distributor agrees to settle an account with an exhibitor, subdistributor or other licensee for some round dollar amount when such accounts involve more than one film. Recognizing that the distributor will not likely accept such language, create a written record of the submission of such language (e.g., in one of the drafts to the distribution agreement or in a proposed written rider). This may help to create evidence that the contract is a contract of adhesion or that the refusal of the distributor to include such language (i.e., its omission) was an unconscionable act.

Trust me. At some point in the conversation between representatives of film distributors and film producers, it is very likely that the distributor will say something to the effect of "Trust me" or "There is going to have to be a certain amount of trust here." When that happens, the producer should look the distributor in the eye, smile and say, "Trust is for emergencies. So long as we have the opportunity to communicate, negotiate and express in writing the way we think this transaction ought to occur, there is no need for trust. And even when a situation comes up that was not anticipated, there is no reason why we cannot communicate about that. Only in the rare circumstances that do not permit negotiation or consultation, should either of the parties to a film distribution agreement rely on trust."

Revenue allocation. The distribution agreement negotiations should include some discussion of an objective standard on which to base such revenue allocations, such as the box office performance of the movie in single exhibition. Film distributors and exhibitors have come up with a formula to help handle allocation issues as between them. The formula is labeled "SPFRE" (same percentage as film rentals earned). This financial arrangement is sometimes negotiated between a film distributor and exhibitor so that the exhibitor agrees to pay the same percentage of the week's advertising cost for the movie as the exhibitor's percentage of the box office receipts received by the exhibitor in that same week. The producer should argue that a similar provision should be used in the feature film distribution deal (i.e., the SPFRE concept should be used in place of the distributor's "discretion" to make allocations among films licensed as a package).

Revenue allocation problems also occur in syndicated film packages. Producers may want to negotiate for an approval right over any such syndication formula used by a distributor on that producer's film when and if the producer's film is included in a syndicated package. The producer should seek to impose reasonable limits on the distributor's ability to sell or license a producer's picture as part of a package unless a mechanism is established for providing a fair valuation of such picture compared to the others in the package.

Allocation of revenues in outright sales. In situations involving outright sales of film packages (i.e., packages of several films licensed for a lump sum price) in a territory, to a network or in syndication, the producer should seek language that limits the ability of the distributor to engage in such outright sales unless the provision includes a mechanism for providing a fair valuation of such picture compared to the others in the package.

Charitable contributions. If the distributor seeks language in the distribution agreement authorizing it to make charitable contributions out of the revenues generated by a motion picture being distributed, the producer should seek to limit such charitable contributions to those associated with a charity premiere of the movie or other appropriate promotional/charity opportunities associated with the movie. In addition, the producer should insist on authorizing the producer or the director to choose which charity will benefit from the proceeds of such a charity premiere. If, in addition, the distributor seeks to retain language in the distribution agreement authorizing it to claim such a charitable contribution as a deductible distribution expense and as a U.S. income tax deduction, then the producer should insist that an amount corresponding to the charitable contribution be included in gross receipts as revenues, so that all net and gross profit participants receive some potential benefit from such revenues, not just the distributor.

Foreign receipts or overseas rentals. When the distribution agreement is negotiated, the producer should take the position that foreign receipts which have been remitted or which are remittable be included in gross receipts. The phrase "remitted or remittable" means already sent back or that which are able to be sent back. With respect to foreign receipts for the exploitation of a motion picture in international territories, the question often arises as to whether a net profit participant should receive the benefit of monies collected in the foreign territory and that could be remitted back to the United States but which have not yet been sent back. Again, the typical major studio/distributor definition of the term gross receipts excludes foreign receipts until they are collected and converted into dollars here in the U.S. The phrase "remitted or remittable" ought to be added, so as to remove the distributor's discretion to delay inclusion of such amounts in its gross and net profit calculations.

Blocked or restricted currencies. Producers should seek to negotiate a provision in the distribution deal that clarifies whether blocked or restricted currencies will be included in the distributor's definition of gross receipts. Obviously the producer should take the position that blocked currencies should be included in gross receipts; after all they do represent revenues earned by the producer's film. In addition, even though blocked currencies may not be taken out of the country in which they were earned, they do have value to the distributor. Distributors accumulate blocked currencies in certain countries over a period of time until there is enough there to produce a film locally or until they can sell the blocked funds at a discount to someone else who wants to utilize the local currency for some other business venture. Thus the producer should argue that blocked funds should be included as distributor gross receipts, or in the alternative, the share of such blocked funds that would have otherwise been paid to such gross and net profit participants be placed in a segregated bank account in the foreign country in trust for such persons, so that they can benefit from whatever value such funds may have in the future. This alternative approach has its own problems but is still better than not including blocked funds in distributor gross receipts.

Prompt payment. The producer should seek to negotiate language in the distribution agreement that will reasonably limit the distributor's discretion to hold payments for television and cable sales until actual play dates and not include these funds in the net and gross profit calculations until then. Such funds should be included in gross receipts when received by the distributor. This is more of a timing issue but could have an adverse impact on the interests of gross and net profit participants in any given accounting period. The distributor should not have the discretion to include such payments in its gross receipts whenever it chooses.

Video royalties. The producer should inquire when negotiating the distribution agreement as to whether the distributor owns or has any financial interest in the video company to be used as the video manufacturer/wholesaler. If so, the producer should insist, first that the video revenue stream be handled on a distributor fee basis like most of the other film revenue streams and not on a royalty basis. If that is not acceptable to the distributor (and it is not likely to be), then the producer should take the position that the revenues deducted by the video company not be deducted at such a high percentage (i.e., the 80 percent typically retained by the video wholesale/manufacturer). The other side of the same argument is that the royalty fee paid to the distributor, if that's what it is called, should not be so low (i.e., only 20 percent). The distributor's royalty fee should be more than the arbitrary 20 percent. After all, the distributor is also getting to participate in the revenues of its affiliated video manufacturer/wholesaler. The amount deducted should be something more along the lines of what a subdistributor's fees are. It would actually be more fair to reverse the 80/20 split, (i.e., have the video manufacturer/wholesaler retain 20 percent and remit 80 percent to the film distributor). Under any circumstances, since the distributor in this video revenue arena does not have to spend any time, money or expertise looking for an interested video company to distribute its film in the video market, does not have to negotiate an arm's length video license agreement (it's already set up) and is participating in the video company's profits anyway, it is outrageous for the distributor also to charge the 30 percent distributor's fee, thus the distributor's fee should also be negotiated downward.

Reserves for video returns. The film producer should demand that the distributor provide reliable statistics developed by a third party authority on the typical levels of such videocassette returns to determine whether the percentage being sought by the film distributor is reasonable. Assuming the distributor is asking for a reserve authorization that is not warranted by any reliable statistical data on the number of returns that can be reasonably expected, the producer should seek to limit the distributor to a more reasonable reserve percentage.

Ancillary rights. The producer should take the position that all revenues generated by the exploitation of the subject film in all ancillary markets or media be included in the distributor's gross receipts, and the producer should see that the distribution agreement reflects this position.

Discounts, rebates, and kickbacks. Producers should seek to negotiate a fair provision in the distribution agreement that includes the prorated value of discounts and rebates in the profit participation calculations, arguing that without the producer's film and the films of other producers, the distributor would not be able to get such discounts and rebates in the first place. Even if a producer is successful in negotiating such a provision, it is not unthinkable for a distributor who has a particularly close relationship with a given exhibitor or other film licensee to have the rebate shifted (on paper) to another producer's film and/or included as part of an overall settlement as between the distributor and the licensee, in which case the distributor may have the discretion to allocate the amount of the settlement among various films distributed by the distributor on behalf of several different producers. Producers and their profit participation auditors (or litigating attorneys) have to watch also for indications of kickback arrangements in all of the distributor's relationships with the providers of services that the distributor pays for and deducts the costs of as distribution expenses (e.g., outside advertising agencies, film labs, trailer production firms, exhibitors in cooperative advertising arrangements, distributor employees and facilities, distributor editing, censorship approvals, checking services, screening expenses, industry assessments, residuals and banking costs).

Trailer revenues. Do not allow the distributor to insert language in the distribution agreement authorizing the distributor to exclude revenues allocated to film shorts or trailers from distributor gross receipts. If that is not possible, then the producer should argue that the distributor should not be allowed to recoup any portion of the expense associated with the production of such trailers or film shorts from the revenue stream of the same film. A distributor may incur substantial expenses in preparing trailers and advertising accessories. If such expenses are charged against the distributor's proceeds as expenses of distribution, then any amounts of revenues derived from trailers and advertising accessories should be included in gross receipts to the distributor for purposes of calculating profit participations. Such payments may be made by exhibitors in certain territories. If the distributor wants to keep its revenues from trailers and accessories, it should not be able to deduct costs associated with the preparation of such items as distribution expenses.

Distributor commercials and product placements. Provide that if the distributor receives a fee or any form of compensation for a distributor commercial, trailer or product placement appearing before, after or during the producer's feature film, the amount should be included in the distributor's gross receipts. This issue can get a bit tricky because of the all the different available arrangements for financing, producing and distributing a film.[2] For example, if a project is an in-house production, the producer will have little or no say with regard to such matters. On the other hand, in other film finance/distribution scenarios, if the producer negotiates the product placement, the distributor might seek to share in the revenues. In the alternative, if the distributor in some way negotiates a product placement or other form of distributor commercial, the producer and other net and gross profit participants should seek to have revenues generated in that fashion included in the distributor's gross receipts.

Product tie-ins. The producer should confirm that revenues (advances and royalties) generated from product tie-ins are included in the distributor's gross receipts.

Stock footage. The producer should seek to include a prorated share of the revenues generated by the sale of stock footage in the distributor's gross receipts.

Sales of physical properties. The producer should negotiate to include revenue generated from the sale of any physical properties associated with the producer's movie in the distributor's gross receipts for that movie. In film finance situations in which the studio gets to recoup its negative cost or in which the production cost was not provided by the studio/distributors, such an exclusion is not appropriate.

Salvage exclusion. The producer should seek to include revenues generated by the sale of physical properties for salvage in the distributor's gross receipts for the movie from which the physical property came.

Uncollectible indebtedness or bad debts. The producer should seek to limit the distributor's discretion and include more objective language in the distribution agreement with respect to the circumstances under which the distributor may write off a bad debt. And in such situations, the audit provision in the distribution agreement should provide the producer's net profit participation auditor with expanded rights to determine whether the distributor's claims regarding uncollectible indebtedness is bona fide.

Ownership/film library. If the producer cannot get the distributor to agree that the producer will continue to own the copyrights to the picture and that certain limited rights are merely being licensed to the distributor or that the distributor's rights are limited to a term of years, the producer and counsel should seek to provide in the distribution agreement that any monies generated from the sale or licensing of the picture as part of the distributor's film library will be included in the distributor's gross receipts for purposes of calculating the financial interests of the producer and other profit participants.

Net recoveries. Certainly, if litigation and related expenses are deducted as a distribution expense, then the producer along with all gross and net profit participants should be allowed to benefit from any net recoveries by having such recoveries included in the distributor's gross receipts. Negotiate to include in gross receipts all revenues from any settlement, court judgment or decree relating to (a) any claims for unauthorized exhibition, distribution or other use of the film and/or (b) for any infringement, plagiarism or other interference by any party with the copyright of the film or (c) for breach of contract in connection with the distribution and/or exhibition of the film.

Scrapping of prints. Notwithstanding the fact that only a relatively small amount of money is involved and that such revenues will still have to be allocated amongst the many different films that are scrapped at the same time, the producer should not allow the distributor to exclude arbitrarily such revenues from the distributor's gross receipts on the producer's film. The producer should seek to negotiate language in the distribution agreement that either includes the revenues thus generated or that reduces the distributor's costs of making prints by the reasonable value of the prints as salvage.

The distributor actually receives most of the revenues listed above, thus all other net and gross profit participants should argue that such monies should be included in the distributor's gross receipts.

Distribution Fees

Services provided. The producer should see that the distribution agreement provides a very precise definition of what distributor services are paid for by means of the distribution fee, so that such amounts are not being paid twice, first as part of the distributor's fee and second as part of the distributor distribution expense recoupment (and/or distributor overhead). Also, provide reasonable distribution fees in each market. Reasonableness, in this regard, should be primarily based on what services are provided by the distributor, not what other distributors are charging for the same service, since in this industry, in particular, such a comparison may be very unrealistic.

The threshold question with respect to a film distributor's fees is whether they are reasonable, and reasonableness in this context can only be determined by clearly establishing what the fee compensates the distributor for and then comparing the distribution fees and corresponding deals with other distributors. Of course, since the major studio/distributors do not appear to operate in a true free market system (rather a shared monopoly or mature oligopoly) and they pretty much conduct their business in a similar manner, such an inquiry still may not tell us what is reasonable with respect to their distribution fees.

Unfortunately, there has been no extensive survey and analysis of the distribution fees charged by the various major studio/distributors or their independent counterparts conducted and published in recent years. In addition, based on the experience of some researchers seeking similar business related information from the major studio/distributors, reliable statistics relating to such items as distribution fees are not likely to be provided without a court order, and that might not even do the trick.

Retroactive distribution fee increases. When the distribution agreement provides for retroactive distribution fee increases, it is important to limit or segregate the revenues from which the retroactive recoupment can be extracted. If the distribution agreement does not address this point, the distributor will most likely take its retroactive increase from 100 percent of the subsequently accruing revenues (i.e., after the triggering event occurs, the distributor will take all of the next revenues to pay for the increase in its distribution fees back to the first dollar). Thus, the susceptible payment corridor from which the retroactive increase is paid should be limited in some reasonable manner (e.g., 50 percent of gross receipts), which allows the production company and other participants to continue receiving their percentage participations while the distributor is recouping retroactively.

Subdistribution fees. Clarify in the distribution agreement under what circumstances and in which markets the distributor will utilize the services of a subdistributor. To the extent that the distributor utilizes the services of a subdistributor, see that such subdistributor's fees are paid by the distributor out of its distribution fees and not in addition to its distribution fee. In other words, the distributor should not receive its full distribution fee for distribution services actually being handled by a subdistributor and for which a subdistributor also charges a distribution fee. Thus the producer should seek to have the primary distributor absorb the distribution fee of the subdistributor within its own distribution fee while retaining the balance as a supervision fee or have the fees of the subdistributor passed through without markup. In the alternative the producer may seek to negotiate a minimal override for the primary distributor on the distribution fees of subdistributors.

Distributor failure to license. The producer should see that the distribution agreement contains language which applies to situations where a distributor fails to issue licenses relating to the exploitation of the film in certain territories within a specified period of time. In such instances, the producer should have the authority to make deals directly with subdistributors in those territories. This provides an additional incentive to the distributor to see that the film is distributed in every available territory. To be fair, the distributor should have the right to match the deal obtained by the producer or lose the territory.

Distribution Expenses

Production or distribution expense. The producer or the producer's counsel should carefully review the items listed in the distribution expense definition section of the film distribution deal to make certain that all expenses listed (which are to be recouped by the distributor out of the distributor's gross receipts before any net profit participants receive any backside participations on the film) can be reasonably characterized as distribution expenses. Producers may discover, for example, that the definition of distribution expenses for the production-financing/distribution deal differs from the definition of distribution expenses for the negative pickup and pure acquisition deals, because in the former, the distributor is also able to collect interest and overhead charges on the production costs but not on its distribution outlays.

Direct distribution expenses. Specific categories of direct expenses that the distributor may deduct should be itemized. Distributors know what their expenses are. Other "indirect expenses" such as the distributor's general administrative overhead and similar internal costs should be regarded as a normal cost of doing business for the distributor and not recoupable from the picture's proceeds, or at least the producer should negotiate for as small a percentage of such expenses to be charged to the picture as possible. Otherwise the producer should be certain that the word "direct" is inserted in front of the general description of what kind of expenses are to be deducted as distribution expenses.

Maybe some relationship should be established between that percentage and the number of films distributed by the distributor in the course of a year.

Thus, the producer should seek to limit the distributor's recoupment of its distribution expenses to 100 percent (not more than 100 percent) of its out-of-pocket expenses occurring as a "direct" result of its distribution of the picture (i.e., not permitting overhead charges, facilities allocations or other similar charges to be deducted by the distributor as distribution expenses). Distributor overhead, if any, should be considered paid out of the distributor's fees just as in any other business. Items like trade-association fees and assessments, along with market research should be considered indirect or at most allocated amongst several films that benefit from such expenditures.

Even if the distribution agreement limits distributor expense deductions to direct expenses, the profit participant auditors still have to be concerned with ferreting out indirect expenses that are claimed by the distributor as direct expenses. Quite often the distributor's staff accountants do not read the distribution agreement. They simply handle each accounting issue in their usual and customary manner, shifting the burden onto the net profit participants' auditor to raise questions regarding whether the accounting practices actually implemented are consistent with the accounting practices authorized in the distribution agreement.

Off-the-top expenses. At least two of the typical major studio/distributor off-the-top expenses ought to be questioned, residual payments to guilds and trade association dues and assessments. Unfortunately, the major studio/distributors are committed as a group to pay the guild residuals out of gross receipts, thus the distributor cannot change that arrangement for a specific distribution deal. But producers should work with other net profit participants (outside the framework of the distribution agreement itself) to see that guild payments are not made before net profit participations. When they are, the effect is that guild members have a built-in gross participation while the film's producer and others only have a net profit participation. In the alternative, the producer and other net profit participants should take the position that they should receive their contingent compensation at the same time as anyone else who worked on the film (i.e., they should get a gross floor).

The producer should also raise the question as to why the MPAA gets paid a percentage of the distributor's gross receipts when the film's producer and other net profit participants have to wait to see if anything is left. The MPAA should not be the beneficiary of a windfall when a film is a huge financial success. The people who made the film ought to be the beneficiaries. MPAA dues and assessments ought to be flat fees paid by the distribution companies themselves and not tied in anyway to the performance of each film released by such distributors. The MPAA dues and assessments arrangement is merely another technique through which the major studio/distributors prevent the people who actually produced the film (writers, producers, directors and actors) from benefiting when the film is a financial success.

Checking costs. Producers and participants may want to audit for documentation of such costs and consider double checking with the checking services. Profit participants may also want to seek a cap on such costs (e.g., deductions of such costs shall not exceed 1 percent of the gross receipts for the picture). In a rent-a-distributor situation a producer may want to hire its own checking service to conduct random checks of attendance at theatres where the producer's film is being exhibited.

Collection costs. The producer may want to seek to place a reasonable ceiling on the distributor's collection costs and demand that the audit provision require the distributor to provide adequate information from which the auditor can fairly judge the reasonableness of the distributor's claimed collection expenses.

Foreign taxes. To the extent that the distributor actually pays any gross receipts or similar taxes in any foreign country based on the exhibition of the picture, the producer should allow the distributor to deduct its payment of such taxes from the film's gross receipts as a distribution expense. The distributor will be claiming a U.S. tax credit on such payments. Since the IRS Code (Sec. 901) and Treasury regulations (Sec. 1.90-1) only permit the credit to be claimed by the person or entity on whom the foreign tax was imposed, it is necessary for the producer negotiating with a film distributor to eliminate language which allows the distributor to also deduct its payments of such taxes as a distribution expense.

Residuals and royalties. On the one hand, the producer may not want the distributor to deduct residual and royalty payments out of the distributor's gross receipts, which means residual and royalty recipients are being paid as contingent compensation before the producer and other net profit participants (assuming the producer is a net profit participant). On the other hand, the producer does not want the distributor to shift the burden of paying residuals and royalties to the producer out of the producer's share because producers are not typically set up to handle such calculations and payments and they do not want their share of net profits to be diminished by such payments. Thus, the ideal compromise would be to get the distributor to handle such payments but out of the film's net profits and on a pari passu (pro rata and concurrent) basis with the payment of all net profit participations to the producer and other net profit participants. Unfortunately, again, these payments are prescribed by guild rules, thus the individual producer has no freedom to negotiate such issues. Changes, if any, will have to occur at a different level (i.e, pursuant to guild contract negotiations). Since there is no organization that represents the interests of independent producers in collective bargaining negotiations with the guilds, no wonder the interests of such producers have been overlooked.

Another useful approach may be for the producer to negotiate a royalty provision (in addition to or as opposed to a net profit participation) on the assignment of rights to the screenplay and/or movie when such rights are assigned or transferred in some other manner to the distributor. Then the producer may be in a position to seek payment of the producer royalty out of distributor gross receipts as an off-the-top distributor expense.

Dues and assessments. Producers may want to seek to negotiate a cap on the amount of dues and assessments that are paid by the distributor to industry trade associations to which it belongs. Also, the producer may want to stipulate that such trade association dues are not to be used to defray the costs associated with lobbying activities that favor the major studio/distributor over the independent producers or that help defend antitrust actions against association member companies unless a similar dues deduction is set aside in a fund that may be claimed by a duly organized association of independent feature film producers who may also use such association dues (deducted from the gross receipts revenue stream generated by independently produced films) to help defray the costs associated with prosecuting such antitrust actions or lobbying activities favorable to independent producers. It would seem only fair that if an association of independent feature film producers were formed, then each film produced by a member production company and distributed by an MPAA distributor would contribute a portion of its gross receipts to the independent producer's association as association dues at the same time that the MPAA and other distributor trade organization dues were being deducted and paid. In addition, independently produced films that were distributed by AFMA member distributors would also contribute an allocable portion to the support of such an organization. Again, this is a remedy that goes outside the distribution agreement and is thus outside the scope of this presentation. In any case, a producer should seek to negotiate a flat-dollar cap on the amount of gross receipts that may be deducted for association dues, (e.g., $50,000).

Sometimes, if the point about the theatrical revenue stream paying for expenses to protect the video revenue stream is raised, the distributor will agree to allocate a greater portion of these dues and assessments to the video revenue stream where it belongs. In other words, "the domestic theatrical revenue stream should not carry the greatest economic burden for association dues and assessments most of which are used to protect the video revenue stream."[3]

Conversion and transmission costs. The producer may want to seek a cap on such costs. Also, such distributor expenses must be carefully audited to verify their reasonableness. Thus, the importance of a strong auditing provision that favors the net profit participants is essential.

Adjusted or accountable gross. The producer should seek to eliminate or avoid any distributor or producer commitments to pay gross participations,

thus the necessity for defining any category of revenues as adjusted or accountable gross becomes moot.

Off-the-bottom expenses. Again, if the producer could succeed in negotiating away any gross profit participations, there would be no need for concepts
such as off-the-top expenses, adjusted gross, accountable gross or off-the-bottom expenses. This murky area of studio accounting could be eliminated as
superfluous.

Improperly claimed expenses. The producer should seek to build in some
sort of penalty provision for improperly claimed expenses (e.g., the distributor
must pay the auditor's fees or put back into the gross receipts revenue stream
twice the amount wrongfully deducted. Since the major studio/distributors
routinely insert such overbudget penalty provisions into their production-
financing/distribution agreements and negative pickup agreements, it is only
fair that producers be allowed to reciprocate. Without a penalty provision, distributors have less reason to be careful to avoid the "mistakes" that typically
seem to work in their favor.

Account number. When a film is produced by a studio, it is assigned an
account number and all charges incurred on behalf of the film are allocated to
that account number. Unfortunately, the studios have been known to loosely
guard those account numbers and persons on the lot have been able to make
unauthorized charges to a film's budget. In a studio financing context, profit
participants or their representatives must carefully review studio charges to
make certain they are all authorized. Although beyond the scope of this presentation (which only deals with the distribution deal itself), the studio's corporate shareholders must also see that the board of directors creates a finance
committee that really oversees and implements strict corporate financial controls. The major studio/distributors have a reputation in the film industry for
loosely adhering to any sort of financial controls and such board of director
finance committees have a reputation for being controlled by studio management.

Anticipated expenses. The producer should seek to place a reasonable limit
or producer approval on the amounts that can be set aside as reserves by the
distributor for such anticipated distributor expenses, otherwise the distributor
will be in a position to eliminate net profits for any given accounting period
merely by overestimating future expenses.

Allocated or apportioned expenses. The producer should seek to add language to the distribution agreement that removes the distributor's discretion to
allocate or apportion expenses. A mutually satisfactory method of allocating
such expenses must be determined. In other words, the parties will have to
determine whether the expenses should be allocated and on a per capita, gross
to gross or other basis. The producer should also try to make sure the audit

rights of the producer and/or profit participants include access to such documentation (i.e., do not allow the distributor to limit access to documents that relate to the amount of money to be received, but also permit auditor access to documents relating to monies that might have been received as distributor gross receipts on a given film, except for the distributor's discretion to allocate or apportion such expenses).

Advertising costs. Film advertising costs, the direct expenses incurred in preparing and producing advertising for motion pictures, must be closely examined to make sure they are reasonable whether the advertising for a movie is handled in-house by a distributor's advertising department or by an outside advertising agency. Profit participants or their representatives should watch for "sweetheart" deals where an outside advertising agency artificially inflates the costs of its services on one producer's movie and gives the studio or distributor a more favorable rate on its in-house productions, or in another variation, actually pays some form of "kickback" to the distributor or an individual on the distributor's staff. In other instances, some studio/distributors may charge a 10 percent advertising fee simply for administering a movie's advertising program when the program is actually conceived, planned, created and implemented by an outside advertising agency. Determine at the distribution agreement negotiation stage whether such fees will be charged and question whether the fee is necessary and whether the percentage is fair and/or reasonable.

The producer must seek to negotiate language in the distribution agreement that allows the auditor to review the distributor's claimed advertising expenses on films distributed at or about the same time as the independently produced film on which the audit is being conducted. The profit participants' auditor must have access to the information upon which to make a judgment as to the fairness of cost allocations relating to the licensing of films in a package for television, whether for network or syndication, and in foreign distribution when films are sold in packages. In the alternative, the distribution agreement should provide for a fair or objective method of allocation (e.g., to base the allocation on the films' theatrical performance). Distributor allocation of expenses must be based on some negotiated and objective criteria, and the distributor must be required to disclose to the producers of independently produced films what percentages of specific expenses were allocated to which films.

Cooperative advertising costs. The producer should insure that his or her auditor has the authority to examine exhibitor/distributor contracts and all relevant records of all parties relating to cooperative advertising expenses.

Combination and cooperative ads. The producer's auditor must be able to review both sides of this transaction (i.e., be able to see how much of the cost was allocated to the other film and how much of the cost was paid by the exhibitor on both films). Language providing such authority for the auditor must be negotiated and included in the distribution agreement, otherwise the auditor has no power to insist on reviewing all of the relevant expense records.

Inflated advertising costs. The producer may want to seek to include a ceiling on the amount of money that can be charged against the film for advertising. The producer should also see that the auditor is authorized to examine all records having any relationship to the costs of advertising for the movie in question, not just the records of the distributor.

Excessive advertising ("buying a gross"). The producer, again, should seek to place a contractual ceiling on the amount of money that can be spent by the distributor on advertising the film.

Advertising fee. If studio/distributors want to charge back some of their costs in overseeing the implementation of a film's advertising by an outside advertising agency, the advertising fee should be imposed on a flat fee basis, otherwise, the distributor gets a windfall on the higher budgeted pictures. Further, if the distributor charges such an advertising fee, the distributor should not be allowed also to charge its full overhead fee.

Advertising overhead. Net profit participants may have a reasonable basis to question this charge, but in lieu of eliminating or limiting the amount of the advertising overhead charge altogether, net profit participants may choose to seek to impose a flat dollar ceiling on the amount that can be charged by the studio or distributor. If an advertising overhead charge cannot be avoided altogether, negotiate for the payment of an actual prorated overhead charge as opposed to an arbitrary percentage and if stuck with a percentage negotiate a flat dollar ceiling on such charges. A percentage based on a film's revenues has no relationship to the actual allocated overhead expense that would be determined by dividing the studio's indirect costs by the number of films released in a given year.

Distributor employee time allocations (shared employee salaries). In situations where the distribution agreement permits the distributor to allocate the time that its publicity people or other studio employees spend on a specific movie and to charge that time against the prints and advertising or other parts of the budget for the film, the distributor's fee and/or overhead charge, if any, should be reduced. To the extent that a studio makes employee time and other similar allocations, there is less justification for a distributor overhead charge.

Contractual distributor overhead. If a distributor is allowed to deduct some of its indirect expenses as distribution expenses and on a flat percentage basis, the producer should seek to negotiate a smaller percentage for such charges, or in the alternative have the categories of such expenses specifically itemized and carefully monitor the reasonableness of such charges. In addition, the producer's auditor must watch for situations in which the distributor improperly characterizes distribution expenses as production expenses in an effort to increase the amount of interest that may be charged against the negative cost of the picture (this concern would not apply on a pure acquisition deal or in a rent-a-distributor situation).

In view of the fact that distributors are generally permitted to recoup at least 100 percent of their direct distribution expenses and distribution fees for distributing a film in various media and markets, the producer may want to take the position that such indirect distribution or other expenses should not be charged against a specific film at all, either on an actual cost or percentage basis, but rather such studio/distributors should cover such costs as most businesses do with their earned fees.

Distributor cost allocations. Require that any distributor expense or gross receipts allocations for purposes of cooperative advertising or other advertising, employee time, film packages, co-features or other similar arrangements be based on an objective standard negotiated in advance and set out in the distribution agreement and that the net profit participation auditor will have access to the information necessary to confirm the fairness of such allocations.

Facilities allocations. In studio or distributor financed films, the producer should consider negotiating (1) to exclude facilities allocations from the permissible distribution expense deductions, (2) to place a limit on the percentage of such allocations, and (3) to carefully review such allocations to make certain they are reasonable and that they do not duplicate costs covered by a broader contractual distributor overhead charge.

Below-the-line fringes. The producer or the auditor must determine exactly what the below-the-line fringes are and how much they cost, otherwise the studio/distributor may be able to overstate such expenses, thus increasing the amount of the distributor's expense deductions and thereby further reducing a film's net profits or its chances of achieving net profits.

Exhibitor allowances. The producer needs to negotiate language in the distribution agreement that requires the distributor to provide adequate information upon which the producer's auditor can determine whether exhibitor allowances are reasonable and to allow the auditor to review documentation on both sides of the transaction. The producer's auditor must be sure that exhibitor allowances permitted by the distributor are not excessive in what amounts to a disguised attempt to cross-collateralize one movie's revenue with others the distributor is distributing or will distribute.

Overreported travel expenses. The producer must make sure that the distribution agreement audit provision provides adequate authority for the auditor to review such expenses and check for receipts.

Print costs. The producer should see that the distribution agreement provides a precise definition of what actually goes into the print cost category. The distribution agreement must also provide broad authorization allowing the auditor to review carefully the print cost item on the distributor's statement to determine whether such costs appear to be reasonable considering the reported number of theatres in which the film ran. The auditor will also need to make judgments regarding what other cost items are included with the actual cost of prints in the print cost item on the distributor's statement.

Unauthorized distribution costs. As with any distribution expense, such costs must be carefully reviewed, confirmed and adjudged reasonable to prevent overstated expenses. The producer may want to ask the distributor if it anticipates any such costs beyond industry assessments for such activities.

Ongoing distribution expenses. In addition to negotiating a specific commitment from the distributor with respect to the minimum expenditures for prints and advertising, it may also be in the producer's best interests to seek a reasonable ceiling on the amount of money the distributor can spend in distributing the film (at least an upper limit beyond which the distributor cannot go without the approval of the producer). If not, the distributor may choose to spend more money than necessary to promote the film in its domestic theatrical release (buying a gross) in an effort to create more value in the subsequent video release where the distributor gets a better deal and has a better chance of making more money anyway. In the meantime, the producer and other net profit participants are so far in the hole because of the excessive expenditure of distribution funds in the domestic theatrical marketplace that no net profits will ever be realized.

Interest

Interest plus profit participation. If a studio/distributor is being paid a fair rate of interest on its borrowed funds, it should certainly not be permitted to participate in the motion picture's net profits[4] or any other defined level of the film's revenue stream beyond the deduction of its distribution fee and direct expenses. Less interest would be required if the producer was able to convince the studio/distributor to allow interest on production funds to be paid and the negative cost to be recouped prior to deduction by the distributor of its distribution fees and distribution expenses. The reason that is not allowed is that the studio will make more interest if the payment of interest on the negative cost is delayed, and since this is not an issue that the studio/distributors will even consider for negotiation and it is extremely favorable to the stronger party, it is probably fair to consider such a provision unconscionable. Studio/distributor conglomerates providing production and distribution financing should discount both their interest rates and distribution fees since they are making money on both. In today's Hollywood, the studio/distributors actually charge higher interest rates and distribution fees, a position that would clearly not be acceptable to any negotiating party who had the strength of bargaining position to require a more fair arrangement.

Excessive interest rates. The producer should seek to negotiate interest rates on funds provided by the major studio/distributor that are lower than the cost of those funds to the studio. After all, the studio/distributor is making money in other areas on the project. In the alternative, the producer should negotiate rates that are the same as or only slightly above the studio's cost of funds.

Delayed interest payments on negative cost balances. If a studio wants to act like a bank and charge interest on borrowed funds, then it ought to also allow a priority position for the recoupment of negative costs so as not to extend unfairly the repayment of the loaned amount thereby increasing the total interest charges. In such situations, the studio/bank is guilty of self-dealing, and this arrangement might well be struck down as being unconscionable, after the fact, if anyone ever raised the question in a court of law.

Interest on advances. The producer should seek to negotiate a provision in the distribution agreement with respect to interest on advances that allows the advance to be included in the distributor's gross receipts for purposes of calculating net profits if the distributor is also going to charge interest on the advance.

Interest on monies not yet spent. The producer should seek to negotiate a provision in the distribution agreement requiring a consistent accounting policy with respect to paying interest on expenses. For example, interest should not begin to accrue until production expenses are actually paid, otherwise, the studio is getting interest on monies not yet spent.

Premature deductions from gross receipts. A similar accounting policy should also be carried over to the distribution expenses, since if distribution expenses are reported on the distributor's accounting statement at the time such expenses are incurred (as opposed to when paid), the amount of the distributor's gross receipts can be prematurely reduced, thus eliminating monies that may have been used to recoup the film's negative cost, thus also reducing the time period over which interest is paid on the negative cost and ultimately reducing the amount of interest paid on such negative costs.

When interest charges stop. It is in the interest of the producer and other net profit participants for interest charges to stop when monies representing negative cost recoupment are actually received by the studio and not wait until the end of the accounting period, however many months that might involve. In the alternative, the studio's accounting policy should at least be consistent with respect to when interest charges start and stop. It is unconscionable for the distributor to start interest accruals at the beginning of an accounting period even though the expense did not occur until sometime during the accounting period, then on the other hand, to stop the accrual of interest at the end of the accounting period when the monies recouping the expense on which the interest is being paid were received at some earlier time during the accounting period.

Interest on overhead. The producer should seek to eliminate or reduce the percentages used for production overhead, or in the alternative see that the production overhead charge does not incur interest. In addition, the distributor should not be allowed to deduct a distribution overhead charge as a distribution expense, and the producer should be careful that the distributor does not improperly characterize distribution overhead as a cost of production.

Simple versus exact interest. The producer should seek to negotiate language in the production-financing/distribution agreement that calls for exact interest as opposed to simple interest.

Interest on gross participations. The producer should seek to negotiate language in the distribution agreement which either characterizes gross participations as an expense of distribution or as some other accounting item other than an interest-bearing production expense.

Production Cost Issues

Gross participants. Since in a negative pickup deal the independent producer will typically control the gross participation issue as opposed to the studio/financier, he or she should not allow any other individuals or entities to participate in gross receipts besides the distributor. This means that the producer will have to stand up to the agents and attorneys representing directors, actors, actresses and others who demand a gross profit participation. Allowing anyone to siphon off a percentage of the distributor's gross receipts either at some defined level of pure, accountable or adjusted gross will substantially decrease the likelihood that any net profits will ever materialize. In the absence of a gross floor being negotiated for the net profit participants, even a single gross participant can eliminate the possibility of a movie's revenue stream ever generating net profits. It would be better for the producer to stand up for the interests of all net profit participants at the time of negotiating for high-priced star talent and refuse to grant gross points.

In opposing a gross participation for Richard Dreyfuss on *Close Encounters of the Third Kind*, producer Julia Phillips claims she told Dreyfuss in the presence of his agent: "We have been killing ourselves for two years while you have been gigging around and making money. You don't have near the personal investment. We don't mind you making a lot of money, but you ain't making more money than us." Julia Phillips reports that Dreyfuss accepted the role of Roy Neary without the gross participation.[5] The next question to ask is whether the elimination of the Dreyfuss gross profit participation was enough to facilitate the payment of net profits on that film?

If the gross participations cannot be avoided, then the producer should work to convert all net profit participations into gross participations or include with the net profit participations alternative gross floors similar to the gross floors that distributors use with exhibitors. Also, if the gross participations cannot be prevented, the producer should seek to characterize such participations as something other than production costs, so as to avoid the application of interest and production overhead charges to the gross participations. The distributor is not limited to classifying such costs as either costs of production or as distribution expenses. It could in all fairness to all other parties involved consider the gross participation as neither, that is, a category all its own, a "gross participation" of all things, to which no interest or production overhead charges are applied.

In a similar approach, entertainment attorney Peter Dekom has called "on the industry to adopt a new standard whereby the non-cash-advance portion of any gross participation paid to an actor or director be deducted off the top without the application of a distribution fee, interest or overhead, and let the studio charge a distribution fee on remaining gross in accordance with the past net profits definitions."[6]

Negative costs. It is very important to define clearly in any production-financing/distribution agreement the distinction between production costs and distribution expenses (and to monitor vigorously the studio's classification of expenses), since a studio financier will typically seek to charge interest on the cost of producing the negative (production expenses) as well as apply the overhead percentage against the production cost total. The producer and other profit participants, therefore, must insist that no expenses that are actually distribution costs be classified by the studio as production costs since such a practice would tend to delay any net profit participation. In those situations where the studio is providing property or services for the production of the film, the producer should seek to limit the excessive charges the studios typically extract for such property or services. After all, if the film is charged an inflated price for a light, a camera, a set, or a light bulb, each extra dollar paid represents a further reduction in the chance that net profits will be achieved and will be available for distribution.

Production overhead. Producers may be able to avoid some overhead costs by avoiding the studio/distributors or by negotiating a smaller percentage for such charges by specifically listing the deductible charges or in the alternative by closely monitoring such charges for reasonableness. "The net profit participant must ask . . . what services, facilities and materials are included for the overhead fee, and whether these items are to be charged separately."[7]

Producers should also try to avoid the ambiguity represented by the Buck Houghton quote: "If you are shooting with a studio affiliation, the stage space and the shooting equipment is part of your overhead charge (a percentage of dollars spent directly)."[8] This statement does not clarify whether the stage space and shooting equipment is being charged individually or as part of the studio's production overhead or both. Also, as pointed out above, the producer should specifically seek language in the distribution agreement that prohibits the studio from charging interest on the studio's production overhead charge.

Creative Control Issues

Approved elements. Producers and directors must not forget about the distributor's approval rights as the film is produced. If the distributor does not like the film, the distributor is not likely to forget. Recognizing that it is important for a studio/distributor to have certain approval rights relating to key elements of the film on P-F/D and negative pickup deals, the producer should also provide in that same distribution arrangement for a mechanism to permit changes in those elements under certain circumstances. The producer may also want to try to limit distributor approvals to the producer, director, shooting script, budget and principal members of the cast.

Script changes. Some effort ought to be made in negotiating the distribution agreement to define further what departures from the approved script will be allowed by the distributor and to provide for some mechanism to obtain quickly distributor approvals on changes along the way. The producer should seek to include a mechanism for approving subsequent changes and for determining which changes during production require distributor approval. Otherwise the producer risks creating a situation in which the distributor may avoid its obligations under the distribution agreement because it does not like the film, while officially claiming that substantial authorized script changes were made. In addition, when a completion guarantee has been provided, it typically does not cover budget overruns caused by script changes. The producer, however, should at least insist on a provision in the completion guarantee that covers script changes prompted by uninsured events that are beyond the control of either the producer or the director.

Editing rights. Although, it may be necessary to allow the distributor the limited right to edit the film to meet the requirements of foreign censors and the MPAA Ratings Board, do not allow the distributor to exercise its sole discretion to make editing changes on the film. In other words, limit the distributor's right to edit the picture only to circumstances required to meet government censorship requirements and/or MPAA rating requirements. Even those distributor edits should be done subject to producer approval.

Censorable material. The producer should try to develop more specific language than the typical producer warranty relating to censorable material (i.e., the producer promises not to include any "censorable material" in the film). In the alternative, this provision should not be drafted as a producer warranty, or it should be stated so that the producer is committing to use its best or reasonable efforts depending on the standard used by the distributor for its commitments.

Cast member approvals. Even though the distributor will insist on approval rights for key cast members, the producer may also want to seek advance approval for other possible cast choices in the event one or another preferred cast member is not available for any reason or has to be replaced on short notice.

Running time. The producer should make sure that the agreed upon running time for the film is something that can be accomplished considering the script that is to be shot. The producer must also work with the director to make sure that the film planned and produced can and does fall within the prescribed running time.

Producer consultation rights. Try to be more clear in exactly what is expected of the distributor when consulting with the producer with respect to issues for which production consultation is provided in the distribution agreement. Also, the producer should do everything possible to project the image and in fact be a producer who can be relied on as a continuing source of quality film product. The producer that is perceived as a future and continuing source of quality film product will typically have more leverage when it comes to producer consultation rights on that producer's most recent film.

Waiver of droit moral. Unless the producer and/or director is satisfied with the provisions of the distribution agreement with respect to the distributor's editing rights, as discussed above, the producer should consider deleting any attempted waiver of droit moral rights.

Television cover shots. The producer should ask that the distributor designate which scenes it wants covered for purposes of television, so as to avoid giving the distributor another opportunity to avoid distribution in that market.

Marketing campaign approval rights. Although not a creative control issue with respect to the production of the film, marketing campaign approval rights relate to what kind of film the prospective audience thinks it is going to see. The producer should seek to provide for approval rights of the producer for the marketing campaign prepared by the distributor. If not, the distributor may use unethical or misleading ads just to get people in the theatre seats and the producer's reputation may be adversely affected. In addition, in most instances, the producer better understands what the film is all about and can work with the distributor to develop a marketing campaign that will both effectively sell the picture to its potential audience and accurately reflect the true nature of the film.

General Contractual Provisions

Distributor discretion. In negotiating with distributors, independent producers should seek to eliminate unnecessary or unreasonable distributor discretion (sole, unfettered or otherwise). Pay particular attention to the provisions that include the following words or phrases which indicate someone, usually the distributor, is being allowed to exercise its discretion: allocation, apportion, best efforts, commonly understood, customarily kept by the distributor, customarily provided by the distributor, customary in the industry, customary practices, customary terms and conditions for agreements of this nature in the motion picture industry, deem, discretion, good faith, industry standards, latitude, long-standing and well-established practices in the industry, ordinary course of business, reasonable, reasonable and customary, reasonable efforts, reasonably, usual, usual and customary manner and well-established practices in the industry.

A distribution agreement filled with these terms is not much of an agreement from the perspective of the producer and other net profit participants. The use of any of these terms in a feature film distribution agreement should be examined for reasonableness and should not be used if there is any way that more specific language could be negotiated. From the producer's point of view, a more objective method for determining the truth or circumstances involved in any matter that is considered in the film distribution relationship or any standard of conduct for the distributor is likely to be more preferable than the use of such vague terms and therefore should be negotiated where possible. When such words or phrases are used, determine whose discretion is involved and then consider whether it is possible to negotiate and draft language that provides a more objective standard with which to comply. Some discretion will almost always be necessary, but discretion can also be an invitation for abuse, especially film distributor discretion.

With respect to a film distribution agreement (and other motion picture documentation), producers must recognize that the use of such vague and subjective terms are just that, "vague and subjective." Their use imposes very little on the studio/distributor and such standards of conduct can only be enforced after the fact, if at all.

Distributor Commitments

Producers should seek to negotiate reasonable commitments with distributors and see that they are met.

Theatrical commitment. It is extremely important that the word "theatrical" be used as a modifier of the word "release" in a film distribution deal since without the word "theatrical" the film distributor would be free (assuming the film is a disappointment to the distributor) to merely sell the motion picture to cable without its being exhibited at theatres.

Domestic theatrical release. Do not overlook the word "domestic" when describing the distributor's theatrical release commitment. Also, try to obtain a distributor commitment to release the film in its domestic theatrical release in a specific number of key cities or markets.

The producer should check with video companies in advance to determine what level of release commitment from the distributor in the domestic theatrical release will create value in the property from the video company's point of view. At a minimum, the producer should see that the distribution agreement guarantees a theatrical release. However, distributors will generally resist guaranteeing the type or pattern of release of a picture. They feel that even the use of a broad standard such as "reasonable business judgment" or "best efforts" may invite litigation if the distributor uses incorrect judgment in its selection of a distribution pattern. The producer should, however, seek minimum specific commitments for prints and advertising, particularly for theatrical distribution, since such amounts demonstrate the distributor's commitment to exploitation of the film. For low- to medium-budget pictures, it is not unusual for P&A commitments to equal 50 to 100 percent of the film's budget. In addition to the guarantee of a theatrical release, the producer may seek distributor commitments for producer consultation and approval rights relating to the release pattern, a theatrical release in certain cities and specified limits on distribution expenses. It would seem that, if the distributor would work with the producer on such issues and obtain producer approvals of its release plan, there would be fewer grounds for litigation.

Prints and ads commitment. Producers may want to seek a commitment from the distributor regarding specified minimum levels of expenditures for prints and ads along with a specific minimum number of prints.

Trailer commitment. Obtain some form of commitment, even if just a "best-efforts" commitment to see that the film's trailer is exhibited a minimum number of times.

Release window commitment. Get the distributor to commit to release the picture within a specified period (e.g., 60–90 days) after delivery of the picture to the distributor.

Conflicting films. Obtain commitments from the distributor not to distribute so many other movies during the subject picture's domestic theatrical release or movies that are so similar to the subject picture that such distributor activities would likely distract from the distributor's commitment to support the picture.

Best efforts versus reasonable efforts. Do not allow the distributor to use a "reasonable efforts" standard of conduct in lieu of the "best efforts" standard. Although, still quite vague, "best efforts" imposes a higher standard of conduct than "reasonable efforts." In both cases, however, the distributor will be interpreting such language as it sees fit. The producer and other net and gross profit participants can only challenge the distributor's interpretation after the fact through audit demands, arbitration and/or litigation. If other more objective standards of conduct are available, use those in place of best efforts or reasonable efforts.

Deferments or deferrals. The producer should seek to clarify in the distribution deal who pays such deferments as between the distributor and producer, when they are to be paid and in cases where such deductions are made from the film's revenue stream, whether they are considered expenses of distribution, an interest-bearing production cost or some other noninterest-bearing category of expense. Talent deferments are payments that would have ordinarily been made to talent during the production of a film; thus it would be reasonable for the producer to negotiate the payment of such deferments to talent out of the film's revenue stream prior to distributor deductions for its fees or expenses, since after all such monies have been at risk longer than any money put up by a distributor for its distribution expenses. Unfortunately, distributors are not likely to agree to such priority payments for talent deferrals.

Grant of rights. The producer must confirm that the grant of rights provision accurately sets out the grant actually being made.

Ownership. The producer should seek to provide that the producer owns the copyrights to the picture, that certain limited rights are merely being licensed to the distributor. In the alternative, the producer may choose to provide that any monies generated from the sale or licensing of the picture as part of a film library be included in the distributor's gross receipts for purposes of calculating the interests of net profit participants.

Term of agreement. In situations where the producer does not transfer ownership to a film to the distributor and retains the right to exploit the property in specified markets or media, the producer should seek to limit the term of the distributor's rights to exploit the film in whatever markets and media the distributor has been granted. Thus, at the end of the term for the distribution agreement, such rights will revert to the producer and whatever value the film may have at that point (e.g., as part of the producer's library of films) will accrue to the producer instead of the distributor.

Most favored nations clause. The producer should seek to include in the distribution agreement a most favored nations clause. This provision is crucial to those participants who find themselves in the same category (e.g., net profit participants). If two such participants are supposed to be paid a specified percentage of net profits, but the definitions of net profits in their respective agreements differ, without the most favored nations clause one may prevent the other from being paid at that level or at all.

Cross-collateralization. The producer should learn to recognize the varying and many forms of distributor cross-collateralization. In situations, where the distributor has the right to exploit a single film in all markets and all media in perpetuity, it may not be reasonable for the producer to expect the distributor not to cross-collateralize profits and losses on that film, as between markets and media. However, in situations where multiple films of a single producer or production company are being distributed by a single distributor, the producer may want to negotiate language that prohibits the direct or indirect cross-collateralization of the profits and losses of such films. In some instances, no provision is made in the distribution agreement regarding cross-collateralization (at any level) and thus the distributor may choose to use its discretion with regard to this issue. It would be a better practice for the producer to negotiate specifically a cross-collateralization provision and specifically limit the ability of the distributor to cross-collateralize profits and losses to specified circumstances. In still other instances, the producer must carefully monitor the activities of the distributor to be certain that it is not effectively cross-collateralizing the financial performance of the producer's film with the performance of the films of other producers.

Offset rights. The producer should seek to place a reasonable limit on the discretion of the distributor to adjust accounting records to compensate for a credit or loss incurred by another party with which it deals. Such a limit should be included in the offset rights provision to prevent the offsetting party from abusing its discretion to make such deductions. These adjustments can adversely affect the financial interests of net profit participants and result in a subtle form of cross-collateralization since they may cover more than one film.

Outright sales. The producer may want to negotiate for a provision prohibiting outright sales in the major foreign territories where films are more likely to generate gross receipts for the distributor beyond the guarantee and thus more revenue for percentage participants. The major foreign territories are France, the United Kingdom, Germany, Australia, Japan, Spain, Sweden and Italy.

Foreign markets and split rights deals. The producer may choose to negotiate split-rights deals in which the domestic and foreign markets are handled by separate distributors. To the extent that the domestic and foreign markets are handled separately, this strategy eliminates cross-collateralization between such markets.

Holdback periods. The producer may want to negotiate a holdback schedule in order to ensure that the picture has an opportunity for maximum revenues in each medium of exploitation. If the producer has reserved certain rights, on the other hand, the distributor may seek holdback provisions. Typical holdback periods might include: videocassette rights—9–12 months after initial theatrical release; cable and pay tv—3 months after start of videocassette distribution; free television—2 years after initial theatrical release.

Liability limitation. The producer, particularly if the distribution rights granted are limited, should see that such limits do not protect the distributor against willful misconduct or gross negligence and possibly even negligent conduct, because such limits may not provide enough incentive for the distributor to act conscientiously to protect the copyright.

Errors and omissions insurance. If the producer's errors and omissions insurance coverage is expanded to include possible distributor error, the distributor should be charged with its pro rata share of the premiums. Also, the distributor should not be allowed to withhold sums of money from distribution proceeds to pay for the anticipated expenses associated with claims covered by the E&O policy, unless there is a reasonable likelihood that such claims will exceed the limits of the insurance coverage. The producer should discuss the E&O requirements as set out in the distribution deal with his or her insurance agent or carrier to make sure the distributor is not obligating the producer to provide coverage that is not available in the current marketplace.

Outside service agreements. The producer should require that any distributor negotiations and agreements with subdistributors, controlled theatres, video companies, outside advertising agencies and other individuals or entities providing support services to the distributor be conducted in an arm's length manner or that distributor fees in such situations be reasonable considering the special relationships involved. In addition, if such relationships provide anything of value to the distributor in relation to the distribution of a specific film, that film's gross receipts ought to be credited with an amount equal to such value. The producer should also see that the language in the distribution agreement provides that such agreements may be reviewed by the auditor for the net profit participants.

Distributor credit. The producer should seek to include language in the distribution agreement which prohibits an extension of distributor credit that affects the financial interest of the producer and other net profit participants beyond a reasonable or specified term.

Distributor contingencies. In negotiating the negative pickup distribution agreement, the producer should try to avoid or minimize contingencies to the distributor's performance. The producer should try to eliminate as many grounds as possible that the distributor may be able to use as a basis for refusing delivery of the film on subjective grounds (e.g., the final picture reflects insignificant differences from the approved script).

Distributor assignment rights. In the event the distribution agreement allows the distributor to assign parts of the agreement to subdistributors and other companies for purposes of meeting its distribution obligations, the producer and other net profit participants should insist on language requiring the distributor to remain liable for performance of the obligations of the agreement even if they are assigned. In many cases, the producer may also want to require the distributor to handle the first general release itself and not pass its distribution obligations on to an entity that was not a party to the distribution agreement. In addition, the producer should preserve his or her ability to assign the right to receive proceeds resulting from the exploitation of the film and otherwise to enforce provisions of the distribution agreement.

Assignment of profit participation interest. Do not provide the distributor with a right of first refusal to acquire the net profit participant's interest. Make the net profit participation interest freely assignable, although in the event of multiple assignees, the distributor should be allowed to appoint a disbursing agent. If the distributor gets a right of first refusal to acquire the net profit participant's interest, such a provision will limit the ability of the profit participant to assign its interest in net profits, and the value of such an interest will be reduced. Through such a restriction on assignment, the distributor may simply be trying to keep the net profit participations in the hands of people in the film industry (i.e., people who are less likely to litigate).

Covenant of good faith and fair dealing. See that explicit language imposing a covenant of good faith and fair dealing on the distributor is inserted into the distribution agreement. A favorably worded covenant of good faith and fair dealing might prove more helpful than an implied covenant.

Good faith. When possible, language in the film distribution agreement which provides that the distributor will perform a certain task in good faith or act in good faith with respect to a particular matter (in instances other than the specific covenant of good faith and fair dealing) should be replaced in the distribution agreement with a more precisely defined standard of conduct.

Warranties. To the extent possible, the producer should require all warranties in the feature film distribution deal to be mutual. In other words, where applicable, they should apply both to the producer and the distributor. Other warranties specifically applying to the distributor also should be included in the distribution agreement (e.g., a warranty as to the financial capacity of the distributor properly to undertake and perform its obligations under the agreement). Another useful distributor warranty might impose an obligation on the distributor to settle all accounts with exhibitors, subdistributors and all other licensees on terms that maximize the financial interests of profit participants.

Warranty of quiet enjoyment. If the distributor wants this warranty and representation included in the distribution agreement, the producer should seek to insert language limiting the warranty to matters known as of the date the agreement was signed.

Overbudget penalties. The producer should refuse to allow the double add-back overbudget penalty on the grounds that it is unconscionable. Notwithstanding the fact that unreasonable contractual penalties may not be enforceable, this studio overbudget policy raises a question as to whether such overbudget costs, when added twice, bear interest and overhead charges the second time around. Also, a determination has to be made as to whether the increased costs are due to certain factors excluded from the calculations relating to the question "was the overbudget threshold exceeded." Thus, the producer should also seek to include language in any overbudget penalty provision that excludes such costs as losses covered by insurance, losses caused by events of force majeure, changes initiated by or approved by the studio, third-party breaches, currency fluctuations, union increases and/or lab increases. In other words, expenses beyond the control of the producer and director should not be allowed to force the producer or director to have to pay an overbudget penalty. If the distributor uses overbudget penalties, the producer should also seek reciprocal provisions that apply to the distributor in the event the distributor makes mistakes or contract misinterpretations that cost the producer and other net profit participants money.

Delivery. The delivery requirements section of a film distribution agreement must be carefully drafted so that the distributor will not be able to refuse delivery of the completed film on subjective grounds. Subjective terms are words or expressions used in contracts that are subject to or likely to be interpreted differently by different individuals, as opposed to more objective terms whose meaning may be more readily agreed upon. Subjective terms should be clearly defined or eliminated in the negotiation of such contracts, particularly in the delivery requirements section. Subjective language should be replaced with objective delivery requirements, which are quantifiable and time-specific standards that must be met by a film's producer in delivering various elements of a completed feature film to a distributor. Such delivery requirements should not be based on some subjective approval of the distributor; thus producers should avoid language in the distribution agreement that calls for an artistic judgment by the distributor. Also, examine the delivery schedule carefully with all providers of items on the list (e.g., film lab and E&O insurance carrier) to make certain that each item can be provided. In addition, see that the delivery schedule is presented in chronological order for the convenience of those obligated to meet its requirements. Draft the delivery schedule so that it can be a useful and working document, not something that is signed and forgotten. Also, distributors sometimes want access to the producer's original delivery materials, but the producer may want to insist that those original materials being provided through a lab remain at the producer's laboratory, assuming that the producer actually selected the film lab. If the delivery requirements provision is not carefully drafted, a negative pickup agreement may not be acceptable to a lender, investors or other motion picture financiers.

Profit participation audits. The producer or profit participant should insist on broad auditing rights in any agreement that controls participation in film profits. Broad auditing rights may be defined as a film producer's negotiated authority to audit the books and records of a distributor with few restrictions. The producer should try to insert language in the audit rights provision that reduces distributor restrictions and limitations on the ability of the producer's representative to conduct an audit. It is not likely that an audit on behalf of motion picture profit participants will rise to the level of a complete audit that is so thoroughly executed that the auditor's only reservations have to do with unobtainable facts. In a complete audit, the auditor examines the system of internal control and the details of the books of account, including subsidiary records and supporting documents, while reviewing legality, mathematical accuracy, accountability and the application of accepted accounting principles. "Complete audit" is a technical accounting term establishing audit standards (same as unqualified audit). Producers can raise the question of a complete or unqualified audit in negotiations for audit rights although such audits are not likely to be permitted.

The producer should check with a profit participation audit firm in advance of signing the distribution agreement to determine what language in the distribution agreement would provide the auditor with the most freedom to conduct a useful audit. Also consider hiring the audit firm to review the distribution agreement before signing it. Provide that if amounts discovered by the auditor to be due the net profit participants exceed 10 percent of what was actually paid, the distributor must pay the auditor's fees and twice the amount due. Statements relating to the accounting reports furnished by the distributor should also require that such reports provide sufficient detail (i.e., enough information to permit a full understanding) of how the accompanying payment was determined.

Experienced entertainment attorneys recommend that profit participants audit any motion picture that has any likelihood of going into profits. The cost of an audit of studio books for a domestic theatrical release may fall in the $20,000 to $30,000 range, but few if any such audits, do not pay for themselves. Audits of major studios have uncovered millions of dollars in errors, most of which seem to be in the studio's favor. Profit participation auditor Steven Sills, whose firm conducts some 200–300 audits a year, says "$30,000 will generally cover the cost of a full blown audit of a major motion picture. The cost will be allocated among the net profit participants and generally recoveries are in the millions."[9] Laventhol and Horwath's Ben Newman agrees that audits "invariably pay for themselves." Newman says that "virtually all successful movies are audited. His largest recovery for a client has been $1 million."[10] Individual producers should make sure they have the funds available to pursue vigorously such audit rights and set aside $25,000 or so to cover the costs of an initial profit participation audit of the distributor (see the list of profit participation auditors at Appendix B).

Unfortunately, and contrary to what the profit participation auditors suggest, auditing is not the final answer to distributor problems. There are clearly limits to how much money an auditor can recover from a distributor. For example, many of the film distributor expenses deducted from the distributor's gross receipts in order to arrive at net profits are considered hard to audit expenses (i.e., they are difficult to verify or judge as to reasonableness). For this reason alone, it might better serve the overall film community for the entire system relating to the deduction of distribution expenses to be abandoned in favor of negotiated across-the-board gross participations for all participants. In addition, when the auditor makes a demand on the distributor the distributor may accept and pay on some of such issues but will not agree with most of the demands by the auditor. Thus, the distributor will almost always leave the net profit participants in the position of either accepting an amount far less than what should have been paid or going to court.

Third party disbursing agent. Negotiate with the distributor and arrange to have a third party, preferably a profit participation auditor, serve as the disbursing agent for all parties who are supposed to receive revenues generated by the exploitation of the film.

Takeover provisions. In negotiating with the distributor and/or completion guarantor, the producer may want to insert a more objective formula for triggering the takeover rights of either of those parties. In addition, the producer may want to provide that in the event of takeover, the distributor does not have the authority to change the producer's compensation, credit or continuing creative involvement when the takeover is prompted by factors beyond the control of the producer.

Substitution clauses. When seeking a preproduction distribution agreement from a small independent distributor, the producer may want to insert a substitution clause, which will allow the producer to select an alternate distributor under certain circumstances.

Litigation disclaimer. The producer should modify his or her litigation disclaimer slightly to state that he or she is not aware of any pending litigation, instead of stating that there is no litigation pending. The producer should also obtain corresponding representations and warranties from the distributor with respect to pending litigation, along with an indemnification provision that offers financial protection to the producer in the event that such litigation is pending and ultimately harms the ability of the distributor to exploit the producer's film or pay the producer amounts owed.

Final judgment. The producer should, at a minimum, see that language requiring the producer to reimburse the distributor for legal fees if the producer files a lawsuit against the distributor but fails to obtain a final judgment against the distributor is reciprocal. If possible, it would be even more favorable to the producer if the distributor's "final judgment" language could be eliminated since most lawsuits are settled prior to "final judgment" and substantial legal fees may have been incurred. In the alternative, this provision could specifically state that both parties assume the burden of paying their own legal fees.

Arbitration. The producer should seek to insert an arbitration clause in the distribution agreement, so that this more informal and less expensive form of dispute resolution can be utilized in lieu of going to court.

Entire agreement clause. Producers negotiating with various representatives of distributors should make notes of any oral representations made by such persons and systematically see that such representations are incorporated into the distribution agreement since otherwise they may be worthless. Oral representations are spoken statements as opposed to written communications. Since the distribution agreement will inevitably include an "entire agreement clause," systematically check to be certain that all oral promises made to the producer or negotiator by any authorized representative of the distributor that are being relied on by the producer are set out in the distribution agreement. Make notes of such promises following each discussion with the distributor's representatives.

The negotiating journal. A producer negotiating with a feature film distributor should maintain a journal in which all distribution agreement provisions offered by the producer but rejected by the distributor are entered during the course of the distribution deal negotiations. Thus, in the event that the deal has to go to litigation, the producer will be able to provide the court with a complete written history of the negotiations. Such evidence will prove helpful in determining whether the distribution deal was a contract of adhesion and whether some of its provisions were unconscionable.

The Limits of Negotiating

If after making a good faith attempt to negotiate some of the above issues with a friendly distributor, the producer and his or her attorney come away with the distinct feeling that there is definitely a limit to what can be accomplished at the negotiating table when the producer is in an inferior bargaining position and that the producer just signed a contract of adhesion filled with unconscionable provisions, it is probably because that is exactly what happened. And when it turns out that neither the producer nor any of his or her fellow net profit participants receive any significant net profits for their efforts they may want to consider other remedies beyond negotiation (remedies that are defined and discussed in *Film Finance and Distribution—A Dictionary of Terms*[11] and are further explored in this book's companion volume *Motion Picture Industry Reform*).

Some persons familiar with film industry distribution agreements suggest in their writings that the solution to the problems associated with the distribution agreement lie in negotiating a better agreement. For example, Robert Freedman says that since "the terms of the distribution contract will determine the financial returns of the motion picture, the producer should understand all terms of the agreement and negotiate those terms that are not to the producer's advantage. The key word is 'negotiate,' for it is unlikely that the producer will be able to get all of the terms changed to his or her advantage."[12]

Hillary Bibicoff also sees the net profit problem as something that can be solved through negotiations. She quotes from former studio accountant David Leedy, who says "participation agreements are complex, and in most cases due to the lack of commercial success, unnecessary . . . in those few instances where a motion picture is a commercial success, proper understanding of the business and careful drafting of the participation agreement can be worth hundreds of thousands (if not millions) of dollars."[13] Bibicoff also suggests that a "potential participant should use [the Bibicoff] article as a guide in attempting to negotiate some changes in his or her agreement with a studio. A potential participant should be aware of exactly what he or she is getting, which may well be nothing. If negotiations regarding the profit participation agreement are impossible, the participant may want to ask for more money up front. The key is—do not be drawn in by dreams of gold, but enter these agreements, if at all, with open eyes."[14]

Unfortunately, the truth is that the inequities in the strength of the bargaining positions of the parties to these agreements generally do not permit a negotiated solution to the vast majority of these problems. This book goes much further than any of these prior writings on the net profit problem, and probably is closer to the truth, when it states that it is very unlikely that the producer will be able to negotiate successfully most of the terms of a feature film distribution agreement. That is exactly what makes such agreements unconscionable. Thus, contrary to the somewhat misleading statements put forth by David Leedy, Hillary Bibicoff, Mark Litwak, Robert Freedman and others, negotiating a better distribution agreement is not the answer to the problems of film distribution.

Notwithstanding the foregoing film industry distribution deal checklist that might on the surface look somewhat encouraging, very few feature film producers or other net profit participants have sufficient leverage with film distributors to obtain favorable results on the vast majority of the issues discussed. Even those who do have such leverage in negotiating the deal may have no effective way to ensure that the distributor will properly implement the negotiated terms of that deal. Such producers must still rely on the inadequate remedies of auditing and litigation to obtain anything close to a proper accounting from a film distributor, and even then an accurate accounting is not likely. In addition, the leverage of those few producers who do have relevant power with the distributors is generally based on their status as insiders in the film industry (see *Who Really Controls Hollywood*) and/or the perception of the major studio/distributor executives that such persons are consistent suppliers of quality films (a subjective judgment at best). Additional remedies beyond negotiation are covered in *Motion Picture Industry Reform*, which is merely a book that discusses reform of the motion picture industry or FIRM (the Film Industry Reform Movement). Neither this book, nor others cited herein, will by themselves bring about significant change. It will take the combined efforts of many concerned industry professionals and private citizens working together. In the meantime, good luck in negotiating and implementing the feature film distribution deal.

Appendixes
Notes
Selected Bibliography
Index

APPENDIX A

Motion Picture Industry Overview

T HE THEATRICAL MOTION picture industry in the United States has changed substantially over the last three decades and continues to evolve rapidly. Historically, the so-called "major studio/distributors" financed, produced and distributed the vast majority of American-made motion pictures seen by most moviegoers. More recently, approximately half of the motion pictures released by the major studio/distributors have been produced by independent producers. Other movies are also released by independent distributors (i.e., those not otherwise associated with the major studio/distributors).

The following general description is a simplified overview of the complex process of producing and distributing motion pictures and is intended to be an aid to those not involved in the motion picture business to understand this unique industry. This overview, however, does not describe what will necessarily occur in the case of any particular motion picture.

Production of Motion Pictures

During the film-making process, which may take approximately twelve to twenty-four months from the start of the development phase to theatrical release, a film progresses through several major phases. These four primary stages of motion picture production are (1) development, (2) preproduction, (3) principal photography and (4) postproduction. A brief summary of each stage follows.

Development deal. Typically, a development deal is an agreement by a studio or production entity to provide early funding for a producer during the development of a motion picture project or projects. Development funds may also be provided to directors or screenwriters. The major studios commonly fund the development costs of many screenplays that are never approved for production, and those costs are recouped from the budgets of the movies that are produced as part of the studio's overhead charge.

Development hell. A film project that enters the development process, never actually gets production funding, but is not actually placed in turnaround either, can be said to be in development hell.

Development

In the development stage, underlying literary material for a motion picture project is acquired, either outright, through an option to acquire such rights or by engaging a writer to create original literary material. If the literary material is not in script form, a writer must be engaged to create a script. The script must be sufficiently detailed to provide the production company and others participating in the financing of a motion picture with enough information to estimate the cost of producing the motion picture.

Preproduction

During the preproduction stage, the production company usually selects (to the extent not chosen during the development stage) a director, actors and actresses, finalizes the budget and secures the necessary financing. Preproduction activities are usually more extensive than the development process. In cases involving unique or desired talent, commitments must be made to keep performers available for the principal photography.

Principal Photography

The process of principal photography (the actual filming of a motion picture) and the creation of special effects is the most costly stage of the production of a motion picture. Principal photography generally takes from six to twelve weeks to complete. Bad weather at locations, the illness of a cast or crew member, disputes with local authorities or labor unions, a director's or producer's decision to reshoot scenes for artistic reasons and other often unpredictable events can seriously delay the scheduled completion of principal photography and substantially increase its costs. If a motion picture reaches the principal photography stage, however, it usually will be completed.

Postproduction

During the postproduction stage, the editing, scoring and mixing of dialogue, music and sound effects tracks of a motion picture take place and master prints are prepared. These activities often require technically sophisticated editing, sound and effects work.

Distribution of Motion Pictures

Motion picture revenue is derived from the worldwide licensing of a motion picture: (a) for theatrical exhibition; (b) for nontheatrical exhibition (viewing in airplanes, hotels, military bases and other facilities); (c) for reproduction on video cassettes (and videodiscs) for home video use; (d) to pay television systems for delivery to television receivers by means of cable, over-the-air and satellite delivery systems; (e) to commercial television networks; and (f) to local commercial television stations. Revenue is also derived from licensing "ancillary rights" to a motion picture for creation of books, published music, soundtrack albums and merchandise.

The timing of revenues received from the various sources varies from film to film. Typically, theatrical receipts from United States distribution are received approximately 90 percent in the first twelve months after a film is first exhibited and 10 percent in the second twelve months. Theatrical receipts from the rest of the world are typically received 40 percent in the first year following initial theatrical release, 50 percent in the second year and 10 percent in the third year. Home video royalties are typically received 80 percent in the first year following theatrical release and 20 percent in later years. Pay and cable license fees are typically received 65 percent in the third year, 25 percent in the fourth year and 10 percent in the fifth year following theatrical release. The majority of syndicated domestic television receipts are typically received in the fourth, fifth and sixth years after theatrical release if there are no network television licenses and the sixth and seventh years if there are network licenses. The markets for film products have been undergoing rapid changes due to technological and other innovations. As a consequence, the sources of revenues available have been changing rapidly, and the relative importance of the various markets as well as the timing of such revenues has also changed and can be expected to continue to change.

Expenses incurred in distributing a motion picture are substantial and vary depending on many factors. These factors include the initial response by the public to the motion picture, the nature of its advertising campaign, the pattern of its release (e.g., the number of theatres booked and the length of time that a motion picture is in release).

The following is a brief summary of each of the sources of revenue of motion pictures and the distribution/licensing process associated with such sources.

United States Theatrical Distribution

In recent years, U.S. theatrical exhibition has generated a declining percentage of the total income earned by most pictures, largely because of the increasing importance of cable and pay television, home video and other ancillary markets. Nevertheless, the total revenues generated in the U.S. theatrical market are still likely to account for a significant percentage of revenues for a particular film. In addition, performance in the U.S. theatrical market generally also has a profound effect on the value of the picture in other media and markets.

Motion pictures are distributed to theatrical markets through numerous branch offices or subdistributors. Theatrical distribution requires the commitment of substantial funds in addition to a motion picture's negative cost. The distributor must arrange financing and personnel to: (a) create the motion picture's advertising campaign and distribution plan; (b) disseminate advertising, publicity and promotional material by means of magazines, newspapers, trailers and television; (c) duplicate and distribute prints of the motion picture; (d) "book" the motion picture in theatres; and (e) collect from exhibitors the distributor's share of the box office receipts from the motion picture. A distributor must monitor carefully the theatres to which it licenses its picture to ensure that the exhibitor keeps only the amounts to which it is entitled by contract and promptly pays all amounts due to the distributor. Distributors will sometimes reach negotiated settlements with exhibitors as to the amounts to be paid, and such settlements may relate to amounts due for several pictures.

For a picture's initial theatrical release, a U.S. theatre exhibitor will usually pay to a distributor a percentage of gross or net box office receipts that is negotiated based on the expected appeal of the motion picture and the stature of the distributor. The percentage remitted to the distributor is known as "film rentals" and customarily diminishes from week to week during the course of a picture's theatrical run. Typically, the distributor's share of total box office receipts over the entire initial theatrical release period will average between 60 to 35 percent; the exhibitor will retain the remaining 40 to 65 percent. The exhibitor will also retain all receipts from the sale of food and drinks at the theatre. Occasionally, an exhibitor will pay to the distributor a flat fee or percentage of box office receipts against a guaranteed amount. Pay television and new home entertainment equipment (such as video games, computers and videocassette players) offer competitive alternatives to motion picture theatres.

The major studio/distributors are often granted the right to license exhibition of a film in perpetuity, and normally have the responsibility for advertising and supplying prints and other materials to the exhibitors. Under some arrangements, the distributor retains a distribution fee from its gross receipts (i.e., the revenues generated from the exploitation of the film in all media and markets), which averages approximately 33 percent of the gross receipts, and recoups the costs incurred in distributing the film. The principal costs incurred are advertising and for duplicating the negative into prints for actual exhibition. The parties providing the production financing are then generally entitled to recover the cost of producing the film.

The amount the major studio/distributors spend on prints and advertising is generally left to the discretion of the distributor. In some instances, however, minimum expenditures are negotiated. In some instances, it may also be to the advantage of the producing entity to place a cap on the prints and advertising expenses, if possible.

Foreign Theatrical Distribution

While the value of the foreign theatrical market varies due to currency exchange rate fluctuations and the political conditions in the world or specific territories, it continues to provide a significant source of revenue for theatrical distribution and appears to be growing. Due to the fact that this market is comprised of a multiplicity of countries and, in some cases, requires the making of foreign-language versions, the distribution pattern stretches over a longer period of time than does the United States theatrical market. The major studio/distributors usually distribute motion pictures in foreign countries through local entities and the distribution fees for such entities usually vary between 35 percent and 40 percent depending on the territory or financial arrangements. These local entities generally will be either wholly owned by the distributor, a joint venture between the distributor and another motion picture company or an independent agent or subdistributor. Such local entities may also distribute motion pictures for other producers, including other major studio/distributors. Film licensing agreements with foreign exhibitors take a number of different forms, but they typically provide for payment to a distributor of a fixed percentage of box office receipts or a flat amount. Risks associated with foreign distribution include fluctuations in currency values and government restrictions or quotas on the percentage of receipts that may be paid to the distributor, the remittance of funds to the United States and the importation of motion pictures into a foreign country.

Home Video Rights

The home video market in the United States has experienced substantial growth in the past decade, and film industry analysts predict a period of continued growth (although at a slower rate) in the United States. Certain foreign territories, particularly Europe, have seen an increased utilization of home video units due to the relative lack of diversified television programming. Consequently, sales of videocassettes have increased in such markets in recent years. Although growth in this area may be reduced because of an increase in television programming in such foreign territories, receipts from home video in these markets can be expected to continue to be significant.

Films are generally released on home video six to nine months after initial domestic theatrical release of the picture, but before the exhibition of the picture on cable/pay or network television.

United States Television Distribution

Television rights in the United States are generally licensed first to pay television for an exhibition period following home video release, thereafter to network television for an exhibition period, then to pay television again, and finally syndicated to independent stations. Therefore, the owner of a film may receive payments resulting from television licenses over a period of six years or more.

Cable and Pay Television

Pay television rights include rights granted to cable, direct broadcast satellite, microwave, pay per view and other services paid for by subscribers. Cable and pay television networks usually license pictures for initial exhibition commencing six to twelve months after initial domestic theatrical release, as well as for subsequent showings. Pay television services such as Home Box Office, Inc. ("HBO") and Showtime/The Movie Channel, Inc. ("Showtime") have entered into output contracts with one or more major production companies on an exclusive or nonexclusive basis to assure themselves a continuous supply of motion picture programming. Some pay television services have required exclusivity as a precondition to such contracts.

The pay television market is characterized by a large number of sellers and few buyers. However, the number of motion pictures utilized by these buyers is extremely large and a great majority of motion pictures that receive theatrical exhibition in the United States are, in fact, shown on pay television.

Network Television

Although not such an important revenue source today, the broadcast network rights have been granted in past years to ABC, CBS, NBC or other entities formed to distribute programming to a large group of stations. These commercial television networks in the United States would license motion pictures for a limited number of exhibitions during a period that usually commenced two to three years after a motion picture's initial theatrical release. During recent years, only a small percentage of motion pictures have been licensed to network television, and the fees paid for such motion pictures have declined. This decline is generally attributed to the growth of the pay television and home video markets, and the ability of commercial television networks to produce and acquire made-for-television motion pictures at a lower cost than the license fees previously paid for theatrical motion pictures.

Television Syndication

Distributors also license the right to broadcast a motion picture on local, commercial television stations in the United States, usually for a period commencing five years after initial theatrical release of the motion picture, but earlier if the producer has not entered into a commercial television network license. This activity, known as "syndication," has become an important source of revenues as the number of, and competition for, programming among local television stations has increased.

Foreign Television Syndication

Motion pictures are now being licensed in the foreign television market in a manner similar to that in the United States. The number of foreign television stations as well as the modes of transmission (i.e., pay, cable, network) have been expanding rapidly, and the value of such markets has been likewise increasing and should continue to expand.

Producers may license motion pictures to foreign television stations during the same period they license such motion pictures to television stations in the United States; however, governmental restrictions and the timing of the initial foreign theatrical release of the motion pictures in the territory may delay the exhibition of such motion pictures in such territory.

Relicensing

The collective retained rights in a group of previously produced motion pictures is often a key asset, as such pictures may be relicensed in the pay and commercial television, home video and nontheatrical markets, and occasionally may be rereleased for theatrical exhibition.

Although no one can be certain of the value of these rights, certain older films retain considerable popularity, and may be relicensed for theatrical or television exhibition. New technologies brought about by the continuing improvements in electronics may also give rise to new forms of exhibition that will develop value in the future.

Other Ancillary Markets

A distributor may earn revenues from other ancillary sources, unless the necessary exploitation rights in the underlying literary property have been retained by writers, talent, composers or other thirdparties. The right to use the images of characters in a motion picture may be licensed for merchandising items such as toys, T-shirts and posters. Motion picture rights may also be licensed for novelizations of the screenplay, comic book versions of the screenplay and books about the making of the motion picture. The soundtrack of a motion picture may be separately licensed for soundtrack records and may generate revenue in the form of mechanical performance royalties, public performance royalties and sheet music publication royalties.

APPENDIX B
Profit Participation Audit Firms

THIS IS A list of the accounting firms in the Los Angeles area that are active in providing the highly specialized auditing services relating to film distribution. Such services are referred to in the industry as motion picture and television profit participation audits or participation/royalty/residual investigations.

1. Deloitte & Touche   310/551-6700
   2029 Century Park East
   Suite 300
   Los Angeles, CA 90067   Contact: Daryl Jamison

2. Gelfand Rennert Feldman   310/553-1707
   1880 Century Park East
   Suite 900
   Los Angeles, CA 90067   Contact: Wayne Coleman

3. Phillip Hacker and Company 310/553-6588
   1875 Century Park East
   Suite 2050
   Los Angeles, CA 90067   Contact: Phillip Hacker

4. Kenneth Levanthal & Company 310/277-0880
   2049 Century Park East
   Suite 1700
   Los Angeles, CA 90047   Contact: Jack Rodman

5. Nigro Karlin Segal   310/277-4657
   10100 Santa Monica Blvd.
   Suite 2460
   Los Angeles, CA 90067   Contact: Mickey Segal

6. Price Waterhouse   310/553-6030
   1880 Century Park East
   Century City
   West Los Angeles, CA 90067 Contact: Michelle Morgan

7. Sills and Adelman   310/201-8750
   2049 Century Park East
   Suite 3700
   Los Angeles, CA 90067   Contact: Steven Sills

APPENDIX C

ADI (Top 50) Market Rankings*

Rank	Market	ADI TV Households
1	New York (Kingston, Poughkeepsie & Bridgeport)	7,075,000
2	Los Angeles (Corona & San Bernardino)	5,036,000
3	Chicago (La Salle)	3,135,900
4	Philadelphia (Allentown, Reading, Vineland, Wildwood & Wilmington, DE)	2,736,000
5	San Francisco–Oakland–San Jose (Santa Rosa & Vallejo)	2,223,600
6	Boston (Derry, Manchester & Worcester)	2,115,500
7	Dallas–Ft. Worth	1,757,700
8	Detroit	1,726,700
9	Washington, DC	1,718,600
10	Houston	1,483,200
11	Cleveland (Akron, Canton & Sandusky)	1,445,100
12	Atlanta (Athens & Rome)	1,421,300
13	Tampa–St. Petersburg (Lakeland & Sarasota)	1,357,700
14	Minneapolis–St. Paul	1,355,000
15	Miami–Ft. Lauderdale	1,326,100
16	Seattle–Tacoma (Bellingham)	1,311,600
17	Pittsburgh	1,156,800
18	St. Louis (Mt. Vernon)	1,111,600
19	Denver (Steamboat Springs)	1,048,400
20	Phoenix (Prescott & Kingman)	1,029,900
21	Sacramento–Stockton	1,025,600
22	Baltimore	945,700
23	Hartford–New Haven (New London)	911,400
24	Orlando–Daytona Beach–Melbourne (Leesburg)	909,100
25	San Diego	906,400
26	Indianapolis (Marion)	873,800
27	Portland, OR	814,900
28	Milwaukee (Kenosha & Racine)	773,400

29	Kansas City (Lawrence)	763,500
30	Cincinnati	752,000
31	Charlotte (Hickory)	744,100
32	Nashville (Cookeville)	711,900
33	Columbus, OH (Chillicothe)	690,600
34	Raleigh–Durham (Fayetteville & Goldsboro)	683,000
35	Greenville–Spartanburg–Asheville (Toccoa)	650,900
36	New Orleans	641,700
37	Buffalo (Jamestown)	614,300
38	Memphis	609,600
39	Grand Rapids–Kalamazoo–Battle Creek (Muskegon)	604,500
40	Oklahoma City	600,000
41	Salt Lake City (Cedar City)	597,700
42	San Antonio (Kerrville)	588,800
43	Norfolk–Portsmouth–Newport News–Hampton	577,000
44	Harrisburg–York–Lancaster–Lebanon	564,400
45	Providence–New Bedford (Vineyard Haven)	559,600
46	West Palm Beach–Ft. Pierce-Vero Beach	533,800
47	Louisville	530,400
48	Greensboro–Winston-Salem–High Point (Burlington, NC)	522,2009
49	Birmingham (Gadsden)	518,600
50	Charleston–Huntington	511,900

*These areas of dominant influence (ADI) television market rankings are based on Arbitron estimates of U.S. television households as of January 1, 1991. Markets in parentheses have no ADI of their own.

AFMA Member List, 1992–1993

ABC Distribution Company
ADN Associates Limited
Alice Entertainment, Inc./Kidpix Entertainment
Allied Vision Limited
American First Run Studios
Angelika Films, Inc.
Arista Films, Inc.
Atlas International Film GMBH
Beyond Films Limited
Blue Ridge Entertainment
Broadstar Entertainment Corporation
Carolco Service, Inc.
Castle Communications PLC
Cinetel Films, Inc.
Cinetrust Entertainment Corporation
Cinevest Entertainment
Concorde-New Horizons
Cori International Film & Television
Crown International Pictures, Inc.
Curt/Esquire Films
Davian International Ltd.
Dino De Laurentiis Communications
Distant Horizon Ltd.
Double Helix Films
Filmark International Ltd.
Filmexport Group SRL.
Film Four International
Fries Distribution Company
Full Moon Entertainment
G.E.L. Distribution
Goldcrest Films & Television Limited
Golden Harvest/Golden Communications
Hemdale Pictures Corporation

Hills Entertainment Group
IFD Films and Arts Limited
Image Organization, Inc.
Imperial Entertainment B.V.
I.N.I. Entertainment Group, Inc.
Inter-Ocean Film Sales, Ltd.
I.R.S. Media International
ITC Entertainment Group
J & M Entertainment
Kings Road Entertainment, Inc.
Kodiak Films, Inc.
Largo Entertainment
Lone Star Pictures International, Inc.
Lway Productions
Majestic Films and Television
Manley Productions, Inc.
Mayfair Entertainment International
MCEG Sterling
Media Home Entertainment
Melrose Entertainment, Inc.
Metro-Goldwyn-Mayer, Inc.
Miracle Films
Miramax International
Moonstone Entertainment
Morgan Creek International
Motion Picture Corporation of America
Movie Acquisition Corporation Limited
The Movie Group
The Movie House Sales Company Limited
New Line Cinema Corporation
New World Entertainment
New Zealand Film Commission
Noble Productions, Inc./Noble Film

The Norkat Company, Ltd.
Norstar Entertainment, Inc.
North American Releasing, Inc.
Odyssey Distributors, Ltd.
Omega Entertainment Ltd.
Overseas Filmgroup
Paul International, Inc.
P.C. Films Corporation
Penta International
Playpont Films Ltd.
Promark Entertainment Group
Puzon Creative Entertainment of
    America
Pyramid Distribution
Quixote Productions
Rank Film Distributors
Rapi Films
Reel Movies International, Inc.
Republic Pictures International
The Robert Lewis Company
Saban Pictures International

Safir Films Limited
The Sales Company
SC Entertainment International
Scotti Brothers Pictures
Shapiro Glickenhaus Entertainment
Silver Star Film Corp.
Smart Egg Pictures
Spelling Films International
Starway International Corporation
The Summit Group (M.E.V.)
Sunny Film Corporation
Trans Atlantic Entertainment
Trimark Pictures
Troma, Inc.
Turner Pictures Worldwide
21st Century Film Corporation
Universal City Studios, Inc.
Viacom Pictures/Showtime Networks
Vision International
World Films, Inc.

Production-Financing/Distribution Agreement

THIS AGREEMENT ("Agreement") consists of the following documents:

"Deal Terms"
"Schedule I—Standard Terms and Conditions"
"Inducement Letter"
Exhibit "A" ("Net Proceeds Definition")
Exhibit "A-l" ("Gross Receipts Definition")
Exhibit "B" ("Delivery Schedule")
Exhibit "C" ("Pre-Approved Elements")
Exhibit "D" ("Cash Flow Schedule")
Exhibit "E" ("Assignment Agreement")
Exhibit "F" ("Laboratory Pledgeholder Agreement")
Exhibit "G" ("Production Account Takeover Letter")

all attached hereto and hereinafter collectively as the "Agreement Documents."

A. PARTIES—Filmright, Incorporated (the "Production Company"), Rocky Roundtree (the "Artist"), the Artist Lender Company, Inc. (the "Lender") and Worldwide Pictures, a division of Worldwide Studios, Inc. (the "Studio/Distributor").

B. PICTURE—The feature-length motion picture currently entitled "Invasion From Chunga" ("the "Picture" #00679) based on the screenplay of the same title written by John Q. Screenwriter (the "Screenplay").

C. DATE OF AGREEMENT—As of June 25, 1993

DEAL TERMS

1. CONTINGENCIES—This Agreement and the Studio/Distributor's obligations hereunder are subject to the satisfaction of all of the following:

a. Clearance by the Studio/Distributor of the Production Company's chain-of-title to the rights of the Picture; and

b. Signature and delivery of the Agreement Documents to the Studio/Distributor.

2. PICTURE SPECIFICATIONS—The Production Company shall produce, complete and deliver to Studio/Distributor the Picture pursuant to the terms hereof.

a. Basic Elements—(1) Underlying Material/Screenplay—Original screenplay entitled "Invasion From Chunga," written by the Artist.

(2) Director—Artist.

(3) Producer—Artist.

(4) Principal Cast—Tentatively, Artist as "Nigor," Rebecca Everyday as "Mame," Gerald McCormick as "Rend," Webber Feet as "Lauren" and James Dee as "Mondo." The Studio/Distributor shall have mutual approval with the Production Company of the actors and actresses engaged to play the roles set forth in the preceding sentence (persons named above being pre-approved). The Production Company shall select all other cast members in its sole discretion; provided, however, that the aggregate compensation required therefor shall not exceed the aggregate compensation provided therefor in the Approved Production Budget.

b. Production/Delivery Requirements:

(1) Production Specifications

(a) Start Date—On or about August 20, 1993.

(b) Production Schedule—Approximately eleven (11) comprised of five (5) day work weeks with two (holidays off, for a total of fifty-three (53) production days.

(c) Locations—Numerous locations in Wyoming. The Studio/Distributor shall have a right of consultation with respect to such locations.

(d) Production Legal Responsibility—The Law Offices of John J. Jingleheimer, III, P.C., Attention: John Jingleheimer.

(e) Studio/Distributor Production Executives—Randy Reminder and Edward Numbers.

(2) Delivery Specifications:

(a) Delivery Date—June 3, 1993 (the "Delivery Date"), which date shall be extended for up to thirty (30) days for any Extrinsic Event or due to any location requirements, producer, director and/or cast unavailability, weather conditions and/or other similar contingencies. Prior to the Delivery Date, the Production Company shall deliver certain items to the Studio/Distributor, or take certain actions, as follows:

(i) On or Before April 22, 1993—A print of the "locked" Picture together with a temporary magnetic sound track, i.e. a work print of the finished Picture of such quality that screening prints may be made therefrom for viewing by potential exhibitors;

(ii) On or Before May 1, 1993—A final "answer print" of the Picture, i.e., a final approved composite answer print of the finished Picture of such quality that interpositives may be made therefrom, and one (1) two-track print master.

After Production Company approval of the final answer print, the Production Company shall order an interpositive from the Laboratory;

(iii) On or Before May 10, 1993 — The Artist, on behalf of the Production Company, or in the event the Artist is not available, the director of photography or editor of the Picture (whichever of the two the Artist designates), shall approve the "check print" made from the internegative ordered by the Studio/Distributor. If the Artist appoints a designee and the Artist's designee fails to approve such check print, the Studio/Distributor, upon notice to the Production Company, shall have the right to thereafter approve the check print, unless within thirty-six (36) hours from such notice, the Artist makes himself available to approve the check print.

(iv) On or Before May 20, 1993 — The Dialogue and Cutting Continuity, item l(g) of the Delivery Schedule, 35mm 4 channel STEREO Magnetic MUFX master, item 2(d) of the Delivery Schedule, 35mm textless background original negative and print therefrom, item l(k) of the Delivery Schedule, and

(v) On or Before June 10, 1993 — The remaining Delivery Items as set forth on the Delivery Schedule.

(b) Laboratory — Film Laboratories, Inc., Studio City, California.

c. Controls/Approvals/Obligations — Except as specifically provided elsewhere in this Agreement, the Production Company shall have exclusive control and responsibility for all day-to-day production decisions and activities of the Picture.

d. Production Company's Right of Consultation — The Studio/Distributor shall consult in good faith with the Production Company regarding the distribution pattern and ad campaign for the initial U.S. theatrical release; provided, however that the Studio/Distributor's decisions with respect thereto shall be final.

3. FINANCING:

a. Approved Production Budget: Five Million Dollars ($5,000,000) ("Approved Production Budget"), inclusive of the "Artist's Fee," as defined in clause 3.b below, but exclusive of a contingency fund of Five Hundred Thousand Dollars ($500,000) (the "Contingency"). The Contingency shall be available as and when required by the Production Company in connection with production of the Picture.

b. Budgeted Fee Payable to Artist — Six Hundred Fifty Thousand Dollars ($650,000) shall be paid to the Artist for the writing, producing, directing and acting services of the Artist ("Artist's Fee"). The Artist's Fee shall be increased to a total of Eight Hundred Thousand Dollars ($800,000) by payment of a bonus of an additional Two Hundred Thousand Dollars ($200,000) (the "Bonus") if the actual production cost of the Picture does not exceed Five Million Dollars ($5,000,000). For such purposes, the calculation of the Picture's actual production cost shall exclude:

(i) Non-Budgeted Union Costs, in accordance with clause 3.c below, and

(ii) Costs resulting from changes requested in writing by the Studio/Distributor in the Approved Screenplay and/or Approved Production Schedule, i.e., changes which increase the Approved Production Budget, provided, however, that such costs shall not include:

(a) Any additional costs associated with supplying the Studio/Distributor with necessary "cover shots" in accordance with clause A.2.b(7) of Schedule I, or

(b) Any costs resulting from the Studio/Distributor's failure to fund the Picture in accordance with the terms hereof after the Production Company's signature is affixed to this Agreement (provided however, that the Production Company has notified the Studio/Distributor in writing in advance of the anticipated incursion of such costs and given the Studio/Distributor seventy-two (72) hours to cure such failure, and any other matter as to which the Studio/Distributor agrees in writing shall constitute breakage);

The above stated Bonus shall be reduced on a dollar-for-dollar basis by an amount equal to the amount that the actual production costs of the Picture exceed the Approved Production Budget.

The Bonus shall be payable, if at all, out of the first dollars of the Contingency. In that regard, the Studio/Distributor shall, upon delivery of the Picture, request that all Studio/Distributor departments submit their costs to the Studio/Distributor's production comptroller, who shall review the same, prepare and submit to the Production Company a final cost statement for the Picture. Such final cost statement shall set forth the remaining Picture costs to be paid for from the Approved Production Budget and Contingency. The Production Company, likewise, shall expeditiously collect all costs associated with the Picture, including the aforementioned final cost statement, as soon as possible after delivery thereof. The Production Company shall thereafter provide the Studio/Distributor with a final cost statement for the Picture when all material costs have been paid and advise the Studio/Distributor of the amount of the Bonus and within thirty (30) days therefrom, the Studio/Distributor will authorize the Production Company to pay any Bonus due the Artist from the remaining balance in the "Production Account", as defined below, or pay the Artist the same (or any balance due) directly.

The Artist's Fee, including the Bonus, if any, shall be fully credited against all sums payable to the Production Company as Participations pursuant to clause 4.b below.

c. Non-Budgeted Union Costs—To the extent that non-budgeted union costs are incurred, pursuant to provisions of the DGA Basic Agreement which may hereafter become applicable with respect to individuals employed on the Picture, the Studio/Distributor shall be responsible for such additional non-budgeted union costs and they shall be added to both the Approved Production

Budget and the "Picture Price," as defined below. In no way shall any portion of the Bonus payable to the Artist be used for the payment of such union costs nor shall the computation or payment of the Picture Price or payment of the Bonus be in any way affected by such union-costs.

d. Production Funds—The Studio/Distributor shall advance funds to the Production Company for the production of the Picture up to the total amount of the Approved Production Budget, and if required thereafter, up to and including the Contingency, in fixed installments and consistent with a cash flow schedule to be mutually approved by the Production Company and the Studio/Distributor [a copy of which is attached hereto as Exhibit "D"] (the "Production Funds"). The Production Company shall be deemed to have repaid the Production Funds upon delivery of the Picture.

e. Take-Over—If, based on the information available (including, but not limited to, the weekly reporting papers furnished by the Production Company), the Studio/Distributor reasonably believes that the estimated cost of production of the Picture will exceed the Contingency ("Projected Overage"), then:

(1) Efforts to Reduce Projected Overage—The Studio/Distributor and the Production Company shall confer for a period of not more than three (3) days on a method to reduce the Projected Overage to a point which will not exceed the Contingency;

(2) Reduction Plan—If the Studio/Distributor and the Production Company agree to a reduction plan that will ensure that the Contingency will not be exceeded, such reductions shall become part of the Approved Production Budget; but

(3) Take-Over—If, however, the parties are unable to agree upon such a reduction plan within said three (3) day period, the Studio/Distributor shall have the right to "take over" the Picture, pursuant to the provisions of clause 2.a.(11) of Part A of Schedule I hereof.

f. Studio/Distributor's Security Interest—To secure the Studio/Distributor's advance of the Production Funds to the Production Company hereunder, the Production Company assigns to the Studio/Distributor as security all right, title and interest in and to the Picture (including, without limitation, all interest in the results and proceeds of the services of all persons engaged in connection with the Picture), whether now owned or hereafter acquired, including, but not limited to, the copyright, all negatives, film, tape and other physical properties created or acquired for the Picture. The Production Company agrees to execute UCC-1 financing statements, an assignment in the form attached hereto as Exhibit "E" and a Laboratory Pledgeholder Agreement in the form attached hereto as Exhibit "F." The Studio/Distributor shall have the right to file and/or record the financing statements and assignments with governmental entities (including the United States Copyright Office) that the

Studio/Distributor may determine. The security interest granted to the Studio/Distributor hereby shall be prior to all other security interests, other than any security interests in favor of guilds, unions and laboratories. At the request of the Studio/Distributor, the Production Company shall execute and deliver all such further documents as the Studio/Distributor may deem necessary or appropriate to perfect the security interest created by this instrument and the Studio/Distributor's rights pursuant to this clause 3.f.

4. CONSIDERATION—a. Picture Price—The amount actually expended by the Production Company in connection with the Production Company's production of the Picture, but in no event shall such amount exceed the Approved Production Budget and Contingency (the "Picture Price"), which amount shall, as aforementioned, be advanced, as the Production Funds to the Production Company during the course of production of the Picture, if and when needed.

b. Participation—The Studio/Distributor shall pay the Production Company the following:

(1) Gross Receipts at First Breakeven—Twenty Percent of "Gross Receipts," as defined in and payable pursuant to Exhibit "A-l" attached hereto, from first dollar until "Cash Breakeven," as defined below, is achieved ("First Breakeven");

(2) Gross Receipts at Second Breakeven—Thereafter ten percent (10%) of Gross Receipts in excess of First Breakeven until an additional twenty percent (20%) of Gross Receipts is achieved ("Second Breakeven").

(3) Gross Receipts After Second Breakeven—Thereafter, five percent (5%) of Gross Receipts in excess of Second Breakeven until "Initial Actual Breakeven," as defined below, is achieved; and

(4) Additional Gross Receipts or Net Proceeds—Thereafter, the greater of five percent (5%) of Gross Receipts or thirty percent (30%) of Net Proceeds, out of which the Production Company will bear (in either case) all contingent participations payable to third parties.

For purposes hereof, Cash Breakeven shall mean that point at which Net Proceeds is reached, as defined in Exhibit "A" attached hereto, but with a fifteen percent (15%) distribution fee in lieu of any other distribution fee set forth therein. Initial Actual Breakeven shall mean that point at which Net Proceeds is reached pursuant to Exhibit "A."

Except as provided in this clause 4.b., no other participations may be granted by the Production Company in connection with the Picture except to the extent paid by the Production Company out of the consideration otherwise payable to the Production Company hereunder. The Studio/Distributor agrees to pay directly to third party participants any share of the Production Company's share of Gross or Net Proceeds as assigned by the Production Company; provided, however, that no such third party shall have independent audit rights with respect to such participations as otherwise granted the Production Company in Exhibit "A" and Exhibit "A-l" attached hereto.

c. Soundtrack Album Advance and Producer's Royalty—Two-thirds of the amount of any advance from the record company acquiring the soundtrack distribution rights ("Record Advance") in excess of the cost of production of the soundtrack and soundtrack album for the Picture (the "Soundtrack Album") (including, but not limited to, producer advances, artist's advances, third party costs and all other costs which are customarily recognized in the phonograph record industry) shall be payable to the Production Company for its own account; the remaining one-third shall be payable to the Studio/Distributor. The Production Company may elect to utilize any portion of its share of such excess of the Record Advance to cover costs of production of the Picture in excess of the Approved Production Budget except that such monies may not be used to pay the Production Company compensation for services rendered in connection with the production of the Picture (as opposed to the Soundtrack Album) in excess of that provided for in such Approved Production Budget. In the event of such election by the Production Company, the Studio/Distributor shall proportionately contribute a similar amount toward such excess costs of production from its share of any such advance.

If after all royalties payable to any and all third parties rendering services in connection with the Soundtrack Album have been deducted there remain further royalties payable, the Production Company shall be entitled to up to ten percent (10%) of the suggested retail list price (or the wholesale equivalent thereof) derived from the exploitation of the Soundtrack Album for the Artist's services as producer of the Soundtrack Album. The next twenty percent (20%) of record royalties shall be payable to the Studio/Distributor and the balance of such royalties remaining thereafter shall be divided equally between Studio/Distributor and the Production Company.

5. RIGHTS:

a. Rights Granted/Reserved:

(1) Granted: Subject to Clauses 5.a.(2), 7.a.(2) and 7.b.(2) below:

(a) Rights Acquired—Effective upon delivery of the Picture by the Production Company to the Studio/Distributor and payment of the Picture Price by the Studio/Distributor to the Production Company, as between Studio/Distributor and the Production Company, the Studio/Distributor shall own all rights in the Picture, including, without limitation, rights specified in Clauses A.5.a and A.5.b of Schedule I. The Production Company reserves no rights of any kind or nature in the Picture. In that regard, the parties hereto understand that there may be certain composers who will wish to retain certain publishing rights in connection with the original compositions they create for use in or in connection with the Picture. Accordingly, the Studio/Distributor shall consult with the Production Company regarding the engagement of such composers, but the Studio/Distributor's decision shall be final.

(b) Soundtrack Album Right of Approval—The Studio/Distributor shall have approval (not to be unreasonably withheld) of the record company with which the Soundtrack Album for the Picture is placed and the terms of the agreement therefor.

(2) Reservation of Book Publishing Rights—The Production Company shall have the right to create a "making of" book of the Picture containing an essay and other materials prepared by the Artist (including the Underlying Material). The Studio/Distributor reserves the right to approve the contents of such book (such approval not to be unreasonably withheld). The Studio/Distributor shall have a right of first negotiation to acquire the publication rights to such book. If pursuant to such right of first negotiation, the parties cannot agree on terms offered by the Production Company, the Studio/Distributor shall have a continuing right of first refusal with respect to any terms less favorable to the Production Company which the Production Company is thereafter willing to accept. Subject to the foregoing, the Production Company shall retain all revenue payable from the publisher in connection with such publication. If pursuant to the terms of the WGA Basic Agreement, the Artist would be accorded sole separation of rights were the Artist a member of the WGA, the Studio/Distributor will grant Artist all benefits to which writers accorded sole separation of rights are entitled under the WGA Agreement, including, but not limited to, all benefits pertaining to novelization rights. If no other writer is engaged to perform writing services in connection with the Picture prior to the completion of principal photography thereof, the Artist shall be deemed to be entitled to sole separation of rights for purposes of this sub-clause (2).

   b. Distribution Term—Perpetuity.

   c. Distribution Territory—The Universe.

   d. Copyright Ownership—Worldwide.

6. NOTICES AND PAYMENTS:

a. To Production Company:	Filmright, Incorporated 850 Montana Avenue, Suite 305 Santa Monica, CA 90031
with a courtesy copy to:	John J. Jingleheimer, III, Attorney 89045 Wilshire Blvd., Suite 405 Los Angeles, CA 90045
b. To Studio/Distributor:	Worldwide Pictures 100 Worldwide Plaza, Suite 500 World City, California 98765 Attention: Feature Law Department.

7. SPECIAL PROVISIONS:

a. Production Company Special Provisions:

(1) The Studio/Distributor's Print and Ad Commitment—The Studio/Distributor shall spend no less than $7,000,000 for Prints and advertising expenses in connection with the Picture as such expenses are defined in clause A.6 of Exhibit "A" attached hereto.

(2) Remakes and Sequels:

(a) Theatrical Remakes and Sequels—If the Studio/Distributor determines at any time hereafter to exercise its theatrical Derivative Distribution Rights granted hereunder, the Studio/Distributor, the Production Company and the Artist shall then negotiate with each other for their mutual participation in a theatrical production based on such rights on terms no less favorable to the Production Company and the Artist than those contained herein. If no agreement is reached within thirty (30) days after such negotiations have commenced, all such rights shall be frozen.

(b) Television Remakes and Sequels—If the Studio/Distributor determines at any time to exercise its television Derivative Distribution Rights granted hereunder, the Studio/Distributor, the Production Company and the Artist shall then negotiate with each other for their mutual participation in a television production based on such rights in whatever format (including but not limited to a T.V. special, movie-of-the-week, pilot, multi-part series or series). If no agreement is reached within thirty (30) days after such negotiations have commenced, or if the network fails to approve the participation of any of the foregoing parties, all such rights shall be frozen.

(3) Premieres—The Studio/Distributor shall make the Picture available for one premier benefit in Jackson Hole, Wyoming, subject to the Studio/Distributor's approval of the recipient of the charitable funds derived therefrom.

b. The Production Company's and the Artist's Special Provisions:

(1) Artist's Cutting Rights—The Artist shall be entitled to the cutting rights as set forth below, which rights shall be solely personal to the Artist and not transferable to any other individual:

(a) Preconditions—All cutting rights granted to the Artist hereunder are conditioned upon the following:

(i) The cost of production must not exceed 110% a of the Approved Production Budget and Contingency; provided however, that the following costs shall be excluded from the determination of such excess, if any:

(A) Costs caused by an Extrinsic Event;

(B) Costs reimbursed by insurance coverage on the Picture;

(C) Costs resulting from the addition of new scenes at the request of the Studio/Distributor not required by the Approved Screenplay;

(D) Costs resulting from changes required by the Studio/Distributor in the

Approved Screenplay or Production Schedule after the Production Budget has previously been approved by the Studio/Distributor; and

(E) Non-Budgeted Union Costs, in accordance with clause 3.c above, costs resulting from changes requested in writing by the Studio/Distributor in the Approved Screenplay and/or Approved Production Schedule which increase the Approved Production Budget, any costs resulting from the Studio/Distributor's failure to fund the Picture in accordance with the terms hereof after the authorized Production Company representative has signed this Agreement, provided, however, that the Production Company has notified the Studio/Distributor in writing in advance of the anticipated incursion of such costs and given the Studio/Distributor seventy-two (72) hours to cure such failure, and any other matter as to which the Studio/Distributor agrees in writing shall constitute breakage.

(ii) The Picture as delivered hereunder must in all events substantially and materially conform to the Screenplay as approved by the Studio/Distributor hereunder;

(iii) The Picture must have a running time of not less than 95 nor more than 110 minutes with a rating no more restrictive than "R";

(iv) The Picture (and all major delivery items) must be fully delivered on the dates required hereunder; and

(v) The Artist is ready, willing and able and does so exercise such rights within the Studio/Distributor's time release schedule, bidding and distribution requirements, provided, however, that in no event shall the requirements of this sub-clause (v) entitle the Studio/Distributor to accelerate the Delivery Date.

(b) U.S. Theatrical Cut—The Artist shall be entitled to determine the final cut of the Picture intended for its initial U.S. Theatrical release.

(c) Other Versions—The Artist shall have the first opportunity to cut the other versions of the Picture enumerated below:

(i) Additional Pre-conditions—All additional cutting rights granted the Artist in this clause 7(c) are additionally conditioned upon the following:

(A) No Additional Cost to Studio/Distributor—The exercise of such rights shall not be at any additional expense to the Studio/Distributor; and

(B) Studio/Distributor Has Final Determination—The Studio/Distributor shall communicate its objections (if any) to the Artist's creative decisions with respect to the exercise of his additional cutting rights hereunder as and when such decisions are communicated to the Studio/Distributor; provided, however, that if there is any disagreement between the Studio/Distributor and the Artist with respect to such cuts under this clause 7(c), the Studio/Distributor shall make the final determination in its sole discretion.

(ii) U.S. Free Television Version—The United States television version (in which connection the Artist will have shot alternative scenes when it was reasonably foreseeable that such scenes shot for the version referred to in (2) above are not likely to be acceptable for such network television version), further subject to time and network standards and practices requirements;

(iii) In-Flight Version—The U.S. "in-flight" exhibition version, further subject to the exhibitor's time and rating requirements;

(iv) Syndication Version—The U.S. television syndication version, subject to time and standards and practices requirements, which version shall be furnished to the Studio/Distributor's licensees (and for which the Studio/Distributor will not be responsible for such licensees failure to broadcast the version furnished);

(v) Pay and Cable Television Version—The U.S. pay and cable television versions, further subject to time requirements.

(vi) U.K. Version—A different English language version for distribution in the U.K. (if such is required) provided that such version is edited in the United States. Notwithstanding the foregoing, if the Production Company pays for all transportation and other living expenses incurred in connection with the cutting of the U.K. version of the Picture by the Artist in the U.K., the Artist shall have the right to do so in the U.K.

(2) First Negotiation Right for Artist's Next Theatrical Motion Picture Project—The Studio/Distributor and the Production Company shall exclusively negotiate in good faith with respect to their mutual participation in the production and distribution of.the Artist's next theatrical motion picture project. If no agreement is reached within thirty (30) days after such negotiations have commenced, neither party shall have any further obligations to the other with respect thereto. Subject to the provisions of clause 7.a.(2) of the Deal Terms, the following motion pictures are excluded from the provisions of this sub-clause (2):

(a) Remakes and Sequels—Any remakes and sequels of the Picture; and

(b) Outside Offered Projects—Motion picture projects not developed by the Artist with respect to which the Artist is offered employment in the capacity of producer, director, player and/or writer.

(3) First Negotiation Right for Artist's Writing, Performing and Directing Services on Live Stage Productions—If at any time the Studio/Distributor elects to exercise its live stage rights hereunder, the Studio/Distributor and the Production Company shall exclusively negotiate in good faith with respect to the Artist's writing, performing and directing services on any live stage productions produced in connection with such exercise. If no agreement is reached within thirty (30) days after such negotiations have commenced, such live stage rights shall be frozen.

(4) Credit—In lieu of a possessory credit for the Artist's directing services, the Artist shall be accorded credit above the regular and artwork title in sub-

stantially the form: "A Rocky Roundtree Picture" on all the positive prints of the Picture and in paid advertising for the Picture (including in the billing block which shall appear on all jackets of video cassettes of the Picture) and the credit "A Rocky Roundtree Picture" shall be accorded to the Artist above the regular title on all positive prints of the Picture and in paid advertising for the Picture (including in the billing block which shall appear on all jackets of videocassettes of the Picture) in the following size of type:

(a) Positive Prints—75% of title on screen in the main titles (to be set forth on two separate cards).

(b) Paid Advertising—100% of non-artwork title with a floor of 25% of the average size of the artwork title type.

(5) Videocassette—For the Production Company when commercially available.

(6) Transportation and Expenses:

(a) Transportation—One (1) round-trip fare, first class, if available, and if used, for the Artist. One (1) additional round-trip fare, first class, if available and if used. Also, exclusive ground transportation to and from the airport.

(b) Expense Allowance—Two thousand dollars ($2,000) per week in major cities such as such as London and Los Angeles; elsewhere One Thousand Five Hundred Dollars ($1,500).
per week.

c. Single Picture License—The Studio/Distributor hereby grants to the Production Company a one-picture license in the Underlying Material/Screenplay, as set forth in clause 2.a.(1) above, and any other rights that the Studio/Distributor may now or hereafter own or control in connection with the Picture for the sole purpose of the production of the Picture. Said license shall terminate automatically upon delivery of the Picture to the Studio/Distributor or upon the Studio/Distributor's election to take over the Picture under Clause 3.e above.

8. DEFINITION OF TERMS—Terms of art used in these Deal Terms which are not defined herein shall have the meaning set forth in the other Agreement Documents. Terms of art not defined in the Agreement Documents shall be defined as commonly understood in the entertainment industry.

9. MISCELLANEOUS PROVISIONS—(a) Entire Agreement—The Agreement Documents constitute the entire agreement between the parties hereto and supersede all prior agreements, representations and warranties, if any, made with respect to the subject matter hereof.

(b) Amendments—This Agreement may be amended only by written agreement executed by all of the parties.

(c) Inconsistent Provisions—To the extent any terms or conditions of the Standard Terms and Conditions are inconsistent with the Deal Terms, the Deal Terms shall govern.

PRODUCTION COMPANY—Filmright, Incorporated
By: _____
    James W. Producer, President

STUDIO/DISTRIBUTOR—Worldwide Pictures,
a Division of Worldwide Studios, Inc.
By: _____
    Jeffrey Wilson, Vice President

The signature of the undersigned is to acknowledge its agreement to the foregoing only in its capacity as lender of the directing services of the Artist. The Artist Lender Company, Inc.
By: _____
    Rocky Rountree, President

Schedule I
STANDARD TERMS AND CONDITIONS

The Standard Terms and Conditions of the Agreement dated as of June 25, 1993 by and between Worldwide Pictures, a division of Worldwide Studios, Inc. (the "Studio/Distributor"), a California corporation, and Filmright, Incorporated (the "Production Company"), and the Artist Lender Company, Inc., for the services of Rocky Rountree (the "Artist").

A.
STANDARD P-F/D PROVISIONS

1. CONTINGENCIES/APPROVAL OF CHAIN OF TITLE—To clear the chain-of-title, the Production Company must establish that the Production Company is the sole owner of the Underlying Material (defined below) free of any claim, lien, limitation or condition of any kind to the extent necessary for Studio/Distributor to fully exploit all rights granted the Studio/Distributor hereunder. As used herein, the term "Underlying Material" (if not specifically otherwise identified in the Deal Terms) shall mean any and all literary, dramatic or musical material (excluding material created by the Studio/Distributor or directly acquired by the Studio/Distributor from an independent third party) that is:

    a. written or composed for use in the Picture;

    b. acquired, supplied or assigned by the Production Company (or by any other person that produced or was associated in the production of the Picture) for or in connection with the Picture;

    c. included in the Picture; and/or

    d. on which the Picture is based in whole or in part.

2. PRODUCTION/DELIVERY SPECIFICATIONS—a. Production Spe-

cifications—If the Picture has not been produced as of the date hereof, the following terms and conditions shall govern (if and where applicable):

(1) Start Date—Principal photography of the Picture shall commence on or about the Start Date set forth in the Deal Terms, if any.

(2) Production Schedule—If there is a Production Schedule set forth in the Deal Terms, there shall be no substantial deviations therefrom unless approved in writing by the Studio/Distributor.

(3) Locations—If locations are specified in the Deal Terms, principal photography of the Picture shall take place at such locations unless otherwise agreed to by the Studio/Distributor in writing.

(4) MPAA—The Picture shall be produced in accordance with the Production Code of the Motion Picture Association of America or any successor thereto, if any.

(5) Dailies—The Production Company shall, upon the Studio/Distributor's reasonable request from time to time, permit the Studio/Distributor as the financier/distributor of the Picture to view and otherwise examine, prior to the delivery of the Picture, any materials or properties relating to the Picture which the Studio/Distributor may designate (including, without limitation, "dailies" and then existing edited versions of the Picture), provided that such viewing or examination does not materially interfere with the production of the Picture or violate the rights of any person under any applicable collective bargaining agreement to which the Studio/Distributor is a signatory.

(6) Records—The Production Company shall maintain accurate records of all of the Production Company's operations in accordance with generally accepted accounting principles and practices in the motion picture industry. The Studio/Distributor shall have the right to audit such records at any reasonable time after three (3) days notice of its intent to do so.

(7) Weekly Cost Reports—Commencing no later than the Start Date, the Production Company shall submit weekly cost reports on the Picture to the Studio/Distributor until delivery of the Picture hereunder.

(8) Insurance—(a) Types of Insurance Obtained by Production Company—The Production Company agrees to maintain the insurance coverage set forth below. Except to the extent indicated otherwise, all such insurance shall have such limits of liability, be subject to such deductions and exclusions, and be maintained during such periods, as may be customary in the motion picture industry.

(i) Cast Insurance;

(ii) Negative Film Insurance;

(iii) Extra Expense Insurance;

(iv) Production Company Errors and Omissions—Such policy shall:

(A) Liability Minimum—Have limits of liability of not less than $1,000,000 per claim and $5,000,000 in the aggregate;

(B) Primary Coverage—Pursuant to its terms provide primary errors and omissions coverage and not contributory coverage, notwithstanding any other errors and omissions insurance which the Production Company and/or the Studio/Distributor may obtain or maintain; and

(C) Minimum Coverage Period—Be maintained in full force and effect by the Production Company, at the Production Company's sole cost and expense commencing on the date hereof and continuing for a period of not less than three (3) years following the initial theatrical release of the Picture in the Distribution Territory, it being understood that in the event of cancellation or non-renewal, the Production Company shall obtain and maintain a substitute policy therefor (and promptly deliver to the Studio/Distributor evidence of the maintenance of such substitute policy), the terms of which shall be in accordance with the provisions of this clause A.2.a.(8). The Production Company agrees to give the Studio/Distributor not less than thirty (30) days prior written notice of any cancellation or non-renewal of such insurance policy.

(v) Comprehensive General and Automobile Liability—Such policy shall have limits of liability of not less than $1,000,000 per claim.

(vi) Third Party Property Damage—Such policy shall have limits of liability of not less than $500,000 per claim.

(vii) Miscellaneous Equipment Floater;

(viii) Props, Sets and Wardrobe All-Risk Floater;

(ix) Workers' Compensation or Equivalent

(x) Employer's Liability.

(b) Approved Carriers—All such insurance shall be placed with Pacific Indemnity Company, Lloyds of London, Fireman's Fund Insurance Company or other insurance carriers approved by the Studio/Distributor.

(c) Evidence of Insurance—The Production Company shall cause the Studio/Distributor to be added as a named insured, as its interest may appear, under the insurance policies referred to above in (a)(i) through (viii), inclusive, and shall, as soon as practicable (but in any event prior to the commencement of principal photography of the Picture) provide the Studio/Distributor with written evidence satisfactory to the Studio/Distributor of the maintenance of such insurance policies and of the provisions thereof (including evidence that the Studio/Distributor has been named as a named insured as aforesaid).

(9) Production Cash Flow Schedule—The Production Company immediately shall prepare and deliver to the Studio/Distributor a Production Cash Flow Schedule based upon the Approved Production Budget. The Production Company agrees that there shall be no acceleration of the Production Cash Flow Schedule without the prior written consent of the Studio/Distributor's Vice President in charge of production (presently Donna Q. Dingleberry).

(10) Production Account/Production Account Take-Over Letters—The Production Company shall maintain a production account (the "Production

Account"), account number BDX8796200LD in the name of the Production Company at the World Film Bank, located at 123 Fort Hill Road, Jackson Hole, Wyoming 89089, which Production Account shall be separate from the Production Company's other funds; all funds to be advanced pursuant to this Agreement shall be deposited in the Production Account. No sums shall be paid from the Production Account other than for production of the Picture, unless and only to the extent that such items are specified in the Approved Production Budget. The Production Company shall obtain and furnish to the Studio/Distributor written confirmation, in the form of Exhibit "G" attached hereto, from said bank of its waiver of any right of "set-off" or similar right with respect to the Production Account. The Studio/Distributor will not exercise any of its rights thereunder to take over the Production Account unless it has taken over production of the Picture. The Studio/Distributor may, at any time after it has taken over production of the Picture, require that copies of all bank statements with respect to the Production Account be delivered to it.

(11) Take-Over—(a) Production Company's Self Help Right—At any time after the provisions of clause 3.e.(3) of the Deal Terms take effect, the Studio/Distributor shall have the right, but not the obligation, to take over production of the Picture. Prior to taking over production as aforesaid, the Production Company may, but need not, advance funds in an amount deemed by the Studio/Distributor in the exercise of its good faith sound business judgment to be sufficient to cover the Projected Overage, and accordingly, thereafter, the Studio/Distributor shall not have the right to take over production of the Picture. If the Production Company advances additional funds as aforesaid, the Studio/Distributor shall have the right to take over the Picture subsequently if the Picture again is in a position where the Studio/Distributor would have the right hereunder to take over production.

(b) Take-Over Rights—If the Studio/Distributor takes over production, it shall be deemed to do so as the assignee of the Production Company. The Production Company shall, concurrently with the execution hereof, execute the Production Account take over letter in the form of the attached Exhibit "G" and deliver the same to the bank referred to therein placing such account at the disposal of and under the sole control of the Studio/Distributor in the event of take over. In addition, upon take over of production by the Studio/Distributor, the Production Company shall, to the extent such persons and/or equipment are within its control, place at the Studio/Distributor's disposal and under its control all persons and equipment employed or used by the Production Company in connection with the Picture.

For such purposes, the Production Company hereby irrevocably constitutes and appoints the Studio/Distributor as the Production Company's attorney-in-fact, with full power of substitution and revocation, if the Studio/Distributor shall exercise its take over rights, in the name of the Production Company, or otherwise, to make withdrawals from and otherwise deal with the Production Account (as more fully set forth in Exhibit "G" hereto), to expend funds from the production account previously not expended in or in connection with the production of the Picture, to borrow money, to enforce, modify release, compromise or terminate any contract or other right or obligation of the Production Company, to engage and discharge personnel, and to enter into or terminate any contract for services, provided that such action shall not breach the Production Company's contractual obligations in connection with the Picture, to acquire or lease and dispose of equipment and other real or personal property, to make claims under any policy of insurance, to endorse and collect any checks or other instrument payable to the Production Company, and in general to do any act which the Production Company might do, all to the extent that the foregoing relates to the production of the Picture.

The Studio/Distributor shall indemnify the Production Company and hold the Production Company harmless from and against any and all claims, actions, judgments and demands, together with all losses, liabilities, damages, costs and expenses incident thereto (including, without limitation, reasonable lawyers' and accountant's fees) from the Studio/Distributor's aforesaid acts or failure to act.

(c) Contractual Obligations—If the Studio/Distributor should take over production of the Picture, the Studio/Distributor shall have the right to elect not to take over any contract or obligation of the Production Company which the Studio/Distributor has not previously approved after reasonable notice thereof and which the Studio/Distributor reasonably considers to be unduly onerous and inconsistent with the Approved Production Budget. The foregoing shall not apply to customary union agreements, music performance or freelance agreements calling for compensation under One Thousand Dollars ($1,000) per week unless the Studio/Distributor has not previously approved such agreements or they are not consistent with the Approved Production Budget or Approved Production Schedule. Contracts not previously approved and not disapproved within five (5) business days of receipt by the Studio/Distributor shall be deemed approved.

(d) Reservation of Rights—In the event of a take over of production by the Studio/Distributor, each of the parties hereto reserves its rights with respect to the actions of the other. The Studio/Distributor shall utilize experienced production personnel to supervise such production. The Studio/Distributor in such event shall indemnify the Production Company against claims by third parties resulting from actions taken by the Studio/Distributor.

(e) Production Company Remedy—If, after a take over of production of the Picture by the Studio/Distributor, the Production Company shall deposit or cause to be deposited in the Production Account for the Picture such funds (or furnish a guaranty for such funds to be paid as and when required in form and substance satisfactory to the Studio/Distributor) as will, in the good faith sound business judgment of the Studio/Distributor, remedy any breach of this Agreement theretofore occurring on the part of the Production Company and cover adequately any liability which the Studio/Distributor in the exercise of its good faith sound business judgment believes will arise, then the Production Company may resume responsibility for production and completion of the Picture. No such resumption of responsibility by the Production Company shall prejudice the right of the Studio/Distributor thereafter to take over production pursuant to this clause 11 by reasons of the later occurrence of any event described in 3.e of the Deal Terms.

(f) Individual Producer(s) Remain Intact—If the Studio/Distributor shall take over production, the Studio/Distributor shall not replace the individual producers of the Picture, provided they promptly follow all instructions and directions with respect to the Picture given by the Studio/Distributor directly or through its representatives, which instructions and directions shall be determined by the Studio/Distributor in the exercise of its sole discretion. The Studio/Distributor shall have the right to replace such producers immediately should they fail or refuse to promptly follow such instructions or directions. There shall be no cure period with respect to such failure or refusal.

b. Delivery Specifications—The Production Company shall deliver the Picture conforming to the specifications and requirements of this Agreement, fully cut, edited, scored, titled and ready for exhibition and release in all respects by making complete delivery of all items set forth in Exhibit "B" hereof and all other materials required under the terms of this Agreement. The Production Company acknowledges that time is of the essence with respect to the Delivery Date. In connection with delivery of the Picture, the following shall apply:

(1) Technical Specifications—The Picture shall be an entirely new and original sound and talking motion picture photoplay of first class quality, telling a continuous story. Except to the extent specifically specified otherwise in the Deal Terms, the Picture shall be photographed in color, and will be originally recorded in the English language and in synchronization with the lip movements of the actors speaking or singing such dialogue.

(2) Length—A running time of not less than ninety-five (95) nor more than one hundred ten (110) minutes.

(3) Commercial Material—None of the materials to be delivered by the Production Company to the Studio/Distributor may contain any commercial material, inserts for commercials or other material extraneous to the Picture.

(4) Copyright—The Picture when delivered shall contain a copyright notice in the name of the Studio/Distributor or another related entity designated

by the Studio/Distributor in the form required by the requirements of the Universal Copyright Convention, the United States Copyright Act, as amended, and the Pan American Convention and shall contain the following legend:

"THIS PICTURE IS PROTECTED UNDER LAWS OF THE
UNITED STATES AND OTHER COUNTRIES. UNAUTHORIZED
DUPLICATION, DISTRIBUTION OR EXHIBITION MAY RESULT
IN CIVIL LIABILITY AND CRIMINAL PROSECUTION."

Said legend shall be located on the end title of the Picture, at or near the cast listing.

(5) MPAA Rating—The Picture shall qualify and receive a rating no more restrictive than "R" by the MPAA Ratings Board or an equivalent mark of approval or rating by any similarly constituted authority which may succeed the MPAA Ratings Board. In no event shall a rating of "X," "NC-17" or "G" by any such authority be permitted.

(6) Credits—The negatives and positive prints of the Picture as delivered to the Studio/Distributor hereunder shall contain all required screen credits in conformity with all contractual specifications.

(a) Submission of Credits—As soon as practicable, but not later than thirty (30) days prior to the date on which screen credits for the Picture are to be photographed, the Production Company shall deliver to the Studio/Distributor a complete written statement showing the exact form and manner in which the Production Company proposes to make up the main and end titles of the Picture together with a complete written statement showing the full text of all screen and advertising credit obligations. In no event shall such statement contain inconsistent requirements for credit.

(b) Form of Credits—The Studio/Distributor shall consult with the Production Company with respect to paid advertising credits. The Studio/Distributor shall determine in its sole discretion, the information to be contained in all credits to appear in the main and end titles of the Picture (except the Artist shall determine the color, style and size of type of such credits) and in all advertising thereof subject to the following:

(i) Guilds—The requirements of the applicable collective bargaining agreements;

(ii) Third Party Contracts—The credit provisions of all contracts pursuant to which an agreement to accord credit has been made with respect to the Picture (provided such agreement is not in violation of any other term of this Agreement);

(iii) Industry Practices—General practices with respect to credit in the Entertainment Industry.

(iv) This Agreement—All other applicable provisions of this Agreement.

(c) Remedies—(i) Inadvertent Failure by the Studio/Distributor—Any inadvertent failure of the Studio/Distributor to comply with any such credit obligations, or failure due to the acts or omissions of third parties, shall not constitute a breach by the Studio/Distributor, or entitle the Production Company to any relief at law or in equity against the Studio/Distributor. In the event of any such failure to comply with such credit obligations, the Studio/Distributor shall upon written notice from the Production Company use its best efforts to correct its failures and use reasonable efforts to cause third parties to correct their failures (it being understood that any such correction shall be made only on a prospective basis) as follows:

(A) Correction Required—To the extent such failure is required to be corrected or efforts are required to be made to correct such failure pursuant to the terms of any agreement between the Production Company and a third party relating to the Picture, which agreement was delivered to the Studio/Distributor in accordance with the terms hereof, or (B) Correction Not Required—In the event that such failure is not required to be corrected or efforts are not required to correct such failure pursuant to any such agreement, to the extent the Studio/Distributor determines, in the exercise of its business judgment, that such correction is practical.

(ii) Indemnity by the Studio/Distributor—The Studio/Distributor shall defend and indemnify the Production Company against any claims or suits arising out of any breach by the Studio/Distributor of its credit obligations.

(iii) No Injunctive Relief—Notwithstanding anything to the contrary herein contained, the Production Company's sole remedy for any breach by the Studio/Distributor pursuant to clause A.2.b.(6)(c)(i) shall be for damages in an action at law, and the Production Company shall not be entitled to equitable relief, by way of injunction or otherwise.

(7) Cover Shots—The Production Company shall cause the director of the Picture to prepare all "cover shots" or alternate scenes in accordance with the Screenplay to make the Picture acceptable for exhibition on U.S. prime-time network television and airlines. The Production Company hereby acknowledges that the Studio/Distributor has communicated to the Production Company all "cover shots" or alternate scenes necessary to make the Picture acceptable for such exhibition.

(8) Foreign Versions—Delivery of the Picture shall include all of the Production Company materials (if any) relating to foreign dubbed or substituted versions of the Picture which materials shall be delivered no later than sixty (60) days after the initial U.S. theatrical general release of the Picture.

(9) IRCA—The Production Company shall provide evidence that the Production Company has fully complied with all the requirements of the Immigration Reform and Control Act of 1986, including but not limited to having complied with the Immigration Verification Employment Eligibility Provisions required by such Act.

(10) Contracts—The Production Company shall provide the Studio/Distributor with executed copies of all agreements entered into by the Production Company with respect to the Picture promptly upon the Production Company's receipt of the same, but in no event later than the completion of principal photography on the Picture. All such agreements shall be freely assignable by the Production Company.

Upon delivery of the Picture, the Production Company shall execute, in form and substance satisfactory to the Studio/Distributor an assignment to the Studio/Distributor (i) of the Production Company's rights under all agreements entered into by the Production Company with respect to the Picture, and (ii) of all right, title and interest in and to the Picture, in perpetuity, throughout the universe, including the copyright therein and all component parts thereof (including all original music and lyrics created for the Picture unless the Studio/Distributor agrees to waive the foregoing requirement of the assignment of the copyright in such original music and lyrics). Such agreements shall be free of any lien or encumbrance of any kind or nature whatsoever. If, within a reasonable time after the Studio/Distributor's written request therefor, the Production Company fails to execute such an assignment, the Studio/Distributor may do so in the Production Company's name, and for that purpose the Production Company irrevocably constitutes the Studio/Distributor as the Production Company's attorney-in-fact.

The Studio/Distributor shall assume the obligation to pay all residual and other additional or supplemental payments required to be made thereafter by reason of the distribution or other exploitation of the Picture by the Studio/Distributor in the Distribution Territory pursuant to the terms of any applicable collective bargaining agreement to which the Studio/Distributor is a party. In addition, the Studio/Distributor shall pay to the person(s) engaged by the Production Company to compose the music and lyrics for the Picture any royalties payable in connection with the Studio/Distributor's distribution of the Picture provided that such royalties are not in excess of the usual and customary royalties payable for such use. The Studio/Distributor shall also assume any and all other executory obligations under the agreements entered into by the Production Company with respect to the Picture which are normally assumed by the distributor in the distribution of the rights granted the Studio/Distributor hereunder to the extent such agreements have not been disapproved by the Studio/Distributor. All residual, supplemental and royalty payments by the Studio/Distributor pursuant to this clause shall constitute a recoupable distribution expense. Except as set forth above in this sub-clause (1) or elsewhere in this Agreement, the Production Company shall remain liable for all other executory contractual obligations to third parties.

(11) Laboratory—All laboratory work in connection with the distribution of the Picture, shall be performed by such laboratory or laboratories as set

forth in the Deal Terms. Concurrent with the execution hereof, the Production Company shall execute the Studio/Distributor's standard laboratory access letter granting the Studio/Distributor customary access to the items delivered to such laboratory.

(12) Insurance—The Production Company agrees to maintain negative film insurance and errors and omissions insurance pursuant to the terms and conditions of clause A.2.a.(8) above.

(13) Talent Options—In the event any agreements entered into by the Production Company for personal services in connection with the Picture contain options for such services in any other motion pictures, then the Production Company shall assign to the Studio/Distributor all its rights in such options.

(14) Advance Delivery—To allow the Studio/Distributor to plan and prepare its ad campaign for the Picture as well as make arrangements for the exhibition thereof, the Production Company shall use its best efforts to furnish the Studio/Distributor with such advertising and print materials as and when reasonably requested by the Studio/Distributor in advance of the Delivery Date.

c. Studio/Distributor Approvals—As sometimes noted elsewhere herein and to the extent not specifically identified in the Deal Terms, the Studio/Distributor shall have approval of the elements set forth below and any substitution and/or material changes thereto (unless the Deal Terms specifically indicate such element is not subject to the Studio/Distributor's approval):

(1) If the Picture Has Not Yet Been Produced—(a) Locations—Locations in addition to or different from those set forth in the Deal Terms, if any;

(b) Merchandising—Subject to the Artist's rights pursuant to clause A.5.a.(2) below, grants of merchandising rights (and the terms thereof) from all Principal Production Personnel (defined below);

(c) Principal Production Personnel—To the extent deemed necessary by the Production Company to engage in connection with the Picture, the following above-the-line production personnel (hereinafter "Principal Production Personnel"): principal cast, composer, location auditor and additionally, executive producer, associate producer and production manager (provided, however that the Studio/Distributor shall solely have a right of consultation, and not right of approval, with respect to the three (3) Principal Production Personnel listed immediately preceding this parenthetical) and all agreements for the services of such personnel the terms of which shall be consistent with the terms of this Agreement, the stature of the respective personnel in the entertainment industry and the Studio/Distributor's customary method of doing business. Any agreement submitted for approval pursuant to this sub-clause (e) shall be deemed approved unless disapproval thereof has been communicated by the Studio/Distributor within five (5) business days of its receipt thereof;

(d) Production Budget—The Picture's Production budget which shall be prepared on the Studio/Distributor's then current standard production budget form. In addition to all customary production budget costs, the production budget shall include, but not be limited to, all costs of insurance (as required hereunder), guaranteed (not contingent) deferments and production legal fees;

(e) Production Schedule—Production schedule which shall be based upon the screenplay as approved pursuant to this clause A.2.c.(1);

(f) Production Cash Flow Schedule; and

(g) Screenplay.

(2) Regardless of Whether the Picture Has Been Produced—(a) Chain of Title;

(b) Credits—All screen credits above or before the title or of a size equal to 50% or more of the size of the title and all paid advertising credits;

(c) Insurance—Pursuant to clause A.2.a.(8) above;

(d) Laboratory—Pursuant to clause A.2.b.(11) above; and

(e) Participations—Any participation based upon the receipts of the Picture (the deferments set forth in Clause 4.b. of the Deal Terms are hereby approved by the Studio/Distributor).

d. Studio/Distributor Consultation—The Production Company shall consult with the Studio/Distributor with respect to the individuals engaged in all key crew capacities.

3. FINANCING—As provided in the Deal Terms.

4. CONSIDERATION—a. Condition/Full Consideration—All consideration set forth in clause 4. of the Deal Terms is conditioned upon the Picture being produced in accordance with the requirements of this Agreement and being completely delivered on the Delivery Date. Such consideration shall be deemed full consideration for all rights granted and services performed by the Production Company hereunder.

b. Participation—The Production Company Participation in the revenues derived from the Picture (if any, as granted in the Deal Terms) shall be defined, computed, accounted for and paid in accordance with Exhibit "A" and Exhibit "A-1" attached hereto. If the Deal Terms provide that the Participation payable to the Production Company is "reducible," such Participation shall be reduced by all third party net proceeds participations on a percentage point by percentage point basis and thereafter by the dollar amount of all third party gross participations.

If the Deal Terms provide for a "Soft Floor" in connection with the reduction of the Production Company Participation, such term shall mean that the dollar amount of all third party participations not utilized in reducing the Production Company's participation prior to reaching the Soft Floor shall be deducted "off the top." A "Hard Floor" shall mean that no further reductions or deductions shall be made of the Production Company's Participation once the Hard Floor has been reached; provided, however, that notwithstanding the foregoing, if the aggregate Participations granted in connection with the Picture (including the Production Company's Participation) exceed a sum equal to sixty percent (60%) of the Net Proceeds, the Production Company's Participation hereunder shall be reduced by an amount equal to such excess so that the Studio/Distributor shall retain for itself a sum equal to no less than forty percent (40%) of 100% of the Picture's Net Proceeds.

5. RIGHTS—a. Basic Rights—The rights granted the Studio/Distributor hereunder shall include all right title and interest in and to the Picture including the negative, positive prints, copyrights therein, revenues therefrom, and the exclusive right to distribute the Picture during the Distribution Term in the Distribution Territory including without limitation, the sole and exclusive right and license to release, exhibit, distribute, exploit, market, advertise, issue, reissue and otherwise dispose of and use all or any part of the Picture, and any and all cut, re-cut, edited, re-edited, dubbed, re-dubbed and other versions thereof. Without limiting the generality of the foregoing, and to the extent not specifically limited in the Deal Terms, the Studio/Distributor shall have the right to:

(1) All Media—To release, exploit, advertise, distribute, exhibit, license, sell and perform the Picture and trailers thereof, in 35mm, 16mm, 8mm, other sizes, gauges, forms (including tapes, discs, records and cassettes) and in all media whether now known or hereafter created, and in connection therewith to reproduce the Picture and/or the sound and music synchronized or recorded in or with the Picture.

(2) Portions—Except to the extent limited by the agreements with third parties rendering services on the Picture as approved by the Studio/Distributor hereunder, to broadcast, transmit or reproduce, separately from other portions of the Picture, the visual portion, sound or music contained in the Picture, or excerpts, dramatizations or summaries of such visual portion, sound or music or of the Underlying Material, or any part or combination of all or any part of the foregoing.

(3) Advertising & Publicity Publications—To publish, in such form and publications as the Studio/Distributor may desire (including newspapers, fan magazines and trade periodicals), and to copyright in the Studio/Distributor's name or in the name of its nominee, synopses, novelizations, serializations, dramatizations, sketches and other adaptations of and selections from the literary property on which the Picture is based and from the Screenplay of the Picture, and to use excerpts from such literary property and the Picture in heralds, programs, booklets, posters, lobby displays, pressbooks and all other media of advertising and publicity.

(4) Name and Likeness—To use the names and likenesses of the cast, and any other person who rendered services or granted rights in or for the Picture, and to use the name and trademark of the Production Company, in and in

connection with the Picture and the advertising and exploitation of the Picture, including commercial tie-ups, subject to all reasonable and customary restrictions in written contracts with such persons that have been approved in advance by the Studio/Distributor. The Studio/Distributor agrees and hereby approves that the contract for the personal services of the Artist hereunder shall prohibit the Studio/Distributor's use of the Artist's name, voice or likeness in any commercial tie-ups without the Artist's prior written consent except to the extent the Artist's name appears in the billing block used in connection with such commercial tie ups. As used herein, the term "commercial tie-up" refers to a type of advertising or exploitation in which some product, service or commodity (in addition to the Picture) is advertised.

(5) Commercial Tie-Ups—Subject to the Artist's approval rights pursuant to clause A.5.a.(4) above and the agreements for the services of any third party rendering services in connection with the Picture, to enter into and exploit to commercial tie-ups with respect to the Picture

(6) Underlying Material—Subject to the rights reserved pursuant to clause 5.a of the Deal Terms, to all rights in and to the Underlying Material and the Screenplay including but not limited to all General Distribution Rights, Allied Rights, Music Rights including, but not limited to the masters embodied in the soundtrack and soundtrack album of the Picture and Music Rights and Derivative Distribution Rights therein.

(7) Advertising—To make all determinations with respect to the advertising, exploitation and publicizing of the Picture, provided however, that the Studio/Distributor shall consult with the Production Company with respect to the initial U.S. advertising campaign and release pattern for the Picture. No advertising or publicity relating to the Picture shall be released without the Studio/Distributor's prior consent (except that which is casual, incidental and non-derogatory in nature). Subject to the Studio/Distributor's control of all such advertising and publicity, the Production Company shall cooperate fully with the Studio/Distributor in connection with all such advertising and publicity, such as participating in a reasonable number of publicity interviews (with the principal cast) relating to the Picture. The Studio/Distributor shall also have the right to broadcast by radio or television, with living actors or otherwise, announcements of or concerning the Picture, and dramatic episodes taken from, based on or adapted from the Screenplay of the Picture or from the Underlying Material.

(8) Music—All rights as described in clause A.5.b.(3) hereof.

(9) Title—To take any steps to register, protect, or acquire rights or consents in connection with any such title. The Production Company shall have mutual approval with the Studio/Distributor as to any change in the English language title of the Picture. The Studio/Distributor shall have the right to translate the title into foreign languages for foreign exhibition purposes and in

connection with such right, the Studio/Distributor may change the title itself, as so translated, to the extent the Studio/Distributor, deems such change necessary in good faith.

(10) Copyright—The Studio/Distributor may in its own name, or in the name of the copyright proprietor or otherwise, take such steps as the Studio/Distributor reasonably deems appropriate by action at law or otherwise, to prevent any unauthorized reproductions, exhibition or distribution of the Picture, or any infringement of the copyright on the Picture or to prevent any impairment of, encumbrance on, or infringement upon the rights of the Production Company or the Studio/Distributor under this Agreement.

(11) Trademark—To use its name, logos, trademark and other identification or those of any of its sub-distributors, in and in connection with the Picture and the advertising and exploitation thereof, in such manner, position, form and substance as the Studio/Distributor may elect. In no event shall the Studio/Distributor have the right to use the trademark version of "Filmright, Incorporated" or "Forever Films Company, Inc." except to the extent necessary to accord credit as required hereunder.

(12) Prints and Physical Properties—To cause negatives, prints, trailers, videocassettes, videodiscs, and other physical properties relating to the Picture to be made, transported and stored. The Studio/Distributor shall own all such physical items, and have exclusive rights to their possession and control, together with the right to destroy any such items.

b. Definition of Rights Designated in Deal Terms—The rights granted the Studio/Distributor and reserved to the Production Company, if any, pursuant to the Deal Terms are defined as follows:

(1) General Distribution Rights—All theatrical distribution rights, free, pay, cable and pay-per-view television rights and home video rights of every kind and nature;

(2) Allied Rights—All allied and ancillary rights of every kind and nature including but not limited to all live stage, merchandising rights and print publication rights. Notwithstanding the foregoing sentence, the use of Artist's name, voice and likeness in the exercise of any merchandising rights in connection with the Picture shall be subject to the Artist's prior written consent except to the extent that the Artist's name appears in the billing block appearing on any merchandising item.

(3) Music Rights—(i) All rights of ownership throughout the world in perpetuity in and to all music and sound recordings thereof created for use in, or in connection, with the Picture, and the royalty free right (except to the extent soundtrack album royalties are agreed to in advance by the Studio/Distributor) to publish, administer and exploit all such music and sound recordings for use in or in connection with the Picture, or otherwise, including, but not limited to the soundtrack album produced therefor, which musical compositions

shall be subject to the applicable record distributor's standard "controlled compositions" clause. The rights hereinabove specified shall include the royalty free right to use the aforementioned music and sound recordings in all promotional materials created in connection with the Picture, including, but not limited to trailers, televisions spots, "making of" documentaries, etc.

(ii) The royalty free right (except to the extent soundtrack album royalties are agreed to in advance by the Studio/Distributor) to use pre-existing music and pre-existing sound recordings thereof licensed for use in or in connection with the Picture, including but not limited to, the Soundtrack Album produced therefor, and in any and all media where the Picture is exploited. The rights hereinabove specified shall include the royalty free right to use the aforementioned music and sound recordings in all promotional materials created in connection with the Picture, including, but not limited to trailers, televisions spots, "making of" documentaries, etc.

(4) Derivative Distribution Rights—Sequel rights (all rights in theatrical or television motion pictures which contain substantially the same leading characters, but a substantially different story from that contained in the Picture) and remake rights (all-rights in theatrical or television motion pictures which contain substantially the same story and leading characters as contained in the Picture) and spinoff rights.

6. SPECIAL PROVISIONS—a. CREDIT—Except as specifically provided otherwise in the Deal Terms, all other aspects of the credit to be accorded pursuant to clause 7.b.(4) of the Deal Terms shall be determined by the Studio/Distributor in its sole discretion, subject to the following:

(1) Paid Advertising—The Studio/Distributor's obligation hereunder, if any, to accord credit in paid advertising shall be limited to advertising issued by or under the direct control of the Studio/Distributor and shall not include: (a) group, list or institutional advertising; (b) teaser or special advertising; (c) outdoor advertising; (d) promotional material for exhibitors; (e) publicity, advertising or exploitation relating to the story or literary or dramatic material on which said Picture is based, its title, the authors or writers, the music, the composers or conductor, the director, any members of the cast, or similar matters; (f) any advertising or publicity written in narrative form; (g) a listing in the nature of a cast of characters; (h) trailer or other advertising on the screen; (i) radio or television advertising or exploitation; (j) newspaper or magazine advertising of eight (8) column inches or less; (k) window or lobby displays or advertising; (1) advertising relating to subsidiary or ancillary rights in the Picture (including without limitation, novelizations, screenplay and other publications, products or merchandising, soundtrack recordings, videocassettes, videodiscs and other home video devices and the covers, packages, containers or jackets therefor); (m) advertising in which no credit is accorded other than credit to one (1) or two (2) stars of the Picture and/or the Studio/Distributor

and/or any other company financing or distributing the Picture; (n) advertising, publicity and exploitation relating to by-products or commercial tie-ups; and (o) other advertising not relating primarily to the Picture.

Notwithstanding the foregoing, the Studio/Distributor shall accord the credit "A Filmright Motion Picture" in any excluded advertising set forth above in which a presentation credit is accorded the Studio/Distributor.

(2) Title—If both artwork and non-artwork titles are used, position and size references to title herein shall apply to the non-artwork title only; provided, however, that in no event shall the credit accorded hereunder be less than twenty-five percent (25%) of the size of type of the artwork title.

b. Videocassettes—The videocassette copy of the Picture granted the Production Company in the Deal Terms shall be provided the Production Company at such time, if ever, as the Picture is offered for sale to the general public in the United States on videocassette and shall be subject to the Production Company's execution of the Studio/Distributor's standard agreement limiting the Production Company's use of such videocassettes to private home use only.

c. Transportation and Expenses—Any right of the Production Company to transportation and expenses pursuant to the Deal Terms shall be effective, when and only when the Artist is required by the Studio/Distributor to travel more than seventy-five (75) miles from the Artist's principal place of residence. Any weekly expense allowance provided the Lender under the Deal Terms shall be prorated at 1/7 thereof per day.

B.
STANDARD CONTRACT PROVISIONS

1. REPRESENTATIONS AND WARRANTIES—The Production Company and Artist jointly and severally represent and warrant that:

a. Corporation/Ability to Perform—The Production Company is a corporation, organized and incorporated under the laws of the state of incorporation indicated in clause A in the preamble of this Agreement; that Production Company is in good corporate standing and will remain so until the Picture is delivered to Studio/Distributor hereunder; and that the Production Company has the power and authority to execute and perform this Agreement.

b. Underlying Material—With respect to the Underlying Material, when the Picture is delivered hereunder the Production Company will have acquired and the Studio/Distributor will acquire from the Production Company all rights in and to the Underlying Material necessary for the Studio/Distributor's exercise and enjoyment of all rights granted to the Studio/Distributor hereunder. Such rights shall include but not be limited to royalty-free synchronization and performance rights in all media whether now or hereafter known (except to the extent royalties or limitations on media are agreed to in advance by the Studio/Distributor) in any music and lyrics for the entire world including all countries where the royalty or performance fee is paid by or chargeable to motion picture producers as well as all other exclusive motion picture rights in all of the Underlying Material other than music and lyrics.

c. No Violation of Third Party Rights—The Picture, and its distribution by the Studio/Distributor hereunder, shall not violate or infringe any right of a third party including without limitation, any copyright (whether, literary, dramatic, musical or otherwise), "droit d'auteur," patent, trademark, trade name, or contract, property or personal right, or right of privacy or other right of any person, or constitute an act of unfair competition, or a libel or slander of any person. Without limiting the foregoing, with respect to the "droit d'auteur," the Production Company, understanding the needs and customs of the exhibition and exploitation of programs, waives the enforcement of the "droit d'auteur", on its own behalf and on behalf of all of its officers, directors and shareholders.

d. No Claims—To the best of the Production Company's knowledge, there are no claims, liens, encumbrances or rights in or to the Picture or any part thereof.

e. Suitable For Exhibition—The Picture is (or when delivered hereunder shall be) fully synchronized with dialogue, music and sound, main and end titles (except for the Studio/Distributor's name and trademark), completed and ready and suitable for exhibition throughout the Distribution Territory.

f. Conformity with Law—The Picture has been or will be produced in accordance with all applicable laws and requirements with the force of law.

g. Duration of Representations and Warranties—The Production Company's representations and warranties hereunder shall continue in full force and effect, notwithstanding the delivery by the Production Company, or acceptance or approval by the Studio/Distributor, of the Picture, or any items, elements or documents of any kind, and notwithstanding any termination of this Agreement.

2. INDEMNIFICATION—a. Indemnity by Production Company—The Production Company shall indemnify and hold harmless the Studio/Distributor, its affiliated companies and their shareholders, directors, officers, employees, licensees, agents, successors and assigns, against and from any and all claims, or demands reduced to judgment, causes of action, judgments, liabilities, losses, costs and expenses (including, without limitation, reasonable attorney's fees) that may arise out of or result from the breach of any of the Production Company's warranties and representations herein contained or that may arise out of or result from any other claim, lien or encumbrance pertaining to the exploitation of the rights granted the Studio/Distributor hereunder resulting from the Production Company's act or failure to act regardless of whether or not the Production Company has warranted the absence of any such claims, liens or encumbrances hereunder. The Studio/Distributor will promptly give

the Production Company notice of any claim or action which is or may be covered by the preceding sentence and which comes to the Studio/Distributor's attention, and the Studio/Distributor will promptly deliver or cause to be delivered to the Production Company photocopies of any and all letters, proceedings, complaints or other documents in the Studio/Distributor's possession relating to any such claim or action and cooperate with the Studio/Distributor in all other matters relating to the defense of any such claim or action.

b. No Waiver of Indemnity—Neither the receipt, inspection nor retention by the Studio/Distributor of any copy of any document or documents delivered pursuant to this Agreement nor any written approval by the Studio/Distributor of the Production Company's chain of title and rights in and to the Picture, nor approval by the Studio/Distributor of the Picture, nor any act by either party, nor any omission by the Studio/Distributor to exercise any right of the Studio/Distributor's, nor the expiration or termination of this Agreement, nor the election by the Studio/Distributor or the Production Company to participate in or conduct the defense of any claim or action shall impair, modify or discharge any of the Production Company's warranties and representations or obligations herein contained.

c. Indemnity by Studio/Distributor—The Studio/Distributor warrants and represents that it has the right to enter into this Agreement and that it will not exceed the rights granted to the Studio/Distributor hereunder. The Studio/Distributor shall indemnify and hold harmless the Production Company, and its subsidiary companies, and their respective shareholders, directors, officers, employees, licensees, agents, successors and assigns, and each of the foregoing, against and from any and all claims, or demands reduced to judgment, causes of action, judgments, liabilities, losses, costs and expenses (including, without limitation, reasonable attorney's fees) that may arise out of or result from the breach of any of the Studio/Distributor's warranties and representations herein contained. The Production Company will promptly give the Studio/Distributor notice of any claim or action which is or may be covered by the preceding sentence and which comes to the Production Company's attention, and the Production Company will promptly deliver or cause to be delivered to the Studio/Distributor photocopies of any and all letters, proceedings, complaints or other documents in the Production Company's possession relating to any such claim or action and shall cooperate with the Studio/Distributor in all other matters relating to the defense of any such claim or action.

3. DEFAULT—a. Default By Production Company—(1) Events of Default—The occurrence of any of the following shall constitute a Production Company's Default:

(a) General Default—A material breach by the Production Company of the performance of any material term, condition or covenant hereunder including any representation or warranty and failure to cure such breach within five

(5) working days after written notice thereof (except with respect to delivery of the Picture, as to which no cure period shall apply);

(b) Financial Default—If at any time prior to delivery of the Picture to the Studio/Distributor, the Production Company shall:

(i) Bankruptcy—Be adjudicated a bankrupt, or petition for or consent to any relief under any bankruptcy, reorganization, receivership, liquidation, compromise or arrangement or moratorium statutes; or

(ii) Assignment to Creditors—Make an assignment for the benefit of its creditors; or

(iii) Receivership—Petition for or be subjected to the appointment of a receiver, liquidator, trustee or custodian for all or a substantial part of its assets who is not discharged within sixty (60) days from the date of appointment thereof; or

(iv) Levy on Picture—If the Picture or any portion thereof is attached or levied upon and such attachment or levy is not released within thirty (30) days after such levy; or

(v) Abandon Production—If the Production Company abandons production of the Picture; or

(vi) Inability to Pay Debts—If the Production Company admits in writing its inability to pay its debts generally when due.

(2) Studio/Distributor's Remedies—In the event of the Production Company's default the Studio/Distributor may do one or more of the following:

(a) Termination—Terminate this Agreement in its entirety and be relieved of the obligation (if any) to loan or advance or cause to be loaned or advanced any further monies for the Picture. The Production Company shall repay the aggregate of any sums advanced by the Studio/Distributor with accrued interest thereon, on such termination.

(b) Debt Acceleration—Accelerate and declare due and payable the Production Company's indebtedness to the Studio/Distributor (if any) plus interest thereon.

(c) Takeover—Exercise its right of takeover hereunder, if any.

(d) Remedies Cumulative—All rights and remedies granted to the Studio/Distributor under this Agreement are cumulative and the exercise of one shall not limit its rights concurrently or subsequently to exercise any other rights or remedies at law or in equity (including, but not limited to injunctive relief), under this Agreement or otherwise.

b. Default by Studio/Distributor—The sole right of the Production Company for any breach hereof by the Studio/Distributor shall be the recovery of money damages, if any, and the rights herein granted by the Production Company shall not terminate by reason of such breach. In no event may the Production Company terminate this Agreement or obtain injunctive or other equitable relief with respect to any breach of the Studio/Distributor's obligations hereunder.

4. NON-WAIVER—The waiver by any party of any breach hereof shall not be deemed a waiver of any prior or subsequent breach hereof. The Production Company's or the Studio/Distributor's failure to enforce any provision hereof on any occasion shall not be deemed to be a waiver of any preceding or succeeding breach of such provision or any other provision hereof.

5. CONFORMITY—Nothing in this Agreement shall be construed so as to require any illegal act. Any conflict between any provision hereof and any law or requirement with the force of law or any collective bargaining agreement ("Guild Agreement") to which the Studio/Distributor is a signatory shall be restricted to the extent necessary to bring it within the applicable requirements. Any invalid provision(s) hereof shall be severed, and of no effect, and the remaining provisions shall continue in full force and effect, as if the invalid provision(s) had never been contained herein.

6. NOTICES AND PAYMENTS—Any notice hereunder may be given orally unless required hereunder to be in writing. Any notice by the Production Company to the Studio/Distributor shall be given in writing. Either the Production Company or the Studio/Distributor may hereafter designate a substitute address by written notice to the other.

a. To Production Company—A written notice to the Production Company shall presently be given by delivery to the Production Company or to the Lender's agent, by mail or by transmission through cable, telegraph, or facsimile (provided there is confirmation of receipt of such transmission) at the address for the Production Company as set forth in the Deal Terms. The date of mailing or transmission of any such notice to the Production Company shall be deemed the date of service thereof.

b. To Studio/Distributor—A notice to the Studio/Distributor shall presently be given by mail or by transmission by cable, telegraph, or facsimile (provided there is confirmation of receipt of such transmission) to the Studio/Distributor at the address set forth in the Deal Terms section of this Agreement. The date of mailing or transmission of any such notice shall be deemed the date of service thereof.

7. FURTHER INSTRUMENTS—The Production Company shall execute such documents and do such other acts and deeds as may be reasonably required by the Studio/Distributor or its assignees or licensees to further evidence or effectuate its rights hereunder.

8. ASSIGNMENT—The Studio/Distributor shall have the right to freely assign this Agreement and/or any of the Studio/Distributor's rights hereunder to any person, firm or corporation. The Studio/Distributor shall remain secondarily liable to the Production Company unless such assignment is to a so-

called "major" motion picture studio or distributor or similarly financially responsible third party or to any entity with which the Studio/Distributor is merged or consolidated or by which the Studio/Distributor is acquired and such assignee accepts the Studio/Distributor's obligations hereunder. The Production Company shall not have the right to assign this Agreement except as provided in clause A16 of Exhibit "A."

9. GOVERNING LAW—This Agreement shall be construed in accordance with the laws of the state of California applicable to agreements which are executed and fully performed within the state of California. Any legal proceeding of any nature brought by any party hereto shall be submitted for trial before any court of competent jurisdiction within the state of California. The parties hereto expressly consent and submit to the jurisdiction of any such court and agree to accept service of process outside the state of California, in any matter to be submitted to any such court pursuant hereto.

10. HEADINGS—The headings of the sections and clauses of this Agreement are for convenience only, and they shall not be of any effect in construing the contents of the respective sections or clauses.

11. RELATIONSHIP OF PARTIES—This Agreement is a license agreement under copyright and shall not constitute a trust, partnership or joint venture.

INDUCEMENT LETTER

June 25, 1993
Worldwide Pictures
100 Worldwide Plaza, Suite 500
World City, California 98765
Attention: Feature Law Department

Gentlepersons:

As an inducement to you to enter into the Production-Finance/Distribution Agreement ("P-F/D Agreement") executed concurrently herewith, by and among Filmright, Incorporated (the "Production Company"), Rocky Roundtree (the "Artist"), the Artist Lender Company, Inc. (the "Lender") and you (Worldwide Pictures, a division of Worldwide Studios, Inc., otherwise referred to in such P-F/D Agreement as the "Studio/Distributor") with respect to the motion picture entitled "Invasion From Chunga," I represent, warrant and agree as follows:

1. That the Lender is now, and will be at all times during the term of said P-F/D Agreement and at all other times when my services may be rendered or required thereunder, authorized to furnish my personal directing services as therein provided;

2. That I will keep and perform all of the terms and conditions pertaining to the Lender of said P-F/D Agreement and will perform my services in accordance with the terms and conditions thereof; and if for any reason my employment contract with the Lender should expire or be terminated, I will keep and perform all of the terms and conditions thereof pertaining to the Lender, as though I were a party to said P-F/D Agreement and had executed in place of the Lender;

3. That you shall be entitled to apply for equitable relief, by injunction or otherwise, to prevent a breach of the Lender's or my obligations under said P-F/D Agreement hereunder;

4. That all notices served on the Lender in accordance with the provision of said P-F/D Agreement shall be deemed to be notices to me of the contents thereof; and

5. That my social security number is 123-45-6789.

Very truly yours,

Rocky Rountree

Exhibit "A"
NET PROCEEDS DEFINITION

This exhibit is attached to and is part of the agreement dated June 25, 1993, by and among Filmright, Incorporated (the "Production Company"), Rocky Roundtree (the "Artist"), the Artist Lender Company, Inc. (the "Lender") and Worldwide Pictures, a division of Worldwide Studios, Inc., (the "Studio/Distributor") relating to the motion picture entitled "Invasion From Chunga" (hereinafter referred to as the "Picture"). Net proceeds of the Picture, with respect to which any Net Proceeds Participant may be entitled to contingent compensation under the agreement to which this exhibit is attached, shall be computed, and such contingent compensation shall be accounted for and paid, as provided in this exhibit.

A1. Definitions—As used in this exhibit, the following terms and their respective equivalents, unless the context expressly provides t the contrary, have the following meanings:

(a) "Agreement" means the agreement to which this exhibit is attached, together with this exhibit and any other attached provisions, riders, exhibits and schedules, as they have been or may hereafter be amended or supplemented.

(b) "British Territory" means the United Kingdom of Great Britain and Northern Ireland, the Republic of Ireland, the Isle of Man, the Channel Islands, Malta, Gibraltar, and ships and aircraft flying the British flag, and camps wherever situated where British forces are stationed.

(c) "Canadian Territory" means Canada, together with any other countries which are licensed by or through the Studio/Distributor's distributors for Canada. Any receipts derived by the Studio/Distributor's distributors for Canada shall be deemed to have been derived from the Canadian Territory, whether or not the respective exhibitions are in the Canadian Territory.

(d) "Cost of Production" means the aggregate of all costs, charges and expenses paid or incurred in connection with the production of the Picture, calculated according to the Studio/Distributor's method of accounting applicable to motion pictures produced at the time the Picture is produced, including those items supplied by the Studio/Distributor at the respective rates specified in its rate card in effect at the time such items are supplied, plus an administrative fee of 15% of the aggregate of all items of cost of production other than such administrative fee. For purposes of computing such administrative fee, participations shall be deemed included in cost of production (whether or not such participations are payable from the first dollar of gross), but only if and to the extent that the Studio/Distributor's obligation to pay the respective participation accruals before any Net Proceeds (as defined in clause A9(b) have been derived.

(e) "Country" means a nation, or any other area (anywhere in the universe) for which the Picture is licensed.

(f) " Domestic Territory" means the United States, together with any other countries which are licensed by or through the distributing organization(s) servicing the United States for the Studio/Distributor. Any receipts derived by such distributing organization(s) servicing the United States shall be deemed to have been derived from the Domestic Territory, whether or not the respective exhibitions are in the Domestic Territory.

(g) "Foreign Territory" means all countries other than the Domestic Territory, the Canadian Territory and the British Territory.

(h) "Four-Wall Engagement" means engagements for the exhibition of the Picture in Theatres hired and/or operated by the Studio/Distributor for the respective engagements. Income received by the Studio/Distributor from each four-wall engagement in any country shall be included in Accountable Gross from the respective country, but only if and to the extent that such income exceeds the expenses of hiring and/or operating the theatre for that engagement (such as theatre rental and salaries of theatre help); all other expenses of four-wall engagements (such as advertising expenses) shall be deducted under the appropriate provisions of clause A6 herein. If the expenses of hiring and/or operating the theatre for any such four-wall engagement exceed such income from that engagement, the excess shall be deducted under clause A6, as a distribution expense.

(i) "Franchised Sub-Distributor" means a person (other than the Studio/Distributor) licensed by the Studio/Distributor to distribute or sub-license the Picture for exhibition in a particular geographic area outside of the Domestic Territory, with an obligation of such person to account for or report to the Studio/Distributor the amount of any income or expenses of such distribution or sub-licensing, regardless of whether any amounts payable to the Studio/Distributor by such person for such license are fixed, or are on a percentage, guaranteed or other basis, or are computed or determined in any other manner or by any combination of any of the foregoing. The Studio/Distributor's television distributor in the United States (which is now BWB Television Limited, a Studio/Distributor Affiliate) shall also be deemed to be a franchised sub-distributor. Subject to clause A4(c), (i) all income and expenses (relating to the Picture) of each franchised sub-distributor, accounted or reported to the Studio/Distributor, shall be treated for all purposes of accounting and computation hereunder as though they were income and expenses of the Studio/Distributor; and accordingly (ii) the contractual or other licensing arrangement between the Studio/Distributor and each franchised sub-distributor, and the amounts and methods of computation and payment thereunder, shall be of no relevance hereunder.

(j) "Here-" as a prefix in words such as "herein," refers to this agreement.

(k) "Include" (or any equivalent, such as "included" or "including") is illustrative and not limitative.

(l) "Outright Sale" means a license to any person, by the Studio/Distributor or any franchised sub-distributor, to distribute the Picture for theatrical exhibition, in a particular geographic area and for a particular period of time (other than any such license for a period of less than one year for theatrical exhibition in a part of any country), without any obligation of such person to account for or report to the Studio/Distributor or such franchised sub-distributor the amount of any proceeds or expenses of such distribution or sub-licensing. The Studio/Distributor's present or future arrangements for the non-theatrical distribution of the Picture, such as distribution to any government's armed forces, or to any transportation companies, steamship companies, airlines, non-profit organizations, industrial companies, schools or institutions, including any such arrangements with "Movies En Route," "Inflight Motion Pictures, Inc." or other similar agencies, shall not be considered outright sales; accordingly, the Studio/Distributor's receipts from the distribution of the Picture pursuant to any such arrangement shall constitute Accountable Gross from the respective territory under, and be subject to the distribution fee provided for in clause A2(a), A2(b), A2(c) or A2(d).

(m) "Participant" means any Person entitled to receive contingent compensation (as opposed to fixed compensation) pursuant to the Agreement to which this exhibit is attached.

(n) "Participation" or "Participations" mean contingent compensation (as distinguished from fixed compensation).

(o) "Person" means any corporation, partnership, joint venture, trust or any other business entity or firm, as well as any natural person.

(p) "Receipts" means the rentals, license fees, royalties or other charges received for the license or privilege to exhibit the Picture including reissues of the Picture, but excluding remakes and sequels) or trailers of the Picture in any way, including theatrical and non-theatrical exhibitions, and exhibitions on or by means of television and including exhibitions by any other process now known or hereafter devised, whether on film or by means of magnetic tape, wire, cassettes, discs or any other devices now known or hereafter devised, but excluding any amounts received from outright sales.

(q) "Restricted Currency" means a foreign currency which is or becomes subject to moratorium, embargo, banking or exchange restrictions, or restrictions against remittances to the United States.

(r) "Studio/Distributor" means Worldwide Pictures (which is a division of Worldwide Studios, Inc.) together with Worldwide Studios, Inc. and all of its other divisions and its wholly-owned and partially-owned subsidiaries. None of such subsidiaries or other divisions shall have any obligations or liabilities hereunder.

(s) "Studio/Distributor Affiliate" means any corporation controlling (either directly or indirectly) or under common control with the Studio/Distributor. No Studio/Distributor Affiliate shall have any obligations or liabilities hereunder.

(t) "Such as" is illustrative and not limitative.

(u) "United States" means the states of the United States of America, together with the District of Columbia.

A2. Accountable Gross—Subject to clause A3 and A4, Accountable Gross shall be only the aggregate of all of the Studio/Distributor's receipts, and the net sums received by the Studio/Distributor from sub-distribution. The Studio/Distributor's distribution fee with respect to the Accountable Gross described in each sub-clause of this clause A2 shall be the percentage specified in the parentheses immediately following the heading of the respective sub-clause:

(a) Domestic (30%): All of the Studio/Distributors receipts derived from the Domestic Territory.

(b) Canadian (30%): All of the Studio/Distributor's receipts derived from the Canadian Territory.

(c) British (35%): All of the Studio/Distributor's receipts derived from the British Territory.

(d) Foreign (40%): All of the Studio/Distributor's receipts derived from the Foreign Territory.

(e) Outright Sales (15%): The net sums received by the Studio/Distributor from outright sales.

Except as otherwise provided in clause A1(g) (with respect to four-wall engagements), the moneys received by any exhibitor (such as a theatre or group of theatres, a television station or a television network) shall not be included in Accountable Gross, whether or not the respective exhibitor is owned, operated or controlled by the Studio/Distributor or any Studio/Distributor Affiliate. Moneys received from the sale or other disposition of still photographs, novelties, commercial articles or advertising or sales materials, or accessories, or from music royalties, phonograph records, books or other publications, stock footage, or any other rights or materials (literary, musical, physical or otherwise) taken from the Picture or on which the Picture is based in whole or in party shall not be included in Accountable Gross.

A3. Exclusions—(a) The amounts of all adjustments, credits, allowances (other than advertising allowances), rebates and refunds, given or made to sub-distributors, exhibitors and licensees, shall be excluded from Accountable Gross. To the extent that such amounts represent a return of amounts previously included in Accountable Gross, an appropriate adjustment shall be made by a corresponding reduction in Accountable Gross, and also in the Studio/Distributor's distribution fees with respect to the amount of the reduction.

(b) Moneys in the nature of security deposits, or advance or periodic payments, shall not constitute Accountable Gross until they have actually been earned (such as by the exhibition of the Picture) or forfeited.

A4. Foreign Currency—(a) Except as provided in this clause A4, (i) all accountings, reports, statements, computations and determinations hereunder shall be made and expressed in United States currency units; and (ii) no moneys shall be included in Accountable Gross unless they have been paid in United States dollars in the United States, or are payable in a foreign currency which is not a restricted currency and have been remitted in United States dollars to the United States, or could be if the Studio/Distributor so desired. The conversion of such foreign currency into United States dollars shall be made at the average weighted rate of exchange at which remittances have been received by the Studio/Distributor during the accounting period in which such remittances are received.

(b) Moneys which would otherwise be included in Accountable Gross, except that they are payable in a foreign currency which is a restricted currency, are herein called "restricted proceeds." Restricted proceeds shall be included in Accountable Gross only as follows, or on such other basis as the Studio/Distributor may adopt from time to time with respect to motion pictures then distributed by the Studio/Distributor:

(i) Where remittances in United States dollars are received in the United

States from a country where a quota of remittances is authorized for a fixed period, then a fraction of the total restricted proceeds of the Picture in such country during the period fixed by the quota shall be included in Accountable Gross. The numerator of such fraction shall be the amount of that restricted currency which is converted into remittances for such period which are received by the Studio/Distributor in United States dollars in the United States, or could be if the Studio/Distributor so desired, and the denominator shall be the total amount which became available to the Studio/Distributor in that restricted currency during such period and which could have been used for such remittances during such period if no exchange restrictions were in effect. The conversion into United States dollars of the amount of that restricted currency to be so included shall be made at the average weighted rate of exchange at which such quota remittances were received during such period.

(ii) Where remittances from a country are received in United States dollars in the United States, under authorization granted from time to time for remittance of a portion of the total restricted currency accumulated by the Studio/Distributor in such country, then each remittance shall be deemed to have come from the oldest restricted currency accumulated by the Studio/Distributor in such country, until such time as all accumulations of that restricted currency which are earlier (than the first such accumulation of restricted proceeds of the Picture) have been exhausted. Thereafter, all restricted proceeds of the Picture in such country, up to the date to which the restricted currency for the purchase of each remittance was accumulated, shall be included in Accountable Gross in accordance with the formula provided for in clause A4(b)(i), at the rate of exchange at which such remittance was received by the Studio/Distributor.

(iii) As and when contingent compensation becomes payable to the Participant under this Agreement, the Participant may notify the Studio/Distributor in writing that the Participant elects to require settlement of the Participant's share of the restricted proceeds of the Picture remaining in any country and not yet included in Accountable Gross under any provision of this clause A4(b), in the currency of such country. Such notice shall also include a designation of a bank or other representative in such country, to whom payment may be made for the Participant's account. Such payment shall be made to such representative as and when the Participant has obtained any required permission. Such payment shall be made at the Participant's expense and shall, to the extent thereof, be deemed the equivalent of the inclusion in Accountable Gross of the restricted proceeds of which such payment represents the Participant's share, and satisfy the Studio/Distributor's obligations to the Participant with respect to such restricted proceeds and the Participant's share thereof.

(c) No moneys shall be included in Accountable Gross on account of the income of any franchised sub-distributor unless the net sums payable to the

Studio/Distributor on account of such income of the respective franchised sub-distributor have been remitted or paid to the Studio/Distributor in United States dollars in the United States or could be if the Studio/Distributor so desired. If any such net sums are payable in a restricted currency, (i) the determination as to whether and when such respective net sums are remitted shall be made as provided in clause A4(b); and (ii) if a fraction of such respective net sums is so remitted, then an equivalent fraction of such moneys shall be included in Accountable Gross.

(d) On the Participant's written request, the Studio/Distributor shall report to the Participant the amount of restricted proceeds (if any) which under any provision of this clause A4 have not yet been included in Accountable Gross, as of the closing date of the most recent statement which has then been furnished to the Participant under clause A10.

A5. Distribution Fees—Distribution fees shall be computed and payable from the first dollar of Accountable Gross in each classification, at the respective percentage rates specified in clause A2, and the Studio/Distributor shall be entitled to deduct such distribution fees from Accountable Gross and retain them for its own account.

A6. Distribution Expenses—The Studio/Distributor shall be entitled to deduct and retain for its own account, from the Accountable Gross remaining after the continuing deduction of its distribution fees, the aggregate of all sums paid or advanced, and all costs and charges incurred, by the Studio Distributor, directly or indirectly, in connection with the distribution, exhibition, marketing and/or exploitation of the Picture, which are not included in cost of production (all such deductible amounts being herein collectively called "distribution expenses"), including any such sums, costs and charges for or in connection with any of the following:

(a) Taxes—Taxes, excises and imposts (and payments and expenses in contesting, compromising or settling any of them, together with any interest and penalties on any of them) imposed by any taxing authority (regardless of any doubt as to the legality or applicability of any of them, and regardless of how they may be designated or characterized by the respective taxing authority or any other taxing authority), on or with respect to:

(i) the Picture and any trailers thereof;

(ii) Any prints and physical properties of the Picture;

(iii) advertising accessories, for free distribution, relating to the Picture;

(iv) Exhibition, distribution or other use of the Picture, trailers thereof or physical properties thereof;

(v) any Accountable Gross, receipts or other revenues or credits from the Picture or trailers thereof, or from the exhibition, distribution or other use thereof, or the remittance of payment of all or any portion thereof.

The taxes, excises and imposts deductible under this clause A6(a) shall include the so-called Canadian "remittance tax," and other remittance taxes, and all personal property, turnover, sales, use, film hire, excise, stamp, gross income and gross receipts taxes, and taxes computed on a portion of receipts, revenues or remittances (but excluding all net income, franchise, excess profits and corporation taxes). In preparing and filing their corporate tax returns, the Studio/Distributor and its distributors and Studio/Distributor Affiliates shall have the right to take the full amount of any credits, deductions or other benefits that may be available to them with respect to, or relating to, any such taxes, excises and imposts, without any accounting, payment or other liability or obligation to the Participant. Notwithstanding anything contained in clause A10, or elsewhere in this Agreement, the Participant shall have not right to inspect or copy any tax return of the Studio/Distributor or any of its distributors, or to require the Studio/Distributor or any of its distributors to produce any such tax return or any information contained therein.

(b) Prints and Physical Properties—Prints, replacement prints, master discs and records; laboratory work; titles; dupe negatives and fine grain prints, redubbed tracks and foreign versions, including a version or versions synchronized with music or sound effects; substandard reductions; re-editing, re-cutting, rerecording and changes of or in the Picture; copyright protection, registration and renewal; and insurance premiums (or an equivalent charge, if and to the extent that the Studio/Distributor provides coverage itself) with respect to any of the foregoing items or with respect to any other physical properties relating to the Picture. If the methods or media of exhibition, transmission, projection or communication, or procedures, techniques or practices in connection with any of the foregoing, should be modified or changed, the corresponding costs of the new, substitute or changed methods, media, procedures, techniques or practices shall be deductible under this clause A6(b).

(c) Advertising—Advertising, marketing, promoting, exploiting and publicizing the Picture in any way, including the following:

(i) Publications, such as trade publications, fan magazines, newspapers, organization publications, and other space and display advertising, national and local.

(ii) Cooperative advertising and advertising allowances to exhibitors (whether effected by credits against or deductions from film rentals, by direct reimbursement, or otherwise). No such allowances shall reduce Accountable Gross for the purpose of computing distribution fees.

(iii) Commercial tie-ups.

(iv) Field exploitation, including salaries of employees and allowed living costs and traveling expenses, fees and charges, whether paid to the Studio/Distributor employees or other persons.

(v) Radio and television advertising, including cost of time and program and commercial preparation, recording and prints and tapes.

(vi) Tours and personal appearances of personalities connected with the Picture, including salaries of employees and allowed living costs and traveling expenses, fees and charges, whether paid to the Studio/Distributor employees or other persons.

(vii) Previews and screenings.

(viii) Traveling and living expenses (but not salaries) of the Studio/Distributor's publicity, advertising and exploitation executives, but only for trips directly attributable to or occasioned by the Picture.

(ix) Entertainment, such as of press and personalities.

(x) Art work, cuts and engravings.

(xi) Promotional material, such as souvenirs; and the preparation, manufacture and dissemination of press books, and of any other advertising accessories or materials, for free distribution.

(xii) Production of trailers and the manufacture of prints of such trailers for the Picture utilizing scenes from the Picture or material from other sources.

(xiii) The cost of advertising overhead, which shall be an amount equivalent to 10% of the aggregate of all other amounts which are deductible under this clause A6(c).

(d) Checking—Checking percentage engagements and licenses of the Picture.

(e) Transportation, Duties and Censorship—Freight, shipping, transportation, reels and containers, storage, duties, tariffs, customs charges, import taxes and censorship (including voluntary and involuntary censorship, classification and rating by governmental bodies or other persons or organizations, such as religious, ethnic and veteran's groups and organizations, and networks and other exhibitors or groups and organizations of exhibitors).

(f) Royalties and Guild Payments—Synchronization, recording, performing, patent and trademark royalties, and all other required payments (to any person, including any guild or union) and expenses, for or with respect to the exhibition or exploitation of the Picture, theatrically or on television or otherwise.

(g) Trade Associations—Dues, fees and contributions (to the extent reasonably allocated by the Studio/Distributor to the Picture or the distribution thereof) to MPAA, AMPTP and MPEA or any similarly constituted or substitute authorities or organizations, or their respective successors, wherever located; and fees for industry public relations activities, and for protection against copyright infringements.

(h) Quota Losses—Quota losses and quota expenditures in foreign countries sustained or incurred on account of the Picture. Such quota losses and expenditures shall be apportioned (i) by allocating to the Picture the same percentage of the total quota losses and expenditures, for the particular country and for the particular fiscal period concerned, that the cost of production of the Picture is of the total cost of production of all motion pictures to which such respective quota losses and expenditures are allocated; or (ii) on such other basis as the Studio/Distributor may adopt from time to time with respect to motion pictures distributed by the Studio/Distributor.

(i) Claims and Litigation—The gross amount paid for the settlement of any claims (or on account of any judgment or decree in any litigation relating to any claims); such as for infringement, unfair competition, violation of any right of privacy, right of publicity, defamation or breach of contract, or arising out of other matters in connection with the Picture (such as the literary, dramatic or musical material on which the Picture is based), or the distribution, exploitation or exhibition thereof, including all expenses, court costs and reasonable attorneys' fees in connection with any such claims or litigation, or in connection with the investigation, assertion, prosecution or defense of any other claims or litigation relating to the Picture or its distribution, exhibition or exploitation; and insurance premiums (or an equivalent charge, if and to the extent that the Studio/Distributor provides coverage itself) with respect to any of the foregoing. Any sum received from the settlement of claims (or from judgments) for any unpaid amounts constituting (or which, if paid, would constitute) Accountable Gross shall be treated in the same manner in which a payment from the respective person would have been treated in the absence of a claim or action. The Studio/Distributor may set up appropriate reserves (subject to adjustment by the Studio/Distributor from time to time) for any distribution expenses, uncollectible accounts, or any other matters relating to the Picture, which the Studio/Distributor reasonably anticipates will be deductible from Accountable Gross under this clause A6.

A7. Participations—The Studio/Distributor shall also be entitled to deduct from Accountable Gross all sums (whether described as a deferment, a gross participation or otherwise), which the Studio/Distributor may be contractually obligated to pay to any person(s), including the Participant, for rights or services in connection with the Picture and which are based or dependent on all or any part or percentage of the gross receipts of the Picture (irrespective of the manner in which gross receipts are defined or computed) other than (i) sums which are based or dependent on and computed as a percentage of the net proceeds of the Picture, (ii) sums included in the computation of cost of production, and (iii) royalties and guild payments which are covered under clause A6(f) hereof. The sums which the Studio/Distributor is entitled to deduct pursuant to the preceding sentence are herein collectively called "participations." In computing the Producer's Share, (i) each of such participations shall be deductible hereunder if, when and to the extent that the Studio/Distributor's obligation to pay it accrues, whether or not such payment has then become due or been made; and (ii) participations may be deductible before, during or after the Studio/Distributor's recoupment of cost of production, under clause A9(a), depending on the respective contractual provisions applicable to them.

A8. Producer's Share Defined—As used herein, "producer's Share" means the Accountable Gross remaining after the deduction, on a continuing basis, of the aggregate of (i) the Studio/Distributor's distribution fees, under clause A2 and A5; (ii) distribution expenses, under clause A6; and (iii) participations (if any), under clause A7.

A9. Application of Producer's Share—The Producer's Share shall be applied by the Studio/Distributor as follows:

(a) Recoupment—The Studio/Distributor shall own and retain all of the Producer's Share until all unrecouped amounts of cost of production of the Picture have been entirely recouped, together with interest (at the rate herein specified) computed monthly on all such unrecouped production costs from the month in which such respective costs were paid or accrued. Interest chargeable hereunder shall be 125% of the prime interest rate per annum quoted by the Bank of America (at the respective times at which such interest is computed hereunder). Any Producer's Share available for recoupment hereunder shall first be applied to any interest then due, after which the remaining Producer's Share (if any) shall be applied to the recoupment of the cost of production.

A10. Accountings—(a) The Studio/Distributor shall give the Participant statements semi-annually for the first two years after the date of the first general release of the Picture in the United States, as such date is established by the Studio/Distributor and reflected in its records in accordance with its usual practices; however, if the Picture should be exhibited theatrically in the United States before such first general release date in engagements for which tickets are sold in advance on a reserved seat or reserved performance basis, then such two-year period shall instead commence on the date of the first such exhibition. After the expiration of such two-year period, such statements shall be given annually (if percentage compensation is then payable to the Participant hereunder, and otherwise only on the Participant's written request); no request under this sentence shall be effective unless it is made at least one year after the last previous such request (or after the last statement was given, if no such request was made previously). Such statements shall (i) conform with the end of the Studio/Distributor's corresponding accounting period, and be given within ninety (90) days thereafter; and (ii) be accompanied with payment of the amount, if any, shown to be due the Participant.

(b) The Studio/Distributor shall keep full, true and accurate books of account pertaining to the production and distribution of the Picture. Said books of account, insofar as they relate to the Picture, and have not become incontestable, may be examined on behalf of the Participant for the purpose of verifying the accuracy of any statement given the Participant hereunder, during reasonable business hours, by either (i) a national firm of certified public accountants of a stature qual to Price Waterhouse & Company or Haskins and Sells, or (ii) such other first-class reputable firm of certified public accountants as the Studio/Distributor in its sole discretion may approve. No audit may go into any transactions reported in any statement rendered prior to the commencement of any earlier audit. No audit may continue for longer than forty-five (45) consecutive business days, nor shall audits be made more frequently than once annually.

(c) Whenever Accountable Gross is derived from a transaction involving the Picture and one or more other motion pictures, in which the payment for each motion picture is not separately stated, the Studio/Distributor shall have the right to make an allocation between the Picture and such other motion picture(s), based on the Studio/Distributor's own reasonable opinion of the relative values in, and at the time of, such transaction. Whenever costs are incurred with respect to the Picture and one or more other motion pictures, and the cost attributable to each motion picture is not separately stated, the Studio/Distributor shall have the right to make an allocation of such costs between the Picture and such other motion picture(s), based on the Studio/Distributor's reasonable opinion.

(d) Statements given the Participant hereunder shall be subject to correction or amendment by the Studio/Distributor at any time. The Studio/Distributor agrees to keep its books of account with respect to the Picture for at least eighteen (18) months after the respective transactions or activities on which they are based, but may destroy such books of account after such respective eighteen (18) month periods. Each statement shall be deemed correct, and conclusive and binding on the Participant, on the expiration of a period of eighteen (18) months after it is given, and the inclusion in any statement of information or items which appeared in a previous statement shall not render any such information or items contestable or recommence the running of such eighteen (18) period with respect thereto; however, if the Participant delivers a written notice to the Studio/Distributor, objecting to any such statement or item within such eighteen (18) month period, and if such notice specified in detail the particular items to which the Participant objects and the nature of the Participant's objections thereto, then insofar as such particular items are concerned, such statements shall not be deemed correct or conclusive or binding on the Participant. Any objection to any statement given the Participant hereunder shall be deemed to have been waived unless action based thereon is instituted by the Participant against the Studio/Distributor within six (6) months following the expiration of such eighteen (18) month period.

(e) All statements and payments shall be sent to the Participant at the Participant's then current address for notices under the agreement to which this exhibit is attached.

A11. Creditor-Debtor Relationship—The relationship between the Participant and the Studio/Distributor is that of creditor and debtor with respect to the payment of any moneys due the Participant hereunder. Nothing contained in this agreement shall be construed to create a trust or specific fund with respect to Accountable Gross or net proceeds of the Picture or the Participant's portion thereof, or with respect to any other moneys, or to prevent or preclude the Studio/Distributor from commingling any such Accountable Gross or net proceeds or any moneys due the Participant hereunder with any other moneys or funds, or to give the Participant a lien on the Picture or an assignment of the proceeds thereof; the Participant waives any right to make any claim to the contrary. The Studio/Distributor shall have no fiduciary obligation to the Participant under this agreement, and the Studio/Distributor shall not be deemed to have received any moneys as the Participant's agent or trustee or for the Participant's account. The Studio/Distributor's obligation to pay any moneys to the Participant hereunder shall not bear interest, nor shall the Participant acquire any right, title or interest in any increments or gains that may accrue to funds payable to the Participant under this agreement.

A12. No Representations—Nothing contained in this exhibit shall be deemed to obligate the Studio/Distributor to produce the Picture, or to release or distribute it. If the Picture is produced, released and distributed, it is expressly acknowledged that the Studio/Distributor has not made and is not required to make any representations or covenants with respect to the amount of Accountable Gross or Net Proceeds which will or may be derived from the Picture, or with respect to the amount of contingent compensation which will or may become payable to the Participant hereunder.

A13. No Joint Venture—Nothing contained in this Agreement shall be deemed to constitute a partnership or joint venture between the Participant and the Studio/Distributor, or to make the Participant the Studio/Distributor's agent, and neither the Participant nor the Studio/Distributor shall be or become liable or obligated to any third party by any representation or act of the other. The Participant waives any right to make any claim to the contrary, notwithstanding any acts of the parties of either of them.

A14. Distribution of the Picture—As between the Participant and the Studio/Distributor:

(a) The Studio/Distributor shall have exclusive control of the distribution, exploitation, marketing, reissuing and sale or other disposition of the Picture and all versions thereof, by the Studio/Distributor or any persons designed by the Studio/Distributor (whether or not any such person is a Studio/Distributor Affiliate), perpetually and without territorial or other limitation. In the Studio/Distributor's sole discretion, at any time or from time to time, the Studio/Distributor may withhold or withdraw the Picture or any such versions from distribution, either entirely or with respect to all or any part of any country or medium of exhibition.

(b) The Picture may be distributed under any plan or plans which the Studio/Distributor deems proper or expedient. Without limiting the foregoing, (i) the Studio/Distributor may distribute the Picture in groups with other motion pictures, whether or not the Studio/Distributor or any Affiliate of the Studio/Distributor has any ownership interest or participation in any such other motion pictures; (ii) the Studio/Distributor may make all booking, leasing and rental contracts for the exhibition of the Picture, and sell it and territorial rights in it outright, and grant to others the right to distribute and exhibit the Picture or any part thereof; and (iii) the Studio/Distributor may make and cancel contracts in connection with any of the foregoing, and adjust and settle disputes, and give allowance and credits, with and to distributors, licensees, exhibitors and other persons (whether or not any such distributor, licensee, exhibitor or other person is a Studio/Distributor Affiliate, or is owned, operated or controlled by the Studio/Distributor or any Studio/Distributor Affiliate).

(c) The Studio/Distributor shall own all rights in the Picture, and in Accountable Gross and Net Proceeds thereof, including the right to hypothecate them, and the Participant shall have no right, title or interest therein; however, nothing contained in this clause A14(c) or in any such hypothecation shall release the Studio/Distributor from its obligation to make any payment to which the Participant may become entitled hereunder.

(d) The Studio/Distributor and each franchised sub-distributor may use its own judgment in determining the extent (if any) to which it will audit, check or verify the computation of any payments to it, or press for the collection of any unpaid amounts constituting (or which, if collected, would constitute) Accountable Gross. Neither the Studio/Distributor nor anyone else shall be required to sue or otherwise press for, or file claims in any bankruptcy or insolvency proceedings for, any such amounts.

A15. Sale of All Rights in the Picture—If the Studio/Distributor sells all of its right, title and interest in the Picture, the Participant may elect either of the following alternatives:

(a) The net sums received by the Studio/Distributor from such sale shall constitute Accountable Gross, and shall be treated in the same manner as Accountable Gross described in clause A2(e), but the income of the purchaser would not be included in Accountable Gross; or

(b) No amounts received by the Studio/Distributor from such sale shall be included in Accountable Gross (and accordingly the terms of such sale and the amounts paid to the Studio/Distributor thereunder would be of no relevance hereunder), but (i) all income and expenses (other than the purchase price paid to the Studio/Distributor) of the purchaser, relating to the Picture, shall be treated for all purposes of accounting and computation hereunder as though they were income and expenses of the Studio/Distributor; and (ii) upon the assumption by the purchaser of all of the Studio/Distributor's obligations hereunder, such sale shall be deemed a novation, so that the Studio/Distributor shall not be liable to the Participant for the payment of any contingent compensation which may thereafter become payable hereunder based on any such income of the purchaser, but the Participant shall look solely to the purchaser for any such payment.

The Participant may make such election by written notice to the Studio/Distributor, served within one (1) week after the Studio/Distributor notifies the Participant, in good faith and in writing, that it proposes to make such sale; if the Participant fails to notify the Studio/Distributor of the Participant's election within such one-week period, the Participant shall be deemed to have elected alternative (a). The Studio/Distributor's notice shall identify the purchaser and specify the purchase price. If such purchase price has changed at the time such sale is made, the Studio/Distributor shall be obligated to notify the Participant again (in which event the same procedure would again be followed) if and only if the change is substantial and adversely affects the elected alternative.

A16. Assignment by Participant—The Participant may assign the Participant's right to receive contingent compensation hereunder, at any time after the release of the Picture. However, the Studio/Distributor shall only be obligated to honor one such assignment, and then only if it is an assignment of all (as distinguished from part) of the Participant's right to receive such contingent compensation thereafter. Nothing herein contained shall be deemed to preclude the Participant from making a partial assignment or to preclude the first assignee (of all of the Participant's said right) from making a subsequent complete or partial assignment, however, the Studio/Distributor shall not be obligated to pay in accordance with any such partial or subsequent assignment unless a single person is designated as a disbursing agent, to whom the Studio/Distributor may make all such payments thereafter, regardless of any further assignment(s). The Studio/Distributor's obligation to pay in accordance with any such assignment or designation of a disbursing agent, shall be further conditioned on the Studio/Distributor's receipt of written notice thereof, in form satisfactory to the Studio/Distributor. The Studio/Distributor's payment in accordance with any such assignment or designation shall be deemed to be the equivalent of payment to the Participant hereunder. The Participant's rights to inspect and audit the Studio/Distributor's books of account shall not be assignable without the Studio/Distributor's prior written consent.

A17. Headings—The headings of the clauses and sub-clauses of this exhibit are for convenience only, and they shall not be of any effect in construing the contents of the respective clauses or sub-clauses.

Exhibit "A-1"
GROSS RECEIPTS DEFINITION

This exhibit is attached to and is part of the agreement dated June 25, 1993, by and among Filmright, Incorporated (the "Production Company"), Rocky Roundtree (the "Artist"), the Artist Lender Company, Inc. (the "Lender") and Worldwide Pictures, a division of Worldwide Studios, Inc., (the "Studio/ Distributor") relating to the motion picture entitled "Invasion From Chunga" (hereinafter referred to as the "Picture").

Net proceeds of the Picture, with respect to which any Net Proceeds Participant may be entitled to contingent compensation under the agreement to which this exhibit is attached, shall be computed, and such contingent compensation shall be accounted for and paid, as provided in this exhibit.

A1. Definitions—As used in this exhibit, the following terms and their respective equivalents, unless the context expressly provides t the contrary, have the following meanings:

(a) "Agreement" means the agreement to which this exhibit is attached, together with this exhibit and any other attached provisions, riders, exhibits and schedules, as they have been or may hereafter be amended or supplemented.

(b) "British Territory" means the United Kingdom of Great Britain and Northern Ireland, the Republic of Ireland, the Isle of Man, the Channel Islands, Malta, Gibraltar, and ships and aircraft flying the British flag, and camps wherever situated where British forces are stationed.

(c) "Country" means a nation, or any other area (anywhere in the universe) for which the Picture is licensed.

(d) "Here-" as a prefix in words such as "herein," "hereof" and "hereunder," refers to this agreement.

(e) "Include" (or any equivalent, such as "included" or "including") is illustrative and not limitative.

(f) "Person" means any corporation, partnership, joint venture, trust or any other business entity or firm, as well as any natural person.

(g) "Receipts" means the rentals, license fees, royalties or other charges received for the license or privilege to exhibit the Picture including reissues of the Picture, but excluding remakes and sequels, or trailers of the Picture in any way, including theatrical and non-theatrical exhibitions, and exhibitions on or by means of television and including exhibitions by any other process now known or hereafter devised, whether on film or by means of magnetic tape, wire, cassettes, discs or any other devices now known or hereafter devised, but excluding any amounts received from sub-distribution.

(h) "Restricted Currency" means a foreign currency which is or becomes subject to moratorium, embargo, banking or exchange restrictions, or restrictions against remittances to the United States.

(i) "Road Show Engagements" means (i) engagements for the exhibition of the Picture in theatres hired and/or operated by the Studio/Distributor for the respective engagements; and (ii) engagements, for the exhibition of the Picture, for which tickets are sold in advance on a reserved seat or reserved performance basis. The net sums received by the Studio/Distributor or losses resulting to the Studio/Distributor from road show engagements, after the payment of all expenses incurred for or attributable to such road show engagements, shall be included or deducted (as the case may be) in or from Accountable Gross. The expenses referred to in the preceding sentence shall include but not be limited to all expenses of hiring and/or operating such theatres for such road show engagements (including theatre rental and salaries of theatre help), all expenses of checking road show engagements, and all advertising expenses incurred for or attributable to such road show engagements (whether such advertising expenses represent amounts paid or incurred directly by the Studio/Distributor, or reimbursements or allowances to exhibitors, sub-distributors or licensees), such as: expenses of advertising through newspapers, billboards, television, radio. exploitation material, lobby displays, marquees, bus cards, area magazine advertising, and a pro rata share (as allocated by the Studio/Distributor, based on the Studio/Distributor's reasonable opinion) of national magazine advertising; telegraph and cable charges, and long distance telephone charges, in connection with specific advertising campaigns; costs of production of advertising material, such as newspaper ads, trailers, stills, lithograph paper and other material shipped to exhibitors for use in connection with specific engagements; and salaries and expenses of field men and of group sales personnel, and printing costs, for group sales activities, publicity and star tour engagements, and special promotion and exploitation events.

(j) "Studio/Distributor" means Worldwide Pictures (which is a division of Worldwide Studios, Inc.) together with Worldwide Studios, Inc. and all of its other divisions and its wholly-owned and partially-owned subsidiaries. None of such subsidiaries or other divisions shall have any obligations or liabilities hereunder.

(k) "Studio/Distributor Affiliate" means any corporation controlling (either directly or indirectly) or under common control with the Studio/Distributor. No Studio/Distributor Affiliate shall have any obligations or liabilities hereunder.

(l) "Such as" is illustrative and not limitative.

(m) "United States" means the states of the United States of America, together with the District of Columbia.

A2. Accountable Gross—Subject to clause A3 and A4, Accountable Gross shall be only the aggregate of all of the Studio/Distributor's receipts, and the net sums received by the Studio/Distributor from sub-distribution. Except as otherwise provided in clause A1(g) (with respect to road-show engagements), the moneys received by any exhibitor (such as a theatre or group of theatres, a television station or a television network) shall not be included in Accountable Gross, whether or not the respective exhibitor is owned, operated or controlled by the Studio/Distributor or any Studio/Distributor Affiliate. Moneys received from the sale or other disposition of still photographs, novelties, commercial articles or advertising or sales materials, or accessories, or from music royalties, phonograph records, books or other publications, stock footage, or any other rights or materials (literary, musical, physical or otherwise) taken from the Picture or on which the Picture is based in whole or in party shall not be included in Accountable Gross.

A3. Exclusions—(a) The amounts of all adjustments, credits, allowances (other than advertising allowances), rebates and refunds, given or made to sub-distributors, exhibitors and licensees, shall be excluded from Accountable Gross. To the extent that such amounts represent a return of amounts previously included in Accountable Gross, an appropriate adjustment shall be made by a corresponding reduction in Accountable Gross, and also in the Studio/Distributor's distribution fees with respect to the amount of the reduction.

(b) Moneys in the nature of security deposits, or advance or periodic payments, shall not constitute Accountable Gross until they have actually been earned (such as by the exhibition of the Picture) or forfeited.

A4. Foreign Currency—(a) Except as provided in this clause A4, (i) all accountings, reports, statements, computations and determinations hereunder shall be made and expressed in United States currency units; and (ii) no moneys shall be included in Accountable Gross unless they have been paid in United States dollars in the United States, or are payable in a foreign currency which is not a restricted currency and have been remitted in United States dollars to the United States, or could be if the Studio/Distributor so desired. The conversion of such foreign currency into United States dollars shall be made at the average weighted rate of exchange at which remittances have been received by the Studio/Distributor during the accounting period in which such remittances are received.

(b) Moneys which would otherwise be included in Accountable Gross, except that they are payable in a foreign currency which is a restricted currency, are herein called "restricted proceeds." Restricted proceeds shall be included in Accountable Gross only as follows, or on such other basis as the Studio/Distributor may adopt from time to time with respect to motion pictures then distributed by the Studio/Distributor:

(i) Where remittances in United States dollars are received in the United

States from a country where a quota of remittances is authorized for a fixed period, then a fraction of the total restricted proceeds of the Picture in such country during the period fixed by the quota shall be included in Accountable Gross. The numerator of such fraction shall be the amount of that restricted currency which is converted into remittances for such period which are received by the Studio/Distributor in United States dollars in the United States, or could be if the Studio/Distributor so desired, and the denominator shall be the total amount which became available to the Studio/Distributor in that restricted currency during such period and which could have been used for such remittances during such period if no exchange restrictions were in effect. The conversion into United States dollars of the amount of that restricted currency to be so included shall be made at the average weighted rate of exchange at which such quota remittances were received during such period.

(ii) Where remittances from a country are received in United States dollars in the United States, under authorization granted from time to time for remittance of a portion of the total restricted currency accumulated by the Studio/Distributor in such country, then each remittance shall be deemed to have come from the oldest restricted currency accumulated by the Studio/Distributor in such country, until such time as all accumulations of that restricted currency which are earlier (than the first such accumulation of restricted proceeds of the Picture) have been exhausted. Thereafter, all restricted proceeds of the Picture in such country, up to the date to which the restricted currency for the purchase of each remittance was accumulated, shall be included in Accountable Gross in accordance with the formula provided for in clause A4(b)(i), at the rate of exchange at which such remittance was received by the Studio/Distributor.

(iii) As and when contingent compensation becomes payable to the Participant under this Agreement, the Participant may notify the Studio/Distributor in writing that the Participant elects to require settlement of the Participant's share of the restricted proceeds of the Picture remaining in any country and not yet included in Accountable Gross under any provision of this clause A4(b), in the currency of such country. Such notice shall also include a designation of a bank or other representative in such country, to whom payment may be made for the Participant's account. Such payment shall be made to such representative as and when the Participant has obtained any required permission. Such payment shall be made at the Participant's expense and shall, to the extent thereof, be deemed the equivalent of the inclusion in Accountable Gross of the restricted proceeds of which such payment represents the Participant's share, and satisfy the Studio/Distributor's obligations to the Participant with respect to such restricted proceeds and the Participant's share thereof.

(c) On the Participant's written request, the Studio/Distributor shall report to the Participant the amount of restricted proceeds (if any) which under any provision of this clause A4 have not yet been included in Accountable Gross, as of the closing date of the most recent statement which has then been furnished to the Participant under clause A7.

A5. Deductible Items—The Studio/Distributor shall be entitled to deduct and retain for its own account, from Accountable Gross, the aggregate of all sums paid or advanced, and all costs and charges incurred by the Studio/Distributor, directly or indirectly, for or in connection with any of the following:

(a) Taxes—Taxes, excises and imposts (and payments and expenses in contesting, compromising or settling any of them, together with any interest and penalties on any of them) imposed by any taxing authority (regardless of any doubt as to the legality or applicability of any of them, and regardless of how they may be designated or characterized by the respective taxing authority or any other taxing authority), on or with respect to:

(i) the Picture and any trailers thereof;

(ii) Any prints and physical properties of the Picture;

(iii) advertising accessories, for free distribution, relating to the Picture;

(iv) Exhibition, distribution or other use of the Picture, trailers thereof or physical properties thereof;

(v) any Accountable Gross, receipts or other revenues or credits from the Picture or trailers thereof, or from the exhibition, distribution or other use thereof, or the remittance of payment of all or any portion thereof.

The taxes, excises and imposts deductible under this clause A6(a) shall include the so-called Canadian "remittance tax," and other remittance taxes, and all personal property, turnover, sales, use, film hire, excise, stamp, gross income and gross receipts taxes, and taxes computed on a portion of receipts, revenues or remittances (but excluding all net income, franchise, excess profits and corporation taxes). In preparing and filing their corporate tax returns, the Studio/Distributor and its distributors and Studio/Distributor Affiliates shall have the right to take the full amount of any credits, deductions or other benefits that may be available to them with respect to, or relating to, any such taxes, excises and imposts, without any accounting, payment or other liability or obligation to the Participant. Notwithstanding anything contained in clause A10, or elsewhere in this Agreement, the Participant shall have not right to inspect or copy any tax return of the Studio/Distributor or any of its distributors, or to require the Studio/Distributor or any of its distributors to produce any such tax return or any information contained therein.

(b) Prints and Physical Properties—Prints, replacement prints, master discs and records; laboratory work; titles; dupe negatives and fine grain prints, re-dubbed tracks and foreign versions, including a version or versions synchronized with music or sound effects; substandard reductions; re-editing, re-cutting, rerecording and changes of or in the Picture; copyright protection, registration and renewal; and insurance premiums (or an equivalent charge, if and to the extent that the Studio/Distributor provides coverage itself) with respect to any of the foregoing items or with respect to any other physical properties relating to the Picture. If the methods or media of exhibition, transmission, projection or communication, or procedures, techniques or practices in connection with any of the foregoing, should be modified or changed, the corresponding costs of the new, substitute or changed methods, media, procedures, techniques or practices shall be deductible under this clause A6(b).

(c) Advertising—Advertising, marketing, promoting, exploiting and publicizing the Picture in any way, including the following:

(i) Publications, such as trade publications, fan magazines, newspapers, organization publications, and other space and display advertising, national and local.

(ii) Cooperative advertising and advertising allowances to exhibitors (whether effected by credits against or deductions from film rentals, by direct reimbursement, or otherwise). No such allowances shall reduce Accountable Gross for the purpose of computing distribution fees.

(iii) Commercial tie-ups.

(iv) Field exploitation, including salaries of employees and allowed living costs and traveling expenses, fees and charges, whether paid to the Studio/Distributor employees or other persons.

(v) Radio and television advertising, including cost of time and program and commercial preparation, recording and prints and tapes.

(vi) Tours and personal appearances of personalities connected with the Picture, including salaries of employees and allowed living costs and traveling expenses, fees and charges, whether paid to the Studio/Distributor employees or other persons.

(vii) Previews and screenings.

(viii) Traveling and living expenses (but not salaries) of the Studio/Distributor's publicity, advertising and exploitation executives, but only for trips directly attributable to or occasioned by the Picture.

(ix) Entertainment, such as of press and personalities.

(x) Art work, cuts and engravings.

(xi) Promotional material, such as souvenirs; and the preparation, manufacture and dissemination of press books, and of any other advertising accessories or materials, for free distribution.

(xii) Production of trailers and the manufacture of prints of such trailers for the Picture utilizing scenes from the Picture or material from other sources.

(xiii) The cost of advertising overhead, which shall be an amount equivalent to 10% of the aggregate of all other amounts which are deductible under this clause A6(c).

(d) Checking—Checking percentage engagements and licenses of the Picture.

(e) Transportation, Duties and Censorship—Freight, shipping, transportation, reels and containers, storage, duties, tariffs, customs charges, import taxes and censorship (including voluntary and involuntary censorship, classification and rating by governmental bodies or other persons or organizations, such as religious, ethnic and veteran's groups and organizations, and networks and other exhibitors or groups and organizations of exhibitors).

(f) Royalties and Guild Payments—Synchronization, recording, performing, patent and trademark royalties, and all other required payments (to any person, including any guild or union) and expenses, for or with respect to the exhibition or exploitation of the Picture, theatrically or on television or otherwise.

(g) Trade Associations—Dues, fees and contributions (to the extent reasonably allocated by the Studio/Distributor to the Picture or the distribution thereof) to MPAA, AMPTP and MPEA or any similarly constituted or substitute authorities or organizations, or their respective successors, wherever located; and fees for industry public relations activities, and for protection against copyright infringements.

(h) Quota Losses—Quota losses and quota expenditures in foreign countries sustained or incurred on account of the Picture. Such quota losses and expenditures shall be apportioned (i) by allocating to the Picture the same percentage of the total quota losses and expenditures, for the particular country and for the particular fiscal period concerned, that the cost of production of the Picture is of the total cost of production of all motion pictures to which such respective quota losses and expenditures are allocated; or (ii) on such other basis as the Studio/Distributor may adopt from time to time with respect to motion pictures distributed by the Studio/Distributor.

(i) Claims and Litigation—The gross amount paid for the settlement of any claims (or on account of any judgment or decree in any litigation relating to any claims); such as for infringement, unfair competition, violation of any right of privacy, right of publicity, defamation or breach of contract, or arising out of other matters in connection with the Picture (such as the literary, dramatic or musical material on which the Picture is based), or the distribution, exploitation or exhibition thereof, including all expenses, court costs and reasonable attorneys' fees in connection with any such claims or litigation, or in connection with the investigation, assertion, prosecution or defense of any other claims or litigation relating to the Picture or its distribution, exhibition or exploitation; and insurance premiums (or an equivalent charge, if and to the extent that the Studio/Distributor provides coverage itself) with respect to any of the foregoing. Any sum received from the settlement of claims (or from judgments) for any unpaid amounts constituting (or which, if paid, would constitute) Accountable Gross shall be treated in the same manner in which a payment from the respective person would have been treated in the absence of a claim or action. The Studio/Distributor may set up appropriate reserves (subject to adjustment by the Studio/Distributor from time to time) for any distribution expenses, uncollectible accounts, or any other matters relating to the Picture, which the Studio/Distributor reasonably anticipates will be deductible from Accountable Gross under this clause A6.

A6. Gross Receipts Defined—As used here, "gross Receipts" means the Accountable Gross remaining after the deduction on a continuing basis of the items specified in clause A5.

A7. Accountings—(a) The Studio/Distributor shall give the Participant statements semi-annually for the first two years after the date of the first general release of the Picture in the United States, as such date is established by the Studio/Distributor and reflected in its records in accordance with its usual practices; however, if the Picture should be exhibited theatrically in the United States before such first general release date in engagements for which tickets are sold in advance on a reserved seat or reserved performance basis, then such two-year period shall instead commence on the date of the first such exhibition. After the expiration of such two-year period, such statements shall be given annually (if percentage compensation is then payable to the Participant hereunder, and otherwise only on the Participant's written request); no request under this sentence shall be effective unless it is made at least one year after the last previous such request (or after the last statement was given, if no such request was made previously). Such statements shall (i) conform with the end of the Studio/Distributor's corresponding accounting period, and be given within ninety (90) days thereafter; and (ii) be accompanied with payment of the amount, if any, shown to be due the Participant.

(b) The Studio/Distributor shall keep full, true and accurate books of account pertaining to the production and distribution of the Picture. Said books of account, insofar as they relate to the Picture, and have not become incontestable, may be examined on behalf of the Participant for the purpose of verifying the accuracy of any statement given the Participant hereunder, during reasonable business hours, by either (i) a national firm of certified public accountants of a stature qual to Price Waterhouse & Company or Haskins and Sells, or (ii) such other first-class reputable firm of certified public accountants as the Studio/Distributor in its sole discretion may approve. No audit may go into any transactions reported in any statement rendered prior to the commencement of any earlier audit. No audit may continue for longer than forty-five (45) consecutive business days, nor shall audits be made more frequently than once annually.

(c) Whenever Accountable Gross is derived from a transaction involving the Picture and one or more other motion pictures, in which the payment for each motion picture is not separately stated, the Studio/Distributor shall have the right to make an allocation between the Picture and such other motion picture(s), based on the Studio/Distributor's own reasonable opinion of the relative values in, and at the time of, such transaction. Whenever costs are incurred with respect to the Picture and one or more other motion pictures, and the cost attributable to each motion picture is not separately stated, the Studio/Distributor shall have the right to make an allocation of such costs between the Picture and such other motion picture(s), based on the Studio/Distributor's reasonable opinion.

(d) Statements given the Participant hereunder shall be subject to correction or amendment by the Studio/Distributor at any time. The Studio/Distributor agrees to keep its books of account with respect to the Picture for at least eighteen (18) months after the respective transactions or activities on which they are based, but may destroy such books of account after such respective eighteen (18) month periods. Each statement shall be deemed correct, and conclusive and binding on the Participant, on the expiration of a period of ten (10) months after it is given, and the inclusion in any statement of information or items which appeared in a previous statement shall not render any such information or items contestable or recommence the running of such eighteen (18) period with respect thereto; however, if the Participant delivers a written notice to the Studio/Distributor, objecting to any such statement or item within such eighteen (18) month period, and if such notice specified in detail the particular items to which the Participant objects and the nature of the Participant's objections thereto, then insofar as such particular items are concerned, such statements shall not be deemed correct or conclusive or binding on the Participant. Any objection to any statement given the Participant hereunder shall be deemed to have been waived unless action based thereon is instituted by the Participant against the Studio/Distributor within six (6) months following the expiration of such eighteen (18) month period.

(e) All statements and payments shall be sent to the Participant at the Participant's then current address for notices under the agreement to which this exhibit is attached.

A8. Creditor-Debtor Relationship—The relationship between the Participant and the Studio/Distributor is that of creditor and debtor with respect to the payment of any moneys due the Participant hereunder. Nothing contained in this agreement shall be construed to create a trust or specific fund with respect to Accountable Gross or net proceeds of the Picture or the Participant's portion thereof, or with respect to any other moneys, or to prevent or preclude the Studio/Distributor from commingling any such Accountable Gross or net proceeds or any moneys due the Participant hereunder with any other moneys or funds, or to give the Participant a lien on the Picture or an assignment of the proceeds thereof; the Participant waives any right to make any claim to the contrary. The Studio/Distributor shall have no fiduciary obligation to the Participant under this agreement, and the Studio/Distributor shall not be deemed to have received any moneys as the Participant's agent or trustee or for the Participant's account. The Studio/Distributor's obligation to pay any moneys to the Participant hereunder shall not bear interest, nor shall the Participant acquire any right, title or interest in any increments or gains that may accrue to funds payable to the Participant under this agreement.

A9. No Representations—Nothing contained in this exhibit shall be deemed to obligate the Studio/Distributor to produce the Picture, or to release or distribute it. If the Picture is produced, released and distributed, it is expressly acknowledged that the Studio/Distributor has not made and is not required to make any representations or covenants with respect to the amount of Accountable Gross or Net Proceeds which will or may be derived from the Picture, or with respect to the amount of contingent compensation which will or may become payable to the Participant hereunder.

A10. No Joint Venture—Nothing contained in this Agreement shall be deemed to constitute a partnership or joint venture between the Participant and the Studio/Distributor, or to make the Participant the Studio/Distributor's agent, and neither the Participant nor the Studio/Distributor shall be or become liable or obligated to any third party by any representation or act of the other. The Participant waives any right to make any claim to the contrary, notwithstanding any acts of the parties of either of them.

A11. Distribution of the Picture—As between the Participant and the Studio/Distributor:

(a) The Studio/Distributor shall have exclusive control of the distribution, exploitation, marketing, reissuing and sale or other disposition of the Picture and all versions thereof, by the Studio/Distributor or any persons designed by the Studio/Distributor (whether or not any such person is a Studio/Distributor Affiliate), perpetually and without territorial or other limitation. In the Studio/Distributor's sole discretion, at any time or from time to time, the Studio/Distributor may withhold or withdraw the Picture or any such versions from distribution, either entirely or with respect to all or any part of any country or medium of exhibition.

(b) The Picture may be distributed under any plan or plans which the Studio/Distributor deems proper or expedient. Without limiting the foregoing, (i) the Studio/Distributor may distribute the Picture in groups with other motion pictures, whether or not the Studio/Distributor or any Affiliate of the Studio/Distributor has any ownership interest or participation in any such other motion pictures; (ii) the Studio/Distributor may make all booking, leasing and rental contracts for the exhibition of the Picture, and sell it and territorial rights in it outright, and grant to others the right to distribute and exhibit the Picture or any part thereof; and (iii) the Studio/Distributor may make and cancel contracts in connection with any of the foregoing, and adjust and settle disputes, and give allowance and credits, with and to distributors, licensees, exhibitors and other persons (whether or not any such distributor, licensee, exhibitor or other person is a Studio/Distributor Affiliate, or is owned, operated or controlled by the Studio/Distributor or any Studio/Distributor Affiliate).

(c) The Studio/Distributor shall own all rights in the Picture, and in Accountable Gross and Net Proceeds thereof, including the right to hypothecate them, and the Participant shall have no right, title or interest therein; however, nothing contained in this clause A14(c) or in any such hypothecation shall release the Studio/Distributor from its obligation to make any payment to which the Participant may become entitled hereunder.

(d) The Studio/Distributor and each franchised sub-distributor may use its own judgment in determining the extent (if any) to which it will audit, check or verify the computation of any payments to it, or press for the collection of any unpaid amounts constituting (or which, if collected, would constitute) Accountable Gross. Neither the Studio/Distributor nor anyone else shall be required to sue or otherwise press for, or file claims in any bankruptcy or insolvency proceedings for, any such amounts.

A12. Sale of All Rights in the Picture—If the Studio/Distributor sells all of its right, title and interest in the Picture, the Participant may elect either of the following alternatives:

(a) The net sums received by the Studio/Distributor from such sale shall constitute Accountable Gross, and shall be treated in the same manner as Accountable Gross described in clause A2(e), but the income of the purchaser would not be included in Accountable Gross; or

(b) No amounts received by the Studio/Distributor from such sale shall be included in Accountable Gross (and accordingly the terms of such sale and the amounts paid to the Studio/Distributor thereunder would be of no relevance hereunder), but (i) all income and expenses (other than the purchase price paid to the Studio/Distributor) of the purchaser, relating to the Picture, shall be treated for all purposes of accounting and computation hereunder as though they were income and expenses of the Studio/Distributor; and (ii) upon the assumption by the purchaser of all of the Studio/Distributor's obligations hereunder, such sale shall be deemed a novation, so that the Studio/Distributor shall not be liable to the Participant for the payment of any contingent compensation which may thereafter become payable hereunder based on any such income of the purchaser, but the Participant shall look solely to the purchaser for any such payment.

The Participant may make such election by written notice to the Studio/Distributor, served within one (1) week after the Studio/Distributor notifies the Participant, in good faith and in writing, that it proposes to make such sale; if the Participant fails to notify the Studio/Distributor of the Participant's election within such one-week period, the Participant shall be deemed to have elected alternative (a). The Studio/Distributor's notice shall identify the purchaser and specify the purchase price. If such purchase price has changed at the time such sale is made, the Studio/Distributor shall be obligated to notify the Participant again (in which event the same procedure would again be followed) if and only if the change is substantial and adversely affects the elected alternative.

A13. Assignment by Participant—The Participant may assign the Participant's right to receive contingent compensation hereunder, at any time after the release of the Picture. However, the Studio/Distributor shall only be obligated to honor one such assignment, and then only if it is an assignment of all (as distinguished from part) of the Participant's right to receive such contingent compensation thereafter. Nothing herein contained shall be deemed to preclude the Participant from making a partial assignment or to preclude the first assignee (of all of the Participant's said right) from making a subsequent complete or partial assignment, however, the Studio/Distributor shall not be obligated to pay in accordance with any such partial or subsequent assignment unless a single person is designated as a disbursing agent, to whom the Studio/Distributor may make all such payments thereafter, regardless of any further assignment(s). The Studio/Distributor's obligation to pay in accordance with any such assignment or designation of a disbursing agent, shall be further conditioned on the Studio/Distributor's receipt of written notice thereof, in form satisfactory to the Studio/Distributor. The Studio/Distributor's payment in accordance with any such assignment or designation shall be deemed to be the equivalent of payment to the Participant hereunder. The Participant's rights to inspect and audit the Studio/Distributor's books of account shall not be assignable without the Studio/Distributor's prior written consent.

A14. Headings—The headings of the clauses and sub-clauses of this exhibit are for convenience only, and they shall not be of any effect in construing the contents of the respective clauses or sub-clauses.

Exhibit "B"
DELIVERY SCHEDULE

This exhibit is attached to and is part of the agreement dated June 25, 1993, by and among Filmright, Incorporated (the "Production Company"), Rocky Roundtree (the "Artist"), the Artist Lender Company, Inc. (the "Lender") and Worldwide Pictures, a division of Worldwide Studios, Inc., (the "Studio/Distributor") relating to the motion picture entitled "Invasion From Chunga" (hereinafter referred to as the "Picture").

A. The Production Company shall deliver, in the manner herein provided, each of the items described in this exhibit (all of which items are of, or relate to, the Picture), except for those items which, pursuant to the terms hereof, are to be made or procured by Studio/Distributor. Except as otherwise specifically provided in the agreement to which this exhibit is attached, all of the items to be delivered by the Production Company hereunder shall be delivered on or before the delivery date specified in clause 2.b.(2)(a) of said agreement.

B. The Studio/Distributor may, in a notice served on the Production Company following the completion of principal photography of the Picture, request that one or more of said items be delivered prior to said delivery date, in which event the Production Company shall, subject to the Production Company's reasonable production requirements relative to the item(s) specified in the Studio/Distributor's said notice, deliver the item(s) so specified by the Studio/Distributor promptly following Studio/Distributor's said request.

C. All items to be delivered by the Production Company hereunder shall (a) at the time of delivery (i) conform to all specifications set forth in the agreement to which this exhibit is attached and otherwise conform to accepted, standard specifications for theatrical feature productions; (ii) be of first-class technical quality and in first-class condition; (iii) where applicable, be fully edited, cut, main and end titled, scored, re-recorded, leadered, identified, assembled and conformed in all respects to the answer print; (iv) be in numbered containers suitable for the protection of the contents; and (v) be accompanied by a separate inventory identifying the contents of each container in detail; and (b) be addressed and delivered to the specific person, laboratory or department designated in this exhibit with respect to the item concerned or to such other person, laboratory or department which the Studio/Distributor may hereafter designate in a notice served on Production Company.

D. Any item which, pursuant to the terms hereof, is to be made or procured by the Studio/Distributor shall be so made or procured at such time as the Studio/Distributor determines appropriate, it being understood that if the Studio/Distributor, at any time, determines that such item is not required for the distribution of the Picture, the Studio/Distributor shall have no obligation to make or procure same. The Studio/Distributor's obligation (if any) to make or procure any item(s) hereunder shall be subject to the delivery hereunder by the Production Company of any materials necessary to manufacture such items(s).

E. Notwithstanding anything to the contrary set forth in this exhibit, in the event that the Production Company fails, refuses or neglects to deliver any item(s) to be delivered by the Production Company hereunder, the Studio/Distributor shall have the right (but not the obligation) to make or procure same.

F. All costs incurred in connection with the manufacture and/or delivery of the items hereinafter described (including, without limitation, any item[s] made or procured by the Studio/Distributor pursuant to this exhibit) shall be borne by the Production Company, it being understood that to the extent that the Studio/Distributor pays any costs in connection with the manufacture and/or delivery of any such item(s), (a) the Production Company shall pay to the Studio/Distributor an amount equal to such costs promptly following the Studio/Distributor's request therefor; and (b) the Studio/Distributor shall have the right to deduct and retain for its own account, from any sums payable to the Production Company pursuant to the agreement to which this exhibit is attached, an amount equal to the aggregate of the costs so paid by the Studio/Distributor (to the extent that such costs have not been paid by the Production Company to the Studio/Distributor as aforesaid); provided, however, that in no event shall the Production Company be obligated to so pay to the Studio/Distributor, or shall the Studio/Distributor so deduct and retain, on account of the manufacture of such item(s) an amount in excess of the sums which are then customarily charged by established laboratories (or other established manufacturers of such item[s]) in the vicinity of Los Angeles, California, in connection with manufacture of such item(s).

G. Any material not delivered to the Studio/Distributor and held temporarily or permanently by the Production Company for whatever reasons shall be stored in a recognized film vault and letters of access for each such item shall be delivered to the Studio/Distributor's Editorial Department Head.

Items to be delivered as soon as possible and no later than the delivery date:

1. Screenplay/Script—One (1) each of the final screenplay and shooting script.

2. Publicity Material—All written publicity material, including a final set of cast and production credits, a detailed synopsis of the Picture, detailed production notes pertaining to the making of the Picture, complete biographies of starring and key feature players, 1 1/2 page feature stories on key stars and filmmakers (not less than six features) and a minimum of three pages of column items, or "shorts."

3. Credit Statement—The written statement to be provided by the Producer to the Distributor setting out all main-and-end title billing, paid-advertising billing and all requirements regarding paid advertising.

Items to be delivered within two (2) weeks after the completion of principal photography:

1. Black & White Photographs—Original black and white negatives and three (3) sets of contact sheets, and any other special pre-production portrait photos related to the Picture, each with identification of persons and subject matter therein, including at least the following:

A. A total of 100 production stills depicting production scenes of the Picture with members of the cast appearing there;

B. A total of 50 informal or casual photographs of principal members of the cast and key production team members (i.e., the producer, director and director of photography); and

C. A total of 25 gallery or portrait sitting photographs, in and out of character, of the principal cast members for the Picture.

2. Color Photographs—Original negatives (if negative color is used) or all original color positive transparencies of production photography (2 1/4" × 2 1/4") or 35mm, with appropriate identifications, including at least the following:

A. A total of 150 production color shots depicting scenes in the Picture with members of the cast (including principals) appearing therein;

B. A total of 50 candid color shots of principal members of the cast and key production team members as designated above; and

C. A total of 35 portrait shots of principal cast members.

Items to be delivered on delivery date:

1. Answer Print—Final answer print made from Item 2 below;

2. Original Picture—Original Picture negative and composite optical soundtrack negative;

3. Interpositive—A 35mm color corrected unused interpositive made from the original Picture negative and conformed in all respects to the delivered answer print;

4. Television Cover Shots and Scenes—The materials referred to in Items 1–3 above (excluding the composite optical soundtrack negative) and Items 8 and 9 below with respect to all Cover Shots and/or additional scenes needed to permit a two (2) hour U.S. Network television broadcast of the Picture;

5. Internegative—One (1) 35mm internegative manufactured from the interpositive and one (1) composite optical soundtrack negative, conformed in all respects to the delivered answer print, along with one (1) composite spliceless check print from each such internegative and composite optical soundtrack negative (for the Library of Congress);

6. Titles—A 35mm textless background negative and a 35mm interpositive therefrom of the main and end titles and all descriptive titles conformed in all respects to the delivered answer print.

7. Music, Dialogue and Sound Items:

A. Master—A three-track or four-track 35mm magnetic master including separate mixed dialogue, separate mixed music and separate mixed sound effects tracks conformed in all respects to the delivered answer print;

B. Mixed Music and Sound Effects—A 35mm magnetic master of the separate mixed music and separate mixed fully filled sound effects conformed in all respects to the delivered answer print;

C. Dolby Sound—In the event that either Picture is recorded in Dolby Sound, the following materials must be delivered in lieu of Items A & B above:

(1) Access to the original 35mm magnetic four-track Dolby stereo master with surrounds (if surrounds were recorded);

(2) The original 35mm magnetic two-track Dolby stereo master with surrounds (if surrounds were recorded);

(3) A 35mm mag Dolby stereo music and fully filled effects only track (i.e., without dialogue); and

(4) A 35mm magnetic mono three-track master.

D. Music Master Recordings—A quarter (1/4) or one-half (1/2) inch magnetic tape (15 ips with 6ohz sync pulse) derived from the master recordings of all music recorded in connection with the Picture and/or any phonograph recordings thereof;

E. Music Cue Sheets—One (1) copy of the music cue sheets specifying the title of each composition contained in the Picture, and with respect to each composition, specifying the performer, composer, publisher, copyright owner, the affiliated performing rights society, usages (whether instrumental, instrumental-visual, vocal, vocal-visual or otherwise) and the place and number of such uses showing the film footage and running time for each cue;

F. Agreements—One (1) copy of the signed composers, lyricist and/or publishing agreements pertinent to all music embodied in the Picture along with one (1) copy of the signed agreements pertaining to all music embodied in the Picture granting pertinent synchronization and performing rights licenses and the necessary corresponding master use licenses;

G. Music Sheet—An original piano, vocal and rhythm lead sheet (music sheet) in 8 × 10 format of all songs utilized in the Picture;

H. Composer's Original Score—One (1) copy of the composer's original score and the band parts of all music written in connection with the Picture and/or any phonograph recordings thereof;

8. Film and Soundtrack Materials—All film and soundtrack materials for use in the manufacture of release prints, trailers, promo reels and television spots;

9. Screen Credits—Screen credit obligations, with a list of credits as they appear in the main and end titles, and paid advertising obligations, and including any restrictions as to the use of such names and likenesses;

10. Dialogue/Continuity—One (1) copy of a detailed dialogue and action (or combined) continuity of the Picture;

11. Laboratory Letter—A laboratory access letter (in the form of the Laboratory Access Letter accompanying this Agreement as Exhibit "F") granting the Distributor access to all items listed in this Exhibit "B" which are to be provided through the laboratory;

12. MPAA Certificate—The MPAA Certificate of Approval with the rating as specified elsewhere in this Agreement;

13. Certificate of Insurance—A certificate of insurance for Producer's Errors and Omissions insurance, as required to be maintained by the accompa-

nying Agreement, along with evidence showing that the premium for such policy has been paid for the current term of such policy;

14. Residuals—All information necessary for the calculation of all residuals payable in connection with the Picture (e.g., SAG final cast list, writers cast list and directors cast list).

15. Title and Copyright—One (1) copy each of the title report and copyright search report, along with all chain of title documents for all literary materials upon which the Picture is based; also one (1) copy of the copyright registration for the Picture, if an wherever registered by the Producer in the Territory.

Items to be delivered when and if ordered by the distributor:

1. Soundtrack Album Materials—All music materials necessary for making a soundtrack album of the Picture;

2. Work Print—A lab print from the developed original; and

3. Outakes—The negative and positive prints of all cut outs, trims, second takes, lists, sound effect tracks, dialogue tracks and music tracks made in connection with the Picture, whether or not included in the completed Picture.

Exhibit "C"
PRE-APPROVED ELEMENTS

This exhibit is attached to and is part of the agreement dated June 25, 1993, by and among Filmright, Incorporated (the "Production Company"), Rocky Roundtree (the "Artist"), the Artist Lender Company, Inc. (the "Lender") and Worldwide Pictures, a division of Worldwide Studios, Inc., (the "Studio/Distributor") relating to the motion picture entitled "Invasion From Chunga" (hereinafter referred to as the "Picture").

The following elements shall be deemed pre-approved under this Agreement or the Studio/Distributor shall have been accorded its necessary consultation rights with respect therewith:

1. Arty McCormick to prepare artwork for the one-sheet for an amount of compensation to be negotiated between the Studio/Distributor and Mr. McCormick which compensation shall be a distribution expense. Additionally, the following terms and conditions shall apply to Mr. McCormick's services:

a. First Proposal—At such time as deemed necessary by the Studio/Distributor to accommodate its distribution activities hereunder, Mr. McCormick shall submit to the Studio/Distributor his proposal for the one-sheet artwork. and the Studio/Distributor shall have the right in its sole discretion to accept or reject such proposal.

b. Second Submission—If the Studio/Distributor rejects such first proposal, the Studio/Distributor shall communicate to Mr. McCormick the basis of its objections and Mr. McCormick shall have five (5) calendar days thereafter to prepare and submit a second proposal. The Studio/Distributor shall have the right in its sole discretion to accept or reject such proposal.

c. Third Proposal—If the Studio/Distributor rejects such second proposal, the Studio/Distributor shall communicate to Mr. McCormick the basis of its objections and Mr. McCormick shall have five (5) calendar days thereafter to prepare and submit a third proposal. The Studio/Distributor shall have the right in its sole discretion to accept or reject such third proposal. Thereafter, the Studio/Distributor shall have no further obligations to Mr. McCormick with respect to the Picture (other than any unpaid compensation as previously negotiated) and the Studio/Distributor shall have the right to utilize the results and proceeds of all of Mr. McCormick's services in whole or in part as the Studio/Distributor may elect.

2. Chuck Holland as line producer of the Picture pursuant to terms and conditions to be agreed upon between Mr. Holland and the Production Company within the parameters of the Approved Production Budget.

Exhibit "D"
CASH FLOW SCHEDULE

TO: Filmright, Incorporated   July 6, 1993
FROM: Studio/Distributor
SUBJECT: Revised Cash Flow Without Completion Bond

Attached is the revised cash flow for the production of "Invasion From Chunga":

Wire transfers should be initiated from California no later than noon (Pacific time) on each Tuesday of the week indicated to insure that the funds are available for the check exchanges with the payroll service on Thursdays.
The dates and dollar amounts due are:

Tuesday	June 22	$	934,000
	June 29	$	934,000
	July 6	$	934,000
	July 13	$	934,000
	July 20	$	934,000
	July 27	$	934,000
	August 3	$	934,000
	August 10	$	934,000
	August 17	$	934,000
	August 24	$	2,456,000
	August 31	$	2,456,000
	September 7	$	2,456,000
	September 14	$	2,456,000

September 21	$ 2,456,000
September 28	$ 2,456,000
October 5	$ 2,456,000
October 12	$ 2,456,000
October 19	$ 2,456,000
October 26	$ 2,456,000
Post Production	$ 2,034,000
Direct Costs	$35,000,000
Contingency	$ 3,500,000
TOTAL	$38,000,000

Exhibit "E"
ASSIGNMENT AGREEMENT

For good and valuable consideration, receipt of which is hereby acknowledged, Filmright, Incorporated (the "Production Company") hereby assigns to Worldwide Pictures, a division of Worldwide Studios, Inc. (the "Studio/Distributor"), its successors and assigns the following ("Collateral"):

(a) Copyright—All of the Production Company's right, title and interest in and to the feature-length motion picture presently entitled "Invasion From Chunga" written, produced and directed by Rocky Rountree (the "Picture"), in perpetuity, throughout the universe, including, without limitation, the copyright, in and to the screenplay upon which the Picture is based, the Picture, including, but not limited to, the right to enforce said copyright and to recover damages on account of infringement of said copyright, regardless of the date of such infringement;

(b) Third Party Agreements—All of the Production Company's rights under all agreements with third parties ("Third Party Agreements") entered into by the Production Company with respect to the Picture, and

(c) Collateral—All negatives, film, tape and other physical properties created for the Picture.

The Studio/Distributor hereby assumes, and undertakes to keep and perform, in the place and stead of the Production Company, each and all of the executory obligations, undertakings and agreements on the part of the Production Company to be kept and performed pursuant to the Third Party Agreements, including, without limitation, any obligation to make residual, reuse and other additional or supplemental payments required to be made on or after the date of this Assignment Agreement pursuant to the terms of any applicable collective bargaining agreement by reason of the distribution or other exploitation of the Picture by the Studio/Distributor.

In furtherance of this assignment and for the purposes thereof (and not otherwise), the Production Company hereby irrevocably appoints the Studio/

Distributor as its attorney-in-fact with full power of substitution and revocation, in the name of the Production Company or otherwise, to demand, enforce, collect, receive and receipt and give releases for any payment or indemnity becoming due or arising under or in-connection with any of the Collateral or any policy of insurance relating thereto, to endorse, and collect any checks, drafts or other instruments payable to the Production Company therefor, to file any claims or institute any proceedings which the Studio/Distributor may deem appropriate for the enforcement of any agreements, contracts or rights included in the Collateral and to compromise any such demand, claim or action. The Studio/Distributor shall indemnify the Production Company with respect to claims against the Production Company arising as a result of the Studio/Distributor's use of such power of attorney. The Studio/Distributor shall have no obligation to the Production Company or any other person to take any action to enforce any such agreement, contract or right or to exercise any other right or power granted by this Agreement unless the following conditions have been satisfied: (i) such action shall have been requested of the Studio/Distributor by the Production Company in writing and (ii) the Studio/Distributor shall have received indemnity against costs and expenses which may be incurred in connection with such action in amounts and form satisfactory to the Studio/Distributor.

This Assignment is executed in accordance with and is subject to the terms and provisions of that certain Production-Financing/Distribution Agreement between the Production Company and the Studio/Distributor dated as of June 25, 1993.

PRODUCTION COMPANY—Filmright, Incorporated
By: _____
    James W. Producer, President

Exhibit "F"
LABORATORY PLEDGEHOLDER AGREEMENT

As of June 25, 1993
Film Laboratories, Inc.
67 Beverly Drive
Studio City, CA 90456
Re: "Invasion From Chunga"
Gentlemen:

This refers to the Production-Financing/Distribution Agreement ("Agreement") dated as of June 25, 1993 by and between the Worldwide Pictures, a division of Worldwide Studios, Inc. (the "Studio/Distributor") and Filmright, Incorporated (the "Production Company") relating to the production, financing and distribution of the feature-length motion picture entitled "Invasion From Chunga" (the "Picture") and the transfer of ownership of all rights in and to Picture to the Studio/Distributor, including, but not limited to, the exclusive right to distribute the Picture in all media perpetually throughout the universe.

You hereby confirm that you now have or will have, from time to time, in your possession at the laboratories at the above address, or under your control, all negatives, dupe negatives, fine grain prints, soundtracks, positive prints (cutouts and trims excepted), and sound and other physical properties in connection with the Picture and the trailer for the Picture, whether or not in completed form (collectively the "Original Material").

You are hereby authorized, directed and instructed by the Production Company and you agree to permit Studio/Distributor to have access to and to use the Original Material in accordance with the requirements of the Studio/Distributor. Such access and use by the Studio/Distributor shall be without regard to any liability or obligation of the Production Company and/or any third party to you, and you agree not to look to the Studio/Distributor or its property by reason of work, labor, materials or services which you may have performed for or furnished to the Production Company and/or such third party.

You agree to give the Studio/Distributor prompt written notice addressed to the Studio/Distributor at 100 Worldwide Plaza, Worldwide City, California 91608, c/o Jerry Adept, Editorial Department, of any change of location of the storage of the Original Material and you agree that you will not dispose of the Original Material in whole or in part without the prior written consent of the Studio/Distributor.

As between the Production Company and the Studio/Distributor, nothing herein contained modifies or in any manner changes the right of the Studio/Distributor under the Agreement.

Please confirm your agreement to the foregoing by signing in the space below.

Very truly yours,
Filmright, Incorporated
By:_____
James W. Producer,
President

STUDIO/DISTRIBUTOR—Worldwide Pictures,
a division of Worldwide Studios, Inc.
By: _____
Jeffrey Wilson, Vice President

UNDERSTOOD AND AGREED TO:
Film Laboratories, Inc.
By: _____
       Aaron Developer, President

Exhibit "G"
PRODUCTION ACCOUNT TAKEOVER LETTER
(to be typed on the Production Company's letterhead)

June 25, 1993

Picture:	"Invasion From Chunga" (the "Picture")
Bank:	World Film Bank, N.A.
Branch:	Jackson Hole, Wyoming
Street and Number:	123 Fort Hill Road
City:	Jackson Hole, Wyoming 89089
Account Number:	123456789
Name of Account:	Chunga Production

Gentlemen:

By countersigning this letter, you hereby acknowledge and agree that:

1. The following are the only authorized signatories on the above-captioned account:

For the Production Company, any two of the following:

> James W. Producer
> Robert V. Accountant
> Leslie D. Moneypenny

2. If the Worldwide Pictures, a division of Worldwide Studios, Inc. ("Studio/Distributor") takes over production of the Picture pursuant to its agreement with the Production Company, the Studio/Distributor may require that one or more signatures of the Studio/Distributor will be required on all checks.

3. In consideration of the Studio/Distributor providing financing for the Picture for which this account was established, we have executed an agreement giving the Studio/Distributor authority to exercise its sole control over the account at any time it takes over production of the Picture. Please confirm to the Studio/Distributor that upon their notice to you of their take over of production of the Picture and presentation of a copy of our agreement with them, you, pursuant to their request, will delete our authorized signatories on the above-captioned account, add such additional signatories as may be designated by the Studio/Distributor and thereafter pay only checks signed by the

Studio/Distributor's designees. We hereby release you from any and all claims, demands and liabilities, without limitation arising from your compliance herewith or with the instructions of the Studio/Distributor pursuant to our agreement with them.

4. You will not exercise any right of "set-off" or similar right with respect to the above-captioned account based upon any claims that you may have against us or any third parties.

Kindly acknowledge the within instruction and authorization and your acceptance thereof in the acknowledgement and acceptance space provided below.

Yours truly,

Filmright, Incorporated

By: _____
James W. Producer,
President

ACKNOWLEDGED AND ACCEPTED:
WORLD FILM BANK, N.A.
By: _____
George W. Sheffield, President

APPENDIX F

Negative Pickup Distribution Agreement

THIS AGREEMENT (hereinafter referred to as the "Agreement") is made and entered into as of this the 21st day of April, 1993, by and between Film-right, Incorporated (hereinafter referred to as the "Production Company") and Worldwide Distribution, Inc. (the "Distributor") and such Agreement relates to the production and distribution of a new and original feature-length sound and talking motion picture of first class quality in the English language and currently entitled "Invaders From Chunga" (the "Picture").

In consideration of the mutual covenants and agreements herein contained and for other good and valuable consideration, the parties hereto do hereby agree as follows:

1. THE PICTURE—The Production Company desires to produce the Picture on the terms and conditions hereof, and the Distributor desires to purchase all rights in and to the completed Picture set forth herein, subject to the terms and conditions hereof. During the period commencing on the date of this Agreement and continuing until the delivery of the Picture hereunder to the Distributor, the Production Company shall do, or cause to be done, all things of every kind necessary to develop, create, finance production costs, photograph, edit and otherwise complete and deliver the Picture to the Distributor in accordance with the terms and conditions of this Agreement, including, but not limited to, the terms of clause 2.A hereof requiring the submission to the Distributor for the Distributor's approval, all of the items set forth therein (including, but not limited to, the chain of title documents described in clause 2.A(4) hereof), and the terms of clause 2.b hereof setting forth the specifications for delivery of the Picture.

It is presently contemplated that pre-production of the Picture will commence not later than June 6, 1993 and that principal photography of the Picture will commence not later than September 15, 1993.

2. PRODUCTION REQUIREMENTS—A. Distributor Approvals—The Distributor shall have an absolute right of approval of the following elements of, or relating to, the Picture:

(1) The Picture's cash flow schedule, final budget and the individual items contained therein. The Distributor has heretofore approved a budget of Three

Million U.S. Dollars ($3,000,000 U.S.) (the "Budget"), inclusive of a cash Producer's fee in the sum of Three Hundred and Fifty Thousand U.S. Dollars ($350,000 U.S.) on account of the individual producing services of James W. Producer;.

(2) The final production schedule ("Production Schedule");

(3) The literary and dramatic materials acquired or prepared for use in the Picture, including, without limitation, the screenplay ("Screenplay") for the Picture, and the terms on which they were acquired or prepared;

(4) The chain of title documents pursuant to which the Production Company acquired the rights necessary to produce, distribute, and otherwise exploit the Picture (including, without limitation, the current title thereof) and to grant such rights to the Distributor in accordance with the terms hereof (including, without limitation, any and all settlement agreements, releases and waivers obtained by the Production Company from any third parties with respect to the Screenplay), it being agreed that the foregoing obligations are of the essence of this Agreement;

(5) Any screenwriter(s) who have rendered or who may render services;

(6) The director;

(7) The producer and executive producer. acknowledges that they have heretofore approved James W. Producer as the individual producer of the Picture;

(8) The composer, lyricist and conductor;

(9) The principal cast;

(10) The cinematographer, art director, production designer, film editor, unit production manager, associate producer, unit publicist, still photographer, production auditor, construction coordinator and head of transportation;

(11) Any and all contracts and agreements relating to any and all parties whose services and/or facilities shall be engaged for or utilized in the production of the Picture, including, without limitation, the contracts for the employment of the personnel set forth in Paragraphs 2.A.(5), (6), (7), (8), (9) and (10).

(12) The screen and advertising credits, if any, to be accorded to any person, firm or corporation, irrespective of size or position;

(13) All studios and location sites;

(14) Any special photographic, audio and technical processes to be used;

(15) Any deferments and contingent percentage participations (whether in "gross receipts" or "net proceeds" or otherwise) granted or assigned to any third party, all of which shall be the sole obligation of the Production Company, and not of the Distributor it being understood and agreed that nothing contained herein shall be deemed to create any obligation or liability on the part of the Distributor to pay any such deferments or participations;

(16) All music synchronization licenses and any other agreements or instruments under which any music has been or may be acquired for the Picture;

(17) Releases from all third parties, if any (with the exception of any production money lender) who may provide any sums in connection with production of the Picture, indicating that such third parties shall have no right, title or interest in or to the Picture. The Production Company shall deliver such releases to the Distributor on or before the delivery of the Picture, it being agreed that the foregoing obligation is of the essence of this Agreement;

(18) All post-production facilities for the Picture, including the laboratory and location for Production Company's final mix;

(19) The entity designated as the corporate producer of the Picture;

(20) Any and all contracts and agreements relating to the financing of the Picture, including, without limitation, any and all bank loan, so-called inter-party and completion guarantor agreements and related documents and all terms thereof.

The Distributor's approvals shall be in writing. There shall be no change or deviation from or substitution for any approved element without the Distributor's prior written consent. The Distributor shall not have the obligation to accept delivery of the Picture, and consequently shall be relieved of any payment obligations to the Production Company or its lender hereunder, if the Distributor, for good cause, fails to approve of each and every element set forth in clauses (1) through (20) above.

Whenever either party has a right of approval under this Agreement such right shall be exercised in accordance with the provisions of clause 9.H hereinbelow.

B. Specifications—The Production Company represents, warrants and agrees that, in addition to complying with clause 2.A hereof and the other requirements hereof, the Picture:

(1) Unless otherwise specified by the Distributor shall be photographed (i) in color, using 35mm raw stock negative film designated by the Distributor, (ii) in a standard 1.85/1 aspect ratio, (iii) using a standard academy aperture with the 1.33/1 aspect ratio on academy aperture center line, inside of which aperture the Picture composed for a 1.85/1 composition aspect ratio, having the same vertical center line, and (iv) with lettering on main and end titles not in excess of 71.3', of the width of said 1.85/1 composition with the same vertical center line, so that the lettering shall appear on the television screen in any television exhibition of the Picture; and was or will be recorded, synchronized, dubbed and re-dubbed utilizing such recording system as the Distributor may designate or approve;

(2) Shall have a running time (including main and end titles) of not less than ninety (90) minutes and not more than one hundred twenty (120) minutes;

(3) Shall be an entirely new and original sound film telling a continuous story with all necessary dialogue (which dialogue shall be originally recorded

in the English language, except to the extent otherwise required by the approved. screenplay), music, lyrics and sound effects, fully edited titled, and assembled with the sound track fully synchronized with the photographic action thereof, not containing, without the Distributor's consent in each instance, any stock or reused film or sound recordings; of first class technical quality, with a picture negative and soundtrack from which first-class positive release prints suitable for exhibition in first-class theatres can be made;

(4) Shall have an aggregate certifiable cash negative cost of Three Million U.S. Dollars ($3,000,000 U.S.), it being acknowledged and agreed that prior to payment of the Pickup Price described in Clause 6 below, the Production Company shall furnish the Distributor with the final budget of the Picture, together with the full negative cost statement for the Picture, certified as to its accuracy by an authorized representative of the Production Company;

(5) Shall not depict, show or contain photography of any product, commodity or service in such manner as to constitute express or implied advertising or the endorsement thereof or the representation of the use thereof unless approved by the Distributor, nor unduly emphasize same, nor show or contain photography of any motor vehicle(s) not designated or consented to by the Distributor; nor constitute any violation of any law or administrative regulation or rule nor constitute an invasion, violation or infringement of any right or interest of any third party;

(6) Shall qualify for a rating not more restrictive than "R" (or the equivalent thereof) by the Motion Picture Association of America's ("MPAA") Code and Rating Administration or any successor thereto;

(7) Shall not, either in whole or in part constitute, or contain any material which constitutes, a violation of any law or administrative regulation or rule, or an invasion, violation or infringement of any right or interest of any third party; and

(8) Shall be produced in accordance with all applicable laws, statutes, ordinances, rules, regulations and requirements of all governmental agencies and regulatory bodies, both domestic and foreign, having jurisdiction with respect to the production of the Picture; and, to the extent required pursuant to any applicable law by reason of the Production Company or any other entity's activities. The Production Company and/or such other entity or entities, as the case may be, shall have become signatory to all applicable collective bargaining agreements and the Production Company's activities and those of such other entity or entities in connection with the Picture have not, are not and will not be in violation of such collective bargaining agreements, to the extent same are applicable thereto.

C. Added Scenes, Retakes and Cover Shots—If the Distributor shall request that retakes be made of any scenes or sequences of the Picture or that added scenes be made, the Production Company shall make such added scenes or retakes promptly following such request; if practicable, during principal photography of the Picture and, otherwise, as soon thereafter as possible.

The Production Company acknowledges that it is aware that free and/or pay television networks and/or stations and/or systems in the United States, Canada and/or elsewhere may now or in the future maintain standards to assure that programming transmitted over their facilities be acceptable for viewing by "family" or other audiences. Accordingly, the Production Company shall, at the Production Company's expense, produce, shoot and record and will deliver to the Distributor a "soft version" of the Picture ("Soft Version") which will include so-called "cover shots" or alternative scenes, sound or dialogue (collectively "cover shots") which can be used in lieu of any unacceptable scenes, sound or dialogue for such television broadcasting and for foreign exhibition as described in clause 2.I hereof. Delivery of the Picture shall not be deemed complete unless and until all of the foregoing are delivered to the Distributor. The cost of producing and delivering such cover shots shall be included by the Production Company in the Budget of the Picture.

D. Progress Reports; Production Representative—The Production Company shall prepare and deliver daily to the Distributor's Production Department or its representative copies of all daily call sheets and detailed production reports in a form approved by the Distributor which reports shall reflect the progress of the production of the Picture. The Production Company shall promptly notify the Distributor and Completion Guarantor of any occurrence which delays or interferes with, or might delay or interfere with, the production of the Picture. The Distributor may designate one or more production representatives whom the Production Company will keep advised as to all phases of the production of the Picture and to whom the Production Company shall make available all books, records and other information and data relating to the Picture and the production thereof, the cost of which representative shall be included in the Budget of the Picture.

E. Photography, Rushes, Previews—The Distributor's representatives and/or the Completion Guarantor's representatives may observe the photography of the Picture, may view all daily rushes of the Picture at reasonable times, may examine all negative and positive prints of the Picture and may run or reproduce the most recent rough cuts, sequences and other prints and sound tracks at such time as they may desire. In no event shall any dailies, rushes, rough cuts, cut sequences or any other negative or positive film or sound tracks of the Picture be screened or exhibited by the Production Company except with the prior written consent of the Distributor. If the Picture is produced at a place other than in the vicinity of Los Angeles, California, the Distributor may require daily rushes and other film to Los Angeles, California, or such other place as the Distributor may direct. At any time after delivery of the Picture to the Distributor, said Distributor shall have the sole right (but not the obligation) at such times and places and for such purposes as it may desire, to preview and otherwise exhibit the Picture prior to its release to the general public.

F. Production, Advertising and Publicity—The Distributor shall at all times after the date hereof have the sole and exclusive right to advertise and publicize the production and delivery of the Picture and all elements thereof, and the Distributor's rights with respect thereto shall be exclusive throughout the Territory, as that term is hereinafter defined. The Production Company shall not issue or authorize the issuance of any advertising or publicity relating to the Picture without the Distributor's prior written consent. The Distributor may assign to the Picture such publicity persons and photographers as it may deem advisable.

G. Trailers—All trailers of the Picture shall be prepared or caused to be prepared by the Distributor and not by the Production Company, unless otherwise directed by the Distributor.

H. Cutting and Editing—The Production Company shall have the right to cut and edit the Picture, but only (i) prior to delivery of the Picture to the Distributor, (ii) in consultation with the Distributor and (iii) on a positive print of the Picture unless and until the Production Company shall have notified and consulted with the Distributor concerning final negative cutting. The Distributor's cutting and editing rights are delineated in clause 8.B(2)c below and are subject to any other provisions of this Agreement relating thereto.

I. Delivery of Picture—With the exception of the rights of the Picture's production money lender, the completed Picture shall be delivered free of all liens, claims and encumbrances, fully cut, edited, scored and ready for release in all respects, and complying with all of the terms and conditions hereof. Such delivery shall be made to the Distributor at an address to be specified, at the Production Company's sole cost and expense, on or before September 15, 1993, time being of the essence; provided, however, that on or before October, 15, 1993, or such earlier date as the Distributor may reasonably require, the Production Company shall deliver to the Distributor a work print of the Picture which will be suitable for exhibition in the anti-blind bidding states. In the event that release and marketing requirements are such that earlier delivery of the completed answer print is necessary or desirable, as the Distributor shall determine in its sole discretion, the Production Company will consider in good faith, the Distributor's request for such earlier delivery, but the Production Company's failure to make such earlier delivery shall not be a breach of this Agreement. Delivery shall not be deemed complete until the Production Company has delivered all items enumerated in the Delivery Schedule attached hereto as Exhibit "A" or required by any provision of this Agreement to be delivered to the Distributor [including, but not limited to, a certified statement of the final negative cost of the Picture as described in clause 2.B(4) above] which items shall be of a quality suitable for commercial exploitation.

Notwithstanding anything to the contrary contained herein or in Exhibit "A" attached hereto, the Soft Version of the Picture described in clause 2.C hereof will also be suitable for the purpose of preparing additional theatrical versions of the Picture to be edited for exhibition in certain foreign territories. The delivery obligation of the Production Company hereunder with respect to such Soft Version shall include the delivery (at the Production Company's expense) of duplicate negatives and music and effects tracks necessary for the preparation of release prints of the Soft Version.

3. CONTRACTS—A. Production Contracts—As part of the Production Company's delivery obligations hereunder, the Production Company shall obtain, and deliver to the Distributor, all contracts, assignments and licenses necessary in connection with the production of the Picture and the full enjoyment by the Distributor of its rights hereunder. Without limiting the generality of the foregoing, in the event that any music or lyrics synchronized with or recorded for the Picture are not in the public domain, the Production Company shall obtain from the copyright proprietor thereof (and with respect to music or lyrics synchronized with or recorded for the Picture which are composed by an employee-for-hire of the Production Company or are otherwise owned by the Production Company, the Production Company shall grant to the Distributor) royalty-free synchronization and performing rights licenses pursuant to which the Distributor shall have, among other things, the right throughout the Territory to perform publicly said music and lyrics for profit or non-profit, and to authorize others so to perform same, and otherwise to use said music and lyrics, in connection with the Picture and excerpts therefrom and trailers therefor, as the same may be exploited theatrically, non-theatrically, on television (free, pay, cable and otherwise) and by any and all other means (including, without limitation, by means of video cassettes, video discs or other similar devices) and in any and all media, now known or hereafter devised, at no additional cost or expense to the Distributor.

B. Credits—(1) As soon as shall be practicable, but in no event later than thirty (30) days after completion of principal photography of the Picture, the Production Company shall deliver to the Distributor a complete written statement showing the exact form and manner of the main and end titles of the Picture, together with a complete written statement showing the full text of all screen and advertising credit obligations. Thereafter, the parties will consult with each other with respect to the credits and attempt to agree upon the final form of such credits, having due regard for the Production Company's approved contractual obligations and contractual obligations under collective bargaining agreements or otherwise. If the parties are unable to agree as to such matters, the decision of the Distributor with respect thereto shall be final and conclusive, provided that the Distributor shall comply with any contractual credit obligations which it has theretofore approved. The Production Company shall not prepare the final title cards of the Picture until such credits have been determined as aforesaid.

(2) The Distributor will comply with the credits determined in accordance with the foregoing to the extent that it can do so without violating any applicable agreement with any union, guild or other party. In no event, however, shall the Distributor be liable or responsible for any acts or omissions with respect to credits by any third party exhibitor, distributor or sub-distributor, newspaper, magazine, record company or other person, firm or corporation.

(3) The Production Company shall include in the main and/or end titles of the Picture, in a size, place, form and style designated by the Distributor, presentation and distribution credits together with such copyright notices, seals, emblems, disclaimers, and credits to any party or parties participating in the production, financing and ownership of the Picture and the copyright thereof, as may be designated by the Distributor.

(4) Notwithstanding any provision of this Agreement, the Distributor shall not be obligated to give the Production Company or any third party credit in group, list or so-called teaser advertising; in special advertising; in advertising relating primarily to the source material upon which the Picture is based, or to the author, any member of the cast, the individual, executive or associate producer, the director or any other personnel involved with the production of the Picture; in so-called "award" or "congratulatory" advertisements, including advertisements or announcements relating to consideration or nomination for an award; in advertising on radio or television; in institutional or other advertising not relating primarily to the Picture; in advertising in narrative form; in advertising eight (8) column inches in size or less; in theatre display advertising; in advertising relating to the exploitation of subsidiary or ancillary rights in the Picture or in advertising in which no credit is accorded other than credit to the Distributor and/or any other company financing or distributing the Picture.

(5) All references to the title of the Picture in any provision of this Agreement, or in any agreement between the Production Company and a third party, relating to credit shall be deemed to refer to the so-called "regular" title of the Picture and not to any "artwork" title (as said term is customarily used and understood in the motion picture industry) which may be used in connection with the Picture.

(6) No casual or inadvertent failure of the Distributor to comply with any provision hereof relating to the credit to be accorded to the Production Company or to any third party transferring rights or rendering services in connection with the Picture shall constitute a breach of this Agreement by the Dis-

tributor. The Production Company represents, warrants and agrees that (notwithstanding anything to the contrary contained in agreements with third parties delivered to the Distributor, the rights and remedies of the Production Company or any such third party in the event of any breach relating to credit by the Distributor, shall be limited to the right to recover damages, if any, in an action at law and in no event shall the Production Company or any such party by reason of any such breach have the right to terminate this Agreement or to enjoin or restrain the exhibition or other exploitation of the Picture, or the use, publication or dissemination of any advertising issued in connection with the Picture.

(7) Unless the Distributor shall otherwise consent in writing, each contract entered into by the Production Company in which provision is made for the giving of credit to any party shall limit the obligation to give such credit in the manner and to the extent as hereinabove set forth in this clause. Without limiting the generality of the preceding sentence, each such contract shall (i) contain a clause pursuant to the terms of which the obligation to give such credit shall not apply to the advertising and publicity described in clause 3.B(4) above, (ii) contain an exculpatory clause limiting the rights and remedies of such party in the event of any breach of such credit provision as set forth in Clause 3.B(6) above, and (iii) provide that all references therein to the title of the Picture shall be deemed to refer to the so-called "regular" title thereof and not to any "artwork" title used in connection therewith, as set forth in Clause 3.B(5) above.

(8) The Production Company agrees that the main or end titles of the Picture, as delivered to the Distributor, shall include a copyright notice in conformity with the laws of the United States and the Universal Copyright Convention relating to the form and content of copyright notices, designating the Distributor as the copyright proprietor. The Picture shall also contain the following, such legend to appear on the Picture in accordance with customary practice (i.e., located at the end titles at or near the cast of characters):

"THIS MOTION PICTURE IS PROTECTED UNDER LAWS OF THE UNITED STATES AND OTHER COUNTRIES. UNAUTHORIZED DUPLICATION, DISTRIBUTION OR EXHIBITION MAY RESULT IN CIVIL LIABILITY AND CRIMINAL PROSECUTION."

4. INSURANCE—A. Coverage—As a condition to the Distributor's promise, set forth herein, to distribute the Picture the Production Company agrees to obtain and maintain the following insurance policies as customarily maintained by producers of feature length theatrical motion pictures in the United States:

(i)   cast insurance;

(ii)   negative film insurance;

(iii)   extra expense insurance;

(iv)   producer's errors and omissions;

(v)   comprehensive and general and automobile liability;

(vi)   third party property damage;

(vii)   miscellaneous equipment floater;

(viii) props, sets and wardrobe all risk floaters; and

(ix)   workers' compensation or equivalent employer's liability.

All such insurance shall be placed with Pacific Indemnity Company, Lloyds of London, Fireman's Fund Insurance Company or such other insurance carrier satisfactory to the Distributor.

The policy of producer's errors and omissions insurance referred to in (iv) above shall (a) be delivered to the Distributor prior to the commencement of principal photography, (b) have limits of liability not less than Five Million Dollars ($5,000,000) per each claim or occurrence (with no exclusions whatsoever and with such deductible amounts as are customary and approved in writing by the Distributor, (c) pursuant to its terms provide primary errors and omissions coverage and not contributory coverage, notwithstanding any other errors and omissions insurance which the Production Company and/or the Distributor may obtain or maintain, (d) be maintained in full force and effect by the Production Company in the Territory, at the Production Company's sole cost and expense, for a period of not less than five (5) years following the date upon which the Picture is delivered to the Distributor hereunder, it being understood that in the event of cancellation or non-renewal of said policy of producer's errors and omissions insurance, the Production Company shall obtain and maintain a substitute policy therefor (and promptly deliver to the Distributor evidence of the maintenance of such substitute policy), the terms of which substitute policy shall be in accordance with the provisions of this clause 4, and (e) be satisfactory to the Distributor in all other respects. Without limiting the foregoing provisions of this clause 4, (a) the comprehensive general and automobile liability insurance referred to in (v) above and the third party property damage insurance referred to in (vi) above shall each have limits of liability of not less than One Million Dollars ($1,000,000) and (b) subject to the foregoing provisions of this clause 4, all of the aforesaid insurance shall have limits of liability, be subject to such deductions and exclusions and be maintained during such period, as may be approved by the Distributor.

The Production Company shall cause the Distributor to be added as a named insured, as its interests may appear, under the insurance policies referred to in (i) through (viii) above, inclusive, and shall, before delivery of the Picture or at such earlier time as the Distributor shall specify, provide the Distributor with written evidence satisfactory to the Distributor of the maintenance of such insurance policies and of the provisions thereof (including evidence that the Distributor has been named as an additional insured, as aforesaid). The Production Company shall indemnify the Distributor and the corporations comprising the Distributor from and against all claims, actions, damages and liability and expense (including reasonable attorneys' fees [whether or not in connection with litigation] and court costs) which may be asserted by or on behalf of any employee of the Production Company by reason of injury or death arising out of or in the course of his or her employment; or by or on behalf of any party by reason of accident, injury, death or property damage resulting from any negligence or fault on the part of the Production Company or its employees.

B. Claims and Recoveries—If any claim shall be made against the Production Company and/or the Distributor relating to the errors and omissions insurance on the Picture or any rights relating thereto, the Production Company shall forthwith advise the Distributor in writing of such claim and cooperate with the Distributor and the insurance carriers with respect to such claim, and abide by the Distributor's instructions with respect thereto. The Production Company shall indemnify and hold harmless the Distributor and the corporations comprising the Distributor and its and their officers, directors and employees from and against any and all claims, actions, damages, liability and expense (including reasonable attorneys' fees [whether or not in connection with litigation] and court costs) arising out of or relating to any such claims. The Production Company shall not, without the consent of the Distributor do or fail to do any act or thing which could adversely affect the rights of the Distributor. Any recovery under said errors and omissions policy shall be paid to the Distributor and the Production Company as their interests appear therein.

5. DEFAULT—A. Events of Default—The following shall each constitute an "Event of Default" and give rise to the Distributor's right to take over production of the Picture (such Distributor's right of takeover may be assigned in part or in whole to a completion guarantor):

(1) Any failure, refusal or neglect of the Production Company to perform any of its material obligations under this Agreement or under any other agreement relating to the Picture, including, but not limited to, the Production Company's obligation to complete the Picture in accordance with the terms hereof;

(2) Any breach or default by the Production Company of any representation, warranty or other material term or provision of this Agreement (including, without limitation, the provisions of clauses 2.A and B hereof);

(3) The adjudication of the Production Company as a bankrupt, or the filing of a petition by the Production Company for (or consent by the Produc-

3

tion Company to) any relief under any bankruptcy or other debtor's relief act, or the appointment of a receiver, liquidator, trustee or custodian for all or a substantial part of the Production Company's assets (whether or not at the petition of the Production Company); or

The failure of the Production Company to fully deliver the Picture to the Distributor as herein provided, on or before the delivery date as specified in clause 2.I hereof.

B. Take-Over Rights—(l) In addition to the Distributor's take-over rights if an Event of Default occurs, the Distributor may take-over production of the Picture if, for any reason (other than a force majeure contingency which affects the Distributor to the same extent that it affects the Production Company), any of the following occur, whether or not the respective occurrence constitutes or is caused or accompanied by an Event of Default (again, such Distributor's right of takeover may be assigned in part or in whole to a completion guarantor):

a. The cost of production exceeds 125% of the Budget, or the Distributor has reasonable grounds to believe it will do so; or

b. The cost of production at any time exceeds 125% of the budgeted cost (as reflected in the Budget) for the stage of completion in which the Picture is then; or

c. The progress of production is materially behind the approved production schedule of the Picture: or

d. The Production Company fails, or the Distributor has reasonable grounds to believe the Production Company will fail to deliver the Picture within the time required hereunder.

(2) If the Distributor elects to exercise any take-over rights, the Distributor shall do so by written notice to the Production Company. If the Distributor exercises any such take-over rights:

a. The Distributor may assume supervision and control of the production of the Picture.

b. The Production Company shall turn over to the Distributor the Picture (in whatever stage of completion it may be) any and all physical properties, facilities, supplies and equipment in connection with it.

c. The Distributor may require the Production Company to assign to the Distributor, the Production's Company's rights under any of the Production Company's contracts in connection with the Picture, in which event the Distributor may elect to assume the Production Company's obligations under any such contract.

d. The Production Company shall have no further share in the net proceeds of the Picture.

(3) If the Distributor has the right to take over production of the Picture, then, whether or not the Distributor has previously exercised such take-over

rights, the Distributor may elect to abandon the production of the Picture hereunder and terminate this Agreement.

C. Overbudget Penalty—In the event the final actual negative cost of the Picture exceeds Three Million Dollars ($3,000,000) (except for force majeure events or due to the failure of the Distributor to provide the amounts specified in clause 6.A(l) below), then the Distributor shall be entitled to recoup, in addition to the amounts specified in clause 6.A(l) below, an amount equal to twice the amount of such excess.

D. Distributor's Right to Terminate—If at any time an Event of Default shall occur, the Distributor shall have the right, at any time thereafter, in addition to all of its other rights and remedies hereunder, to terminate this Agreement by notice in writing to such effect to the Production Company.

E. Effect of Termination—If the Distributor terminates this Agreement pursuant to any right of the Distributor so to do, the Distributor shall be released and discharged from all further obligations under this Agreement and the Production Company shall immediately repay all amounts expended or incurred by the Distributor, if any, and hold the Distributor harmless from any and all claims, actions, damages, liability and expense (including reasonable attorneys' fees [whether or not in connection with litigation] and court costs) arising out of or relating to any failure by the Production Company to comply with any obligations set forth herein. The foregoing shall not be deemed to limit any of the Distributor's rights or remedies hereunder.

F. Cumulative Rights and Remedies—All rights and remedies granted to the Distributor hereunder are cumulative and the exercise of one shall not limit or affect the Distributor's right concurrently or subsequently to exercise any other right or remedy, and shall be in addition to such other rights or remedies as the Distributor may have at law, in equity, under this Agreement or otherwise.

G. Default by the Distributor—If, and only if the Distributor shall commit a material breach of this Agreement and shall fail to remedy said material breach within a period of thirty (30) days after receipt by the Distributor of written notice from the Production Company specifying wherein the Distributor breached this Agreement; or if, after delivery of the Picture to the Distributor, the Distributor shall improperly fail to make any payments provided for herein at the time and in the manner herein required and such failure shall continue for a period of thirty (30) days after receipt by the Distributor of written notice from the Production Company or the Picture's production money lender, specifying such failure to make payments then, and in either of such events, the Production Company (or the production money lender) shall have the right to proceed against the Distributor for the monies due to be paid or, with respect to any other breach for damages. The rights and remedies of the Production Company or any party transferring rights or rendering services in connection with the Picture, in the event of any breach of any provision of this Agreement by the Distributor including, without limitation, any provision hereof relating to credit, shall be limited to the right to recover damages, if any, in an action at law, and in no event shall the Production Company or any such party be entitled by reason of any such breach to terminate or rescind this Agreement or to enjoin or restrain or otherwise interfere with the production, distribution or exhibition of the Picture, or the use, publication or dissemination of any advertising issued in connection with the Picture.

6. CONSIDERATION—A. Pickup Price; Net Proceeds—Subject to the terms and conditions hereof, as full and complete consideration for all rights granted to the Distributor hereunder and for all of representations and warranties contained herein, the Distributor agrees to pay the Production Company (or its designed production money lender) and the Production Company agrees to accept the following:

(1) An amount equal to the certified cash negative cost of the Picture, plus interest and fees payable to any lender, such payment not to exceed Three Million Five Hundred Thousand Dollars ($3,500,000) unless approved in writing by the Distributor as payable pursuant to the Budget and Approved Schedule.

(2) A Production Company deferment of Two Hundred Fifty Thousand Dollars ($250,000) payable in first position of all deferments out of first gross receipts received by the Distributor except after the Distributor has recouped the amount expended by the Distributor pursuant to 6.A(l) above, if any, and any overbudget penalty pursuant to clause 5.C above.

(3) If the Production Company shall deliver the Picture to the Distributor in accordance with the provisions of sub-clause (l) above, an amount equal to One Hundred Percent (100%) percent of the "net proceeds" of the Picture, it being understood and agreed that any and all participations of every kind in the revenues derived from the Picture, however denominated (including, without limitation, all participations in net proceeds of the Picture), and any and all deferments of any kind, payable to third parties in connection with the Picture, shall be borne solely by the Production Company, on a dollar for dollar basis, out of the Production Company's share of such net proceeds. For purposes of this Agreement, "net proceeds" shall be defined, computed, accounted for and paid in the same manner as in the agreements between the Distributor and other independent feature film producers with which it does business, i.e., gross receipts minus the Distributor's distribution fees and minus its distribution expenses incurred by the Distributor in connection with the Picture not otherwise recouped pursuant to clause 6.A(1) above.

B. Investment Tax Credit—As between the Distributor and the Production Company, the Distributor shall be entitled to one hundred percent (100%) of any U.S. income tax investment tax credit which may be available, to the full extent such credit may be available to the Distributor relating to the Picture. The Production Company agrees to furnish to the Distributor at any time, at the Distributor's request, any statement and or documentation requested by the Distributor to substantiate the Distributor's entitlement to such investment tax credit with respect to the Picture. The Production Company shall retain all production records including, without limitation, vouchers, checks and payroll records and shall deliver all such production records or copies thereof to the Distributor concurrently with the delivery of the Picture. If the Production Company shall fail or refuse to execute or procure the execution of such statements and or documentation with respect to the investment tax credit for the Picture, including executing and delivering a letter of authorization to the Distributor Director of the Internal Revenue Service (as approved by the Distributor), the Distributor shall have the right to execute such statements and/or documentation in the Production Company's name, and the Distributor is hereby irrevocably appointed the Production Company's attorney-in-fact for that purpose, the same being a power coupled with an interest with unlimited rights of substitution and/or delegation.

7. WARRANTIES AND INDEMNITIES—A. Production Company Warranties—The Production Company warrants and represents that:

(1) The Production Company has the right to enter into this Agreement and to grant and assign to the Distributor all of the rights, licenses and privileges granted and assigned to the Distributor hereunder.

(2) The Distributor shall have all rights in and to all literary, dramatic, musical or other material or services utilized in the production of the Picture and the results and proceeds of all thereof required for the Distributor's full and unfettered exercise and enjoyment of all rights of the Distributor hereunder.

(3) The Production Company warrants that the title of the Picture may be used by the Distributor in connection with the distribution and other exploitation of the Picture without violating or infringing any rights of any third parties.

(4) There are, and will be, no claims, liens, encumbrances, limitations, restrictions or rights of any nature in or to the Picture or any part thereof which can or will impair or interfere with the rights of the Distributor hereunder (including, without limitation, any liens or security interests in favor of any bank, production money lender or other third party which may have provided production financing for the Picture); and the Picture and each and every part thereof, including the sound and music synchronized therewith, and the exercise by the Distributor of any and all rights of the Distributor hereunder with respect thereto, will not violate or infringe upon the trademark, trade-name, copyright, patent, literary, dramatic, music, artistic, personal, civil or property right, right of privacy, or any other right or interest of any party, or constitute a libel or slander or defamation or invasion of privacy or unfair competition of or with respect to any party.

(5) All obligations of the Production Company with respect to the Picture,

and the production, distribution, and exploitation thereof, including, without limitation, all salaries, royalties, residuals, license fees, service charges, laboratory charges and the like, shall have been or shall be fully paid or discharged by the Production Company in a timely fashion and any and all such obligations payable prior to the delivery of the Picture shall have theretofore been paid or discharged, but in no event later than delivery of the Picture. In this regard, the Production Company shall have paid all employer payroll deductions required to have been made to any and all union or guild pension, health or welfare plans and shall have prepared and submitted all reports and other information required in connection with the Picture.

(6) If the Production Company is a corporation, it is a duly organized and existing corporation and is currently in good standing under the laws of the state or country of its incorporation and the execution and delivery of this Agreement does not, and will not, violate any provisions of its Articles or Certificate of Incorporation, its Bylaws, or any contract or other agreement to which it is a party.

(7) The Production Company shall obtain the synchronization and performing rights licenses described in clause 3.A hereof for all of the music to be contained in the Picture, at no cost, at any time, to the Distributor.

B. Indemnity by Production Company—The Production Company shall indemnify and hold harmless the Distributor and the corporations comprising the Distributor and its and their officers, directors and employees from and against any and all liability, damages, costs and expenses (including reasonable attorneys' fees [whether or not in connection with litigation] and court costs) which any of them may sustain or suffer by reason of a breach or claim of breach of any of the covenants, agreements, representations or warranties of the Production Company contained in this Agreement. If any third party files a claim against the Distributor the corporations comprising the Distributor (or any of them), or any officer, director or employee or any such corporation, alleging facts which, if true, would be subject to the Production Company's indemnity hereunder, the Distributor and any such corporation, officer, director or employee shall be entitled to representation by the counsel of its choice in such action and the cost thereof shall be included in the Production Company's indemnity hereunder. In addition to any and all rights and remedies granted to the Distributor hereunder, the Distributor shall have the right to set off against any monies payable to the Production Company hereunder the amount of any such liability, damage, cost or expenses.

8. TERM, TERRITORY, OWNERSHIP AND RIGHTS—A. Term and Territory—This Agreement and all of the Distributor's rights hereunder shall be in full force and effect forever ("Term") throughout the entire universe ("Territory").

B. Ownership and Exploitation Rights—(1) Upon delivery of the Picture to the Distributor and payment by the Distributor to the production money lender of all sums due such production money lender of the Picture, the Distributor shall own (and the Production Company does hereby grant, sell and assign to the Distributor solely and exclusively, throughout the Term and Territory, all right, title and interest in and to the Picture, the copyright (including all renewals and extensions) therein, all literary, dramatic and other material contained in, or upon which the Picture is based or produced or created in connection with the Picture (including, without limitation, the Screenplay and all music and lyrics), all negatives, positive prints and all other physical, tangible and intangible properties, rights and licenses acquired, produced or created in connection with the Picture, and shall have the sole and exclusive right to, and to license others to, exhibit, distribute, market, exploit, sell, advertise, publicize, perform, dispose of, turn to account or otherwise deal in or with any or all of the foregoing in such manner and in and by such media as the Distributor may in its sole discretion determine, without any obligation or liability whatsoever to the Production Company with respect thereto except as herein specifically provided. Concurrently herewith the Production Company is executing and delivering to the Distributor the Copyright Assignment attached hereto as Exhibit "B." Upon delivery of the Picture to the Distributor hereunder, the Distributor shall have the right to date said Assignment (and the Distributor is hereby irrevocably appointed the Production Company's attorney-in-fact for such purpose) and register the Assignment with the United States Copyright Office.

(2) Without limiting the generality of clause 8.B(l) preceding, the Distributor shall have the perpetual right to distribute and exploit the Picture throughout the Territory:

a. To exercise its rights as specified in clause 8.B(1) with respect to the Picture, including, but not limited to, all sound and music contained therein, excerpts therefrom and trailers thereof, in any and all forms and manners, lengths, languages and versions, sizes and gauges of film or other material, by any and every means, method, process or device now known or which may hereafter be discovered, invented, developed, devised or created (including, without limitation, by means of film, tape, wire, discs, cartridges, and cassettes), and in any and all markets, including, without limitation, the theatrical, non-theatrical, television (whether so-called "free," "pay," "cable" or otherwise) or home showings, educational and industrial markets;

b. To select, designate or change the title of the Picture in its discretion and to release the Picture in any and all parts of the Territory under such title or titles as the Distributor may designate;

c. To make any and all changes and modifications in the Picture which the Distributor shall, in its sole discretion, determine to be necessary or desirable, including, without limitation, to: re-cut, edit, re-edit, add to, delete from and re-record, re-score, dub and/or reorganize the Picture or any part or parts thereof (including the main and end titles thereof), and make foreign versions (including titled, super-imposed and dubbed versions) and shorter versions of the Picture, including so-called "featurettes";

d. To use for any purpose, or dispose of, any and all (i) physical properties acquired for the Picture; and (ii) cutouts, trims, second takes, tests, sound effects tracks, dialogue tracks, process keys and background and such portions of the Picture as finally edited as may be desirable by the Distributor for inclusion in stock shot, process shot, sound effects and music libraries;

e. To cause or permit the interpolation of advertising material at intervals during the television, cable or similar exhibition of the Picture and otherwise to conform to the needs, practices and customs of any such exhibition;

f. To announce and include on the positive prints of the Picture and trailers thereof and in all advertising and publicity relating thereto, in such manner position, form and substance as the Distributor may elect the Distributor's name, trademark and presentation announcement; (ii) the designation of the Distributor or any of its subsidiaries, affiliates and licensees as the distributor of the Picture; and (iii) any and all of the credits and matters specified in clause 3.B;

g. To manufacture or cause to be manufactured such positive prints, preprint and other materials and to cause the performance of such laboratory work with respect to the Picture as the Distributor may require and to cause trailers of the Picture to be produced, manufactured, exhibited and distributed by every means, method or device now or hereafter known;

h. To manufacture and distribute or cause to be manufactured and distributed advertising accessories of all types and kinds, which shall be the property solely of the Distributor, and to advertise, publicize and exploit the Picture by such means, methods and devices and in such media, and to such extent as the Distributor in its sole discretion may deem desirable;

i. To issue and authorize publicity and to use, produce, transmit, broadcast, exploit, publicize, exhibit and control in connection with the production, distribution, exhibition, advertising and exploitation of the Picture, the names, photographs, likenesses, voices and other sound effects, as well as recordings, transcriptions, films and other reproductions thereof, of the director, all members of the cast, and all other persons rendering services in connection with the Picture, including all so-called commercial tie-ups and by-product rights; and to broadcast by radio and television, by living actors, electrical transcriptions, filmed or otherwise in any language, the underlying literary material and Screenplay on which the Picture is based, and to publish or cause to be published synopses, resumes, abridgements, fictionalizations or novelizations thereof;

j. To produce or cause to be produced one or more motion pictures, including, without limitation, television motion pictures and series and motion pictures which constitute sequel(s) to or remake(s) of, the Picture (as the terms "sequel" and "remake" are customarily used and understood in the motion picture industry), and to distribute, exhibit and otherwise exploit the same in any and all media (including without limitation, television) throughout the Territory or to dispose of the same as the Distributor may in its sole discretion determine, without any obligations whatsoever to the Production Company with respect thereto;

k. To publish, market and exploit all music or lyrics written for or in connection with the Picture and any and all rights therein;

l. To use and license any other person, firm or corporation to use all or any part of the sound recordings made for the Picture and or all or any part of the musical scores and individual parts used in, or in connection with the Picture for the purpose of producing or reproducing phonograph, tape, wire or other recordings of any kind for any purpose;

m. To use, exercise, employ, merchandise and exploit the name of the Picture and all of the characters, situations, objects, property, wardrobe, designs, equipment or events depicted, described or portrayed in the Picture (including, without limitation, in connection with the licensing, production or other exploitation of toys, comic books, posters, buttons, etc.);

n. To write (or cause to be written), publish, market and exploit, and authorize others to write (or cause to be written), publish, market and exploit, novelizations of, and other publications based upon, the Screenplay or other material based thereon or otherwise written, produced or created in connection with the Picture; and

o. To cause the Picture to be copyrighted in accordance with the Distributor's customary practices, in the name of the Distributor and to cause the renewal and

extension of any such copyright if the Distributor shall so elect. The Distributor shall not be liable to the Production Company or any other person, firm or corporation, if there is any defect in any such copyright. The Distributor may, in its own name or in the name of the copyright proprietor or otherwise, take such steps as the Distributor may deem necessary or appropriate by action at law, or otherwise, to prevent unauthorized reproduction, exhibition or distribution of the Picture, or any infringement of the copyright of the Picture, or to prevent any impairment of, encumbrance on, or infringement upon the rights of the Production Company or the Distributor under this Agreement.

C. Import and Export Licenses, Subsidies and Quotas—The Distributor shall be entitled to all subsidies, prizes and the benefit of all import and/or export licenses and/or quotas and/or similar benefits with respect to the Picture which would entitle the Picture to be imported into or exhibited in any country or territory. The Production Company shall notify the Distributor of such licenses and or quota benefits and transfer and assign the same to the

Distributor upon request. If it is not legally permissible to make such transfer and assignment the same shall be held in trust, for the sole benefit of the Distributor. The foregoing provision shall apply to all future arrangements which may come into being under applicable treaties or other favorable arrangements for the foreign importation or exhibition of films.

D. Distributor Services and Facilities—If the Distributor or any of the corporations comprising the Distributor or any subsidiary or affiliate of any such corporation shall furnish, supply, render, procure, arrange for, or make available to the Production Company for, or in connection with, the Picture any materials, equipment, facilities or services, including, but not limited to, laboratory or studio facilities, transportation, travel, trucking, insurance, hotel accommodations, lodging, catering, advertising, costumes or props, it, or such subsidiary or affiliate, shall be entitled to charge and receive payment therefor in the same manner as if the same were furnished, supplied, rendered, procured, arranged for or made available by persons, firms, or corporations other than the Distributor, the corporations comprising the Distributor, its subsidiaries or affiliates.

E. Talent Options—The Distributor shall control all options acquired by the Production Company to require the services of persons engaged to render services in connection with the Picture.

9. MISCELLANEOUS PROVISIONS—A. Licenses and Permits—The Production Company shall duly and promptly apply for and procure all necessary consents, licenses and permits which may be required from any governmental agencies in connection with this Agreement and the production of the Picture, including, without limitation, the qualification of the Picture for "nationality" of the country (or countries) of production and for all aid, subsidies, licenses, quota and other benefits resulting or accruing therefrom, all work permits, immigration requirements and all permits required for the export of the Picture from the place of production and the import thereof into the United States or other place of delivery designated by the Distributor.

B. Assignments—This Agreement is personal to the Production Company, and no rights hereunder may be sold, transferred, assigned, mortgaged, pledged, hypothecated or otherwise disposed of by the Production Company; no rights hereunder shall devolve by operation of law or otherwise upon any receiver, trustee, or assignee of the Production Company; and the Production Company shall not assign, sub-contract or delegate any of its production obligations hereunder.

C. Supplemental Documents—The Production Company will from time to time, upon the Distributor's request, execute, acknowledge and deliver such instruments as may be necessary and proper to evidence, maintain, effectuate or defend any and all of the rights of the Distributor under any provision of this Agreement. Should the Production Company fail to execute, acknowledge or deliver any such supplemental document upon the Distributor's written request (including, without limitation any document renewing and/or extending the copyright in the Picture), the Distributor shall have, and is hereby granted, the rights for and on behalf of the Production Company, as the Production Company's attorney-in-fact, to execute, acknowledge and deliver such document. The Production Company hereby agrees that the foregoing appointment is irrevocable and constitutes a power coupled with an interest.

D. Relationship of Parties—Nothing herein contained shall constitute a partnership between, or joint venture by, the parties hereto or constitute either party the agent of the other. Neither party shall hold itself out contrary to the terms of this clause, and neither party shall become liable for the representation, act or omission of the other contrary to the provisions hereof.

E. Illegality and Severability—Nothing contained in this Agreement shall be construed so as to require the commission of any act contrary to law, and wherever there is any conflict between any provision of this Agreement and any statute, law, ordinance, order or regulation the latter shall prevail, but in such event any provision of this Agreement so affected shall be curtailed and limited only to the extent necessary to bring it within the legal requirements.

F. Waivers—No waiver of any breach of any provision hereof shall be deemed a waiver of any preceding or succeeding breach.

G. Effect of Termination—Neither the expiration of this Agreement nor any other termination thereof shall effect the Distributor's ownership of the Picture or any other rights or privileges hereunder, or any warranty or undertaking of the Production Company under this Agreement.

H. Power of Attorney—Wherever the Distributor is entitled in this Agreement to act as the Production Company's attorney-in-fact, said appointment shall be a power coupled with an interest and the Distributor shall have full power of delegation and substitution.

I. Notices—All notices, or other documents (collectively "notices") which any party shall be required to or shall desire to give to the other hereunder shall be in writing, unless otherwise specified, and shall be addressed or directed to the party intended to receive the same at its address provided for herein. All such notices shall be given in one of the following ways: (i) by personal delivery, or (ii) by United States mail, postage prepaid, airmail (if available); or (iii) by delivery, toll prepaid to a telegraph or cable company; or (iv) by transmittal by any electronic means whether now known or hereafter developed, including but not limited to, telex, telecopier, or laser transmissions, able to be received by the party intended to receive notice. If so delivered, mailed, telegraphed, cabled, or transmitted, each such notice shall, except as herein expressly provided, be conclusively deemed to have been given when personally delivered or on the date of delivery to the telegraph or cable company or when electronically transmitted or on the first business day following the date of mailing, as the case may be. Any such notice shall be given to the Production Company addressed as follows: Filmright, Incorporated, 850 Montana Avenue, Suite 12, Santa Monica, California 90031 and to the Distributor addressed as follows: Worldwide Distribution, Inc., 802 Beverly Drive, Suite 10, Beverly Hills, California 90025.

J. Governing Law—All matters pertaining to this Agreement (including its validity, performance and breach) shall be governed by the laws of California applicable to contracts made and to be performed entirely in the state of California.

K. Written Approvals—Any approvals given under this Agreement shall be made in writing. The Production Company may not exercise any approval granted to it herein in a manner which might interfere with the production, distribution or exploitation of the Picture.

L. Headings—Section and clause headings as used in this Agreement are for convenience only and are not a part hereof, and shall not be used to interpret, any provision of this Agreement.

M. Amendment—No modification, alteration or amendment of this Agreement shall be valid or binding unless in writing and signed by the party to be charged therewith.

N. Entire Agreement—This Agreement expresses the entire understanding of the parties hereto and replaces any and all former agreements, understandings or representations relating in any way to the subject matter hereof, and contains all of the terms, conditions, understandings and promises of the parties hereto in the premises. No officer, employee or representative of the Distributor has any authority to make any representation or promise not contained in this Agreement, and the Production Company acknowledges that the Production Company has not executed this Agreement in reliance upon any promise or representation not expressly set forth in this Agreement.

IN WITNESS WHEREOF, the parties hereto have executed and delivered this Agreement as of the date first written above.

PRODUCTION COMPANY—Filmright, Incorporated
By: _____
James W. Producer, President

DISTRIBUTOR—Worldwide Distribution, Inc.
By: _____
Jerry Goldmine, Vice President

Exhibit "A"
Delivery Schedule

(see the sample Delivery Schedule set forth at Exhibit "A" in conjunction with the Production-Financing/Distribution Deal above)

Exhibit "B"
Copyright Assignment

KNOW ALL PERSONS BY THESE PRESENTS that, in consideration of Ten Dollars ($10.00) and other good and valuable consideration, receipt of which is hereby acknowledged, the undersigned authorized representative of Filmright, Incorporated (the "Assignor") does hereby sell, grant, convey and assign unto Worldwide Distribution, Inc. (the "Assignee"), its successors, assigns and licensees forever, all right, title and interest including but not limited to the exclusive worldwide motion picture and allied rights of the Assignor in and to that certain motion picture to wit: the feature length motion picture based on the original screenplay written by John Q. Screenwriter and entitled "Invaders from Chunga" ("Picture"), and all revisions, arrangements, adaptations, dramatizations, translations, sequels and other versions of the Picture which may heretofore have been produced or which may hereafter be produced with the sanction of the Assignor.

This instrument is executed in accordance with and is subject to the agreement (the "Negative Pickup Distribution Agreement") between the undersigned and the Assignee dated as of the 21st of April, 1993, relating to the purchase of certain rights in the Picture, which rights are more fully described in said Negative Pickup Distribution Agreement.

Dated this the 25th day of April, 1993.

ASSIGNOR—Filmright, Incorporated
By:
    James W. Producer, President

THE STATE OF   California   }
COUNTY OF   Los Angeles   }

This instrument was acknowledged before me on the 25th day of April, 1993, by James W. Producer, President of the above-named corporation and authorized representative of the Assignor for this document and he is known by me to be the person represented or has been proved to me by sufficient evidence to be such person.

Notary Public in and for
the State of California

(Notary Seal)

Sally P. Notary
Printed Name of Notary

My Commission Expires:
    June 8, 1994

APPENDIX G

Distribution Rights Acquisition Agreement

This agreement (hereinafter referred to as the "Agreement") is entered into on this the 2nd day of April, 1993, by and between Filmright, Incorporated (the "Production Company") and World Wide Distribution, Inc. (the "Distributor").

1. LICENSE—(a) Picture—This Agreement concerns a feature length motion picture now entitled "Invasion From Chunga" (the "Picture") produced by the Production Company as the production entity, produced by James W. Production Company as the individual producer, written by John Q. Screenwriter, directed by X. Lent Director, and starring Very Good Actor as Nigor and Mary Lu Sirkus as Mariene, photographed in color with a running time of not less than ninety (90) minutes and not more than one hundred and ten (110) minutes and qualifying for an MPAA rating not more restrictive than "R."

(b) Distribution Rights—The Production Company grants and licenses to the Distributor the following, collectively referred to as the "Distribution Rights," for the Term and the Territory specified below:

(i) General Grant of Rights—The Production Company hereby grants and licenses to the Distributor, without qualification, the sole and exclusive right and license under copyright to exercise all rights of Theatrical Distribution, Theatrical Exhibition, Non-Theatrical Distribution, Non-Theatrical Exhibition, Free Television Distribution, Free Television Exhibition, Pay Television Distribution, Pay Television Exhibition, Video Cassette Distribution and Video Cassette Exhibition (all as defined herein or in the Glossary attached hereto at Exhibit "A" and all of which are presented herein with initial capitalization) with respect to the Picture and trailers thereof and excerpts and clips therefrom in any and all languages and versions, including dubbed, subtitled and narrated versions, using any form of Motion Picture Copy. The Distributor shall have the right, in connection with the marketing, distribution and exploitation of the Picture, (A) to use and to authorize others to use the title of the Picture or to change such title, (B) to use and perform and to authorize others to use and perform any musical material contained in the Picture, (C) to cut, edit and alter the Picture or any part thereof as the Distributor may deem necessary for the effective marketing, distribution and exploitation of the Picture and/or to conform to censorship, import permit and other legal requirements and/or to conform to time segment or exhibition standards of licensees or exhibitors, and (D) to use the Distributor's name and trademark and/or the name and trademark of any of the Distributor's Sub-distributors and licensees in such manner, position and form as the Distributor, its Sub-distributors or licensees may elect.

(ii) Advertising and Publicity Rights—The Production Company hereby grants to the Distributor for purposes of advertising and publicizing the Picture in connection with the marketing, distribution and exploitation of the Picture the right (A) to publish and to license and authorize others to publish in any language, in any media and in such form as the Distributor deems advisable synopses, summaries, adaptations, resumes and stories of and excerpts from the Picture and from any literary, dramatic or musical material in the Picture or upon which the Picture is based, (B) to use and authorize others to use the name, voice and likeness (and any simulation or reproduction thereof) of any person appearing in or rendering services in connection with the Picture and (C) to broadcast and authorize others to broadcast by radio and television in any language excerpts from the Picture and from any literary, dramatic, or musical material in the Picture or upon which the Picture is based. The Distributor shall comply with the Production Company's written instructions as to contractual obligations relative to advertising and publicity issued by the Distributor or under the Distributor's control provided the Distributor has received such written instructions at least eight (8) weeks prior to delivery of the Picture and that said written instructions conform to the Distributor's standard credit provisions for comparable talent, including the Distributor's standard art work title provisions. This undertaking by the Distributor is solely for the benefit of the Production Company and not for the benefit of any third party. No casual or inadvertent failure by the Distributor or any of its Subsidiaries, Affiliates, Sub-distributors or licensees to comply with contractual obligations relative to advertising and publicity shall constitute a breach of this Agreement.

2. TERM—The period during which the Distributor may exercise the Distribution Rights ("Term") shall commence on the date of this Agreement (i.e., the date first above written) and continue thereafter in perpetuity.

3. TERRITORY—The territory in which the Picture may be distributed ("Territory") shall consist of the entire universe.

4. PRODUCTION COMPANY'S RESERVED RIGHTS/HOLDBACK— The Production Company reserves all rights in the Picture and the literary, dramatic and musical material on which it is based not specifically granted to the Distributor. The exercise of any of such reserved rights, including Literary Publishing Rights, Merchandising Rights, Music Publishing Rights, Sound-

track Recording Rights, Radio Rights, Remake Rights and Sequel Motion Picture Rights in or into the Territory during the Term.

5. PAYMENTS TO PRODUCTION COMPANY—Subject to compliance with each and all of the Production Company's agreements herein and in full consideration for the Distribution Rights and the representations, warranties and agreements contained herein, the Distributor shall pay to the Production Company the following:

(a) Advance—An Advance in the sum of Five Hundred Thousand Dollars ($500,000 U.S.), payable Two Hundred Fifty Thousand Dollars ($250,000 U.S.) within ten (10) days following Delivery of the Picture, One Hundred Twenty Five Thousand Dollars ($125,000 U.S.) within thirty (30) days following the earlier of the Initial Theatrical Release of the Picture or six (6) months following Delivery of the Picture; and One Hundred Twenty Five Thousand Dollars ($125,000 U.S.) within ninety (90) days thereafter. Such Advance shall be recoupable from the first Net Proceeds which would otherwise be payable to the Production Company pursuant to clause 5(b) below.

(b) One Hundred percent (100%) of the Net Proceeds of the Picture, if any. Notwithstanding any other provision herein and without limiting the foregoing, the Distributor hereby agrees that with respect to the Net Proceeds from the Theatrical Exploitation of the Picture, it shall pay the Production Company not less than the following sums:

(i) a sum equal to ten percent (10%) of Gross Theatrical Film Rentals, up to one Million Dollars ($1,000,000 U.S.);

(ii) a sum equal to twenty percent (20%) of the Gross Theatrical Film Rentals in excess of One Million Dollars ($1,000,000 U.S.) up to Five Million Dollars ($5,000,000 U.S.);

(iii) a sum equal to twenty-five percent (25%) of the Gross Theatrical Film Rentals in excess of Five Million Dollars ($5,000,000 U.S.) up to Seven Million Five Hundred Thousand Dollars ($7,500,000 U.S.); and

(iv) a sum equal to thirty percent (30%) of the Gross Theatrical Film Rentals in excess of Seven Million Five Hundred Thousand Dollars ($7,500,000 U.S.).

6. DISTRIBUTION FEES—The distribution fees ("Distribution Fees") to be charged by the Distributor for the entire Territory shall be the following:

Domestic Theatrical	20% 1st week of engagement
	15% 2nd week of engagement
	10% 3rd week of engagement
	7.5% 4th week of engagement and all weeks of engagement thereafter.
Domestic Home Video	22.5%

Domestic Pay Television, Pay Per View, Basic Cable and Network Television	25%
Domestic Television Syndication	30%
Domestic Non-Theatrical	25%
Other Domestic Rights	30%
Foreign Rights	15%

7. DELIVERY—(a) Delivery Date—The Delivery Items specified in sub-clause 7(b) below shall be delivered to the Distributor, at the Production Company's sole cost and expense, at such place as the Distributor shall designate, not later than September 20, 1993, subject to events of Force Majeure.

(b) Delivery Items—Delivery of the Picture shall consist of delivery of all of the items ("Delivery Items") specified in Exhibit "B" attached hereto and delivery of a Laboratory Access Letter in the form of Exhibit "C" attached hereto signed by an authorized representative of the Production Company and the Laboratory.

8. WARRANTIES AND INDEMNIFICATIONS—(a) Rights/Payments/Mutuality—The Production Company warrants, represents and agrees that it has and shall continue to have during the Term, exclusively, all rights necessary to enter into this Agreement free and clear of any and all restrictions, claims, encumbrances, impairments or defects of any nature and that neither the signing of this Agreement nor anything contained in the Picture nor the exercise by the Distributor of any of the Distribution Rights granted herein will violate or infringe upon any rights of any kind of any party nor require the Distributor, its Subsidiaries, Affiliates, Sub-distributors or any of their licensees or agents to make any payment of any kind to any Party for any reason (such payments, if any, being the responsibility and obligation of the Production Company) and that the Picture as delivered will be in all respects ready and of a quality, both artistic and technical, adequate for general Theatrical Exhibition and commercial public exhibition and that the Distributor, its Subsidiaries, Affiliates, Sub-distributors and their licensees and agents will peacefully enjoy and possess each and all of the rights and licenses granted or purported to be granted hereunder throughout the Term without hindrance on the part of any third party.

(b) Copyright—The copyright in the Picture and in the literary, dramatic and musical material upon which it is based or which is contained therein will be valid and subsisting during the Term in each country of the Territory, and no part of the Picture or of any such literary, dramatic or musical material is or will be in the public domain. The Picture when delivered to the Distributor shall contain a copyright notice in the Production Company's name in compliance with the Universal Copyright Convention and the Copyright Law of the United States. The Production Company agrees to secure, register, renew and extend all copyrights in the Picture and all related properties upon eligibility for copyright registration, renewal and extension. The Production Company hereby irrevocably designates the Distributor as its attorney-in-fact to do so if the Production Company fails to do so, and also designates the Distributor as its attorney-in-fact to take reasonable steps to defend said copyrights against any and all infringements thereof. The Production Company agrees that the foregoing designations constitute powers coupled with an interest, are irrevocable throughout the Term and may be exercised at the Distributor's sole discretion. The Distributor shall not be liable to the Production Company for any action or failure to act on behalf of the Production Company within the scope of authority conferred on the Distributor under this clause 8(b) unless such action or omission was performed or omitted fraudulently or in bad faith or constituted wanton and willful misconduct or gross negligence.

(c) Indemnification—The Production Company agrees to indemnify and hold the Distributor, its parent, Subsidiaries, Affiliates and Sub-distributors and their respective officers, agents, directors, employees and licensees harmless from any and all claims, actions or proceedings of any kind and from any and all damages liabilities, costs and expenses (including reasonable legal fees) relating to or arising out of any violation or alleged violation of any of the warranties, representations or agreements or any error or omission in any of the material or information furnished to the Distributor in accordance with this Agreement.

(d) Errors and Omissions Insurance—The Production Company shall obtain and maintain throughout the Term, motion picture producers and distributors errors and omissions insurance in a form acceptable to the Distributor from a qualified insurance company acceptable to the Distributor naming the Distributor and each and all of the parties indemnified herein as additional named insureds. Such insurance shall be for a minimum of One Million Dollars ($1,000,000) with respect to any one claim relating to the Picture, and Three Million Dollars ($3,000,000) for claims relating to the Picture in the aggregate. The policy shall be for an initial period of not less than three (3) years commencing as of the Delivery Date and shall provide for thirty (30) days prior written notice to the Distributor in the event of any revision, modification or cancellation and that it shall be deemed primary insurance and that any insurance obtained by the Distributor shall be excess insurance not subject to exposure until the coverage provided by the Production Company's policy shall be exhausted.

9. DISTRIBUTION AND EXPLOITATION—The Distributor shall have

complete, exclusive and unqualified discretion and control as to the time, manner and terms of distribution, exhibition and exploitation of the Picture, separately or in connection with other motion pictures, in accordance with such policies, terms and conditions and through such Parties as the Distributor in its sole business judgment may determine proper or expedient and the decision of the Distributor in all such matters shall be binding and conclusive upon the Production Company. The Distributor makes no express or implied warranty or representation as to the manner or extent of any distribution or exploitation of the Picture nor the amount of money to be derived from the distribution, exhibition and exploitation of the Picture nor as to any maximum or minimum amount of monies to be expended in connection therewith. The Distributor does not guarantee the performance by any Sub-distributor, licensee or exhibitor of any contract regarding the distribution and exploitation of the Picture. The Production Company shall on request use its best efforts to secure for the Distributor such licenses and permits as may be necessary or desirable for the importation and distribution of the Picture in any geographic area of the Territory.

10. MPEA—The Production Company acknowledges that the Distributor is a member of the Motion Picture Export Association of America, Inc. ("MPEA"), and must abide by any regulations or directives of the MPEA, which has the authority to direct its members not to license or ship motion pictures for distribution or exhibition in any geographic area of the world.

11. CENSORSHIP—If the Distributor is unable to distribute the Picture in any country or area of the Territory because of censorship or any MPEA regulation or directive or any event of Force Majeure, then: (a) the amount of any Advance payable to the Production Company hereunder shall be reduced by that percentage which, on the average, receipts from the distribution of Theatrical Motion Pictures in any affected country or area represent of the receipts from the distribution of Theatrical Motion Pictures in the entire Territory, according to the latest figures generally available from the MPEA, and the Production Company will on demand refund such amount to the Distributor if such amount has already been paid to the Production Company; and (b) if the Distributor has incurred any Distribution Expenses in connection with the distribution of the Picture in the affected country or area, the Distributor may deduct the amount thereof from any sum thereafter due to the Production Company or may, at the Distributor's election, treat such amount as a Distribution Expense in accordance with the provisions of this Agreement.

12. DISTRIBUTOR'S DEFAULT—The Production Company shall not have any right to terminate or rescind this Agreement because of any default or breach of any kind by the Distributor, its Subsidiaries, Affiliates, Sub-distributors or their licensees. The Production Company shall not be entitled to

seek or obtain any injunctive relief with respect to the exercise of the rights granted hereunder by reason of any alleged default or breach by the Distributor or its Subsidiaries, Affiliates, Sub-distributors or their licensees, it being agreed that the only remedy of the Production Company in any such event shall be an action for an accounting or for damages.

13. PRODUCTION COMPANY'S DEFAULT—In the event of any default or breach by the Production Company and the failure of the Production Company to rectify the default or breach within fifteen (15) days after notice, the Distributor shall have the right to terminate this Agreement. If this Agreement is terminated for the Production Company's default or breach, the Production Company shall immediately refund to the Distributor any sums paid hereunder as an Advance without limiting any other right or remedy that the Distributor may otherwise have.

14. DISPOSITION OF DELIVERY ITEMS UPON EXPIRATION OR TERMINATION—All Motion Picture Copies made by or for the Distributor shall be the Distributor's property. Upon expiration or earlier termination of the Term, all Delivery Items, Motion Picture Copies, trailers, advertising materials and accessories which were delivered to the Distributor by the Production Company and which are existing and within the Distributor's control at the time of such expiration or termination shall at the Distributor's election, be returned to the Production Company to such place as the Production Company shall designate at the Production Company's sole cost and expense, or, shall be destroyed with certificates of destruction furnished to the Production Company.

15. WAIVER/REMEDIES—No express or implied waiver by either the Distributor or the Production Company of any provision of this Agreement or of any breach or default of the other shall constitute a continuing waiver, and no waiver shall be effective unless in writing. All remedies contained in this Agreement shall be cumulative and none of them shall be in limitation of any other remedy or right.

16. SECURITY INTEREST—In order to induce the Distributor to enter into this Agreement and to perform its obligations hereunder and in order to secure the completion and delivery of the Picture to the Distributor, the continuing exclusive rights and licenses granted to the Distributor hereunder and the right of the Distributor to recoup monies paid by the Distributor and the right of the Distributor to retain all amounts derived from the exercise of the Distribution Rights granted to the Distributor hereunder other than the amounts payable to the Production Company hereunder, the Production Company hereby grants and assigns to the Distributor a continuing security interest in and copyright mortgage on all of the Production Company's right, title and interest in all elements, properties, copyrights, contract rights, inventories, ac-

counts and general intangibles associated with and relating to the Picture. The Production Company shall sign all further documents the Distributor may reasonably request to perfect, protect, evidence, renew and/or continue the security interest and copyright mortgage hereby granted and/or to effectuate any of the purposes and intents of this Agreement, including without limitation the signing of appropriate financing statements. If the Production Company fails to sign any such document promptly on request, the Production Company hereby appoints the Distributor its irrevocable attorney-in-fact to sign any such document for the Production Company, and the Production Company agrees that such appointment constitutes a power coupled with an interest and is irrevocable throughout the Term.

17. CHOICE OF LAW—This Agreement will be interpreted in accordance with the Law of the state of California, United States of America, applicable to contracts made therein, but without regard to any principles of conflict of laws.

18. LEGAL ACTION/SERVICE OF PROCESS—The Production Company (a) agrees that any legal action or proceeding relating to this Agreement may be instituted in a state or Federal court in the County of Los Angeles, state of California, (b) waives any objection which the Production Company may now or hereafter have to the County of Los Angeles as the venue of any such action or proceeding, and (c) irrevocably submits to the non-exclusive jurisdiction of the United States District Court for the Central District of California, or any court of the state of California located in the County of Los Angeles for any such action or proceeding and any summons, order to show cause, writ, judgment, decree, or other process with respect to any such action or proceeding may be delivered to the Production Company personally outside the state of California, and when so delivered, the Production Company shall be subject to the jurisdiction of such court, and amenable to the process so delivered as though the same had been served within the state of California, but outside the county in which such action or proceeding is pending. Further, the Production Company designates and appoints the Secretary of State of California as its agent In the state of California, upon whom all summonses, notices, pleadings or process in any action or proceedings against the Production Company may be served, with copies thereof to be mailed to the Production Company at the address specified below as its address for notices, and the Production Company hereby irrevocably agrees that such service on said agent shall be of the same legal force and effect and validity as if served on the Production Company personally and with the same effect as if Production Company existed in the state of California.

19. NOTICES—All notices to the Production Company or the Distributor shall be in writing and shall be sent by registered or certified mail to the re-

spective address set forth below or such other address as shall be designated by written notice. The address for all notices to the Distributor shall be:

> Worldwide Distribution, Inc.
> P.O. Box 12345
> Beverly Hills, California 90213

The address for all notices to Production Company shall be:

> Filmright, Incorporated
> 850 Montana Avenue, Suite 23
> Santa Monica, California 90031

20. RELATIONSHIP OF PARTIES—Neither the Distributor nor the Production Company is an agent or representative of the other, and neither shall be liable for or bound by any representation, act or omission whatever of the other. This Agreement shall in no way create a joint venture or partnership nor be for the benefit of any third party. Neither the Distributor nor the Production Company shall have the authority to bind the other or the other's representatives in any way.

21. ASSIGNMENT—This Agreement may be assigned by the Distributor to its parent or any Subsidiary or Affiliate or to any party acquiring all or substantially all of the Distributor's motion picture distribution business. This Agreement may not be assigned by the Production Company, except as to the right to receive payment of all amounts due the Production Company if the Production Company and any assignee execute the Distributor's standard form of Notice of Irrevocable Assignment and Distributor's Acceptance.

22. ENTIRE AGREEMENT—This Agreement and the Exhibits attached hereto embody the entire agreement between the Distributor and Production Company as to the subject matter hereof, and expressly and unequivocally supersedes all previous agreements, warranties or representations, oral or written, which may have been made between the Distributor and the Production Company as to the subject matter hereof. This Agreement may only be amended by a written instrument duly signed by the Distributor and the Production Company.

By signing in the spaces provided below, the Distributor and the Production Company accept and agree to all of the terms and conditions of this Agreement.

DISTRIBUTOR—Worldwide Distribution, Inc.
By: _____

Rory Sanders, President

PRODUCTION COMPANY—Filmright, Incorporated
By: _____

James W. Production Company, President

Exhibit "A"
GLOSSARY

ADVANCE—Any monies or other valuable consideration paid by the Distributor to the Production Company prior to the release of the Picture as set forth at clause 5(a) above. Such Advance shall be recoupable from the first Net Proceeds which would otherwise be payable to the Production Company pursuant to clause 5(b) above.

AFFILIATE—A person or entity that (1) directly, or indirectly through one or more intermediaries, controls or is controlled by or is under common control with the Distributor or (2) a company that owns less than a majority of the voting stock of the Distributor or (3) any company which along with the Distributor are subsidiaries of a third company.

ANCILLARY MARKETS—Geographical or technological areas of demand for the Picture which are auxiliary or supplemental to the theatrical market., including foreign, network and syndicated television, pay cable and home video.

DELIVERY—The voluntary transfer of possession of the Delivery Items specified on Exhibit "B" attached hereto, by the Production Company either directly (or indirectly through the Laboratory) to the Distributor.

FORCE MAJEURE—Any events or forces which delay or prevent performance by either party due to forces outside the control of such party, including but not limited to strikes, labor disturbances or so-called "acts of God."

FREE TELEVISION DISTRIBUTION—Distribution of the Picture for purposes of broadcast television programming which is supported by television commercial sponsors.

FREE TELEVISION EXHIBITION—Exhibition of the Picture as broadcast television programming which is supported by television commercial sponsors.

GROSS RECEIPTS—Gross Receipts shall mean all sums actually received by the Distributor in the United States or in Canada in United States or Canadian dollars as a result of the exploitation of the Distributor's rights hereunder, plus all sums actually received by the Distributor in United States of Canadian dollars in the United States or in Canada from any judgments and/or settlements in connection with third party violations of any rights in and to the Picture, less reasonable costs of collection and reasonable attorney's fees incurred in connection therewith. Advances and security deposits shall not be deemed Gross Receipts unless and until earned by the exploitation of the Picture, or unless such advances and security deposits are non-forfeitable and/or non-refundable, in which event they shall be included in Gross Receipts as and when received. The Distributor agrees to exert its reasonable efforts, consistent with its reasonable business judgment, to maximize Gross Receipts with respect to the Picture and to cause all Gross Receipts to be promptly remitted to the Distributor in the United States in United States dollars. If any Canadian Gross Receipts of the Picture are frozen or unremittable, and such receipts shall be transferred to the Production Company to such effect and upon the Production Company's written request and upon condition that the same shall be permitted by Canadian authorities, the Distributor shall transfer to the Production Company at the Production Company's cost and expense in Canada and in Canadian dollars, such part thereof to which the Production Company would be entitled hereunder if the funds were transmitted and paid in the United States in accordance with the terms hereof, and such transfer shall satisfy all of the Distributor's obligations to the Production Company with respect to such Gross Receipts. The Distributor is not liable in any way for any losses caused by fluctuation of the rate of exchange or because of any failure to confer to remit any particular funds to the United States at any particular time or at a more favorable cost or rate of exchange than the cost or rate of exchange at which such conversion and remittance was accomplished.

GROSS THEATRICAL FILM RENTALS—Gross Theatrical Film Rentals are the gross receipts actually received by the Distributor and any of its Sub-distributors in the United States or in Canada in United States or Canadian dollars from the Theatrical Exploitation of the Picture.

LABORATORY—The company designated by the Distributor or the Production Company with the Distributor's consent which has contracted to develop the exposed motion picture stock for the Picture, for both image and optical sound.

LITERARY PUBLISHING RIGHTS—The right to publish a book about the making of the Picture or for the novelization of the screenplay on which the Picture is based.

MERCHANDISING RIGHTS—The right to manufacture, distribute, license, sell or otherwise exploit characters, names and events appearing in or used in connection with the Picture beyond the motion picture market, including but not limited to T-Shirts, books, posters, jewelry, games, dolls and/or toys.

MOTION PICTURE COPY OR COPIES—All positive prints of the Picture.

MUSIC PUBLISHING RIGHTS—The right to control any musical composition used in conjunction with the Picture and to license such composition for performances, mechanical reproductions and synchronizations and to print, publish and sell sheet music for such composition.

NET PROCEEDS—Net Proceeds are "Gross Receipts" less "Distribution Fees" and "Distribution Expenses" (as defined in Exhibit "D" below) and the "Advance".

NON-THEATRICAL DISTRIBUTION—Distribution of the Picture

amongst institutionalized users as opposed to the general public, including but not limited to in-flight airplanes, hotels, the Red Cross, trains and ships, schools, colleges and other educational institutions, libraries, governmental agency facilities, military installations, business and service organization clubs, shut-in institutions, retirement centers, prisons, museums, film society facilities, churches, offshore drilling rigs, logging camps and remote forestry and construction camps both domestic and foreign.

NON-THEATRICAL EXHIBITION—The exploitation of the Picture through non-theatrical distribution.

PAY TELEVISION DISTRIBUTION—Distribution of the Picture to sub-scriber-paid-for television including satellite-delivery pay cable, over-the-air-subscription television and standard cable.

PAY TELEVISION EXHIBITION—Exhibition of the Picture over sub-scriber-paid-for television including satellite-delivery pay cable, over-the-air subscription television and standard cable.

RADIO RIGHTS—The right to exploit the Picture's screenplay by broad-casting over the radio.

REMAKE RIGHTS—The rights associated with the making of a new production and release of the Picture.

SEQUEL MOTION PICTURE RIGHTS—The right to produce and re-lease a feature film after the Picture which tells a related story that occurred after the story depicted in the Picture.

SOUNDTRACK RECORDING RIGHTS—The right to exploit the phonograph records, tape recordings and compact discs which contain selected portions of the Picture's musical score.

SUB-DISTRIBUTOR—A feature film distributor who handles distribu-tion of the Picture in a specific, limited geographic territory on behalf of the Distributor.

SUBSIDIARY—Any company of which more than 50% of the voting shares are owned by the Distributor.

THEATRICAL DISTRIBUTION—The exploitation of the Picture by means of exhibition in motion picture cinemas, in contrast to the exploitation of motion pictures in other media.

THEATRICAL EXHIBITION—The showing of a the Picture to the public for a charge in a cinema.

THEATRICAL EXPLOITATION—The distribution or exhibition of the Picture in the theatrical marketplace, as opposed to the ancillary markets or the non-theatrical market..

VIDEO CASSETTE DISTRIBUTION—The distribution of the magnetic tapes which are housed in a light-tight magazines and used to record and play back the Picture.

VIDEO CASSETTE EXHIBITION—The exploitation of video cassettes of the Picture either through sales or rental transactions.

Exhibit "B"
DELIVERY ITEMS AND SCHEDULE

(See sample of Delivery Items and Schedule at Exhibit "A" of the Production-Financing/Distribution Agreement above.)

Exhibit "C"
Laboratory Access Letter

February 13, 1993
World Class Film Labs, Inc.
113 Round Robin Lane
Los Angeles, California 90034
                    RE: "Invaders From Chunga" ("Picture")
Gentlemen:
    You acknowledge that you now have, or will have, on deposit with you in the name of the undersigned, certain of the print, preprint and sound materials ("Materials") for the Picture and the trailer ("Trailer") for the Picture. Please be advised that the undersigned and Worldwide Distribution, Inc. (the "Distributor") have entered into an agreement ("Distribution Agreement") pertaining to certain the Distributor's acquisition of rights to distribute the Picture. Under certain circumstances described in the Distribution Agreement, the Distributor shall have the right to order prints and other film and sound track of the Picture and Trailer. Accordingly, it is agreed as follows:
    1. You are hereby instructed and directed upon your receipt hereof (and subject to the making of credit arrangements satisfactory to you) to honor all orders of the Distributor and such others as the Distributor may designate to you in writing.
    2. All services and material ordered by the undersigned (or its designees) shall be at the expense of the person or company ordering the same, and you agree to look solely to such person or company for payment of such charges as may be incurred. The Distributor shall not be responsible for any such charges, except for materials ordered by the Distributor.
    3. You will not look to the Distributor nor assert any claim or lien against it, the Picture or said materials by reason of any work, labor, material or services which you may perform for or furnish to the undersigned or its designees (other than the Distributor), nor will you look to the undersigned nor assert any claim or lien against the undersigned, the Picture or said materials by rea-

son of any work, labor, material or services which you may perform for or furnish to the Distributor or its designees.

4. You will not refuse to honor any of the undersigned's orders by reason of any unpaid charges incurred by the Distributor, its designees or others. You will not refuse to honor any of the orders of the Distributor or its designees by reason of any unpaid charges incurred by any others (including without limitation the undersigned or its designees).

5. Neither the undersigned nor any others shall have the right to remove the Materials from your premises without the written consent of the Distributor.

6. The undersigned hereby waives any claim for damages or otherwise which it may have against you for any actions which you may take pursuant to the direction of the Distributor (or its designees) hereunder.

7. The instructions contained herein are irrevocable and may not be altered or modified except in a writing signed by the undersigned and the Distributor.

Please confirm your understanding of and agreement to the foregoing by signing in the space provided below.

FILMRIGHT INCORPORATED

By: _____

    ("the undersigned")

WORLDWIDE DISTRIBUTION, INC.

By: _____

    ("Distributor")

AGREED AND ACCEPTED:
WORLD CLASS FILM LABS, INC.

By: _____

Exhibit "D"
Definition of Distribution Expenses

The term Distribution Expenses as used in this Agreement shall refer to and include all reasonable and accountable costs and expenses incurred by the Distributor and/or its Subsidiaries, Affiliates, Sub-distributors, licensees and agents in connection with the distribution, exhibition, advertising, promotion, exploitation and turning to account the Picture or in the exercise of any of the

262 | *Appendix G*

rights granted to the Distributor with respect to the exploitation of the Picture in the Territory of whatever kind or nature, including without limitation the following:

(a) All costs of duped and dubbed negatives, sound tracks, prints, release prints, tapes, cassettes, duplicating material, labor and facilities and all other film material manufactured for use in connection with exploitation and release of the Picture in the Territory.

(b) All costs of preparing and delivering the Picture for distribution in the Territory, including, without limitation, all costs incurred in connection with screening and audience testing expenses, the production of foreign language versions of the Picture, whether dubbed, superimposed or otherwise, as well as any and all costs and expenses in connection with changing the title of the Picture, recutting, re-editing, re-recording, rescoring, dubbing and/or remaking and/or reorganizing the Picture or any part or parts thereof or shortening the Picture for release in any Territory or for exhibition on television or other media, or in order to conform to the peculiar national or political prejudices likely to be encountered in any territory, or for any other purpose or reason.

(c) The reasonable and accountable costs of creating materials for and of advertising, promoting, exploiting and publicizing the Picture in any way, including (without limiting the generality of the foregoing) the aggregate of the following (as to all of which the Production Company shall be entitled to the its pro-rata share of any benefit of volume discounts and/or rebates of which the Distributor has the benefit):

(i) All costs incurred to advertise, publicize and promote the Picture in any way (and to create materials therefor), including in connection with publications, radio and television, direct mail, displays, promotional activities, entertainment, commercial tie-ins, promotional materials and printing materials.

(ii) That portion of the advertising costs referred to in the preceding subclause (a) incurred to advertise, publicize and promote the Picture by any and all means (and to create materials therefor), inclusive of national, regional or local publications, radio and television, trailers, direct mail, display advertising, promotional activities, entertainment, and commercial tie ins, in connection with the theatrical exhibition of the Picture, whether engaged in by the Distributor or its Sub-distributors directly or where the Distributor or its Sub-distributors pay, share in or are charged with all or a portion of the costs thereof (whether affected by credits against or deductions from theatre rentals). Any costs of media advertising for theatrical exhibition contributed by exhibitors from exhibitor's share of box office receipts or exhibitor's overhead shall not be deductible as a distribution expense.

(d) All insurance covering or relating to the Picture, including (but not limited to) errors and omissions insurance, and all insurance on negatives, positive prints, sound materials or other physical property, it being understood, that the Distributor shall obtain or maintain customary insurance with respect to distribution of the Picture in the Territory.

(e) All transportation, shipping, packing, delivery, inspection and storage charges on all negatives, prints and other materials in connection with the Picture: the cost of film cases, cans and containers, all duties, customs, taxes, fees, insurance and imposts in connection with shipments and all other costs incidental to providing and delivering prints; telegraph and telephone charges in connection with the distribution of the Picture.

(f) The amount of all sales, remittance, currency conversion and similar taxes and fees, however denominated, imposed in connection with the picture. Nothing herein contained shall be deemed to permit the Distributor to recoup any part of net income, corporate, franchise, excess profit or other similar corporate taxes imposed upon the Distributor as a corporate entity as distinguished from taxes imposed upon the Distributor with respect to the Gross Receipts derived from the distribution of the Picture.

In no event shall the recoupable amount of any tax imposed upon the Distributor with respect to the Gross Receipts or any portion thereof, however denominated, be decreased because of the manner in which such taxes are elected to be treated by the Distributor in filing net income, corporate, franchise, excess profits or similar tax returns.

(g) All reasonable legal expenses and obligations (including, but not limited to, judgments, settlements and attorneys' fees) incurred in connection with any of the matters contained in this Agreement or any litigation instituted by or against the Distributor or any of its Sub-distributors, licensees or agents in connection with the Picture or the distribution, exhibition or exploitation thereof (excluding litigation and disputes between the parties thereto).

(h) The cost of obtaining and renewing copyright or similar registrations in any country or territory of the Territory (which the Distributor shall have the right but not the obligation to do).

(i) The cost of auditing Sub-distributors and sublicensees and the cost of checking box office receipts.

(j) The cost of any compensation or payments (including, but not limited to, payments in connection with television exhibitions) which the Distributor may be or become obligated to make with respect to the Picture by reason of any executive or judicial order, any collective bargaining agreement (such as residuals), any government action or any legal action or otherwise.

(k) All travel and transportation expenses of the Distributor employees, agents or special representatives specifically assigned to sell the Picture reasonably incurred during the period they are so assigned. If more than one picture is handled, then such costs shall be pro-rated among all of the pictures. The

Distributor agrees that excluding those situations in which first class travel in connection with the Picture is required pursuant to contract, guild or other bona fide obligations, air travel expenses incurred in connection with the Picture shall be chargeable at so-called "coach" rather than first class fares.

(l) All distribution fees, commissions or similar charges paid, incurred or retained by any third party, including without limitation any sub-distributor or sales agent in connection with distribution and exploitation of the Picture, provided that in no event shall the Distributor deduct distribution fees payable to the Distributor.

(m) Any other costs, expenses and direct distribution expenses in connection with the exhibition, distribution and exploitation of the Picture, incurred by the Distributor in the exercise of its reasonable good faith business judgment which are properly treated as deductible items of distribution expenses according to good trade practices and any other costs which are recoverable as distribution expenses under the provisions of this Agreement.

APPENDIX H

Distribution Agreement (Rent-a-Distributor Deal)

THIS AGREEMENT is made as of this the 18th day of April, 1993, by and between Filmright, Incorporated, having its principal office at 850 Montana Avenue, Santa Monica, California 90031 (hereinafter referred to as the "Production Company"), and Good Movies International Corp., having its principal office at 3404 Victoria Avenue, Laguna Beach, California 92677 (hereinafter referred to as "Distributor"), with respect to the Pictures owned by the Production Company and to be distributed by the Distributor upon the following terms and conditions:

1. THE PICTURES—The Production Company has produced, or is in the process of producing, and agrees to deliver to the Distributor for distribution the following:

> "Invasion From Chunga"
> "Heartbreak and Cool"
> "Exploitation Flick II"

(hereinafter referred to as "Pictures" whether one or more)

2. GRANT OF RIGHTS—The Production Company hereby grants to the Distributor the exclusive and irrevocable license to rent, lease, exhibit, distribute, reissue, deal in the Pictures and prints or any part thereof, and trailers thereof, and to license others to do so in standard and substandard gauges throughout the territory or territories and for the term set forth in Schedule "A" attached hereto and incorporated herein by this reference as if fully set forth verbatim (hereinafter referred to as the "Licensed Territory" and "Term") by any and all mediums or means whatsoever.

Without in any way limiting the generality of the foregoing, the Distributor shall, pursuant to this Agreement, have and shall be vested during the Term of this Agreement with:

(a) Distribution Rights—The sole and exclusive right to exhibit, distribute, market, exploit, sell, broadcast, transmit, reproduce, and publicize the Pictures, or any portion or element thereof, including the musical soundtracks and reissues thereof and to permit others to do the same throughout the Licensed Territory for any and all purposes whatsoever, including without limitation, theatrically, non-theatrically, commercially, non-commercially, sponsored, non-sponsored, sustaining and in connection with the advertising or exploitation of commercial products or otherwise, on all gauges of film and by every means, method and device now known, or which may hereafter be discovered, invented, devised or created, including radio, television (whether free, pay, closed circuit, CATV, or otherwise), audio visual devices, videotapes, tapes, discs, records, and cassettes, and any and all improvements on any thereof.

(b) Right to Deal—The right to generally deal with the Pictures, the revenues and properties thereof in such manner as the Distributor may elect and deem advisable.

(c) Foreign Language Versions—The right to make, cause to be made and/or authorize others to make foreign versions of the Pictures.

(d) Distributor's Tradename—The right to announce on the Pictures and elsewhere that it is presented by the Distributor and to use its own name and trademark on said Picture and to authorize others to use and attach their own names and trademarks thereon.

(e) Trailers—The right to cause trailers of the Pictures to be manufactured, exhibited and distributed by every means, method and device throughout the Licensed Territory.

(f) Publications—The right to write and authorize others to do the same, in all languages, books and other publications of the Pictures of all kinds and for all uses and purposes whatsoever, including but not limited to the use of the same or any part thereof for advertising and publicity purposes.

(g) Claims—The right in the name of Distributor or otherwise to institute and prosecute all actions or proceedings which the Distributor may deem necessary to institute or prosecute for the purpose of establishing, maintaining or preserving any of the rights herein granted or purported to be granted to the Distributor and similarly to defend any action or proceeding which may be brought against the Distributor or assignees, with respect to the Pictures or any of the rights herein granted or purported to be granted to the Distributor or which in any manner questions or disputes any of the rights of Distributor in and to the said Pictures or any of the rights herein granted to it.

(h) Advertising—The right to publicize and exploit the Pictures and to authorize others to do the same by such means and to such extent as the Distributor may elect.

(i) Right to Broadcast–Persons—The right to issue and authorize publicity in connection with the Pictures, including the names, photographs, likenesses, acts, poses, voices and other sound effects, as well as recordings, transcriptions, films and other reproductions thereof, of the director, the musicians, the writers, the composers, the authors, all members of the cast and all other persons rendering services in connection with the Pictures.

(j) Right To Broadcast–Material—The right to broadcast by any means or authorize others to do so, in any language, adaptations, versions or sketches of the Pictures.

(k) Alterations—The right to make such changes, (including changes in the title of the Pictures), additions, alterations, cuts, interpolations and eliminations as (i) may be required by any duly authorized censorship authority or industry organization; (ii) as may be required for the distribution of the Pictures in television (whether free, pay-per-view, or otherwise), (iii) or otherwise as may be deemed desirable by the Distributor for the distribution of the Pictures.

(l) Disposal—The Distributor may dispose as junk all film and sound recordings delivered and/or paid for by the Production Company hereunder, after they have served their purpose. However, should the Production Company desire to have any or all of such materials, then the Production Company shall notify the Distributor in writing of its desires on or before thirty (30) days prior to the expiration of the term of this Agreement and shall arrange, at the Production Company's sole cost, for the pick-up and shipping of such materials.

3. DELIVERY—It is of the essence of this Agreement that the Production Company make full delivery of the Pictures to the Distributor on or before November, 15, 1993, by the Production Company making physical delivery at the Production Company's sole expense at such address as the Distributor may designate of all those items set forth on Schedule "B" attached hereto and incorporated herein by this reference as if fully set forth verbatim, including, without limitation if requested, a laboratory letter. In the event the Production Company fails to properly deliver any such item on a timely basis, then without limitation of its other rights and remedies, the Distributor shall have the right to (i) prepare, create, and manufacture such items, in which event the Production Company will pay to the Distributor all costs incurred by the Distributor with respect thereto and/or at the Distributor's option the Distributor may deduct such costs from any and all sums otherwise due the Production Company hereunder; or (ii) terminate the term hereof relating back to its inception at any time prior to such full and complete delivery thereof, in which event the Production Company will promptly repay to the Distributor any sum previously paid by the Distributor to the Production Company hereunder.

4. DISTRIBUTOR'S SHARE OF RECEIPTS—The Distributor shall be entitled to receive an amount equal to fifteen percent (15%) percent of the gross sales from the distribution of the Pictures hereunder. Any and all costs of distribution, including but not limited to shipping, duties, customs, insur-

ance, telephone, promotion, film prints, music and effect sound tracks, foreign language dubbing costs, color transparencies and artwork, cassette duplication and film to tape transfer costs, shall be paid entirely by the Production Company.

5. PRODUCTION COMPANY'S WARRANTIES—The Production Company represents, warrants and agrees as follows:

(a) Rights of Production Company—The Production Company has the right to enter into and perform this Agreement and grant to the Distributor all of the rights and licenses herein granted and agreed to be granted to the Distributor; and if the Production Company is a Partnership or a corporation that it is duly organized under the laws of its domicile or state of incorporation, that it has taken all necessary action to authorize the execution and delivery of this Agreement and, that the same does not and will not violate any provisions of its Articles of Partnership or the Articles of Incorporation or By-Laws of the Production Company, or any contract, or any other agreement to which the Production Company is a party.

(b) Claims, Liens, Encumbrances Against the Picture—There are, and will be, no claims, liens, encumbrances or rights of any nature in or to the Pictures or any part thereof which can or will impair or interfere with the rights of any nature in or to the Pictures or any part thereof which can or will impair or interfere with the rights, privileges or licenses of Distributor hereunder.

(c) Trademark, Copyright, Slander Violations—The Pictures and each and every part thereof, including the sound and music synchronized therewith, and the exercise by any party authorized by the Distributor of any right herein granted to the Distributor, will not violate or infringe upon the trademark, tradename, copyright, patent, literary, dramatic, music, artistic, personal, private, civil or property right, right of privacy, or any other right of any person or constitute a libel or slander of any person, and the Pictures will not contain any unlawful or censorable material.

(d) Exclusiveness of Distribution Rights—The Production Company has not and will not sell, assign, transfer, convey or hypothecate to any person or company, any right, title, or interest in or to the Pictures, or any of the other rights granted to the Distributor herein unless such sale, assignment, transfer, conveyance or hypothecation is subject to this Agreement.

(e) Quiet and Peaceful Enjoyment—The Distributor shall quietly and peacefully enjoy and possess, during the entire period of its exclusive rights hereunder, all of the distribution and other rights herein granted and agreed to be granted to the Distributor.

(f) Exhibition Outside the Territory—The Production Company shall not authorize the exhibition of the Pictures, outside of the Licensed Territory, in a place or way that would interfere with the exploitation of any of the Distributor's rights hereunder in the Licensed Territory (such as by advertising in the Licensed Territory, or by telecasting into the Licensed Territory, whether by satellite, CATV or otherwise).

6. INDEMNIFICATION—The Production Company agrees to indemnify and hold the Distributor (and its affiliates, exhibitors, assignees, licensees, and their respective officers and employees) harmless against any liability, damage, cost, expense (including reasonable attorney's fees) occasioned by or arising out of any claim, demand or action inconsistent with any agreement, representation, grant or warranty made or assumed by the Production Company hereunder. The Distributor agrees to give the Production Company notice of any action to which the foregoing indemnity applies, and the Production Company may participate in the defense of the same, at the Production Company's expense, through counsel of its choosing; however, the final control and disposition of the same (by settlement, compromise, or otherwise) shall remain with the Distributor. The Production Company agrees to pay the Distributor on demand any amounts for which it may be responsible under the foregoing indemnity, and/or the Distributor may recoup any such amount from any sum otherwise due the Production Company hereunder, and without limiting any of its other rights or remedies, upon the making or filing of any action, claim or demand subject hereto, the Distributor shall be entitled to withhold sums payable under this or any other agreement between the parties in an amount reasonably related to the potential liability, plus costs and attorney's fees, provided that the Distributor shall not so withhold if the Production Company posts a bond which has been approved in all aspects (form, amount, duration, surety, etc.) by the Distributor.

7. DISTRIBUTOR'S RIGHTS AND OBLIGATIONS—(a) Distributor's Authority—The Distributor shall have complete authority to distribute, exhibit and exploit the Pictures and the rights herein granted in the Licensed Territory, and to license others to do the same, in accordance with such sales methods, policies and terms as it may, in its uncontrolled discretion, determine. The Production Company acknowledges and agrees that the Distributor in the exercise of its rights hereunder may enter into license agreements with third parties which extend in their contract length beyond the term of this Agreement; and, in such event, the Production Company agrees that any such license, subject only to its specific terms and conditions, shall be valid and binding upon the Production Company for its entire term and that the Production Company shall abide by and comply with all of the terms and conditions of any such license agreement. The Production Company acknowledges and agrees that the Distributor makes no representations, warranties, guarantees or agreements as to the gross receipts or net profits, if any, to be derived from the Pictures. In no event shall the Distributor incur any liability to the Produc-

tion Company hereunder based upon any claim by the Production Company that the Distributor has failed to realize receipts or revenue which should or could have been realized.

(b) Transfer of Agreement—It is agreed that the Distributor may transfer or assign this Agreement, or all or any part of the Distributor's rights hereunder, to any person, firm, or corporation, and this Agreement shall inure to the Distributor's benefit and the benefit of the Distributor's successors, transferees and assigns.

(c) Distribution Singly or as a Group—Without in any manner limiting the generality of the foregoing, it is agreed that: (i) the Pictures may be distributed singly or in a group including other pictures, and if distributed or otherwise disposed of as part of a group including other pictures, the gross receipts allocated to the Picture or Pictures shall be reasonably fixed and determined by the Distributor and any such allocation shall be conclusive and binding upon the Production Company in all respects; (ii) the Distributor may make all bookings, leasing and rental contracts for the exhibition of the Pictures, and grant to others the right to distribute and exhibit the Picture or any part thereof; (iii) the Distributor may make and cancel contracts in connection with any of the foregoing and adjust and settle disputes and give allowances and credits with and to the Distributor's licensees, exhibitors, and other persons; and (iv) the Distributor may incur any expenses it deems appropriate in connection with the Picture and the exercise of its rights hereunder.

If the Distributor advertises, publicizes, or promotes the Picture or Pictures with a group of other pictures, the cost of such advertising, publicity and promotion shall be allocated between the Picture or Pictures and such other motion pictures, taking into consideration the proportion that the advertising, publicity and promotion of the Picture or Pictures bears to the total advertising, publicity and promotion used for the entire group of pictures.

(d) Access to Film—The Distributor shall have the right of access to all negative and positive film and soundtrack elements and all negative and positive prints of stills connected with the Picture, and exclusive possession of all materials delivered pursuant to clause 3 hereof.

8. RECORDS AND ACCOUNTS—(a) Distributor's Payments to Production Company, Reports and Settlements—The Distributor will furnish the Production Company with reports showing revenues actually received from completed sales for each accounting period for which each report is furnished. Said reports shall be furnished quarterly during the term of this Agreement. No report shall be due for any quarter in which there is no activity. Each report shall include the computation of gross receipts, distribution fees, distribution expenses, and any payments due the Production Company. Payment of any sums due the Production Company under this Agreement to the extent reflected in such reports shall be made to the Production Company concurrent

with the furnishing of such report and each report shall be furnished approximately forty-five (45) days after the close of the period for which such report is furnished. Any deposits, other than non-refundable deposits, or revenues received from uncompleted sales shall not be deemed to be actually received until all conditions precedent to the Distributor's right to retain such deposits or revenues have occurred.

(b) Keeping of Records—The Distributor agrees to maintain complete and accurate books of account and records of the distribution of the Pictures. The Production Company or a Certified Public Accountant acting on its behalf may examine such books and records during reasonable business hours at the Distributor's place of business once each year.

(c) Finality of Statements—Any statement or report submitted to the Production Company by the Distributor pursuant to this Agreement shall be binding upon the Production Company and not subject to any objection for any reason if not disputed in writing by the Production Company within one (1) year after such statement or report shall have been delivered to the Production Company. If any figures on a statement reappear on, or are included in cumulative amounts on, any later statement, the later statement shall be disregarded in computing the Production Company's time to object.

(d) Assignment—The Production Company shall have no right to sell, assign, transfer, or otherwise dispose or encumber its interest hereunder or its earnings therefrom and any attempt to do the same shall be without force or effect.

9. MISCELLANEOUS PROVISIONS—(a) Force Majeure—Anything herein contained to the contrary notwithstanding, neither party shall be liable to the other in damages because of any failure to perform hereunder caused by any cause beyond its control, including but not limited to fire, earthquake, flood, epidemic, accident, explosion, casualty, strike, lockout, labor controversy, riot, civil disturbance, act of a public enemy, embargo, war, act of God, any governmental ordinance or law, the issuance of any executive or judicial order, any failure or delay or any transportation agency, any failure or delay in respect to any electrical or sound equipment or apparatus, or by any laboratory, any failure without fault, to obtain material, transportation, power or any other essential thing required in the conduct of its business or any similar cause.

(b) Relationship of Parties—Nothing herein contained shall constitute a partnership between or joint venture by the parties hereto, or constitute either party the agent of the other. Neither party shall hold itself out contrary to the terms of this clause, and neither party shall be or become liable by any representation, act or omission of the other contrary to the provisions hereof. This Agreement is not for the benefit of any third party and shall not be deemed to give any right or remedy to any such party whether referred to herein or not.

The Distributor shall not be obligated to segregate gross receipts from the Pictures from its other funds nor shall the Distributor be considered a trustee, pledgeholder, fiduciary or agent of the Production Company by reason of anything done or any money collected by it.

(c) No Continuing Waiver—No waiver by either party of any breach hereof shall be deemed a waiver of any preceding, continuing or succeeding breach of the same, or any other term hereof.

(d) Construction—This Agreement shall be deemed made and is to be construed and interpreted under the laws of the State of California, applicable to contracts entered into and totally performed therein. All obligations herein are enforceable in Orange County, California.

(e) Notices—All written notices, payments, accountings and other data which the Distributor is required or may desire to send the Production Company shall be delivered in person or deposited in the United States mails, telegraph or cable office, postage prepaid addressed to the Production Company at:

Filmright, Incorporated
850 Montana Avenue
Santa Monica, CA 90031

or such other address as the Production Company may designate in writing.

All written notices, payments, accountings, and other data which the Production Company is required or may desire to send the Distributor shall be delivered in person or deposited in the United States mails, telegraph or cable office, postage prepaid, addressed to:

Good Movies International Corp.
3404 Victoria Avenue
Laguna Beach, California 92677

or such other address as the Distributor may designate in writing.

(f) Further Documents—The Production Company agrees to execute and deliver to the Distributor such further documents as the Distributor may reasonably require to effectuate this agreement. If the Production Company fails to execute and deliver any such document promptly following the Distributor's request, the Distributor may do so as the Production Company's attorney-in-fact and the Distributor is irrevocably appointed to do so as the Production Company's attorney-in fact. It is acknowledged that this power of attorney is coupled with an interest.

(g) Entire Agreement—This Agreement supersedes and cancels all prior negotiations and understandings between the parties and contains all of the terms of the parties. No modification shall be valid unless in writing and executed by both parties. No officer, employee or representative of Distributor has any authority to make any representation or promise not contained in this Agreement, and the Production Company has not executed this Agreement in reliance on any such representation or promise.

IN WITNESS WHEREOF, the parties hereto have caused this Agreement to be executed by their duly authorized officers as of the day and year first above written.

PRODUCTION COMPANY—Filmright, Incorporated

By: _____
James W. Producer, President

DISTRIBUTOR—Good Movies International, Corp.

By: _____
Jebediah Shrapnel, President

Schedule A

Licensed Territories: Mexico
                             Panama
                             Peru
                             Paraguay
                             Uruguay
                             Brazil
                             Argentina
                             Chile
                             Bolivia
                             Venezuela
                             Colombia
                             Ecuador

TERM: Commencing on the 1st day of May, 1993 and ending ten years (10) years thereafter, however, the Distributor shall have a one-time option to extend the Term for one (1) additional year. Such option shall be exercised by the Distributor giving written notice to the Production Company of its election to exercise its option hereunder on or before the end of the initial term of this Agreement.

SCHEDULE "B"
DELIVERY MATERIALS

35mm Print ( )	[ ]
16mm Print ( )	[ ]
Music & Effects Soundtrack	[ ]

1 inch NTSC Master Tape (   )   [ ]
3/4 inch Viewing Tape (   )   [ ]
1/2 inch Viewing Tape (   )   [ ]
Out-takes or Trailers (   )   [ ]
"Key" or Poster Art   [ ]
Production Photos:
   Color   [ ]
   Black & White   [ ]
Publicity Book(s)   [ ]
Press Book (s)   [ ]
Dialogue Sheets or Script   [ ]
Synopsis   [ ]
One-Sheets   [ ]
Color Transparencies   [ ]
TV/Radio Advertising   [ ]
Lab Access Letter   [ ]
List of Cast & Crew   [ ]
Publicity Photos   [ ]
Other Printed Material   [ ]
Chain of title documents   [ ]
Copyright Registration documents   [ ]

APPENDIX I
Foreign Distribution Agreement

THIS AGREEMENT ("Agreement") is made and entered into on this the 18th day of April, 1993, by and between Filmright, Incorporated a corporation organized under the laws of California, USA, with offices at 850 Montana Avenue, Santa Monica, California 90031 (hereinafter referred to as the "Licensor"), and Territorial, Inc., a corporation organized under the laws of Egypt and having its principal place of business at 10 Siwa Street, Memphis, Egypt (hereinafter referred to as the "Territorial Distributor").

WITNESSETH:

In consideration of the covenants and conditions hereinafter contained, and other good and valuable consideration, IT IS AGREED:

1. "Picture" as used in this Agreement shall mean the feature length motion picture entitled "Invaders From Chunga" produced by Filmright, Incorporated.

2. "Term" as used in this Agreement, shall mean the period commencing with the date of this Agreement and ending five (5) years from such date.

3. "Territory" as used in this Agreement, shall mean the country of Egypt.

4. GRANT OF LICENSE—The Licensor hereby grants to the Territorial Distributor, throughout the Territory and during the Term, the exclusive license, under copyright and otherwise, to exhibit, distribute and otherwise deal in and exploit the Picture and trailers thereof, on 16mm and 35mm film solely in theatres and similar places generally used for public entertainment where admission fees are charged and, in connection with such use, to use and perform all music, lyrics, and musical compositions contained in the Picture and/or recorded in the sound track thereof. The rights granted to the Territorial Distributor shall include the right:

(a) Only with the Licensor's prior written consent, to authorize others to exercise and to sub-license any of the Territorial Distributor's rights hereunder;

(b) To make at the Territorial Distributor's sole cost such dubbed and/or sub-titled versions of the Picture, and the trailers thereof, as the Territorial Distributor may deem advisable;

(c) To publicize, advertise and exploit the Picture throughout the Territory during the Term and to cause or permit others so to do; and

(d) To order at the Territorial Distributor's cost from the Licensor, or if the Licensor elects, directly from such laboratory as the Licensor may designate holding pre-print or other material relating to the Picture, such number of 16mm or 35mm release prints of the Picture and trailers thereof as the Territorial Distributor may, from time to time, require.

All rights and licenses not specifically granted the Territorial Distributor hereunder, including but not limited to non-theatrical and television distribution rights, are reserved solely to the Licensor. However, the Licensor agrees not to exhibit or cause the exhibition of the Picture by means of television in the Territory during the term of the license period with respect to the Picture.

5. CONSIDERATION—(a) Outright Sale—In consideration of the rights herein granted to the Territorial Distributor, the Territorial Distributor agrees to pay to the Licensor, and the Licensor agrees to accept, the sum of Two Hundred Fifty Thousand U.S. Dollars ($250,000 U.S.), payable as follows:

(i) Fifty Thousand U.S. Dollars ($50,000 U.S.) upon execution of this Agreement; and

(ii) Two Hundred Thousand U.S. Dollars ($200,000 U.S.) as follows: the Licensor shall give the Territorial Distributor written notice to the effect that the Picture is complete and that the Territorial Distributor's orders for release prints can be filled and shipped. Upon receipt of such notice, the Territorial Distributor shall, within thirty (30) days thereafter, furnish to the Licensor an irrevocable clean letter of credit drawn upon a bank acceptable to the Licensor providing for the payment of the foregoing amount, plus the laboratory charges for the Territorial Distributor's initial print order, upon the sole condition that the laboratory manufacturing said prints shall have given said bank written notice that said laboratory shall have shipped to the Territorial Distributor the prints of the Picture initially ordered by the Territorial Distributor. In the event that the Territorial Distributor fails to cause said letter of credit to be opened within thirty (30) days after the licensor's said notice shall have been given, the Licensor shall have the right to terminate this Agreement and all of its obligations hereunder and to retain the sum theretofore paid by the Territorial Distributor the Licensor under sub-clause (i) hereof.

(b) Non-Payment—Payment by the Territorial Distributor to the Licensor of the sum or sums set forth in clause 5(a) above shall be deemed of the essence of this Agreement, and the Territorial Distributor's failure to make payment thereof in the manner therein described shall constitute a material breach hereof, which shall entitle the Licensor to cancel the within Agreement upon ten (10) days' written notice to the Territorial Distributor. Notice hereunder shall be deemed "written" if transmitted by letter, telegram or cable. Unless the Territorial Distributor shall, within said ten (10) day period, fully comply with clause 5(a) above, at the expiration of said period this Agreement shall forthwith be deemed cancelled, null and void. In such event, it being impossible to ascertain exactly the amount of Licensor's damages, any deposit or partial payment made hereunder shall be retained by the Licensor as liquidated damages for such breach, in addition to any other rights and remedies the Licensor may have by reason of such breach.

(c) Censorship—If, in the Territory defined herein, the Picture shall not have been passed by any board of censorship and shall be rejected in part by any such board of censorship, the Territorial Distributor will make such changes in the prints of the Picture as may be required by said board or boards of censorship, shall bear the full cost thereof, and shall give the Licensee notice of the changes made. If, in the Territory, the Picture shall be rejected altogether by any such board of censorship, the Territorial Distributor shall have the right, exercisable by written notice to the Licensor, to terminate this Agreement for the Territory.

6. WARRANTIES AND REPRESENTATIONS—The Licensor warrants and represents that:

(a) The Licensor is the sole owner of, and has the right to grant to the Territorial Distributor, all of the rights granted to the Territorial Distributor under this Agreement;

(b) There are not, and there will not be outstanding at any time during the Term hereof, liens, claims or other encumbrances, which will interfere with any of the rights granted to the Territorial Distributor pursuant to the terms of this Agreement;

(c) Neither the Picture nor the exercise of any right herein granted will violate or infringe any copyright, personal or property right or right of privacy, or slanders or libels, any person, firm or corporation; and

(d) The Territorial Distributor will quietly and peacefully enjoy the rights herein granted to it throughout the Term and the Territory without hindrance on the part of any third party by reason of any act or omission of the Licensor.

7. NO ALTERATIONS ALLOWED—The Territorial Distributor agrees that the Picture shall be exhibited exactly in the form in which the Licensor delivers it to the laboratory which shall manufacture the Territorial Distributor's release prints, and that no changes, addition, alterations, cuts, interpolations, or eliminations shall be made without the prior written consent of the Licensor, except as may be required for censorship purposes. The Territorial Distributor shall not remove or permit the removal of the name of the Licensor, the producer, director, author or members of the cast or any other designation of credit, including notice of copyright, from the prints, advertising materials or accessories utilized by the Territorial Distributor pursuant to this Agreement, and the Territorial Distributor will not alter the order, relative size or manner or presentation of any such credit.

8. OWNERSHIP—Legal title to all prints, trailers, advertising and other materials referred to herein shall remain in the Licensor at all times, subject to

the right of the Territorial Distributor to the use thereof in accordance with and subject to the terms of this Agreement. If the Licensor shall so request, the Territorial Distributor shall secure such copyright registration or other legal registration or protection for the Picture in the Territory in the name of the Licensor, at the Licensor's cost. The Territorial Distributor agrees not to challenge or attack the validity of the Licensor's copyright in the Picture in any manner and the Territorial Distributor agrees to exert its best efforts to fully protect and defend such copyright. The Territorial Distributor shall give the Licensor prompt written notice of any claim or proceeding which may be made or commenced against the Territorial Distributor or Licensor alleging any claim that, if proved, would put the Licensor in material breach of its warranties hereunder. The Licensor shall have the right to dispose of or defend any such claim or proceeding and to control the conduct of any negotiations in the defense of any such proceeding. The Territorial Distributor agrees to fully cooperate in all respects with the Licensor in connection therewith, and in particular to give to the Licensor any information in its possession or control with reference to any such claim.

9. TERMINATION—Upon the conclusion of the term of the license granted hereunder or any sooner termination thereof by reason of the Territorial Distributor's material breach hereof, the Territorial Distributor agrees to ship all prints, advertising materials, accessories or any other materials in its possession with respect to the Picture to the Licensor, at the Licensor's cost therefor, or, if the Licensor shall so request, to destroy all such prints and other materials and to furnish the Licensor with certificates of such destruction, at the Territorial Distributor's cost.

10. MISCELLANEOUS PROVISIONS—(a) Relationship of Parties—Nothing herein contained shall constitute a partnership between or joint venture by, the parties hereto or constitute either party the agent of the other. Neither party shall hold itself out contrary to the terms of this Agreement and neither party shall become liable by reason of any representation, act or omission of the other contrary to the provisions hereof. This Agreement is not for the benefit of any third party and shall not be deemed to give any right or remedy to any such party whether referred to herein or not.

(b) Waiver—No waiver by either party of any breach hereof shall be deemed a waiver of any preceding or succeeding breach hereof.

(c) Assignment—This Agreement and the rights granted hereunder to Territorial Distributor are personal to the Territorial Distributor, and the Territorial Distributor agrees not to assign, transfer to otherwise hypothecate the same in whole or in part without obtaining the prior written consent of the Licensor, nor shall any of said rights or licenses be assigned or transferred by the Territorial Distributor to any third party by operation of law or otherwise. In the event that Licensor shall consent to any such assignment by the Territorial Distributor, the Territorial Distributor shall nevertheless continue to remain fully and primarily responsible and liable to the Licensor for the full performance of all terms of this Agreement; and the Territorial Distributor agrees to submit to the Licensor the names and addresses of all such assignees. The Licensor shall have the right to assign this Agreement in whole or in part. Upon such assignment, the Licensor agrees to give notice of said assignment to the Territorial Distributor in writing.

(c) Notices—All notices and other data required or desired to be given hereunder by either party shall be deposited in the mails in the country of origin, postage prepaid, addressed to the other at the address set forth in the first clause of this Agreement. Either party shall
have the right to designate other or different addresses by a notice given in accordance with the provisions of this clause.

(d) Amendment—This Agreement cannot be amended, modified or changed in any way whatsoever excepting only by a written instrument duly executed by authorized officers of the parties hereto.

(e) Governing Laws—This Agreement shall be deemed made in and is to be construed and interpreted in accordance with the laws of the state of California, USA.

LICENSOR—Filmright, Incorporated
By: _____
James W. Producer, President

Territorial Distributor—Territorial, Inc.
By: _____
Gonzalo Shrevanetza, President

[For copies of additional sample agreements relating to acquisition, development, packaging, financing, production, distribution, licensing and merchandising, see *Film Industry Contracts*, by John W. Cones (self-published, 1993). Those sample agreements are also available on computer diskettes and may be ordered at 310/477-6842.]

Notes

1. Feature Film Net Profits

1. The principal member companies of the Motion Picture Association of America are Disney (Buena Vista, Touchstone and Hollywood Pictures), Warner Bros., MGM/UA, Paramount, MCA/Universal, Columbia/TriStar, Orion and Twentieth Century-Fox.

2. For a more comprehensive listing of these film distributor practices, see *337 Reported Business Practices of the Major Studio/Film Distributors*, a self-published monograph by the same author, or *Film Finance and Distribution—A Dictionary of Terms*, Silman-James Press, 1992, a book by the same author that incorporates all of the business practices previously discussed in the above-referenced monograph.

3. David McClintick, *Indecent Exposure: A True Story of Hollywood and Wall Street*, Dell Publishing, 1983, 512 & 513.

4. Steven D. Sills and Ivan L. Axelrod, "Profit Participation in the Motion Picture Industry," *Los Angeles Lawyer*, April 1989.

5. Hillary Bibicoff, "Net Profit Participations in the Motion Picture Industry," *Loyola of Los Angeles Entertainment Law Journal*, vol. 11, 1991.

6. Adam J. Marcus, "*Buchwald v. Paramount Pictures Corp.* and the Future of Net Profit," *Cardozo Arts & Entertainment Law Journal*, vol. 9, 1991.

7. Peter J. Dekom, "The Net Effect: Making Net Profit Mean Something," *American Premiere*, May–June, 1992.

8. Pierce O'Donnell and Dennis McDougal, *Fatal Subtraction: The Inside Story of Buchwald v. Paramount/How Hollywood Really Does Business*, Doubleday, 1992.

9. David Nochimson and Leon Brachman, "Contingent Compensation for Theatrical Motion Pictures," *The Entertainment and Sports Lawyer*, vol. 5, no. 1, Summer 1986, 3.

10. Most of such terms are defined and discussed in the author's first book, *Film Finance and Distribution—A Dictionary of Terms*, Silman-James Press, 1992; many of such terms also appear in the context of the sample agreements provided in the author's second book, *Film Industry Contracts*, self-published, 1993.

11. Mark Litwak, *Dealmaking in the Film & Television Industry: From Negotiations to Final Contracts*, Silman-James Press, 1994, 256.

12. Melvin Simensky, "Determining Damages for Breach of Entertainment Agreements," *The Entertainment and Sports Lawyer*, vol. 8, no. 1, Spring 1990.

13. Sills and Axelrod.

14. David Robb, "Net Profits: One Man's View from Both Sides," *The Hollywood Reporter*, August 31, 1992, 32.

15. *Los Angeles Times*, July 26, 1987, Calendar, 23.

16. David Robb, "*Buchwald* Ruling Poses Threat to H'wood Deals," *The Hollywood Reporter*, August 24, 1992, 21.

17. O'Donnell and McDougal, 383.

18. Ibid.

19. Pierce O'Donnell and Dennis McDougal, *Fatal Subtraction: How Hollywood Really Does Business/The Inside Story of Buchwald v. Paramount*, Doubleday, 1992, 383.

20. Bibicoff.

21. *Entertainment Weekly*, News & Notes, July 19, 1991.

22. Ibid.

23. *Los Angeles Times*, January 15, 1989, Calendar section at 31, column 1.

24. David Robb, "Net Profits No Myth, But Hard to Get Hands On," *The Hollywood Reporter*, August 17, 1992, 18.

25. Marcus.

26. *Los Angeles Times*, March 23, 1990, Calendar section F, 1, column 4.

27. *Premiere*, June 1992, 24.

28. Dennis McDougal, "A Blockbuster Deficit," *Los Angeles Times*, March 21, 1991, F1; also see James Flanigan, "Big Losses and Big Lessons at the Movies," *Los Angeles Times*, Sunday, March 31, 1991.

29. O'Donnell and McDougal, 410; also see David Robb, "Net Profits No Chimp Change for Murphy," *The Hollywood Reporter*, August 24, 1992, 17.

30. O'Donnell and McDougal, 357.

31. Nicolas Kent, *Naked Hollywood: Money and Power in The Movies Today*, St. Martin's Press, 1991, 241.

32. O'Donnell and McDougal, 357.

33. Ibid, 20.

34. Ibid, 411.

35. Roger Corman and Jim Jerome, *How I Made A Hundred Movies in Hollywood and Never Lost a Dime*, Dell Publishing, 1990, 206.

36. Ibid, 208.

37. O'Donnell and McDougal, 357.

38. William Goldman, *Adventures in the Screen Trade: A Personal View of Hollywood and Screenwriting*, Warner Books, 1983, 237.

39. Steven Bach, *Final Cut: Dreams and Disaster in the Making of Heaven's Gate*, William Morrow and Company, 1985, 287.

40. Mark Litwak, *Reel Power: The Struggle for Influence and Success in the New Hollywood*, William Morrow and Company, 1986, 288.

41. Dana Weschler, "Profits? What Profits?" *Forbes*, February 19, 1990, 38.

42. Corman and Jerome, 127.

43. Ibid, 208.

44. Kent, 241.

45. David Robb, "Net Profits: Breaking Even Is Hard to Do," *The Hollywood Reporter*, September 14, 1992, 1.

46. Ibid, 13.

47. Steven Sills, "Contractual Aspects of Producing, Financing and Distributing Film," UCLA Extension guest lecture, June 9, 1992.

48. Jason E. Squire, *The Movie Business Book: The Inside Story of the Creation, Financing, Making, Selling and Exhibiting of Movies*, 2nd ed., Simon & Schuster, 1992, 65.

49. Robb, "Breaking Even," 12.

50. O'Donnell and McDougal, xv.

51. Quoted in O'Donnell and McDougal, Preface.

52. Dawn Steel, *They Can Kill You . . . But They Can't Eat You: Lessons from the Front*, Pocket Books, 70.

53. Marcus, 582.

54. Sills lecture.
55. O'Donnell and McDougal, 393.
56. Marcus, 566.
57. Ibid, 585.
58. Robb, "Breaking Even," 12.
59. Ibid, 1 & 12.
60. Marcus, 585.
61. Peter J. Dekom, "The Net Effect: Making Net Profit Mean Something," *American Premiere*, May–June 1992, 6.
62. Robb, "No Myth," 17.
63. O'Donnell and McDougal, 352.
64. Ibid, 439 & 440.
65. Ibid, 31.
66. Ibid, 152.
67. Requoted in O'Donnell and McDougal, 420 & 421.
68. Bach, 33.
69. PR Newswire, July 18, 1983.
70. O'Donnell and McDougal, 383.
71. Corman and Jerome, 196.
72. Ibid, 121.
73. Dekom, 6.
74. Squire, 79.
75. Ibid, 129.
76. Dekom, 6.
77. Sills and Axelrod.
78. Stevenson, "The Magic of Hollywood Math," *New York Times*, April 13, 1990, D1.
79. Dekom, 6 & 7.
80. Squire, 59 & 60.
81. O'Donnell and McDougal, 21.
82. Corman and Jim Jerome, vii.
83. O'Donnell and McDougal, 357.
84. Marcus, 583.
85. Goldman, 6.
86. Peter Bart, *Fade Out: The Calamitous Final Days of MGM*, Anchor Books, 1991, 67.
87. Paul Rosenfield, *The Club Rules: Power, Money, Sex, and Fear—How It Works in Hollywood*, Warner Books, 1992, 203.
88. Squire, 163.
89. Ibid, 64.
90. Litwak, 225.
91. Kent, 86.
92. Goldman, 16.
93. Sills lecture.
94. Dan E. Moldea, *Dark Victory: Ronald Reagan, MCA and the Mob*, Penguin Books, 1987, 92 & 93.
95. Marcus, 563.
96. Patrick Robertson, *The Guinness Book of Movie Facts & Feats*, Guinness Publishing, 4th ed., 1991, 78.

97. Neal Gabler, *An Empire of Their Own: How the Jews Invented Hollywood*, Doubleday Anchor Books, 1988, 34.

98. Cass Warner Sperling and Cork Millner, *Hollywood Be Thy Name: The Warner Brothers Story*, Prima Publishing, 1994, 62.

99. Gorham Kindem, "Hollywood's Movie Star System: A Historical Overview," in *The American Movie Industry: The Business of Motion Pictures*, ed. Gorham Kindem, Southern Illinois University Press, 1982, 84.

100. Gabler, 174.

101. Robertson, 78.

102. Frank Brady, *Citizen Welles: A Biography of Orson Welles*, Doubleday, 1989, 200.

103. Ibid.

104. Marcus, 582 & 583.

105. Ibid, 563.

106. Robb, "No Myth," 18.

107. Paul N. Lazarus III, "Ensuring a Fair Cut of a Hit Film's Profits," *Entertainment Law & Finance*, November 1989, 1.

108. Squire, 160.

109. David F. Prindle, *Risky Business: The Political Economy of Hollywood*, Westview Press, 1993, 22.

110. David Nochimson and Leon Brachman, "Contingent Compensation for Theatrical Motion Pictures," *The Entertainment and Sports Lawyer*, vol. 5, no. 1, Summer 1986, 3.

111. O'Donnell and McDougal, 351.

112. Robb, "No Myth," 1.

113. Ibid, 17.

114. Art Linson, *A Pound of Flesh: Perilous Tales of How to Produce Movies in Hollywood*, Grove Press, 1993, 147.

115. Steel, 267.

116. David Robb, "Police Net is Arrested by Boxoffice Drop," *The Hollywood Reporter*, September 8, 1992, 1.

117. David J. Leedy, "Projecting Profits from a Motion Picture," excerpts from an unpublished work, May 8, 1991, 31.

118. Ibid.

119. Ira Deutchman, president of Fine Line Features quoted in Jason E. Squire, *The Movie Business Book: The Inside Story of the Creation, Financing, Making, Selling and Exhibiting of Movies*, 2nd ed., Simon & Schuster, 1992, 326.

120. Nochimson and Brachman, 18.

121. Bibicoff, 25.

122. Ibid, 24.

123. Gunther H. Schiff, "The Profit Participation Conundrum: A Glossary of Common Terms and Suggestions for Negotiation," *Beverly Hills Bar Journal*, Summer 1992, 123.

124. Bibicoff, 24.

125. Schiff, 127.

126. Robb, "No Myth", 17.

127. Squire, 203.

128. Kent, 157 & 158.

129. Squire, 99.

4. Negotiating the Distribution Deal

1. Kurt E. Wilson, "How Contracts Escalate into Torts," Kurt E. Wilson, *California Lawyer*, January 1992.

2. Richard P. Sybert, "Adhesion Theory in California: An Update," *Loyola of Los Angeles Law Review*, 1983.

3. Marcus, 569 & 570; quoting from *Graham* at 820, 623 P.2d at 172073, 171 Cal. Rptr. at 612.

4. Ibid, 567.

5. Ibid, 569.

6. *Graham v. Scissor-Tail, Inc.*, 28 Cal. 3d 807, 819, 623 P.2d 165, 172, 171 Cal. Rptr. 604, 611 (1981).

7. *Buchwald*, 90 L.A. Daily J. App. Rep. at 14483.

8. O'Donnell and McDougal, 466.

9. Steven H. Gifis, *Law Dictionary*, 2nd ed., Barron's Educational Series, Inc., 1984, 495.

10. Teresa A. Garcia, "Feature Film Distribution Agreements: Contracts of Adhesion and the Doctrine of Unconscionability," November 18, 1992, 6.

11. *A&M Produce*, 135 Cal. App. 3d at 484, 186 Cal. Rptr. at 120.

12. Marcus, 573; *Buchwald*, 90 L.A. Daily J. App. Rep. at 14484.

13. Graham v. Scissor-Tail, Inc., 29 Cal. 3d 807, 623 P.2d 165, 171 Cal. Rptr. 604 (1981).

14. Marcus, 573; *Buchwald*, 90 L.A. Daily J. App. Rep. at 14484.

15. Ibid; *Graham*, 28 Cal. 3d at 821, 623 P. 2d at 173, 171 Cal. Rptr. at 612.

16. Cal. Unlawful Contracts Code Section 1670.5 (West 1985; Legislative Committee Comment at 493).

17. Marcus, 573; *Buchwald*, 90 L.A. Daily J. App. Rep. at 14484.

18. Marcus, 571 & 572.

19. U.C.C. Section 2–302 Official Comment.

20. T. Quinn, "Uniform Commercial Code Commentary and Law Digest," Section 2-302[A], at 2-96 (1978).

5. Terms of the Deal Itself

1. *Variety*, January 4, 1956, 84.

2. Nochimson and Brachman, 3.

3. Simon N. Whitney, "Antitrust Policies and the Motion Picture Industry," chapter in *The American Movie Industry: The Business of Motion Pictures*, edited by Gorham Kindem, Southern Illinois University Press, 1982, 183.

4. Litwak, *Reel Power*, 257.

5. Martin Ransohoff quoted in Litwak, *Reel Power*, 257.

6. Frank D. Gilroy, *I Wake Up Screening*, Southern Illinois University Press, 1993, 166.

7. Ibid, 227.

8. Squire, 326.

9. Fred Goldberg, *Motion Picture Marketing and Distribution: Getting Movies into a Theatre Near You*, Focal Press, 1991, 170.

10. Goldberg, 170.

11. Squire, 347.

12. Ibid, 343.

13. Ibid, 349.

14. Harold L. Vogel, *Entertainment Industry Economics: A Guide for Financial Analysis*, 2nd ed., Cambridge University Press, 1990, 76.

15. Leedy, 5.

16. Sills lecture.

17. Whitney, 180.

18. Source: *Art Murphy's Box Office Register*.

19. Source: *Variety Show Business Annual*.

20. Sheila Casey, "Distributor Rentals as a Percentage of Box Office for Top Grossing 1989 Films," December 1992 (unpublished paper); Scott A. Schiff, "Receipt of Film Rentals: The Indies Lose Again (1990)," December 15, 1992 (unpublished paper for Investor Financing of Entertainment Projects course at UCLA Extension); Peter Steriopulos, unpublished paper for UCLA Extension course "The Feature film Distribution Deal," 1992.

21. Sills lecture.

22. Nochimson and Brachman, 3 & 4.

23. Sills lecture.

24. Ibid.

25. Squire, 330.

26. Ibid, 26.

27. *The Hollywood Reporter*, February 20, 1990.

28. Sills lecture.

29. Robb, "No Myth," 18; This quote from the David Robb article is modified with the added material in brackets since video revenues are not actually received by the studio but by the "studio's home video operation."

30. Sills lecture.

31. Ibid.

32. Alex Ben Block, "Is Hollywood Culpable? Paul Newman Lost his Lawsuit, but his Allegation of an Illegal Studio Conspiracy is Still Alive," *Show Biz News*, July 1, 1988, 7.

33. Ibid.

34. Ibid.

35. Nochimson and Brachman, 5.

36. Block, 7.

37. Sills lecture.

38. Dekom, 6.

39. Sills lecture.

40. Nochimson and Brachman, 5 & 6.

41. Ibid.

42. Litwak, *Dealmaking*, 26.

43. Ibid, 28.

44. Roger Ebert, *Roger Ebert's Video Companion*, 1994 ed., Andrews and McMeel, 1993, 551.

45. Ibid, 482.

46. Litwak, *Reel Power*, 242.

47. Bibicoff, 30.

48. Ibid, 31.

49. Ibid, 32.

50. Leedy, 10.

51. Litwak, *Dealmaking*, 258.

52. Goldberg, 197.

53. Ibid.
54. Nochimson and Brachman, 6.
55. Ibid, 15.
56. Leedy, 23.
57. McClintick, 186.
58. Litwak, *Dealmaking*, 261.
59. Lazarus, 5.
60. Nochimson and Brachman, 6.
61. Litwak, *Dealmaking*, 260.
62. Leedy, 13.
63. Goldberg, 31.
64. See Sills and Axelrod.
65. Dekom, 7.
66. Kent, 154.
67. Kent, 87.
68. Ibid, 86.
69. Robb, "No Myth," 17.
70. Kent, 241.
71. Ibid.
72. Dekom, 7.
73. Nochimson and Brachman, 17.
74. *Alperson v. Mirisch Co.*, 250 Cal. App. 2d 84, 58 Cal. Rptr. 178 (1967).
75. Marcus, 546.
76. Linson, 94.
77. Nochimson and Brachman, 14.
78. O'Donnell and McDougal, 147.
79. Buck Houghton, *What a Producer Does: The Art of Moviemaking (Not the Business)*, Silman-James Press, 1991, 164.
80. Sills lecture.
81. Bach, 48.
82. Ibid, 51.
83. Sills and Axelrod.
84. Litwak, *Dealmaking*, 256.
85. Kathleen Neumeyer, "Sue Crazy!" *Los Angeles Times*, May 1989, 103.
86. Litwak, *Dealmaking*, 256.
87. Ibid.
88. O'Donnell and McDougal, 373.
89. Lazarus, 4.

6. Feature Film Distribution Deal Negotiating Checklist

1. Leedy, 20.
2. For an overview of the many forms of film finance, see John W. Cones, *43 Ways to Finance Your Feature Film*, Southern Illinois University Press, 1995.
3. Sills lecture.
4. See Edward E. Colton, "Defining Net Profits, Shares for a Motion Picture Deal," *New York Law Journal*, September 30, 1988.
5. Julia Phillips, *You'll Never Eat Lunch in This Town Again*, Penguin Books, 1991, 223.
6. Dekom, 7.

7. Nochimson and Brachman, 14.

8. Houghton, 162.

9. Sills lecture.

10. Litwak, *Reel Power*, 287.

11. John W. Cones, *Film Finance and Distribution—A Dictionary of Terms*, Silman-James Press, 1992.

12. Robert I. Freedman, "Distribution Contracts," article appearing in *Distributing Independent Films and Videos* (edited by Morrie Warshawaki), The Media Project (Portland) & FIVF (New York), 1989, 136.

13. Leedy, 65 & 66; Bibicoff, 52.

14. Bibicoff, 53.

Selected Bibliography

Articles, Films, Media Reports and Papers

Abode, P. J. "Pick-Ups, Pre-Sales and Co-Ventures." *Montage*. IFP/West publication, Winter 1991/1992.

Achbar, Mark, and Wintonick, Peter. *Manufacturing Consent: Noam Chomsky and the Media*. A documentary film, 1992.

"Antitrust Suit by Theater to Proceed." *The Hollywood Reporter*, January 14, 1992.

Auf der Maur, Rolf. *Enforcement of Antitrust Law and the Motion Picture Industry*. Student paper presented to UCLA Extension class "The Feature Film Distribution Deal," instructor—John W. Cones, 1991.

Barsky, Hertz, Ros, and Vinnick. *Legal Aspects of Film Financing*. April 1990.

Berry, Jennifer. *Female Studio Executives*. A research paper for "Film Finance and Distribution," UCLA Producer's Program, Fall 1994.

Bertz, Michael A. "Pattern of Racketeering Activity: A Jury Issue." *Beverly Hills Bar Journal*, vol. 26, no. 1, Winter 1992.

———. "Pursuing a Business Fraud RICO Claim." *California Western Law Review*, vol. 21, no. 2, 1985.

Bibicoff, Hillary. "Net Profit Participations in the Motion Picture Industry." *Loyola of Los Angeles Entertainment Law Journal*, vol. 11, 1991.

Block, Alex Ben. "Is Hollywood Culpable? Paul Newman Lost his Lawsuit, but his Allegation of an Illegal Studio Conspiracy is Still Alive." *Show Biz News*, July 1, 1988.

Bowser, Kathryn. "Opportunities Knock: Co-Production Possibilities with Japan and Britain." *The Independent*, November 1991.

Brett, Barry J., and Friedman, Michael D. "A Fresh Look At The Paramount Decrees." *The Entertainment and Sports Lawyer*, vol. 9, no. 3, Fall 1991.

Brooks, David. "A Fantasy at the Speed of Sound." *Insight*, May 26, 1986.

Cash William. "Too Many Hoorays for Hollywood." *The Spectator*, October, 1992.

Chrystie, Stephen, Gould, David, and Spoto, Lou. "Insolvency and the Production and Distribution of Entertainment Products." *The Entertainment and Sports Lawyer*, vol. 6, no. 4, Spring 1988.

Cohen, Roger. "Steve Ross Defends His Paychecks." *The New York Times Magazine*, March 22, 1992.

Cohodas, Nadine. "Reagan Seeks Relaxation of Antitrust Laws." *Congressional Quarterly*, February 1, 1986.

Colton, Edward E. "Defining Net Profits, Shares for a Motion Picture Deal." *New York Law Journal*, September 30, 1988.

———. "How to Negotiate Contracts, Deals in the Movie Industry." *New York Law Journal*, September 23, 1988.

———. "What to Include in Pacts Between Author & Film Co." *New York Law Journal*, October 7, 1988.

Cones, John W. "Feature Film Limited Partnerships: A Practical Guide Focusing on Securities and Marketing for Independent Producers and Their Attorneys." *Loyola of Los Angeles Entertainment Law Journal,* 1992.

———. "Maximizing Producers' Negative Pick-Up Profits." *Entertainment Law & Finance*, vol. 8, no. 3, June 1992.

Continuing Education of the Bar, California. *Tax Literacy for the Business Lawyer.* Seminar handout, September 1991.

Corliss, Richard. "The Magistrate of Morals." *Time*, October 12, 1992.

Custolito, Karen, and Parisi, Paula. "Power Surge—Women in Entertainment." *The Hollywood Reporter,* December 6, 1994.

Dekom, Peter J. "The Net Effect: Making Net Profit Mean Something." *American Premiere*, May–June 1992.

Dellaverson, John J. "The Director's Right of Final Cut—How Final Is Final?" *The Entertainment and Sports Lawyer*, vol. 7, no. 1, Summer/Fall 1988.

Denby, David. "Can the Movies be Saved?" *New York Times*, July 21, 1986.

Disner, Eliot G. "Is There Antitrust After 'Syufy'?—Recent Ninth Court Cases Create Barriers to Enforcement." *California Lawyer,* March 1991.

Eshman, Jill Mazirow. "Bank Financing of a Motion Picture Production." *Loyola of Los Angeles Entertainment Law Journal,* 1992.

Farrell, L. M. "Financial Guidelines for Investing in Motion Picture Limited Partnerships." *Loyola of Los Angeles Entertainment Law Journal,* 1992.

Faulkner, Robert R., and Anderson, Andy B. "Short-Term Projects and Emergent Careers: Evidence from Hollywood." *American Journal of Sociology*, vol. 92, no. 4, January 1987.

Feller, Richard L. "Unreported Decisions and Other Developments (RICO and Entertainment Litigation)." *The Entertainment and Sports Lawyer*, vol. 3, no. 2, Fall 1984.

"Film Studios Threaten Retaliation Against States Banning Blind Bids." *Los Angeles Times,* June 1, 1981.

Fleming, Karl. "Who Is Ted Ashley?" *New York Times*, June 24, 1974.

Freshman, Elena R. "Commissions to Non-Broker/Dealers Under California Law." *Beverly Hills Bar Journal*, vol. 22, no. 2.

Gaydos, Steven. "Piercing Indictment, Steven Gaydos." *Los Angeles Reader*, December 1992.

Glasser, Theodore L. "Competition and Diversity Among Radio Formats: Legal and Structural Issues." *Journal of Broadcasting*, vol. 28, no. 2, Spring 1984.

Goldman Sachs. "Movie Industry Update—1991." *Investment Research Report*, 1991.

Gomery, Douglas. "Failed Opportunities: The Integration of the U.S. Motion Picture and Television Industries." *Quarterly Review of Film Studies*, vol. 9, no. 3, Summer 1984.

Goodell, Jeffrey. "Hollywood's Hard Times." *Premiere*, January 1992.

Granger, Rod, and Toumarkine, Doris. "The Un-Stoppables." *Spy*, November 1988.

Greenspan, David. "*Miramax Films Corp. v. Motion Picture Ass'n of Amer., Inc.*: The Ratings Systems Survives, for Now." *The Entertainment and Sports Lawyer*, vol. 9, no. 2, Summer 1991.

Greenwald, John. "The Man With the Iron Grasp." *Time*, September 27, 1993.

Gregory, Keith M. "Blind Bidding: A Need For Change." *Beverly Hills Bar Journal,* Winter 1982–83.

Hammond, Robert A., and Melamed, Douglas A. "Antitrust in the Entertainment Industry: Reviewing the Classic Texts in The Image Factory." *Gannett Center Journal,* Summer 1989.

Hanson, Wes. "Restraint, Responsibility & the Entertainment Media." *Ethics Magazine,* Josephson Institute, 1993.

Harris, Kathryn. "Movie Companies, TV Networks and Publishers Have Been Forced to Audition the Same Act: Cost Cutting." *Forbes,* January 6, 1992.

Honeycutt, Kirk. "Film Producer Mark Rosenberg Dies at Age 44." *The Hollywood Reporter,* November 9, 1992.

Independent Feature Project/West. "Feature Development: From Concept to Production." Seminar, November 1991.

Jacobson, Marc. "Film Directors Agreements." *The Entertainment & Sports Lawyer,* vol. 8, no. 1, Spring 1990.

———. "Structuring Film Development Deals." *Entertainment Law & Finance,* September 1990.

"JFK and Costello." *New York Times,* July 27, 1973.

Kagan, Paul, and Associates. *Motion Picture Investor.* Newsletter, June and December issues, 1990.

———. *Motion Picture Finance.* Seminar, November 1991.

Kasindorf, Martin. "Cant' Pay? Won't Pay!" *Empire,* June 1990.

Kopelson, Arnold. "One Producer's Inside View of Foreign and Domestic Presales in the Independent Financing of Motion Pictures." *Loyola of Los Angeles Entertainment Law Journal,* 1992.

Layne, Barry, and Tourmarkine, Doris. "Court Vacates Consent Decree Against Loews." *The Hollywood Reporter,* February 20, 1992.

Lazarus, Paul N., III. "Ensuring a Fair Cut of a Hit Film's Profits." *Entertainment Law & Finance,* Leader Publications, November 1989.

Leedy, David J. "Projecting Profits from a Motion Picture." Excerpts from an unpublished work, presented Fall 1991, for UCLA Extension class: "Contractual Aspects of Producing, Financing and Distributing Film."

Levine, Michael, and Zitzerman, David B. "Foreign Productions and Foreign Financing: The Canadian Perspective." *The Entertainment and Sports Lawyer,* vol. 5, no. 4, Spring 1987.

Litwak, Mark. "Lessons In Self-Defense: Distribution Contracts and Arbitration Clauses." *The Independent,* 1993.

———. Successful Producing in the Entertainment Industry. Seminar, UCLA Extension, 1990.

Logan, Michael. "He'll Never Eat Lunch In This Town Again!" *Los Angeles Magazine,* September 1992.

Marcus, Adam J. "*Buchwald v. Paramount Pictures Corp.* and the Future of Net Profit." *Cardozo Arts & Entertainment Law Journal,* vol. 9, 1991.

Mathews, Jack. "Rules of the Game." *American Film,* March 1990.

McCoy, Charles W. "Tim", Jr. "The Paramount Cases: Golden Anniversary in a Rapidly Changing Marketplace." *Antitrust,* Summer 1988.

McDougal, Dennis. "A Blockbuster Deficit." *Los Angeles Times,* March 21, 1991.

Medved, Michael. "Researching the Truth About Hollywood's Impact: Consensus and Denial." *Ethics Magazine,* Josephson Institute, 1993.

Moore, Schuyler M. "Entertainment Financing for the '90s: Super Pre-Sales." *Stroock & Stroock & Lavan Corporate Entertainment Newsletter,* vol. 1, q1 1992.

Morris, Chris. "Roger Corman: The Schlemiel as Outlaw." In Todd McCarthy and Charles Flynn, eds., *King of the Bs,* New York: Dutton, 1975.

Nochimson, David, and Brachman, Leon. "Contingent Compensation for Theatrical Motion Pictures." *The Entertainment and Sports Lawyer,* vol. 5, no. 1, Summer 1986.

O'Donnell, Pierce. "Killing the Golden Goose: Hollywood's Death Wish." *Beverly Hills Bar Journal,* Summer, 1992.

Olswang, Simon M. "The Last Emperor and Co-Producing in China: The Impossible Made Easy, and the Easy Made Impossible." *The Entertainment and Sports Lawyer,* vol. 6, no. 2, Fall 1987.

Phillips, Gerald F. "Block Booking: Perhaps Forgotten, Perhaps Misunderstood, But Still Illegal." *The Entertainment and Sports Lawyer,* vol. 6, no. 1, Summer 1987.

———. "The Recent Acquisition of Theatre Circuits by Major Distributors." *The Entertainment and Sports Lawyer,* vol. 5, no. 3, Winter 1987.

Phillips, Mark, C. "Role of Completion Bonding Companies in Independent Productions." *Loyola of Los Angeles Entertainment Law Journal,* 1992.

Powers, Stephen P., Rothman, David J., and Rothman, Stanley. "Hollywood Movies, Society, and Political Criticism." *The World & I,* April 1991.

Pristin, Terry. "Hollywood's Family Ways." *Los Angeles Times,* Calendar Section, January 31, 1993.

Richardson, John H. "Hollywood's Actress-Hookers: When Glamour Turns Grim." *Premiere,* 1992.

Robb, David. "Buchwald Ruling Poses Threat to H'wood Deals." *The Hollywood Reporter,* August 24, 1992.

———. "Net Profits: Breaking Even is Hard to Do." *The Hollywood Reporter,* September 14, 1992.

———. "Net Profits 'Endangered' by Big Budjets." *The Hollywood Reporter,* August 14, 1992.

———. "Net Profits No Chimp Change for Murphy." *The Hollywood Reporter,* August 24, 1992.

———. "Net Profits No Myth, But Hard to Get Hands On." *The Hollywood Reporter,* August 17, 1992.

———. "Net Profits: One Man's View from Both Sides." *The Hollywood Reporter,* August 31, 1992.

———. "Police Net is Arrested by Boxoffice Drop." *The Hollywood Reporter,* September 8, 1992.

Rodman, Howard. "Unequal Access, Unequal Pay: Hollywood's Gentleman's Agreement." *Montage,* October 1989.

Royal, David. "Making Millions and Going Broke: How Production Companies Make Fortunes and Bankrupt Themselves." *American Premiere,* November/December 1991.

Sarna, Jonathan, D. "The Jewish Way of Crime." *Commentary,* August 1984.

Schiff, Gunther, H. "The Profit Participation Conundrum: A Glossary of Common Terms and Suggestions for Negotiation." *Beverly Hills Bar Journal,* Summer 1992.

Sills, Steven. "Contractual Aspects of Producing, Financing and Distributing Film." UCLA Extension guest lecture, June 9, 1992.

Sills, Steven D., and Axelrod, Ivan L. "Profit Participation in the Motion Picture Industry." *Los Angeles Lawyer*, April 1989.

Simensky, Melvin. "Determining Damages for Breach of Entertainment Agreements." *The Entertainment and Sports Lawyer*, vol. 8, no. 1, Spring 1990.

Simon, John. "Film—Charlatans Rampant." *National Review*, February 1, 1993.

Sinclair, Nigel. "How to Draft Multi-Picture Deals." *Entertainment Law & Finance*, January 1987.

———. "Long-Term Contracts for Independent Producers." *Entertainment Law & Finance*, November 1986.

———. "U.S./Foreign Film Funding: Co-Production Tips." *Entertainment Law & Finance*, March 1991.

Sinclair and Gerse. "Representing Independent Motion Picture Producers." *Los Angeles Lawyer*, May 1988.

Sobel, Lionel S. "Financing the Production of Theatrical Motion Pictures." *Entertainment Law Reporter*, May 1984.

———. "Protecting Your Ideas in Hollywood." *Writer's Friendly Legal Guide*, Writer's Digest Books, 1989.

Sperry, Paul. "Do Politics Drive Hollywood? Or do Markets Determine What Studios Make?" *Investor's Business Daily*, March 19, 1993.

Stauth, Cameron. "Masters of the Deal." *American Film*, May 1991.

Sybert, Richard P. "Adhesion Theory in California: An Update." *Loyola of Los Angeles Law Review*, 1983.

Tagliabue, Paul J. "Anti-Trust Developments in Sports and Entertainment Law." *Anti-Trust Law Journal*, 1987.

UCLA Entertainment Law Symposium. "Never Enough: The 'A' Deal, Business, Legal and Ethical Realities." Sixteenth annual symposium, February 1992.

"Vertical Integration, Horizontal Regulation: The Growth of Rupert Murdoch's Media Empire." *Screen*, vol. 28, no. 4, May–August 1986.

Weschler, Dana. "Profits? What Profits?" *Forbes*, February 19, 1990.

Whitney, Simon N. "Antitrust Policies and the Motion Picture Industry." Chapter in Gorham Kindem, *The American Movie Industry: The Business of Motion Pictures*, Southern Illinois University Press, 1982.

Wilson, Kurt E. "How Contracts Escalate into Torts." *California Lawyer*, January 1992.

Wolf, Brian J. "The Prohibitions Against Studio Ownership of Theaters: Are They An Anachronism?" *Loyola of Los Angeles Entertainment Law Journal*, vol. 13.

Zitzerman, David B., and Levine, Michael A. "Producing a Film in Canada: The Legal and Regulatory Framework." *The Entertainment and Sports Lawyer*, vol. 8, no. 4, Winter 1991.

Books

Andersen, Arthur, & Co. *Tax Shelters: The Basics*. Harper & Row, 1983.

Anger, Kenneth. *Hollywood Babylon*. Dell Publishing, 1981.

———. *Hollywood Babylon II*. Penguin Books, 1984.

Armour, Robert A. *Fritz Lang*. Twayne Publishers, 1977.

Bach, Steven. *Final Cut: Dreams and Disaster in the Making of Heaven's Gate*. William Morrow & Co., 1985.

Ballio, T. *The American Film Industry*. 2nd Rev. ed. Madison: University of Wisconsin Press, 1985.

Bart, Peter. *Fade Out: The Calamitous Final Days of MGM*. Anchor Books, 1991.

Baumgarten, Paul A., Farber, Donald C., and Fleischer, Mark. *Producing, Financing and Distributing Film: A Comprehensive Legal and Business Guide*. 2nd ed. Limelight Editions, 1992.

Bayer, William. *Breaking Through, Selling Out, Dropping Dead and Other Notes on Filmmaking*. First Limelight Edition, 1989.

Behrman, S. N. *People In A Diary: A Memoir*. Little, Brown & Co., 1972.

Biederman, Berry, Pierson, Silfen and Glasser. *Law and Business of the Entertainment Industries*. Auburn House, 1987.

Billboard Publications. *Hollywood Reporter Blu-Book*. 1990.

——. *Producer's Masterguide*. 1989, 1990 & 1991.

Blum, Richard A. *Television Writing: From Concept to Contract*. Focal Press, 1984.

Brady, Frank. *Citizen Welles: A Biography of Orson Welles*. Doubleday Anchor Books, 1989.

Brownstein, Ronald. *The Power and the Glitter: The Hollywood-Washington Connection*. Vintage Books, 1992.

Cameron-Wilson, James, and Speed, F. Maurice. *Film Review 1994*. St. Martin's Press, 1993.

Cohen, Sarah Blacher. *From Hester Street to Hollywood*. Indiana University Press, 1983.

Collier, Peter, and Horowitz, David. *The Kennedys: An American Drama*. Warner Books, 1984.

Commerce Clearing House. *Blue Sky Law Reporter*. 1984.

Cones, John W. *The Arrogance of Power: Movies and Antitrust*. Self-published.

——. *Film Finance and Distribution—A Dictionary of Terms*. Silman-James Press, 1992.

——. *Film Industry Contracts*. Self-published, 1993.

——. *43 Ways to Finance Your Feature Film*. Southern Illinois University Press, 1995.

——. *How the Movie Wars Were Won*. Self-published, 1995.

——. *Legacy of a Hollywood Empire*. Self-published.

——. *Motion Picture Biographies*. Self-published.

——. *Motion Picture Industry Reform*. Self-published.

——. *Patterns of Bias in Motion Picture Content*. Self-published.

——. *Politics, Movies and the Role of Government*. Self-published.

——. *337 Reported Business Practices of the Major Studio/Film Distributors*. Self-published, 1991.

——. *Who Really Controls Hollywood*. Self-published, 1995.

Considine, Shawn. *The Life and Work of Paddy Chayefsky*. Random House, 1994.

Corman, Roger, and Jerome, Jim. *How I Made a Hundred Movies in Hollywood and Never Lost a Dime*. Dell Publishing, 1990.

Curran, Trisha. *Financing Your Film*. Praeger Publishers, 1985.

Custen, George F. *Bio/Pics: How Hollywood Constructed Public History*. Rutgers University Press, 1992.

Delson, Donn, and Jacob, Stuart. *Delson's Dictionary of Motion Picture Marketing Terms*. Bradson Press, 1980.

Dinnerstein, Leonard. *Anti-Semitism in America*. Oxford University Press, 1994.

Downes, John, and Goodman, Jordan Elliot. *Dictionary of Finance and Investment Terms*. 2nd ed. Barron's Educational Series, Inc., 1987.

Duncliffe, William J. *The Life and Times of Joseph P. Kennedy*. New York, 1965.

Ebert, Roger. *Roger Ebert's Video Companion*. 1994 ed. Andrews and McMeel, 1993.

Eberts, Jake, and Lott, Terry. *My Indecision Is Final*. Atlantic Monthly Press, 1990.

Eisenberg, Dennis, et al. *Meyer Lansky: Mogul of the Mob*. New York, 1979.

Ephron, Henry. *We Thought We Could Do Anything*. W. W. Norton & Co., 1977.

Erens, Patricia. *The Jew in American Cinema*. Indiana University Press, 1984.

Evans, Robert. *The Kid Stays in the Picture*. Hyperion, 1994.

Farber, Donald C. *Entertainment Industry Contracts: Negotiating and Drafting Guide*. Matthew Bender, 1990.

Farber, Stephen, and Green, Marc. *Hollywood Dynasties*. Putnam Publishing, 1984.

———. *Outrageous Conduct*. Morrow, 1988.

Field, Syd. *Screenplay: The Foundations of Screenwriting*. Dell Publishing, 1985.

Fox, Stuart. *Jewish Films in the United States*. G. K. Hall, 1976.

Fraser, George MacDonald. *The Hollywood History of the World*. Viking Penguin, 1989.

Frederickson, Jim, and Stewart, Steve. *Film Annual: 1992*. Companion Publications, 1992.

Fried, Albert. *The Rise and Fall of the Jewish Gangster in America*. Rev. ed. Columbia University Press, 1993.

Friedman, Lester. *The Jewish Image in American Film*. Citadel Press, 1987.

Gabler, Neal. *An Empire of Their Own: How the Jews Invented Hollywood*. Doubleday Anchor Books, 1988.

Gilroy, Frank. D. *I Wake Up Screening! Everything You Need to Know About Making Independent Films Including a Thousand Reasons Not To*. Southern Illinois University Press, 1993.

Goldberg, Fred. *Motion Picture Marketing and Distribution: Getting Movies into a Theatre Near You*. Focal Press, 1991.

Goldman, William. *Adventures in the Screen Trade: A Personal View of Hollywood and Screenwriting*. Warner Books, 1983.

Gomery, Douglas. *Movie History: A Survey*. Wadsworth Publishing Company, 1991.

———. *The Hollywood Studio System*. Macmillan, 1986; New York: St. Martin's Press, 1986.

Goodell, Gregory. *Independent Feature Film Production*. St. Martin's Press, 1982.

Goodman, Ezra. *The Fifty Year Decline and Fall of Hollywood*. Simon & Schuster, 1961.

Gribetz, Judah, Greenstein, Edward L., and Stein, Regina. *The Timetables of Jewish History*. Simon & Schuster, 1993.

Hearst, William Randolph, Jr., and Casserly, Jack. *The Hearsts—Father and Son*. Roberts Rinehart Publishers, 1991.

Herrman, Dorothy. *S. J. Perelman: A Life*. Simon & Schuster, 1986.

Higham, Charles. *Howard Hughes: The Secret Life*. Berkley Books, 1993.

Hill, Geoffrey. *Illuminating Shadows: The Mythic Power of Film*. Shambhala, 1992

Holsinger, Ralph L. *Media Law*. 2nd ed. McGraw-Hill, 1991.

Houghton, Buck. *What a Producer Does: The Art of Moviemaking (Not the Business)*. Silman-James Press, 1991.

Houseman, John. *John Houseman: Run Through*. Simon and Schuster, 1972.

Hurst, Walter E., Minus, Johnny, and Hale, William Storm. *Film-TV Law:* 3rd ed. Seven Arts Press, 1976.

Johnson, Paul. *A History of the Jews*. Harper & Row, 1987.

Katz, Ephraim. *The Film Encyclopedia*. HarperCollins, 1994.

Kennedy, Joseph P. *The Story of the Films*. W. W. Shaw Company, 1927; reprint, Jerome S. Ozer, 1971.

Kent, Nicolas. *Naked Hollywood: Money and Power in The Movies Today*. St. Martin's Press, 1991.

Kim, Erwin. *Franklin J. Schaffner*. Scarecrow Press, 1985.

Kindem, Gorham. *The American Movie Industry: The Business of Motion Pictures*. Southern Illinois University Press, 1982.

King, Morgan D. *California Corporate Practice Guide*. 2nd ed. Lawpress Corporation, 1989.

Kipps, Charles. *Out of Focus*. Century Hutchinson, 1989.

Koppes, Clayton R., and Black, Gregory D. *Hollywood Goes to War: How Politics, Profits and Propaganda Shaped World War II Movies*. University of California Press, 1987.

Kosberg, Robert. *How to Sell Your Idea to Hollywood*. HarperCollins, 1991.

Kotkin, Joel. *Tribes: How Race, Religion and Identity Determine Success in the New Global Economy*. Random House, 1993.

Lasky, Betty. *RKO: The Biggest Little Major of Them All*. Rountable Publishing, 1989.

Lasky, Jesse, Jr. *Whatever Happened to Hollywood?* Funk & Wagnalls, 1975.

LeRoy, Mervyn, and Kelmer, Dick. *Mervyn LeRoy: Take One*. Hawthorn Books, 1974.

Levy, Emanuel. *George Cukor: Master of Elegance*. William Morris, 1994.

Linson, Art. *A Pound of Flesh: Perilous Tales of How to Produce Movies in Hollywood*. Grove Press, 1993.

Litwak, Mark. *Dealmaking in the Film & Television Industry: From Negotiations to Final Contracts*. Silman-James Press, 1994.

———. *Reel Power: The Struggle for Influence and Success in the New Hollywood*. William Morrow and Company, 1986.

Lucaire, Ed. *The Celebrity Almanac*. Prentice Hall, 1991.

Lyman, Darryl. *Great Jews on Stage and Screen*. Jonathan David Publishers, 1987.

Maltin, Leonard. *Leonard Maltin's Movie Encyclopedia*. Penguin Group, 1994.

Martin, Mick, and Porter, Marsha. *Video Movie Guide: 1989*. First Ballantine Books edition, 1988.

McClintick, David. *Indecent Exposure: A True Story of Hollywood*. Dell Publishing, 1983.

Medved, Michael. *Hollywood vs. America: Popular Culture and the War on Traditional Values*. HarperCollins, 1992.

Medved, Harry, & Medved, Michael. *The Hollywood Hall of Shame: The Most Expensive Flops in Movie History*. Angus & Robertson Publishers, 1984.

Moldea, Dan E. *Dark Victory: Ronald Reagan, MCA, and the Mob*. Penguin Books, 1987.

Monder, Eric. *George Sidney: A Bio-Bibliography*. Greenwood Press, 1994.

Murphy, Art. *Art Murphy's Box Office Register*. 1990.

National Association of Securities Dealers. *NASD Manual.* September 1990.

National Association of Theatre Owners. *Encyclopedia of Exhibition.* 1990.

Navasky, Victor S. *Naming Names.* Penguin Books, 1980.

O'Donnell, Pierce, and McDougal, Dennis. *Fatal Subtraction: How Hollywood Really Does Business.* Doubleday, 1992.

Palmer, James, and Riley, Michael. *The Films of Joseph Losey.* Cambridge University Press, 1993.

Parrish, James Robert. *The Hollywood Celebrity Death Book.* Pioneer Books, 1993.

Penney, Edmund. *Dictionary of Media Terms.* G. P. Putnam's Sons, 1984.

Phillips, Julia. *You'll Never Eat Lunch in this Town Again.* Penguin Books, 1991.

Powdermaker, Hortense. *Hollywood: The Dream Factory—An Anthropologist Looks at the Movie-Makers.* Reprint of 1950 ed.; New York: Ayer, 1979.

Pratley, Gerald. *The Cinema of John Frankenheimer.* A. S. Barnes & Co., 1969.

Prifti, William M. *Securities: Public and Private Offerings.* Rev. ed. Callaghan & Company, 1980.

Prindle, David F. *Risky Business: The Political Economy of Hollywood.* Westview Press, 1993.

Rappleye, Charles, and Becker, Ed. *All American Mafioso: The Johnny Rosselli Story.* Doubleday, 1991.

Ratner, David L. *Securities Regulation.* 3rd ed. West Publishing Company, 1989.

Rawlence, Christopher. *The Missing Reel.* Atheneum, 1990.

Research Institute of America, Inc. *Federal Tax Coordinator.* 2nd ed. 1990.

Reynolds, Christopher. *Hollywood Power Stats: 1994.* Cineview Publishing, November 1993.

Robertson, Patrick. *The Guiness Book of Movie Facts and Feats.* Guiness Publishing. 4th ed. 1991.

Rollyson, Carl. *Lillian Hellman: Her Legend and Her Legacy.* St. Martin's Press, 1988.

Rosen, David, and Hamilton, Peter. *Off-Hollywood: The Making and Marketing of American Specialty Films.* The Sundance Institute and the Independent Feature Project, 1986.

Rosenberg, David. *The Movie That Changed My Life.* Viking Penguin, 1991.

Rosenfield, Paul. *The Club Rules: Power, Money, Sex, and Fear—How It Works in Hollywood.* Warner Books, 1992.

Russo, Vito. *The Celluloid Closet: Homosexuality in the Movies.* Rev. ed. Harper & Row, 1987.

Sachar, Howard M. *A History of the Jews in America.* Vintage Books, 1993.

Scheuer, Steven H. *Movies on TV and Videocassette.* Bantam, 1987.

Schwartz, Nancy Lynn. *The Hollywood Writers' Wars.* McGraw-Hill, 1982.

Shapiro, Michael. *The Jewish 100: A Ranking of the Most Influential Jews of All Time.* Citadel Press, 1994.

Sherman, Allan. *A Gift of Laughter: The Autobiography of Allan Sherman.* Atheneum Publishers, 1965.

Siegel, Eric S., Schultz, Loren A., Ford, Brian R., and Carney, David C. *Ernst & Young Business Plan Guide.* John Wiley & Sons, 1987.

Silfen, Martin E., chairman. Counseling Clients in the Entertainment Industry Seminar book. Practicing Law Institute, 1989.

Simensky, Melvin, and Selz, Thomas. *Entertainment Law.* 1984.

Sinclair, Andrew. *Spiegel: The Man Behind the Pictures.* Little, Brown & Co., 1987.

Sinetar, Marsha. *Reel Power: Spiritual Growth Though Film*. Triumph Books, 1993.

Singleton, Ralph S. *Filmmaker's Dictionary*. Lone Eagle Publishing Co., 1990.

Sklar, Robert. *Movie-Made America: A Cultural History of American Movies*. Random House, 1975.

Sperling, Cass Warner, and Millner, Cork. *Hollywood Be Thy Name: The Warner Brothers Story*. Prima Publishing, 1994.

Squire, Jason E. *The Movie Business Book: The Inside Story of the Creation, Financing, Making, Selling and Exhibition of Movies*. 2nd ed. Simon & Schuster, 1992.

Stanger, Robert A. *Tax Shelters: The Bottom Line*. Robert A. Stanger & Company, 1982.

Steel, Dawn. *They Can Kill You . . . But They Can't Eat You: Lessons from the Front*. Pocket Books, 1993.

Tartikoff, Brandon, and Leerhsen, Charles. *The Last Great Ride*. Random House, 1992.

Trager, James. *The People's Chronology*. Henry Holt & Co., 1992.

Ursini, James. *The Fabulous Life and Times of Preston Sturges*. Curtis Books, 1973.

Van Doren, Charles. *Webster's American Biographies*. Merriam-Webster, 1984.

Vidal, Gore. *Who Makes the Movies?* A collection of essays. "Pink Triangle and Yellow Star." Published by William Heinemann, Ltd., London, 1982.

Vogel, Harold L. *Entertainment Industry Economics: A Guide for Financial Analysis*. Cambridge University Press, 1986 & 1990.

Von Sternberg, Josef. *Fun in a Chinese Laundry*. Mercury House, 1965.

Wakeman, John. *World Film Directors*. Vols. 1 and 2, 1890–1985. 1987.

Walker, John. *Halliwell's Film Guide*. HarperCollins, 1991 and 1994.

Wallis, Hal, and Higham, Charles. *Starmaker: The Autobiography of Hal Wallis*. Macmillan, 1980.

Warshawski, Morrie. *Distributing Independent Films and Videos*. The Media Project, Portland, OR, and Foundation for Independent Video and Filmmakers, New York, 1989.

Waxman, Virginia Wright, and Bisplinghoff, Gunther. *Robert Altman: A Guide to Reference & Reason*. G. K. Hall & Co., 1984.

Wigoder, Dr. Geoffrey. *The New Standard Jewish Encyclopedia*. 7th Ed. Facts on File, 1992.

Writers Guild of America Theatrical and Television Basic Agreement. 1988.

Yule, Andrew. *Picture Shows: The Life and Films of Peter Bogdanovich*. Limelight Editions, 1992.

Index

Retroactive distribution fee increases, 64, 112–13

Revenue allocation, 13, 51–53, 59, 106–7

Robb, David, 2, 9, 22, 81

Robertson, Cliff, 1

Robertson, Patrick, 20, 21

Rocky, 10

Rocky IV, 18

Rolling breakeven, 6, 76, 105

Rosenberg, Lee, 28

Royalties, 54–59, 68, 108–9, 115–16

Running time agreements, 88, 126

Ruthless People, 7

St. Valentine's Day Massacre, The, 11

Salaries, 16, 18, 79–80; net profits as compensation in lieu of, 19–22, 104–5; shared employee, 74, 119

Sales of physical properties, 61, 105, 110–11

Salvage exclusion, 61

Salvage revenues, 105, 111

Samuel Goldwyn, 45–46

Schiff, Gunther, 26–27

Schlossberg, Julian, 44–45

Schneider (Judge), 58, 74

Schwarzenegger, Arnold, 80

Script changes, 86, 125

Second breakeven, 6

Second Restatement of Contracts, on unconscionability, 38–39

Secret Invasion, 15

Selling subject to review. *See* Settlement transactions

Settlement cross-collateralization, 96

Settlement ratio. *See* Settlement transactions

Settlement transactions, 42–47, 96, 105–6; and exhibitor/distributor deal, 49–50; and film rental ratios, 47–49; and outstandings, 50–51

70/30 major deal, 32

Shareholders, and revenue allocation, 53

Shorts, 75, 110

Sills, Steven, 1, 19–20, 47, 52, 57, 85; on value of audits, 134

Sindlinger & Company, 48

Sixty Minutes, 1

Slate cross-collateralization, 95–96

Sliding scale deal, 32

Speed-the-Plow (Mamet), 12

Sperling, Cass Warner, 21

SPFRE (same percentage as film rentals earned), 106–7

Split-rights deals, 130

Stallone, Sylvester, 18

Standards and practices, 87

Star Wars, 28, 100

Stattler, Mel, 20, 22

Steel, Dawn, 12, 24

Stewart, James, 19–20, 21

Sting, The, 56–57

Stock footage, 60, 105, 110

Studio accounting. *See* Creative accounting methods

Subdistribution fees, 64–65, 112–13

Substitution clauses, 94, 135

Surprise, in unconscionable contracts, 38, 39

Syndicated films, 51, 52, 75, 107, 118, 147. *See also* Television

Takeover provisions, 94, 135

Talent: and agencies, 28; deferrals to, 92, 129; gross participations by, 3–4, 80–82, 123–24; salaries for, 16, 18, 79–80

Tanen, Ned, 84

Taxes, 66, 67–68, 72, 76, 107, 115

Television, 54, 108, 130, 143, 146–47; allocation issues regarding, 51, 52, 75, 107, 118; cover shots for, 87, 126

Ten Commandments, The, 9

Term of agreements, 93, 129

Theatrical distribution, 127–28, 131–32, 143–45

They Can Kill You But They Can't Eat You (Steel), 24

Third party disbursing agents, 135

337 Reported Distributor Practices (Cones), 2

Total Recall, 80

Touchstone Pictures, 7

Trade association dues and assessments, 66, 68–69, 76, 114–15, 116

Trailers, 59, 75, 110, 128

Transmission costs, 66, 69, 116

Travel expenses, 75–76, 120

Triad Artists, 28

Turnaround provisions, 93, 105

Twentieth Century-Fox, 11, 28

Twins, 80

Unauthorized cross-collateralization, 95

Unauthorized distribution costs, 76, 121

Uncollectible indebtedness, 61, 111

Unconscionability, 13, 16, 36–39, 106, 121, 132. *See also* Bargaining power; *Buchwald v. Paramount*

Unfair competition, 88

Uniform Commercial Code, 39

JOHN W. CONES is a securities/entertainment lawyer practicing in Los Angeles. He has published several book and journal articles and lectured widely on the film industry under the sponsorship of the American Film Institute, UCLA, USC, state film commissions, and independent producer organizations. Among his previous works are: *Film Finance and Distribution — A Dictionary of Terms* (Silman-James Press, 1992); *Film Industry Contracts* (self-published, 1993); and *43 Ways to Finance Your Feature Film: A Comprehensive Analysis of Film Finance* (Southern Illinois University Press, 1995).

Mr. Cones also publishes a monthly column on film finance and related topics for the Internet Entertainment Network and conducts an ongoing Q&A session at that site on the World Wide Web with users (Internet World Wide Web homepage: http://HollywoodNetwork.com).